D0788404

12·12·75

Territorial Politics and Government in Montana 1864–89

Territorial Politics
and
Government in Montana
1864-89

Clark C. Spence

UNIVERSITY OF ILLINOIS PRESS

Urbana Chicago London

Publication of this work has been supported by a grant from the Oliver M. Dickerson Fund. The Fund was established by Mr. Dickerson (Ph.D., Illinois, 1906) to enable the University of Illinois Press to publish selected works in American history, designated by the executive committee of the Department of History.

LIBRARY OF CONGRESS CATALOGING IN PUBLICATION DATA

Spence, Clark C
 Territorial politics and government in Montana, 1864–89.

 Bibliography: p.
 Includes index.
 1. Montana—Politics and government. I. Title.
F731.S63   320.9′786′02   75–28343
ISBN 0–252–00460–4

FOR TOM

CONTENTS

PREFACE

It was on a crisp spring Sunday in 1971, while I was doing research on this study, that Vivian Paladin drove me out to Forestvale Cemetery, on the north side of Helena. For a moment during that brief visit I almost had the feeling that I had lived among the first generation of Montanans and had now returned to reminisce among old friends and acquaintances. Names I had come to know intimately from the columns of the *Herald* or the *Independent* revived familiar imagery, even when cut in stone. All around lay many of the performers, leading men and bit players alike, who had been involved in Montana's political life during the gaudy territorial half-century: giant Ben Potts, Union hero and governor for half of that period; his major antagonist, proud, unrelenting Wilbur F. Sanders; gentle, erudite Cornelius Hedges, more successful with education than elections; Richard Hickman, veteran legislator who came as a freighter in 'sixty-four; "X" Beidler, stocky, tough-fisted law enforcer whose huge monument was added belatedly by his admirers. These and the other political practitioners of early Montana were a picturesque and human lot and their brand of politics was a personal and human matter. Some were men of energy, ambition and talent; some of but limited ability; a few added the spice of corruption. But together they wrote a fascinating story—a story of grass roots politics intertwined with the federal territorial apparatus; a story significant not only in itself, but also for its part in shaping the course of future state politics and government. This book is an effort to capture the essence of that story.

These pages are the product of the assistance of many people, including the staff members of various repositories: the Bancroft Library, the Huntington Library, the Beinecke Library, the Rutherford B. Hayes Library, the Library of Congress, and the National Archives. I am especially grateful to Vivian Paladin and to Harriett Meloy of the Montana Historical Society for their part in making that one of my favorite oases. Thanks to Mrs. Paladin, some of this material, including an earlier version of Chapter 4, has appeared in *Montana: The Magazine of Western History*. I am also deeply obliged to John Hakola for having shared with me his wide knowledge and understanding of Montana history. Beyond that, I shall always be indebted to that superb teacher, Ernest S. Osgood, who years ago first exposed me to Montana territorial politics and who subsequently introduced me in person to Alice Creek.

ABBREVIATIONS

AG: Attorney General's Papers, Montana, Department of Justice, National Archives

API: Appointment Papers, Department of the Interior, National Archives

APJ: Appointment Papers, Department of Justice, National Archives

APS: Appointment Papers, Department of State, National Archives

BIA: Correspondence, Bureau of Indian Affairs, National Archives

GEC: General Executive Correspondence, Montana Territory, Montana Historical Society

LM: *Laws of Montana*

LT: Letters, Territorial, First Comptroller's Office, Department of the Treasury, National Archives

MHS: Montana Historical Society

SCF: Source-Chronological Files, Montana, Department of Justice, National Archives

TPI: Territorial Papers, Montana, Department of the Interior, National Archives

TPS: Territorial Papers, Montana, Department of State, National Archives

TPUS: Territorial Papers, Montana, United States Senate, National Archives

USSL: *United States Statutes at Large*

INTRODUCTION

The territorial "system" that began with and evolved from the Northwest Ordinance of 1787 has been considered unique, experimental, and a highly successful part of the American political tradition.[1] Its federal administration and operation have been skillfully studied, and several individual territories or blocs of territories have been carefully examined to show the interplay of local and national forces and the seeds of modern western politics in those areas.[2] But others, territories like Montana, have been neglected, and still lacking is any comprehensive, in-depth analysis of the political growth and patterns of western territories in general, although Kenneth Owens's suggestive article of 1970 has established a directional beacon.

The early years of a territory, concludes Owens, were characterized by "a type of disruptive, confused, intensely combative, and highly personal politics that can best be described as chaotic factionalism."[3] The normal result of the stresses of a thinly peopled country with an unsolidified social and political order, this turmoil soon gave way to a more stable, enduring one-party, two-party, or no-party system. In Oregon, Washington, and Dakota, for example, where a dominant

1. Earl S. Pomeroy, "The Territory as a Frontier Institution," *The Historian*, VII (Autumn, 1944), 41; Clarence E. Carter, "Colonialism in Continental United States," *South Atlantic Quarterly*, XLVII (January, 1948), 27–28.

2. Basic to an understanding of the overall territorial structure is Earl S. Pomeroy, *The Territories and the United States, 1861–1890* (Seattle, 1969 ed.). For a thoughtful approach to a region—the Four Corners area—see Howard R. Lamar, *The Far Southwest, 1846–1912* (New York, 1970 ed.). Also outstanding is Lamar's *Dakota Territory, 1861–1889* (New Haven, 1956). Other studies of specific territories include: Lewis Gould, *Wyoming: A Political History, 1868–1896* (New Haven, 1968); Leonard Arrington, *Great Basin Kingdom* (Cambridge, 1958); Jay J. Wagoner, *Arizona Territory, 1863–1912: A Political History* (Tucson, 1970); and Robert W. Larson, *New Mexico's Quest for Statehood, 1846–1912* (Albuquerque, 1968).

3. Kenneth N. Owens, "Pattern and Structure in Western Territorial Politics," *Western Historical Quarterly*, I (October, 1970), 389.

majority with local control of patronage was built on a homogeneous population with a minimum of sectional strife, the one-party pattern prevailed. More rare, the two-party system was likely to be temporary, as in Nebraska or Colorado; or it might, as in the case of Idaho and Arizona, evolve into a mixed and eventually no-party arrangement. Montana, Utah, Wyoming, and New Mexico, according to Owens's analysis, fell firmly into the no-party camp as soon as the "chaotic factionalism" phase was over. In each instance, government came to be managed by a coalition of local interest-groups which cut across party lines: the Mormon Church in Utah; the "Santa Fe Ring" headed by Stephen Elkins and Thomas B. Catron in New Mexico after 1872; Francis E. Warren and Joseph M. Carey, backed by the business community, in Wyoming; and an alliance of entrepreneur Samuel T. Hauser, Delegate Martin Maginnis, and Governor Benjamin Potts in territorial Montana. Such leaders believed that existing governmental machinery alone did not adequately safeguard their own immediate enterprise nor the general material development and welfare of their region. Thus by shrewd alignments, they built small coalitions which represented upper-class interests but were broadly supported by the electorate, and they effectively controlled territorial politics, minimizing in the process the direct influence both of appointed federal officials and voters.

It is with this framework in mind that I wish to view early Montana. Montana was a territory from 1864 to 1889, a quarter-century which spanned much of the Gilded Age, that deceptively complex era of change and adjustment. In that era, industrial capitalism flowered: specialized labor and power-driven machinery brought under a single roof mass-produced goods for broad national (and soon international) markets. Expansion was the byword. Transcontinental railroads pushed westward, bringing settlers and troops, hastening the end of the Indian, and making possible the rapid exploitation of abundant natural resources. American farmers took up nearly as much land in that quarter-century as in all the previous years combined; agriculture not only expanded, but became more mechanized, specialized, and commercialized. If farmers' sons were not drawn west, many were lured to the bright lights of the cities, where they joined the wave of immigrants in adding to the labor force and growing problems of the urban environment.

Earlier historians have characterized the age as one of crass materialism, low national manners and morals, and surrender to the "robber baron" looters who despoiled the nation's resources and nearly pulled down the economic and political structure around their own heads. To be sure, industrial growth did concentrate economic power in the hands of comparatively few, often men of flexible conscience and limited concepts of social responsibility who controlled political as well as business life. But more recent historians have tempered this view, recognizing that while exploitation, corruption, and great emotion characterized the drive for wealth and power, society in general also displayed a lively interest in politics and government and maintained an optimistic belief in the idea of progress. If, through glamourous military leaders, the Republican party tended to dominate the White House and, through a broad program of nationalism and spending, to enhance the role of the central government and to hold a firm grip on the North and the West, the Republicans were not unchallenged. Doggedly clinging to outmoded concepts of local rule and negative protection of individualism, the Democrats provided stiff competition and the two parties were generally closely balanced, although American politics adjusted slowly to new conditions.

Two thousand miles to the west, Montanans were as much a part of the Gilded Age as their New York City counterparts, and their territorial history must be viewed against this national backdrop. They, too, would have their own blend of politics and business, their own formula for regional growth. Economic progress in Montana was tied to population expansion, the amassing of capital, and advancing technology—each of which depended to some extent upon the East or upon the federal government. "Colonialism was—and to a large measure still is—the dominant matrix of Western economic life," says Gene Gressley.[4] Government came to be viewed not merely as a giver of organic and enabling acts, but as an agent of economic growth and prosperity. At election time, national issues like the tariff, currency reform, or civil service reform were by no means ignored, but more basic to Montanans were questions of the public domain, how to pump federal funds into roads, waterways, army posts, civic buildings, or Indian reservations, always with the hope that subsidy would come with a minimum of control, a feature nineteenth-century Americans were more than willing to embrace.[5] If individual political leaders or interest groups benefited, this was not out of keeping with the prevailing national attitudes of the interlocking relations of business and politics.

4. Gene M. Gressley, *West by East: The American West in the Gilded Age* (Provo, 1972), 2.

5. Wallace D. Farnham, " 'The Weakened Spring of Government': A Study in Nineteenth-Century American History," *American Historical Review*, LXVIII (April, 1963), 662–80.

CHAPTER

1

"... Immense Nuggets Wherewith to Dazzle the Eyes of Congressmen": The Creation of a Territory

On Wednesday, May 26, 1864, the tall, gaunt man in the White House affixed his signature to the bill creating a temporary form of government for the Territory of Montana. Thus with a single stroke of his pen, President Lincoln carved out and set aside for future statehood a huge block of more than ninety-two million acres—nearly three times the size of his home state of Illinois.[1] Falling roughly between the forty-ninth parallel on the north, the forty-fifth parallel on the south, the 104th meridian to the east, and the crest of the Bitterroot and Beaverhead mountains in the west, this vast region divided itself historically and geographically into distinct sections. Approximately two-fifths of the new territory lay in the western and southwestern highlands—the "Land of Shining Mountains" as translated from the Indians; the remaining three-fifths east of the Rockies was high, gently rolling plains land, broken by hills, smaller mountain ranges, and wide river valleys. Fully one-fifth of the region belonged to the Pacific Slope, drained by the Columbia and its tributaries; four-fifths, through the sprawling Missouri River system, emptied ultimately into the Gulf of Mexico.[2]

1. Act of May 26, 1864, 13 *USSL*, 85–92; Preliminary Report of the United States Geological Survey of Montana and Portions of Adjacent Territories, *House Executive Document* No. 326, 42 Congress, 2 Session (1871–72), 248.

2. Preliminary Report of the United States Geological Survey of Montana and Portions of Adjacent Territories, 428.

Down to 1863, the history of the area tended to diverge sharply at the watershed of the Continental Divide, that of the region west of the mountains being associated with the Oregon country, and that east of the crest being part of the story of the Louisiana Purchase. For administrative purposes the eastern section became successively a part of Indiana, Louisiana, and Missouri territories, for a time hung in limbo as part of unorganized Indian country, and then was added one time after another to Kansas, Dakota, and Idaho territories. The area between the crest of the Rockies and the top of the Bitterroots north of the forty-fifth parallel had followed a more international course. Part of the Oregon country, it had once been claimed by Spain, Russia, England, and the United States. After Spain and Russia had bowed out and following the period of joint British and American occupation, it gravitated to the United States and was, in turn, attached to the Oregon, Washington, and Idaho territories. Thus, by the signing of his name in 1864, President Lincoln welded the Montana plains and mountains together as a governmental unit for the first time.[3]

During much of the era before the Civil War, the number of people in this vast sprawling wilderness was not great enough to warrant the creation of effective political machinery: only gradually did population grow and pressures develop. Following in the wake of Lewis and Clark, fur traders and trappers invaded the up-river area, planting posts in its very heart. During the 1830s and 1840s, the Jesuits, under the indefatigable Pierre De Smet, began the task of Christianizing the Flatheads of the Bitterroot Valley; occasional adventurers wandered into the region in search of excitement, and in 1850 hardy John Owen presaged the dawn of a new era when he established a trading post in the middle of the Bitterroot country that would provide a nucleus for future settlement.

The movement of pioneers to Oregon, the California gold rush, the Mexican War, and the signing of trade agreements with China in 1844 and with Japan ten years later all helped turn America's eyes to the Far West. It was no accident that the Army appropriations bill of 1853 carried a rider calling for exploration of possible railroad routes to the Pacific. Nor was it chance that one of the routes examined

3. See J. U. Sanders, "Hundred Governors Rule Montana in Two Centuries," *Contributions to the Historical Society of Montana, with its Transactions, Officers, and Members,* 9 vols. (1876–1923), IX (1923), 355–57 (cited hereafter as *Contributions*); Binger Hermann, *The Louisiana Purchase* (Washington, 1898), 51; act of August 14, 1848, 9 *USSL*, 323; acts of March 2, 1853, and May 30, 1854, 10 *USSL*, 172, 277; acts of March 2, 1861, and March 3, 1863, 12 *USSL*, 239, 808–9.

crossed the northern section of the country between the forty-seventh and forty-ninth parallels, and that Isaac Stevens's official report upon it cast credit on Montana and brought the entire Northwest more in focus with the rest of the nation.

By the winter of 1859, enough settlers had filtered into the beautiful valleys between the Bitterroots and the main range of the Rockies to petition the territorial legislature of Washington for the organization of a separate county government for that region.[4] In response, the assembly created Missoula County in December, 1860, to include practically all of that portion of modern Montana lying west of the Continental Divide, with the area tied to Spokane County for judicial purposes. The county seat was located at the trading post of Worden and Company, Hell's Gate, and at the first election in June or July, 1861, seventy-four ballots were cast for local officials.[5] A year later, when the Mullan Road construction crews had moved on, only thirty votes were counted, but Granville Stuart, who was chosen county commissioner, noted in his diary: "We held an election today. Great excitement but nobody hurt except with an overdose of whiskey."[6]

Early in 1859, Brigadier General W. S. Harney, commanding the Department of Oregon, had considered the territory embraced by the upper Clark's Fork, the Bitterroot River, and the headwaters of the Beaver. That country "will not be occupied by the whites for at least twenty-five years," he said. "It is difficult of access, and does not offer the same inducements to the settler that are everywhere presented to him on the coast."[7] What Harney could not foresee, however, was the introduction of new factors. Within five years these very hills and valleys would feel the boots of a small army of whites: not farmers, but prospectors drawn by the magnetic pull of yellow gold.

The discovery of gold in the summer of 1860 by Captain E. D. Pierce and a small party on the Clearwater in what was then Washington Territory (subsequently Idaho), sparked a rush to that region.

4. Twenty-seven men signed the petition. Hubert Howe Bancroft, *The History of Washington, Idaho, and Montana, 1846–1889* (San Francisco, 1890), 618–19.

5. Frank H. Woody, "A Sketch of the Early History of Western Montana," *Contributions*, II (1896), 99. For county organizations of the Bitterroot and Deer Lodge valleys while part of Washington, see *Session Laws of the Territory of Washington*, 1 Session (1854), 472–73; 5 Session (1857–58), 51; 8 Session (1860–61), 7–8, 436–37 (cited hereafter as *Laws of Washington*).

6. Granville Stuart, *Forty Years on the Frontier, as seen in the Journals and Reminiscences of Granville Stuart*, ed. by Paul C. Phillips (Cleveland, 1925), I, 58.

7. Report of Brigadier General W. S. Harney (June 3, 1859), in *Annual Report of the Secretary of War, 1859*, 103.

In September of the following year, new strikes on the Salmon, farther south, attracted thousands from the old diggings and from elsewhere. Next came discoveries in the Boise Basin, along the tributaries of the Snake, and ever hopeful color-hungry prospectors swarmed into the new centers of activity. Although west of Montana proper, these events were important preliminaries to the creation of that territory. The logical route to the new Idaho fields ran either along the old Overland Trail to Fort Hall, then fanned out to the north and west, or it followed a more northern course up the Missouri River to Fort Benton and on across the mountains. The value of the Missouri route was obvious because steam transportation was available to Benton and the head of navigation. At the same time, many a sturdy, vigorous young man might travel a variation of the northern route overland, possibly with one of the four "Minnesota to Montana" expeditions escorted by Captain James L. Fisk between 1862 and 1866.[8]

Many of these migrants worked their way west through the mountains, prospecting as they went. Others, disappointed in the Idaho diggings, wandered eastward over the new Mullan Road, never too occupied to wash a few pans of dirt in the crystal mountain streams. Still others drifted northward from the Colorado mines, victims of severe cases of "quartz on the brain" and confident that their efforts would ultimately reap rewards.

Most were doomed to disappointment but the few exceptions made profound impacts. In July, 1862, John White hit paydirt at Grasshopper Creek, a tributary of the Beaverhead, and the news precipitated a rush and brought Bannack City into existence almost overnight. In the spring of the following year, accidental finds at Alder Gulch, some sixty miles to the east, brought another stampede and the new center of Virginia City soon rivaled Bannack in population and activity. As always, such bustling camps contained not only miners and legitimate businessmen but many who hoped to fleece the unwary. Schooled in cities of the east or in the rough classrooms of Washoe, Central City, or the Fraser River, the newly arrived gamblers, prostitutes, highwaymen, and smooth-tongued vendors of mining stock included talented and unscrupulous drifters from all parts of the world.

At the same time, the new mines were too far from the seat of

8. See Hiram M. Chittenden, *History of Early Steamboat Navigation on the Missouri River* (New York, 1903), II, 270–75; W. Turrentine Jackson, "The Fisk Expeditions to the Montana Gold Fields," *Pacific Northwest Quarterly*, XXXIII (July, 1942), 265–82.

government of Washington, Olympia, or the capital of territorial Dakota, Yankton, to permit any effective protection from those governments, except in name only. Consequently, in response to growing pressures, Congress created the Territory of Idaho in the spring of 1863 in an effort to meet the needs of a rapidly expanding mining population west of the Rockies. The new territory included roughly all of modern Idaho, Montana, and Wyoming;[9] but the distance from Bannack and Alder Gulch to the territorial capital, now Lewiston, even as before was so great, with impassable terrain in the winter, that effective controls or representation were out of the question. True, Governor William Wallace in 1863 did organize Missoula County and the remaining country east of the Rockies into a vast judicial district under Chief Justice Sidney Edgerton, and in January of the following year the Idaho territorial assembly formally created ten counties east of the Bitterroots.[10] But there was a wide gap between the creation and the effective functioning of such local units.

In general, the American territorial structure seems to have been geared to a relatively slow, even development, such as followed agricultural advancement, rather than the rapid, often sporadic and unpredictable convulsions typical of the mineral frontier. Typically the Alder Gulches, the Bannacks, and their many counterparts cropped up practically without warning four or five hundred miles from the nearest seat of organized government. Usually the territorial mechanism proved to weak or too inflexible to adjust quickly enough to meet the exigencies of the situation and extraneous forms of local government came into play until legal authority caught up practically with settlement.

Without precedent in federal statutes, such forms were rooted in necessity and in the tradition of the American frontier. In mining camps generally—and Montana was no exception—two distinct mechanisms were apparent: mining camp law and spontaneous vigilante groups. In the case of the first, when a new discovery was made, one of the first moves of the discoverers was to draw up regulations governing claims and to elect a recorder, a judge, and possibly a sheriff. Typical organization of this type was effected at Bannack in the winter of 1862 and at Alder Gulch the following spring.[11] Within this

9. Act of March 3, 1863, 12 *USSL*, 808–9.
10. Hiram T. French, *History of Idaho* (Chicago, 1914), I, 58; act of January 16, 1864, *Laws of Idaho*, 1 Session (1863–64), 674–77.
11. Stuart, *Forty Years on the Frontier*, I, 232–33; Merrill G. Burlingame, *The Montana Frontier* (Helena, 1942), 96.

structure, cases of all sorts might be tried—mineral and water rights disputes, debt default, robbery, assault, and even murder. Sometimes controversies were brought before a jury, in addition to the judge, with final appeal to an open meeting of all residents. Often, besides acting as a court of final appeal, the assembled miners might make additional rules, elect officers, decide difficult claim questions, and occasionally exercise original jurisdiction over more serious criminal matters.

A second and more severe organ of justice was frequently found in the vigilance committees that rose to meet particular situations. Where the miners' court brought about the arrest of a suspect, then tried him before his peers, vigilante justice first secretly judged and convicted him, then meted out a swift and often harsh brand of punishment. "The first successful uplift movement in Montana," as Jerre Murphy calls the vigilante activity there,[12] was particularly strong and picturesque in large part because the same was true of the criminal element in the early territory. The story of Henry Plummer and the group of well-organized ruffians who terrorized Bannack and Virginia City and the surrounding areas during much of 1863 is well known. Powerless to cope by ordinary means with this band of blackguards, a rowdy element which displayed a remarkable degree of coordination and whose leader was actually elected sheriff, law-abiding citizens resorted to the formation of a secret vigilante committee.

Built around a hard core of Masons and Union Leaguers and headed by men like John X. Beidler (better known as "X"), one of the territory's early heroes; Nathaniel Pitt Langford, soon to become U.S. Collector of Internal Revenue and subsequently historian of the local vigilance group; and Wilbur Fisk Sanders, the uncrowned sovereign of the Montana Republican party for half a century, the vigilantes overwhelmed and completely eliminated Plummer's outlaw band during the early months of 1864. According to Langford, there was no alternative to summary executions in "this Godless country, this country of lawlessness . . . this country where nearly 200 murders have been committed but no man convicted by the Courts. . . ."[13]

Necessary or not, both the miners' courts and the vigilante groups

12. Jerre C. Murphy, *The Comical History of Montana* (San Diego, 1912), 1.
13. Nathaniel P. Langford to J. W. Taylor (Virginia City, May 20, 1866), copy, Nathaniel P. Langford MSS, Minnesota Historical Society. See also Allen Johnson and Dumas Malone, eds., *Dictionary of American Biography* (New York, 1928–), X, 592–93 (cited hereafter as DAB); Nathaniel Langford, *Vigilante Days and Ways* (New York, 1893), I, 323; Thomas J. Dimsdale, *The Vigilantes of Montana* (Virginia City, 1921 ed.), 26–27.

contained inherent weaknesses: their justice was sometimes more rigorous than the crime warranted; decisions were often colored by emotion and sentiment; and it could be argued that mining camp law tended to create petty monopolies in the hands of a few original discoverers to the exclusion of others.[14] Certainly the basic shortcomings of these extralegal organizations accentuated the growing demand for the creation of a new territory that would place formal government on an effective basis. The Idaho governmental unit was much too large. Tradition and the son of Wilbur F. Sanders have it that the first to call for the creation of a separate territory of Montana was the pugilist and saloon-keeper Con Orem, who while in a mellow mood huzzahed a crowd on that subject from the back end of a wagon on a Sunday morning. However that may be, residents of Bannack and Virginia City were concerned about the lack of a formal, effective government, and late in 1863 a number, including Sanders, Langford, Samuel Hauser, and Francis M. Thompson, began to act. Sanders and Hauser, the latter "a hearty, boisterous and talkative young fellow," were instrumental in collecting $2,500 in gold samples, plus cash, to send Sidney Edgerton to Washington to lobby for the cause in Congress.[15]

The chief justice of Idaho, assigned to Bannack and the judicial district east of the mountains, Edgerton was the logical choice. An Ohioan and a Republican of staunch convictions, he had previously represented a constituency from the Buckeye State for two terms in the U.S. House of Representatives, hence could be expected to have the political acumen and contacts required for effective action.[16]

14. Dimsdale, *Vigilantes of Montana,* 79–87; *Montana Post* (December 10, 1864 [published in Virginia City to mid-April, 1868; thereafter in Helena]); John W. Smurr, "Afterthoughts on the Vigilantes," *Montana,* VIII (April, 1958), 8–20.

15. Sidney Edgerton to William M. Hunt (Akron, May 23, 1892); Edgerton to Wilbur F. Sanders (Akron, March 21, 1886), both in Sidney Edgerton Collection, MHS; Martha Edgerton Plassmann, "Biographical Sketch of Hon. Sidney Edgerton," *Contributions,* III (1900), 337; Wilbur E. Sanders, "Montana: Organization, Name and Naming," *ibid.,* VII (1910), 54, 55; Wilbur F. Sanders, "Sidney Edgerton, the First Governor of Montana (Helena, February, 1886), 4–5 unpublished MS, Bancroft Library, University of California.

16. Edgerton (1818–1900) was born in New York and moved in 1844 to Ohio, where he taught school and studied law in the office of abolitionist Rufus Spaulding. A local leader in the anti-slave movement, he was subsequently a delegate to the convention that formed the Free Soil party in 1848 and to the first Republican national convention. Elected to Congress in 1858, he sought to eliminate slavery in the territories and he advocated a transcontinental railroad, but was not a candidate for reelection in 1862. In 1863 he was appointed chief justice of Idaho. Sanders, "Sidney Edgerton," 1–4; *DAB,* VI, 20

After a delay due to the hanging of Plummer and his cohorts, Edgerton left the mines in January, 1864, traveling on horseback through snowy weather to Salt Lake City, carrying in his baggage and in the lining of his overcoat "immense nuggets wherewith to dazzle the eyes of Congressmen and to impress upon their minds by means of an object lesson some adequate idea of the great mineral wealth of this section of the country."[17]

Once in Washington, Edgerton was pleased to find the groundwork already laid, for on December 14, 1863, Representative James M. Ashley of Ohio had introduced a bill to provide a temporary government for the Territory of Montana. This measure had been referred to the House Committee on the Territories, of which Ashley was chairman, and the congressional mill began slowly to grind. Edgerton worked closely with Ashley and entertained other congressmen. His borrowed gold he "flourished gracefully, and incessantly before their covetous eyes and soon got their ears," he recounted later, admitting that he passed off a large piece of retorted gold as a nugget to representatives to whom Idaho, Montana, and Wyoming "were about as little known as the dark continent."[18]

Cooperating with Edgerton was William H. Wallace, formerly governor but now delegate from Idaho, who in March, 1864, presented to the House a memorial from the Idaho legislature "praying for a division of the Territory, and the erection of the eastern portion thereof into a new Territory to be called Jefferson Territory."[19] Pointing to the vastness of the present territory and the mountain barriers separating the eastern mines from the seat of government at Lewiston, more than four hundred miles distant, this petition noted with pride the contribution in mineral wealth made by this area and hastened to emphasize that the region had elected honest, loyal Unionists to the first Idaho legislature. It estimated the population east of the mountains at from fifteen to twenty thousand, a reasonably fair appraisal.[20]

When Ashley's bill was reported out in mid-March, it met little opposition in the House. Proposed boundaries on the west were the

17. Plassmann, "Biographical Sketch of Hon. Sidney Edgerton," 337–38.

18. *Congressional Globe*, 38 Congress, 1 Session (1863–64), 19; Edgerton to Hunt (Akron, May 23, 1892), Sidney Edgerton Collection.

19. *Congressional Globe*, 38 Congress, 1 Session (1863–64), 991; Ansel Wold, comp., *Biographical Directory of the American Congresses, 1774–1927* (Washington, 1928), 1662.

20. Memorial to Congress (December 22, 1863), in *Congressional Globe*, 38 Congress, 1 Session (1863–64), 1168.

Bitterroots, to the delight of the petitioners, though Wallace's support of this line may have cost him the next election.[21] Ashley threw his full weight behind the measure and spoke persuasively on its behalf. A member of an earlier commission to Colorado, he was in genuine sympathy with western sentiments for the creation of new territorial governments. Among other arguments, he pointed out that the estimated cost of a territorial government was $20,000 per year, but that the resulting protection reduced the danger of large-scale Indian warfare and meant an actual economy from the federal administration's point of view.[22]

Michigan representative Fernando C. Beaman eloquently supported Ashley with a reference to the recent vigilante happenings at Bannack and Virginia City, which he said were prima facie evidence of a real need for organized government. Beaman further disclosed that "an unnamed gentleman" had informed him that by summer, 1865, that part of Idaho would have at least 100,000 people.[23]

In the House, opposition was negligible. A brief discussion of the name of the proposed territory consumed as much time as any other aspect of the original debate. It was Ashley who selected the word "Montana." Sunset Cox of Ohio proposed "Shoshone" and facetiously suggested "Douglas Territory" on the theory that it would please the followers of both Frederick Douglass and Stephen A. Douglas. The irascible Elihu Washburne of Illinois jokingly proposed the name "Abyssinia," but no change of name was forthcoming.[24]

Representative Spaulding of Ohio voiced nominal opposition contending that the proposal was uneconomical—that since the Territory of Idaho had been created only during the previous session of Congress and was not yet fully organized, there could be no actual need for splitting it in two and thus doubling administrative expenses. An amendment was suggested by Congressman Davis of New York permitting the president to assign officers already appointed to the Territory of Idaho to the new territory, without new commissions being necessary. This proposed infringement on the Senate's power to confirm territorial appointees elicited criticism, particularly from Thaddeus Stevens of Pennsylvania, who fervently upheld the supremacy of the legislative branch. The Senate, Stevens insisted, must

21. Edgerton to Hunt (Akron, May 23, 1892), Sidney Edgerton Collection.
22. *Congressional Globe*, 38 Congress, 1 Session (1863–64), 1169.
23. *Ibid.*, 1168.
24. *Ibid.*, 1169; James M. Ashley to Hunt (Toledo, April 28, 1892), single letter in MHS.

pass on the transfer of such officials, particularly the territorial judge, for judiciary appointments in the territories were on an entirely different footing from others—they were "congressional courts created by acts of Congress." A colleague from Iowa did not necessarily agree with Stevens, but could see but one reason for the amendment—the benefit of one of the Idaho justices who might wish to remain in the new territory.[25] No names were mentioned, but obviously Chief Justice Edgerton was the one in mind.

But such opposition was minor. The amendment was accepted, and the bill passed the House on March 17, with little trouble. In the Senate, initial discussion augered well. Nesmith of Oregon urged passage on the ground that such action would facilitate taxation of mines and bring in much-needed revenue for the Union war chest. If John P. Hale, the dour senator from New Hampshire, voiced the thrifty virtues of his New England forebears in charging that the real reason behind the bill was the creation of more political offices, his was but a voice in the wilderness. Senator Sumner questioned the name "Montana," and demanded to know its source. "It seems to me it must have been borrowed from some novel or another," he chided. But when someone produced a Latin dictionary and pronounced it "a very classical word, pure Latin," Sumner was mollified.[26]

An amendment was accepted to attach the territory to the surveyor general's district of Kansas and Nebraska for survey purposes, apparently an economy measure, and acceptance of the bill seemed imminent. At this point, however, Morton S. Wilkinson of Minnesota moved an amendment that pushed the race question to the forefront and touched off bitter debate. Where section five of the act prescribed voting qualifications for the first territorial election and restricted suffrage to "every free white male inhabitant above the age of twenty-one years, who shall have been an actual resident of said Territory for thirty days prior to the first election," Wilkinson would amend this section by striking out the words "white male inhabitant" and substituting "male citizen of the United States and those who have declared their intention to become such" in their place.[27]

Clearly the original wording of section five was weak: under it, French-Canadian trappers or other British subjects might conceivably

25. *Congressional Globe*, 38 Congress, 1 Session (1863–64), 1168–69.
26. *Ibid.*, 1169, 1362, 2349, 2350. Years later, Ashley, who selected the name, referred to it as "the Spanish Mexicanized word Montana." Ashley to Hunt (Toledo, April 28, 1892), single letter in MHS.
27. *Congressional Globe*, 38 Congress, 1 Session (1863–64), 1346, 1361–62, 1705.

have been able to participate in Montana's first election. Wilkinson may have been aware of this possibility, but undoubtedly he proposed this particular change with one purpose in mind—to give at least theoretical voting rights to newly freed blacks in the territory to be created. Whatever its intent, the Minnesota senator's amendment brought an extended argument of Negro rights in which the question of Montana as a territory was momentarily obscured. Some saw it as a deliberate attempt to enfranchise the ex-slaves and were aroused from their lethargy to open opposition. Old Reverdy Johnson from the border state of Maryland bellowed like a wounded sea lion at the thought of the black man at the polls, and suggested that blacks might migrate to Montana en masse to gain control of the government. In empassioned debate, the whole question of the Dred Scott decision was aired by both sides, with no more agreement than in earlier years.[28] Most senators were prone to forget that there were few blacks in Montana, and that the voting qualifications under discussion applied only to the first territorial election; qualifications for subsequent elections were to be prescribed by the first legislative assembly in the territory.

When the oratory had subsided, the Senate passed the measure with the Wilkinson amendment and sent it back to the House for concurrence. There, after the unleashing of much verbal artillery, with some, like Pendleton of Ohio viewing the amendment as a test case, challenging the willingness of Congress to give political or social equality to the blacks, the House stood firm and refused to accept the Wilkinson modification. Twice committees of conference were called to effect a compromise: twice they failed. Finally, on the third attempt an agreeable adjustment was made: voting privileges at the first territorial election were to extend to "all citizens of the United States, and those who have declared their intentions to become such, and who are otherwise described and qualified under the fifth section of the act of congress providing a temporary government for the territory of Idaho. . . . ."[29] Since that portion of the Idaho organic act referred to restricting the franchise for the first election to "free white male inhabitants above the age of twenty-one years" who were actual residents,[30] this "compromise" really favored the more conservative element in the House.

To compensate for this, the House agreed to strike out its amend-

28. *Ibid.*, 1346, 1363–64, 1744–45.
29. *Ibid.*, 1364, 1378; act of May 26, 1864, 13 *USSL*, 87–88.
30. Act of March 3, 1863, 12 *USSL*, 810.

ment regarding the transfer of officers from the Territory of Idaho, while the Senate retreated from its position on the location of the survey office, leaving that to the discretion of the Secretary of the Interior. With these points settled, the Senate on May 19 voted its approval, and on the following day the House followed suit.[31] Six days later, President Lincoln added his endorsement and the new Territory of Montana was officially born, with James Ashley and Sidney Edgerton serving as energetic midwives.

At no time did congressional arguments threaten to block the passage of this measure. The withdrawal of southern politicians from Washington at the beginning of the war removed one important barrier to this type of legislation, while a newly established alignment between East and West intended to make Congress more receptive to the establishment of additional territories beyond the Mississippi River. But the debates over the Montana bill did illustrate a common tendency on the part of national lawmakers to lose sight of the territories themselves, and to argue more controversial matters, while western peoples waited impatiently for legislation on their behalf. Montanans would find that during their quarter of a century in territorial status this would be the prevailing pattern.

The territorial organic act served as a framework of government, much like the old colonial charters of two centuries before. Like those of Colorado and Wyoming, that of Montana was modeled on the Wisconsin act of 1836. It was a fairly detailed document of some five thousand words, and it indicated a growing tendency of Congress toward greater objectivity in the "dos" and "don'ts" prescribed for territorial government. Yet it was not, nor was it intended to be, more than a bare outline. If in some respects it provided a rigid yardstick and in others a more plastic one, it remained above all simply a law enacted by a benevolent Congress and, as such, subject to amendment or even revocation, should the parent body desire.

By the terms of the organic act, Montana's boundaries were defined. With the exception of minor adjustments to offset technical errors and to bring the realities of geography in line with the lines on the maps,[32]

31. Act of May 26, 1864, 13 *USSL*, 89; *Congressional Globe*, 38 Congress, 1 Session (1863–64), 2351, 2360.

32. When the Territory of Wyoming was carved out of Dakota in 1868, defective wording left a small area just west of the 111th meridian still technically attached to Dakota but physically separated by hundreds of miles. When the error was discovered, Congress in 1873 legally affixed this land to Montana, which had exercised jurisdiction over it anyway. Act of February 17, 1873, 17 *USSL*, 464; U.S. *Geological Survey Bulletin* No. 817 (1930), 220.

these boundaries would remain unchanged throughout the territorial era and down to the present day. The law also laid down the basic guidelines for establishment and operation of all branches of government—executive, legislative and judicial—following the then standard organization.

Executive power was to be vested in a governor, appointed by the president with the consent and advice of the Senate, who was to hold office for a four-year term and who was to be ex officio superintendent of Indian affairs and commander-in-chief of the territorial militia. Among other powers, the governor had the right to grant pardons and respites for offenses committed against the laws of the territory and to grant reprieves for crimes against federal laws until such time as the president's pleasure could be made known. To the governor were delegated a number of special functions, including the right to organize both judicial and legislative districts prior to the election of the first legislative assembly and the power to appoint, with the consent of the territorial council, all officers not otherwise provided for by the act.[33]

Aiding the governor in his administrative role was the secretary, whose mode of selection and term of office were similar to those of the chief executive. The secretary recorded and transmitted to Congress the proceedings of the legislature and he assumed the duties of governor when that official was absent, but his most important function was as disbursing agent for federal funds in the territory.

Legislative power was to be vested in the governor and in a legislative assembly consisting of a council of seven members and a house of representatives initially of thirteen, but with provision for the size of the house to be doubled in keeping with an expanding population. Per diem payment to members was set, the length of legislative sessions limited, and the extent of legislative powers defined. Generally speaking, these powers were broad and extended to all matters consistent with the Constitution and federal statutes, with specific clauses to preclude any interference with the primary disposal of the public domain, certain inequities of taxation or violation of Indian treaties negotiated by the government in Washington. To the governor was reserved the power to veto legislative bills, but repassage by a two-thirds majority of both houses would override his objections. And, though not expressly written into the organic act,

33. Discussion of provisions here are from act of May 26, 1864, 13 *USSL*, 86–91.

the tacit understanding always existed that Congress might at any time nullify laws enacted by the territorial assembly.

The organic act established the outlines of a judicial system, with district and supreme courts built around three justices who were both territorial and federal judges and who in territorial law exercised both original and appellate jurisdiction. Like the states, Montana was provided with a lower structure of probate courts and justices of the peace. And in the fashion of other territories, she was entitled to elect a delegate to plead her cause, but not to vote, in the national House of Representatives. Lesser federal officials—United States attorney, marshal, and surveyor general—were to be appointed, and their fees, salaries, and duties were prescribed in the law, as were those of the administrative and judicial officers.

With the passage of the organic act, the script was written: next came the selection of the cast. With Sidney Edgerton in Washington were young Sam Hauser and Nathaniel P. Langford. All three had applied for federal posts in the new territory: Edgerton for governor, Hauser for secretary, and Langford for surveyor general.[34] Despite negative sentiments from Minnesota's Wilkinson, who castigated him for leaving his judicial duties in Idaho to lobby in Washington, Edgerton was successful in his campaign for the governorship and received word of his appointment at Salt Lake City on his return, continuing on to Bannack in time to take part in the Fourth of July celebration there.[35] Langford was appointed collector of internal revenue in Montana, but Hauser, who was a Democrat, could not have been surprised when he received nothing from the Republican administration.[36]

34. See "List of Applicants for Montana Appointments" [c. June, 1864], "Memorandum of Appointments" [c. June, 1864], in Roy P. Basler, ed., *The Collected Works of Abraham Lincoln* (New Brunswick, 1953), VI, 371–72. It has been argued that Hauser and Langford went to Washington not so much to seek posts for themselves, but more to make sure that Edgerton and his nephew, Sanders, did not gain too much influence. John W. Hakola, "Samuel T. Hauser and the Economic Development of Montana: A Case Study in Nineteenth-Century Frontier Capitalism" (Ph.D. dissertation, Indiana University, 1961), 24, 28.

35. While Edgerton was in Washington, complained Wilkinson, Idahoans "being left without courts, have without law Arrested and hung over twenty persons Supposed to be guilty of Crimes." Morton S. Wilkinson to Lincoln (Washington, May 20, 1864), Edgerton file, APS. See also Lincoln to Morton S. Wilkinson (Washington, June 20, 1864), Basler, *Collected Works of Lincoln*, VII, 403; *Senate Executive Journal*, XIII, 590, 594; Edgerton to William H. Hunt (Akron, May 23, 1892), MHS; Mary Edgerton to Martha Carter (Bannack, July 13, 1864), Edgerton family MSS, MHS.

36. Hakola, "Samuel T. Hauser," 28–29; *DAB*, X, 592.

The office of territorial secretary was first offered to the Reverend Henry P. Torsey, "Ll.D., President, and Professor of Medical and Moral Philosophy, and Natural Science" at Wesleyan Seminary and Female College in Maine; but Torsey declined on the basis of poor health.[37] John Coburn of Indiana, to whom the position was also offered, also saw fit to reject the honor, and not until early August, 1865, when the colorful Thomas Francis Meagher accepted it, was the vacancy filled.[38] As chief justice, Lincoln selected Hezekiah Lord Hosmer, an active Ohio Unionist who had served as secretary to the House Committee on the Territories that drew up Montana's organic act, though it is clear that Hosmer had long been interested in becoming librarian of Congress.[39] For associate justice, Lincoln appointed Ammi Giddings of Connecticut, who resigned immediately because of his own and his wife's ill health and was replaced by Lyman Ezra Munson, another son of the Nutmeg State.[40] The third member of the judicial triumvirate was Lorenzo P. Williston, a Pennsylvanian who had previously served on the bench of Dakota Territory.[41]

Other federal officers, not territorial in a strict sense, were selected at the same time. In addition to the new collector of internal revenue, Langford, there were Edward B. Neally of Iowa, who became the first U.S. attorney; Minnesotan Cornelius Buck, who was offered the post of U.S. marshal, but resigned in favor of George M. Pinney of Dakota; and Truman C. Everts, who became assessor of internal revenue.[42]

37. Henry P. Torsey to Lincoln (Kent's Hill, Maine, October 14, 1864), TPS.

38. *Senate Executive Journal*, XIII, 590, 594; XIV (Pt. 1), 191, 220, 487. Subsequently, in 1884, Coburn accepted a position as associate justice in Montana. *Ibid.*, XXIV, 182, 188.

39. *Ibid.*, XIII, 591, 637; Ashley to Lincoln (Washington, March 9, 1861), Robert Todd Lincoln MSS, Library of Congress. Hezekiah Hosmer (1814–93) was born in New York, studied law in Cleveland, and after 1835 dabbled in both law and journalism. In 1844 he became associated with the *Toledo Daily Blade*, in 1858 published an *Early History of the Maumee Valley*, and two years later was the author of a novel, *Adela, the Octoroon*. First a Whig, then in 1860 a Republican, he became secretary to the House Committee on the Territories through the influence of James Ashley. *DAB*, IX, 243.

40. Ammi Giddings to Hezekiah Hosmer (Plymouth Ct. [?], May 5, 1865), Hezekiah Hosmer MSS, Beinecke Library, Yale Unversity; *Senate Executive Journal*, XIII, 591, 594; XIV (Pt. 1), 273, 297. A Yale graduate, Munson had practiced law for a number of years in New Haven. Edward L. Munson, "Lyman Ezra Munson," *Contributions*, VII (1907), 199.

41. *Senate Executive Journal*, XIII, 591, 594; Basler, *Collected Works of Lincoln*, VII, 371.

42. *Senate Executive Journal*, XIII, 591, 594; XIV (Pt. 1), 15, 16, 83, 84, 161, 178.

Almost all officers were nonresidents of Montana; only a few had any real experience in territorial government. With the exception of Meagher, the appointee of the Johnson administration, they had in common the fact that they were Republicans. That fact, in a territory where the bulk of the population were Democrats, would sound an ominous note in a setting of wartime strains and animosities.

2

"... The Choice of the Loyal People of Montana": Sidney Edgerton Organizes a Territorial Government

When Sidney Edgerton returned to Bannack in July, 1864, he saw for the first time his fifth child, a daughter named Idaho, born during his interlude in Washington. But his main concern was the infant Montana, a lusty but undisciplined babe, yet to be nurtured to political adulthood. It fell to Edgerton, as the first governor, to take the preliminary steps, as contemplated in the organic act, to breathe life into the machinery of self-government. From his office in a curtained-off corner of his log cabin, which also doubled as a residence and at times a schoolroom, the new chief executive outlined judicial districts, commissioned county officers, named Bannack as the temporary capital (because, according to his wife, there were not so many "Copperheads" there as in Virginia), and ordered a census taken.[1] This hasty population count showed 15,812 people, the bulk of them in Madison County.[2] Edgerton proceeded to establish districts from which members of the legislative council and house would be selected,

1. Pauline Rolfe Archibald, "Mary Wright Edgerton," *Montana*, I (July, 1951), 38–39; Mary Wright Edgerton to Martha Carter (Bannack, November 6, 1864), Edgerton family MSS.
2. James Tufts to Sidney Edgerton (n.p., September 19, 1864), GEC. In September the *Montana Post* estimated the population at 20,000, but soon revised it downward to 15,822, of which 11,493 were in Madison County. *Montana Post*, September 17, October 8, 1864.

and to call a general election for October 24, to elect not only these representatives, but a delegate to Congress as well.[3]

A few months earlier, some of Edgerton's gubernatorial supporters had characterized him as "the choice of the loyal people of Montana . . . a man who knew the country and its needs."[4] This was mere rhetoric, for it is doubtful if Edgerton represented most Montanans or if he fully understood their political complexion. In 1864, when he assumed the governor's office, the territory was comprised of several political factions, but undoubtedly a substantial portion of the population was made up of Democrats, many of whom were of southern antecedents, if not openly anti-Union.

For nearly half a century, St. Louis had been linked with the Upper Missouri country through the fur traders moving up and down the great river highway, a natural tie with border and southern states. A young lady in Bannack wrote her father in 1863, "I verily believe that two-thirds of the people here are infidel and 'secesh.'" Internal Revenue Collector Langford was even less conservative. "Four-fifths of our citizens were *openly declared* Secessionists," he asserted in 1866. Montana, he said, "was a Territory more disloyal as a whole, than Tennessee or Kentucky ever was."[5] Another Edgerton supporter wrote in August, 1864, of his efforts to organize county government for Missoula, noting that there was but one Union man in Deer Lodge County. "The Union timber in this country is so scarce and scatterring [*sic*], that there is not enough eligible to officer the regiment."[6]

Perhaps these were extreme statements, but the evidence is clear that there was a strong pro-Confederate element in early Montana. Confederate Gulch, Jeff Davis Gulch, and the town of Dixie reflected southern impact on place names.[7] This is not to argue the legend that the Left Wing of "Pap" Price's Army retreated to the territory and

3. *Montana Post*, August 26, September 17, 24, 1864.

4. N. P. Langford et al. to Lincoln (Washington, March 17, 1864), Edgerton file, APS.

5. Emily R. Meredith to her father (Bannack, April 30, 1863), in Clyde McLemore, ed., "Bannack and Gallatin City in 1862–1863: a Letter by Mrs. Emily Meredith," *Frontier and Midland*, XVII (Summer, 1937), 285; Langford to J. W. Taylor (Virginia City, May 20, 1866), copy, Langford MSS.

6. Charles Hutchins to Sidney Edgerton (Jocko Agency, August 18, 1864), Charles Hutchins MSS, MHS. See also Robert E. Fisk to Elizabeth Chester (Helena, December 6, 1866), Fisk family MSS, MHS.

7. See Dimsdale, *Vigilantes of Montana*, 76, 270; Langford, *Vigilante Days and Ways*, I, 353–54; *Montana Post*, May 13, 1865; *New York Times*, August 30, 1868.

set out to add it to the Confederacy until halted by Sidney Edgerton, Wilbur F. Sanders, and other staunch Republicans. The situation was never that serious. But it is clear that southern sympathies did exist and that these attitudes were slow to die. That ardent Republicans kept them alive by "waving the bloody shirt" is also clear, but secessionist feeling was more than a "myth" and would color political life in the territory and contribute much to the discomfort of ultra-Unionist officials like Edgerton and James Ashley.[8]

Along with a southern Democratic element, early Montana also had its bloc of northern Democrats. Loyal to the Union, but subject to strong pressures from both Republicans and secessionists, they wavered at times; but in the end, because they were branded as traitors and "Copperheads" by the Unionists, they often cast their lot with the southern Democrats in the formative years.

And much in the minority was the hard core of Union Republicans, drawing their strength from migrants from the upper Midwest, and making up in spirit and vociferation what they lacked in numbers. This group organized the Union League as early as 1863,[9] and its leadership—men like Nathaniel Langford, Wilbur F. Sanders, and Robert Fisk, although representing a minority, were always forces to be reckoned with in the territory.

As the election of October, 1864, approached, it became increasingly clear that national issues would dominate the campaign. The "Union Territorial Ticket" stood four-square behind its candidate for delegate, Wilbur F. Sanders, lawyer, Civil War veteran, and long to be known as the essence of Montana Republicanism. Though he would be defeated four times for the delegateship, Sanders would become one of Montana's first senators when statehood was attained. Robert G. Ingersoll thought him "the keenest blade I have ever crossed"; another could say of him "His soul was as imperious as ever was Caesar's, and his tongue was perpetually firing poisoned arrows. . . . He was not always right, but he always meant to be right. There was no compromise with him."[10]

8. One argument minimizing actual pro-Confederate sentiment and viewing such feeling as more a myth perpetuated by territorial Republicans is James L. Thane, Jr., "The Myth of Confederate Sentiment," *Montana*, XVII (April, 1967), 14–19. A convincing antidote to this point of view is Stanley R. Davison and Dale Tash, "Confederate Back-Wash in Montana Territory," *ibid.*, XVII (October, 1967), 50–58.

9. Langford, *Vigilante Days and Ways*, I, 225–26; A. J. Smith to John Potter (Bannack, March 26, 1867), typescript copy, Langford MSS.

10. Born in Leon, New York, in 1834, Sanders in 1854 moved to Akron where he taught school and studied law with his uncle, Sidney Edgerton, ultimately

His opponent, selected by a territorial Democratic convention presided over by a former governor of Iowa, was "Colonel" Samuel McLean, also a lawyer, a native of Pennsylvania, and in 1860 attorney general of the provisional Territory of Jefferson (Colorado). Sanders observed that Montana was "in the hands of refugees from Price's Army, Missouri having the honor to mother over half our voting population at least. . . ." While not a Missourian, McLean nonetheless espoused "the most radical Pendleton Peace views," Sanders said: he would recognize the Rebels and woo them back into the Union. "Do not regard him I beseech you as an intellectual speciman of our opposition," Sanders wrote James A. Garfield. "They have many better men but he is a very clever old fellow."[11]

Thomas Dimsdale's *Montana Post* made every effort to pull the support of the northern Democrats behind Sanders. "There are but two parties now," argued the editor, "patriots and traitors. Let every Democrat, every Republican, every true lover of his country respond." The choice was between the principles of the Founding Fathers and those of "the arch traitor, Jeff Davis." With the "real" Democrats, the *Post* professed no quarrel: what it condemned was that party organized in the territory "under the *assumed* name of Democrats, whose object is to oppose the government of the United States. . . ." The platform of these "pseudo-Democrats" was the "meanest and most heterogeneous compound ever foisted on the political world of the 19th century." It would be "nothing short of suicide to send any other than a true and reliable Union man" to Washington; a Democratic delegate would be "as utterly unable to fulfill his mission, as a Feejee Islander or a Minnesota Sioux."[12]

So heated was the contest, according to Langford, that McLean "discussed the issues of the campaign, under a *white* flag, on which was embroidered an olive branch." Sanders, too, worked hard to pull

associating with him in his law practice. Serving with the 64th Ohio Infantry during the early part of the Civil War, Sanders resigned because of his health and came to Bannack with Edgerton in 1863. He rode with the vigilantes, was several times a member of the legislature, made numerous trips to Washington on political business, and remained to the end a staunch Republican and baiter of the "Secesh." *DAB*, XVI, 336–37; Michael A. Leeson, ed., *History of Montana, 1739–1885* (Chicago, 1885), 1247–48; A. K. McClure, "Colonel Wilbur Fisk Sanders," 5, undated typescript, MHS; C. C. Goodwin, *As I Remember Them* (Salt Lake City, 1913), 326.

11. Wold, comp., *Biographical Directory*, 1273; Wilbur F. Sanders to James Garfield (Virginia City, November 24, 1864), James A. Garfield MSS, Library of Congress.

12. *Montana Post*, October 1, 8, 15, 1864.

his forces together, but the combined Democratic factions won a victory, "largely by fraud," said Sanders, "but really they could have done it by the *brute* power of numbers which no discipline or organization could overcome."[13] Sanders had carried every county, except the most important—heavily populated Madison—and McLean became Montana's first territorial delegate to Congress. The legislative assembly was divided: the council was Unionist, the house Democratic—in each case by one vote.[14] In explaining the results, the disappointed Dimsdale blamed the Rebels: "The balance of votes in this section were cast by Secessionists, openly claiming to be citizens of Dixie, but voting as citizens of the Northern States."[15] Reelected a year later in an election tainted with fraud, McLean would find his mission in a Republican Congress frustrating and his detractors at home as loud as they were vigorous.[16]

Meanwhile Governor Edgerton kept busy. Because he had no secretary, he personally had to oversee construction of the legislative halls, and because of constant interruptions could find time to work on his message only at night. At noon on December 12, the twenty newly elected legislators convened in Bannack, the House in a two-story log building and the Council in a smaller structure nearby.[17] Instead of a conciliatory approach, Edgerton chose to address the assembly with a severe and tactless denunciation of the Confederacy, in so doing, feeding the fires already smoldering.

> This unhallowed rebellion had its origin in the lust for power and the insane desire to extend and perpetuate human bondage. For years this conspiracy had been plotting, till at length, under the imbecile administration of James Buchanan it threw off all disguise and assumed the defiant attitude of treason. . . . The issue is fully made up between loyalty and treason; the opposing armies are in the field to decide the question by the wager of battle, and between them there is no middle ground.[18]

13. Langford to Taylor (Virginia City, May 20, 1866), copy, Langford MSS; Sanders to Garfield (Virginia City, November 24, 1864), Garfield MSS.

14. The vote for delegate was McLean, 3,896; Sanders, 2,666; rejected ballots, 296. Ellis Waldron, *Montana Politics Since 1864: An Atlas of Elections* (Missoula, 1958), 8; John W. Pace and H. J. Mock, comps., *The Montana Blue Book* (Helena, 1891), 154; *Montana Post*, November 19, 1864.

15. *Montana Post*, November 5, 1864.

16. See *House Journal*, 2 Session (1866), 24; *Montana Democrat* (Virginia City), March 22, 1866; *Montana Post*, March 10, December 1, 1866.

17. Mary Wright Edgerton to Martha Carter (Bannack, November 27, 1864), Edgerton family MSS; Robert L. Housman, "The First Territorial Legislature in Montana," *Pacific Historical Review*, IV (December, 1935), 380.

18. *Montana Post*, December 24, 1864.

Nor was this all: Edgerton further insisted that all members of the assembly subscribe to the "Iron Clad Oath" prescribed by Congress in 1862 for "every person elected or appointed to any office of honor or profit under the government of the United States, either in the civil, military or naval departments of the public service." Despite some question as to its validity for territorial legislators, this oath had been generally accepted in other territories, though not without serious opposition.[19]

At Bannack, the Republican-dominated Council did not hesitate. Indeed, the Council adopted by a strictly partisan vote of six to one a resolution "That we hereby renew our pledges, ever entertained, of loyalty to the Union, and will ever frown indignantly upon any attempt to alienate any portion of our common country from another." In the House, however, a small Democratic bloc led by members from Madison County hesitated, and Edgerton first hinted, then openly proclaimed that without the oath there would be no pay. That, according to the *Montana Post*, "touched the Madison County delegation in a tender place, and with such wry faces as a patient makes who takes distasteful purgatives, and such contortions as one would make after overeating turkey buzzards, they swallowed the 'iron clad.' "[20]

All except one: John H. Rogers of Deer Lodge, who had ridden with Price in Missouri, could not honestly swear that he had never voluntarily borne arms against the United States, as required by the oath. He suggested instead a substitute, pledging his loyalty and to "support, protect, and defend the Constitution and the Government of the United States and the Organic Act of the Territory of Montana," but this satisfied neither Edgerton nor the Unionist members of the House and Rogers was refused his seat, although he was reelected in 1866 and seated without question.[21]

But there was more important work for the first legislative assembly. Largely inexperienced, both houses organized themselves. (The seven-man Council created fifteen committees, including one on "'Federal Relations" and one for "Indian Affairs.") On December 20,

19. Act of July 2, 1862, 12 *USSL*, 502; Housman, "The First Territorial Legislature in Montana," 380; William J. Trimble, *The Mining Advance into the Inland Empire* (Madison, 1914), 220.

20. *Council Journal*, 1 Session (1864–65), 193; *Montana Post*, December 24, 1864.

21. Mary Wright Edgerton to Martha Carter (Bannack, November 27, 1864), Edgerton family MSS; Robert E. Albright, "The Relations of Montana with the Federal Government, 1864–1889" (Ph.D. dissertation, Stanford University, 1933), 61; *House Journal*, 3 Session (1866), 7.

the Council authorized its sergeant at arms to "procure a curtain forthwith" for its front window and to acquire three copies of the Idaho statutes.[22] The organic act did not repeal the laws of Idaho as they applied to Montana; nor did it indicate positively that they were to remain in effect until set aside officially. It was agreed, however, that the Idaho legislation would stand until new laws could be drawn, and that the Idaho statutes should be used as models.[23] On this basis, the assembly set about its work.

One of the assembly's first actions was to stipulate that "the common law of England, so far as the same is applicable and of a general nature, and not in conflict with the special enactments of this Territory, shall be the law and the rule of decision and shall be considered as of full force until repealed by legislative authority."[24] Another of the first acts was a civil practice act, establishing lower courts and prescribing jurisdiction and procedure for civil cases of all types. Along with it came the passage of a criminal practice law, providing means for the indictment and trial of criminal offenders, and defining offenses and penalties thereof. Also passed early was a standard probate act, governing estates, executors, administrators, guardians, and wards.[25]

Previously, Edgerton had divided the territory into three temporary judicial districts, each under the jurisdiction of one of the three federal judges. Now the legislature confirmed this districting, revised the times for holding court, and created a district attorney for each judicial division. At the same time, it sought to more clearly define the right and procedure of procuring the writ of habeas corpus.[26]

In compliance with the organic act, the first legislature prescribed voting qualifications for subsequent elections. With a conservatism in keeping with the times and with the sectional background of its constituents, it adopted an election law that granted the suffrage to "all white male citizens of the United States, and those who have declared their intention to become citizens, above the age of twenty-

22. *Council Journal*, 1 Session (1864–65), 10, 17–18.

23. David Chamberlain, sergeant at arms of the Idaho legislature, brought the laws and bound statutes of Idaho from Lewiston to Bannack and was voted $300 for his services. Langford to Samuel Hauser (Virginia City, March 25, 1865), Samuel Hauser MSS, MHS; act of January 17, 1865, *LM*, 1 Session (1864–65), 573.

24. Act of January 11, 1865, *LM*, 356. See also Gordon M. Bakken, "The English Common Law in the Rocky Mountain West," *Arizona and the West*, XI (Summer, 1969), 110–15.

25. Acts (n.d.), *LM*, 1 Session (1864–65), 43–175, 176–267, 268–325.

26. Acts of January 10 and 11, 1865, *LM*, 352–53, 360–67.

one years," provided that persons thus qualified had resided in the
territory twenty days and in the county ten prior to the election. It
further stipulated that any person elected as delegate, as a member
of the legislature, or to "any territorial office," must have been a resident of the territory for at least a year.[27]

Nine counties were created, their seats of government to be determined by their respective voters. The territorial capital was located
at Virginia City, subject to change on the approval of the general
electorate,[28] a move which began a long series of haggling over a
permanent site, with attempts in nearly every legislative session down
to 1874 to change the location.

Minor laws touched on nearly every phase of normal living. That
lawyers were licensed and regulated may have reflected some of the
typical frontier distrust of the legal profession, but more likely the
law denoted the influence of the large number of lawyers in the territory and in the assembly, for it gave the profession itself control
of admitting new candidates to the bar. The establishment of a school
system and the passing of regulations governing marriage and divorce, prohibiting imprisonment for debt, imposing limited pure food
and drug laws, and restricting usury were but fundamental enactments, basic in all communities.[29]

Civilization as viewed by the legislature meant the banning of concealed weapons, and the enactment of a rather complex statute intended to protect the innocent and unwary from adroit gamblers by
outlawing such nefarious games of chance as "three card monte,"
"noir et rouge," "thimble rig," and "patent safe." But so intricate was
the antigaming law that one correspondent of the *Montana Post* could
complain: "I am a carder and a dicer also. I have bucked the tiger
in San Francisco and have taken the regal Bengal by the mane in
Sacramento. I am an A.M. in the seven damnable sciences, but this
act is above my comprehension, and its provisions are 'past finding
out.' "[30] And he might well have added that enactment was one matter
and enforcement another.

Customary laws[31] dealing with livestock—the control of strays,
regulation of auctions, and prevention of trespass by domestic beasts

27. Act of January 17, 1865, *LM*, 375–76.
28. Acts of February 2 and 7, 1865, *LM*, 432, 528–31.
29. Acts of January 6 and 12; February 6, 7, and 9, 1865, *LM* 345–47, 408–
10, 430–31, 433–43, 470–74, 535.
30. Acts of January 11, 1865, *LM*, 354, 355; *Montana Post*, January 21, 1865.
31. Acts of December 26, 1864; January 9 and 11, 1865, *LM*, 1 Session (1864–
65), 326, 351, 356–60.

on private property—presaged an era in which stockmen would be one of the most important influences in the legislature and indeed the territory. But for the time being, a number of laws reflected the importance of what was obviously the territory's chief industry, mining. Where but in a mineral region would there be a need for a law prohibiting the counterfeiting of gold dust and gold or silver bullion, bars or lumps?[32] The prominence of mining was clearly evident in an act of December 26, which codified and expanded the mineral laws laid down in the various districts, and specifically repealed that part of the Idaho mineral law requiring $100 worth of work to be done on a claim within six months. Notably, this action of the Montana legislature came a full month and a half before other Idaho statutes were invalidated.[33]

If all these and the many other general acts passed during the winter of 1864–65 did not adequately proclaim the arrival of organized government, the tax laws left no doubt. Legislation of February 6 levied an ad valorem tax of four mills on each dollar of assessed value of taxable property and authorized counties to collect an annual fee not exceeding ten mills per dollar of assessed value. In addition, a poll tax was levied on every white male inhabitant between the ages of twenty-one and fifty. Under a separate law, practically all professions—from pawnbroker to physician, from butcher to banker, from hurdy-gurdy to slight-of-hand artist—were subject to license fees.[34]

Soon, as if overcome by a spirit of prosperity, the legislature generously voted to increase the salaries of the governor and the justices by 100 percent, adding $2,500 a year to the stipend already authorized from federal funds. Per diem payment for assembly members was increased even more, with the territory augmenting the $4 a day paid by the national government with an additional $12 of its own.[35] Besides plunging the territory deeply into debt, this expensive legislation would provide a bone of contention over which Democrats and Republicans could wrangle for years to come, each party blaming the other for willful and negligent waste of public funds.

One other aspect of the work of the first legislature should be noted. This was the enactment of many special and private laws during the

32. Act of December 31, 1864, *LM*, 341.

33. Acts of December 26, 1864, and February 9, 1865, *LM*, 329, 715. See also *Montana Post*, October 1, December 24, 1864; Granville Stuart to James Stuart (Virginia City, December 14, 1864), Stuart MSS, Beinecke Library, Yale University.

34. Acts of February 6 and 9, 1865, *LM*, 1 Session (1864–65), 411–29, 523–28.

35. Act of January 24, 1865, *LM*, 391–92.

winter, some 108 such pieces of legislation ranging from the granting of divorces to the chartering of turnpike or townsite companies to the payment of individual for services rendered prior to the creation of the territory.[36] "Numberless bills are introduced and passed, chiefly of charters for roads, ferries, and the like," criticized the *Montana Post*; "everything is ground through on the 'get what you can' principle. . . ." Indeed, said the *Post*, "Funny and foolish things are being done. . . . Travelers in Montana will curse this assembly so long as its monuments remain"—and indeed its monuments were largely in toll gates.[37] Perhaps it is too harsh a judgment to say, as one historian has, "Like so many Montana legislatures since, its members were there not so much to govern as to oversee the slicing of the public pie,"[38] for while the special legislation cannot be ignored nor excused, it should not obscure the positive contributions of the first legislature in laying the foundations of an operating government—no simple task.

On February 9—the final day of its session—the legislature formally repealed all Idaho statutes as they applied to the territory, and dismissed all suits and indictments for collection of revenue then pending against the territory's citizens by its neighbor to the west.[39] Then it adjourned and its twenty exhausted members returned to their homes. "The high comedy which has been on these boards for sixty days, closed Tuesday evening at 10 o'clock," noted one observer. "The spectators were bored, the actors weary, the scenery dilapidated, and the footlights dim."[40]

Yet, considering the circumstances, the performance had been largely a creditable one. Almost to a man, the legislators lacked experience in lawmaking; frequently at odds with the governor, they often as not were political partisans; undoubtedly in their special legislation they succumbed to the blandishments of lobbyists; but they did the best they could with a task that was arduous and complicated. That they achieved as much as they did is surprising.

Many of their errors stemmed from inexperience. The Idaho statutes, enacted only a year before, were followed closely, and many of

36. Included were: wagon road companies, 19; ditch companies, 8; mining companies, 27; townsite companies, 17; municipal incorporations or changes of name, 4; toll bridges or ferries, 13; compensation to individuals, 7; and miscellaneous, 7.

37. *Montana Post*, December 31, 1864; March 4, 1865.

38. Larry Barsness, *Gold Camp: Alder Gulch and Virginia City, Montana* (New York, 1962), 118–19.

39. Acts of February 9, 1865, *LM*, 1 Session (1864–65), 532, 715.

40. *Montana Post*, April 16, 1865.

their faults written into Montana law. Edgerton's successor declared in 1867: "The laws of the Bannack Legislature are imperfect and the compilation still worse."[41] The criminal-practice act, in particular, needed clarification, according to Acting-Governor James Tufts in 1868, and as for the statute of limitations, "Its glaring ambiguity has defied the perceptions of our best lawyers."[42] The county boundary lines as established in early 1865 were vague and misleading and revenue was lost because county officers could not always be certain of their jurisdiction.[43] The United States surveyor general for Montana complained in 1867 that it was only with the greatest of difficulty that "the law and the map could be made to conform. . . ." A strict adherence to the law would place Virginia City in Beaverhead County and Silver City in Deer Lodge, while Helena would be situated in Jefferson.[44]

Such shortcomings are both understandable and excusable, but others are not so easily condoned. Perhaps the most flagrant error committed by the first assembly was a sin of omission, brought about largely by animosity toward the governor. This animosity in turn was engendered in part by Edgerton's strong Unionist proclivities and his unwillingness to compromise on the question of the Iron Clad Oath. Moreover, Edgerton's appointment of county officers alienated members of both parties: Democrats because of his selection of staunch Republicans; Republicans because Edgerton neither asked nor accepted advice or because, in one case, the official "since his appointment has gone over to the Secesh. . . ."[45] If not bad blood, there was at least jealousy between Edgerton and Chief Justice Hosmer;[46] and Edward Neally, the Montana federal attorney, went out of his way to condemn the governor for his poor appointments, as well as his "attempting to run the Territory in his own interest." Wrote Neally, "It is barely possible that when they come to pan him out it will be difficult to find color."[47]

41. "Second Mesage of Governor Green Clay Smith," *Contribution*, V (1904), 150. Codifiers had been W. H. Miller, G. W. Stapleton and Wilbur F. Sanders. *Montana Post*, February 18, 1865.

42. James Tufts to legislature (December 8, 1868), *House Journal*, 5 Session (1868–69), 18, 20.

43. *House Journal*, 3 Session (1866), 256.

44. Report of the Surveyor-General of Montana (October 5, 1867), in *Contributions*, V (1904), 163.

45. Langford to Hauser (Virginia City, March 25, 1865), Hauser MSS.

46. Langford to Hauser (Virginia City, May 8, 1865), *ibid.*

47. Edward B. Neally to Hezekiah Hosmer (Helena, May 7, 1865), Hosmer MSS, Beinecke Library, Yale University.

In any event, Edgerton quickly gained enemies, in the legislature as well as out. Prior to the first election, he had set off election districts in compliance with the terms of the organic act, his divisions based presumably on the rough population count taken in the fall of 1864 under James Tufts. Following this temporary expedient, it was assumed that the legislature would redistrict the territory as the organic act specified. Looking to future population growth, Congress had allowed flexibility by providing for an eventual increase in the number of members of the council to thirteen and of the house to twenty-six, the expansion to be made in proportion to the increase of qualified voters.[48] Unwilling to wait either for emigration or natural births, the legislature enacted a districting bill which increased both houses to maximum size immediately, in so doing using the 1864 census figures, although new discoveries had caused a significant population shift northward from Madison County to the Silver Bow and Last Chance Gulch regions. Although warned that his action would kill the chances of the Union candidate at the next delegate election, Edgerton vetoed the measure on the grounds that it violated the intent of the organic act and the actual pattern of Montana's population and would increase expenses by another $15,000 to $16,000 at a time when the territory could ill afford it. No doubt the governor expected the legislature to reconsider and bring forth a more acceptable bill, but instead, in a moment of resentfulness, without endeavoring to override the veto, the assembly stood firm and without further ado adjourned.[49]

The impact of this failure to provide legislative redistricting was not at first apparent; its consequences were left for subsequent administrations. More than a mere example of lack of cooperation between a federal officer and the representatives of the electorate, it left the territory without legal means of providing for another legislative assembly. The authors of the organic act had assumed that its provisions would be carried out by the first assembly and thus laid down no alternatives in case they were not. Neither they nor Edgerton ever dreamed of the intense political ill will that would be generated by this oversight.

Edgerton had found the legislature almost as difficult to deal with

48. Act of May 26, 1864, 13 *USSL*, 87.
49. Edgerton to Speaker of House (Bannack, February 8, 1865), copy; John P. Bruce to Henry Stanbery (Virginia City, August 20, 1866), both in AG, 1864–70; Langford to Hauser (Virginia City, March 25, 1865); Walter B. Dance to Hauser (n.p., July 14, 1865), both in Hauser MSS; *Montana Post*, February 10, 1865.

as the Indians; as chief executive he was ex officio superintendent of Indian affairs for Montana. This time-honored dualism was a matter of expediency and, it was argued when the territory was created, of economy in handling relations with the Indians.[50] But as both jobs grew increasingly complex, the governor was overburdened and by 1869 the two functions would be separated, so far as Montana was concerned.

Relations with the Indians were potentially explosive. Discontented with government action, displeased by white encroachment, aroused by irresponsible traders, the northern tribes—especially the Blackfeet along the upper reaches of the Teton and Sun and on the eastern slope of the Rockies—were becoming more difficult to handle. A newly arrived agent for the Blackfeet in 1864 called his charges "the most impudent and insulting Indians" he had ever met, and remarked that were it not that their treaty expired the next year, he would recommend that their next annuity be paid "in powder and ball from the mouth of a six-pounder."[51] Even the Flatheads in the Bitterroot Valley "once proverbial for their honesty are growing tricky & worthless," grumbled pioneer John Owen in 1865. "They require rigid & great punishment which will fall upon them Ere they least expect it."[52]

Here Owen was advocating one part of a three-pronged policy accepted by Montanans and frontier residents in general, who felt that lawmakers and eastern administrators did not understand the Indian problem nor the therapeutic value of hot lead and cold steel; what was needed was less coddling and a more resolute, more stringent approach.[53] A second desire was military protection, including the establishment of forts: while Congress early appropriated funds for protection of emigrants along overland routes, not until 1866 were federal troops stationed in the territory.[54] And a third aim of Montana whites, one already begun by earlier treaties, was the reduction and opening to settlement of Indian land holdings. Thus one of the earliest official acts of the first legislature was to send a memorial to the harassed Secretary of the Interior, John P. Usher, complaining that

50. See *Congressional Globe*, 38 Congress, 1 Session (1863–64), 1169; 40 Congress, 2 Session (1867–68), 2800–2801.

51. Report of the Commissioner of Indian Affairs, *Annual Report of the Secretary of the Interior, 1864*, 444.

52. John Owen, *The Journals and Letters of Major John Owen, Pioneer of the Northwest, 1850–1871*, ed. by Paul C. Phillips and Seymour Dunbar (New York, 1927), I, 333.

53. See, for example, *ibid.*, 262; *Montana Post*, June 10, 1865.

54. Act of March 3, 1864, 13 *USSL*, 14; *Annual Report of the Secretary of War, 1867*, 32–49.

"only a small fragment of land imbraced within the boundaries of this Territory" was open for settlement.[55]

Edgerton had troubles with some of the Indian agents, and in the spring of 1865 the Blackfeet killed ten men out of Fort Benton, sending the governor into near panic. "The danger to emigration now enroute up the Missouri River is immense," he wrote the Secretary of War, informing him that he was organizing an expedition of 500 militia and requesting two regiments of troops, plus supplies.[56] But the efforts to raise local volunteers proved a farce. Predicting "the very d–l will be to pay" with the Indians unless the federal government stepped in, Chief Justice Hosmer wrote Samuel Hauser about the "'great fizzle'" in recruiting:

> We had more Generals and Colonels, etc. etc. than there were in the Army of the Potomac, trying, with beat of drum, a great display of flags, and a most melancholy waste of cheap whisky, to raise 500 men. The result was, after a fortnight, recruiting, boys and all, the company numbered about 30, and broke up in disgust, after having pressed into the service, from the Ranches of the Stinking water, about 90 of the hardest looking specimens of horse and mule flesh you ever laid eyes on. It was a tremendous exhibition of windy patriotism, out of which no Buncombe could be made for any body.[57]

Probably Edgerton neglected Indian affairs somewhat; he complained that the duties of superintendent of Indian affairs were illy defined and that there were overlapping jurisdictions where the governor and agents were concerned. Funds were not forthcoming and apparently much of the work with Indian affairs was done by a clerk in the governor's office, whose presence on the payroll he had difficulty in justifying.[58] When Edgerton left the territory, the Indian situation was not critical, but in his absence Acting Governor Meagher would keep problems stirred up, so that the possibility of a full-scale Indian war loomed, and Edgerton, by his neglect of the office would receive some of the blame.[59]

55. Memorial (n.d.), *LM*, 1 Session (1864–65), 721.

56. Edgerton to Edwin M. Stanton (Virginia City, May 30, 1865), copy, letterbook 54, Ulysses S. Grant MSS, Library of Congress; Edgerton to D. N. Cooley (Bannack, August 16, 1865), BIA.

57. Hosmer to Hauser (Virginia City, June 24, 1865), Hauser MSS, MHS.

58. Hutchins to W. P. Dole (Jocko Agency, March 13, October 3, 1865); O. D. Barrett to O. H. Irish (Virginia City, June 1, 1865); Edgerton to James Harlan (Washington, March 31, 1866); Harlan to Cooley (Washington, April 4, 1866); E. B. French to Cooley (Washington, October 25, 1866), all in BIA.

59. Cooley to Harlan (Washington, April 10, 1866); Harlan to William Seward (Washington, April 11, 1866), both in TPS.

For Edgerton, the trials of territorial government were nearly over by the summer of 1865, though his heritage would linger long. No doubt he felt frustrated that he was not selected to run for the delegateship. "Poor Gov is laid on the shelf," wrote a nonadmirer in June, well aware of the chief executive's thwarted ambitions.[60] Moreover, Edgerton had for nearly a year and a half after the creation of the territory been without a secretary and "without one cent of money from the General Government," as he expressed it.[61] Thus when Thomas Francis Meagher accepted the secretaryship and arrived in Bannack in September, 1865, Edgerton was only too glad to hand over the reins of government and depart immediately without resigning or benefit of official leave, heading for Washington "in the line of public duty" and to put his daughter in school.[62]

Except as a visitor, he never returned, and the legacy he left behind was a mixed one. Democrats lumped him with the " 'Union-shrieking,' constitution-breaking, cuffy-loving, office-hungry Radicals," saw him as "a true type of Black Republicanism and meanness," and in 1867 decided to change the name of Edgerton County, created by the first legislature, to Lewis and Clark County.[63] Others branded him "a crank posing as a radical Republican," because he later joined the Democratic party in Ohio.[64] To his friends, he was "a man of more than ordinary ability" who was "grossly misrepresented" and unfairly disliked and whose problems stemmed largely from the ineptness of those around him and from the nature of the roughneck population of early Montana.[65] Whatever he was and however he may have been viewed, he was an important factor in the creation and the organization of the territory, yet in the final analysis, could hardly be considered either an effective politician or a successful governor.

60. Dance to Hauser (n.p., July 14, 1865), Hauser MSS.
61. Edgerton to Seward (Talmadge, Ohio, January 30, 1866), TPS.
62. Edgerton to Andrew Johnson (Washington, March 27, 1866), TPS; Thomas Francis Meagher to Johnson (Virginia City, January 20, 1866), Andrew Johnson MSS, Library of Congress.
63. *Weekly Independence* (Deer Lodge to March, 1874; Helena), August 14, 1868; act of December 20, 1867, *LM*, 4 Session (1867), 130; *The National Cyclopaedia of American Biography* (New York, 1898 –), XI, 78; W. Y. Pemberton, "Changing the Name of Edgerton County," *Contributions*, VIII (1917), 323–26.
64. Vivian Paladin, ed., "Henry N. Blake: Proper Bostonian, Purposeful Pioneer," *Montana*, XIV (Autumn, 1964), 39.
65. Quoted in Thomas Donaldson, "Idaho of Yesterday," 14 (typescript), Bancroft Library; Wilbur F. Sanders, "Sidney Edgerton, the First Governor of Montana," 7–8.

CHAPTER

3

"That Territory Is in a
State of Anarchy":
The "Bogus Legislature" Fiasco

When Secretary Thomas Francis Meagher reached Bannack via Denver and Salt Lake City, after what he called "a very tedious, and somewhat precarious, journey of several weeks over the plains," he was cordially greeted by Governor Edgerton, introduced to local citizens, and after only brief instructions, left on his own as acting governor.[1] The dynamic Meagher brought with him a background of drama and adventure that belied his thirty-five years. An impassioned revolutionist in the Young Ireland movement, he had been sentenced to death in 1848, then banished to Tasmania, whence he had escaped and made his way to the United States by 1852. Here, as a dazzling orator, editor of the *Irish News*, and traveler deluxe, he had made both friends and enemies by the score. During the Civil War, he had led the Irish Brigade through half a dozen major battles, and now this fiery-spirited young warrior arrived in Montana eager to win new laurels, either military or political.[2]

As a northern Democrat and as a former Union officer appointed by

1. Thomas Francis Meagher to Andrew Johnson (Virginia City, January 20, 1866), Johnson MSS.
2. The standard work is Robert G. Athearn, *Thomas Francis Meagher: An Irish Revolutionary in America* (Boulder, 1949). See also James L. Thane, Jr., "An Active Acting-Governor: Thomas Francis Meagher's Administration in Montana," *Journal of the West*, IX (October, 1970), 537–51.

President Johnson, he was not fully in sympathy with his predecessor's fire-eating Radicalism, though he saw fit to compliment Edgerton for "the honest and intrepid discharge of his duties" amid "many embarrassments and vexations." Nor was he initially in complete accord with that group in the territory that was "spuriously called the Democratic Party," to use his words. Delegate McLean, "although the nominee of a faithless faction," he regarded "as an honest and patriotic man, and as a Democrat in the truest and most favourable interpretation of the word." But the bulk of the Democrats, though they now modified their language, were still "favourers and abettors of treason," and stood "in resolute and inveterate opposition to every man and every movement in Montana that bears the decisive stamp of loyalty, or seems calculated to give the new era of freedom and nationality the preponderance over the past one of slavery and Sectionalism."[3] What Montana needed, he confided to a friend, was "a strong infusion of . . . Celtic blood to counteract the acidity and poverty" of that of its present population.[4]

Into Meagher's lap fell the fruits of Edgerton's legislative hassle—the ticklish problem of securing a new legislative assembly after the first session had failed to pass the necessary legislation. This tended to be a political question, with opinions on it drawn along strict party lines. Believing that any legislature convened under the districting carried out by Edgerton in the summer of 1864 would be dominated by the Democrats, who naturally sought statehood while they were in the ascendancy, the Republicans maintained that only a special act of Congress, with reapportionment, could bring together a new assembly. On the other hand, the Democrats, who knew that if representative districts remained as they were they would control the legislature, contended that under the circumstances, the acting governor had the right to call a new election.

Meagher first inclined toward the Republican view that he could do nothing without specific sanction from federal authority. "I came to the conclusion after a mature consultation with United States Judge Munson and Mr. Neallie [sic] United States District Attorney," he said in mid-December, "that the Legislative functions of the Territory had temporarily lapsed, and that it is beyond my power legally

3. Meagher to William Seward (Virginia City, December 11, 1865), TPS.
4. Meagher to Rev. George W. Pepper (Virginia City, January 20, 1866), quoted from *Calendar of the Montana Papers in the William Andrews Clark Memorial Library* (Los Angeles, 1942), 68.

to revive them." Meagher instructed Delegate McLean to work with Edgerton in Washington for congressional relief to provide a legislature fairly representing Montana's population. To the Secretary of State, he expressed his belief that a heavy influx of loyal citizens in the spring would hasten the territory's development, and "just as assuredly, give it, politically, a sounder and nobler life."[5]

But Meagher was a political opportunist. He naturally resented efforts of territorial Republican leaders to stifle him and soon saw his future with the Democratic party—the party that was dominant in Montana, and which, in case of statehood, would control the election of United States senators and representatives.[6] As a result, he early moved over to accommodate his Democratic bedfellows.

As early as mid-January, though still looking to Congress for a way out of the impasse, he condemned the "radicals and extremists of the Republican party of the territory," who were by then engaged "in a cowardly conspiracy" against him.[7] Before another month had passed, Meagher could admit that those Democrats he had formerly characterized as disloyal and anti-Union had now become substantial citizens. "I have frankly to confess I was greatly in error," he acknowledged. "I can truly and safely say, that these very Southerners and Southern sympathizers are now as heartily to be relied upon by the Administration and its friends, as any other men in the Territory." Antagonism to the national party during the Edgerton administration, he concluded, "was in great measure owing to the unrelenting bitterness with which the Republicans, headed by some of the more prominent and authoritarian of the Federal officials, had assailed and endeavored to ostracize it."[8] In a separate communication to the Secretary of State, he confided, "Were it not for the bitter personal animosity of the ultra Republicans (who calculated on my being a miserable and mischievous tool in their hands and whom I have previously disappointed) I should have nothing to complain of in my present position."[9] "The most vicious of my enemies," Meagher said, was Wilbur F. Sanders, "an unrelenting and unscrupulous extremist" who seemed ready "to plunge this most beautiful and prom-

5. Meagher to Seward (Virginia City, December 11, 1865), TPS. "Mr. Neallie" was Edward B. Neally.

6. See Robert E. Albright, "The American Civil War as a Factor in Montana Territorial Politics," *Pacific Historical Review*, VI (March, 1937), 41–42

7. Meagher to Johnson (Virginia City, January 20, 1866), Johnson MSS.

8. Meagher to Seward (Virginia City, February 20, 1866), TPS.

9. Meagher to Seward (Virginia City, February 20, 1866), "private," TPS.

ising Territory into the bitterest and the blackest hot water" and who would soon be in Washington "substantially on a political errand. . . ."[10]

Under Democratic urging, Meagher then reversed his position on the matter of summoning a new legislature. To Secretary Seward he wrote: "On more maturely considering the powers vested in me by the Organic Act, and the laws of the Territory, I came to the conclusion, that a Legislature did legally and constitutionally exist here, and that it was legally and constitutionally within the scope of my prerogatives to summon it into action."[11] Much to the delight of his new-found friends, the "Acting One" called not only a territorial convention to consider statehood, but on February 15, 1866, by proclamation sanctioned the convening of the legislative assembly on March 5.[12]

Meagher credited Helena lawyers with striking away "the fetters and darkness that had for a time fooled and cramped" him and with freeing him from the influence of the "political rascals" who had at first imposed upon him.[13] When he understood, he said, that Montana was "in a state, politically speaking, of imbecility and stagnation," that without a legislature, the territory "would be nothing more than a Government farm, parcelled out among Federal overseers, taxgatherers and bailiffs," he saw no other course but to convoke the assembly.[14]

And despite furious protest, the legislature convened as scheduled. Neil Howie recorded in his diary: "The legislature met to day the Governor called the House to order the Governor very drunk."[15] Clearly the body was thoroughly Democratic in composition and sentiment. (Republicans contended that members of their party simply refrained from voting in the elections.)[16] Certainly the assembly's point of view was reflected in a joint resolution which en-

10. Meagher to Johnson (Virginia City, January 29, 1866), "private," Johnson MSS.
11. Meagher to Seward (Virginia City, February 20, 1866), TPS.
12. *Montana Post*, February 3, 1866.
13. Meagher to Seward (Virginia City, February 20, 1866), TPS; *Montana Post*, February 24, 1866; Meagher to Democratic Convention of Madison County, "Legality of the Legislature," n.d., in John P. Bruce, comp., *Lectures of Gov. Thomas Francis Meagher, in Montana, Together with his Messages, Speeches, &c. to which is added the Eulogy of Richard O'Gorman, Esq., Delivered at Cooper Institute, New York* (Virginia City, 1867), 43.
14. Bruce, comp., *Lectures of Gov. Thomas Francis Meagher*, 47–48; *House Journal*, 2 Session (1866), 125.
15. Entry for March 5, 1866, Diary of Neil Howie, MHS.
16. See Henry N. Blake in *Contributions*, V (1904), 258–59.

dorsed Andrew Johnson's presidential plan of reconstruction for the South and pledged support "so long as he pursues the same direction, and leads on in the beaten path of Democratic Principles. . . ."[17]

But Acting Governor Meagher immediately found himself the center of a storm of controversy, most of the invective directed against him being Republican, although some Democrats were opposed and were moved to join the reorganized Union party.[18] Thomas Dimsdale's *Montana Post* denounced the calling of the constitutional convention and a legislative session as "a mockery, a delusion and a snare" which could only result in a territorial debt so hopeless that Montana scrip would act "as a scarecrow to sane white men, warning them to keep out. . . ."[19] Meagher was "a disgrace to our Territory, and every Democrat of any influence knows it," complained Nathaniel Langford. "Every officer we have hitherto had, has been more desirable, than he has been endurable."[20] The acting governor had surrendered to the "Missouri bushwhackers" and "the traitors with whom this Territory is filled; among decent men of all parties," said Wilbur F. Sanders, he "is dead beyond hope of resurrection. . . . Of course, we will squelch the Legislature by the courts. Those villains must never be permitted to assemble and plot the ruins of this great and glorious territory. . . . We must put a quietous on the doings of this pretender."[21]

Meagher was viciously attacked personally, much capital being made of his fondness for John Barleycorn. It was common knowledge that he was no teetotaler. According to one editor, he twice "lost" his father, necessitating an "Irish wake" each time. Indeed he was accused of having "in fact been drunk nearly every day since he has been in the Territory," and of making the executive office "a place of rendezvous for the vilest prostitutes. . . ."[22]

Meagher early incurred the wrath of the judiciary when he openly

17. Joint resolution (April 13, 1866), *LM*, 2 Session (1866), 52.

18. Nathaniel Langford to Samuel Hauser (Virginia City, February 27, 1866), Hauser MSS; Athearn, *Thomas Francis Meagher*, 151–52.

19. *Montana Post*, February 3, 1866.

20. Langford to Hauser (Virginia City, February 27, 1866), Hauser MSS.

21. Wilbur F. Sanders to James Fergus (Virginia City, February 14, 1866), copy, Allis Stuart Collection, James Fergus MSS, MHS; George M. Pinney to Lyman Trumbull (Helena, June 10, 1866), TPUS; William Chumasero to Andrew Johnson (Helena, February 26, 1866), AG (1864–70).

22. Meagher was also accused of fitting out the legislative halls over "a couple of whiskey shops" at an expense of $7,000 and of contracting to buy paper at $50 per ream. Chumasero to Trumbull (Helena, March 12, 1866), TPS. *Montana Post*, February 3, 1866; September 21, 1867. "He lost another relative said to be a *grandmother* last week and has been on a drunk for some time." Chumasero to Sanders (Virginia City, March 4, 1866), Wilbur F. Sanders MSS, MHS.

told the Democratic convention in Virginia City that "no judge, whatever his powers or consequence, should dispute or disobey" the laws enacted by the second legislature.[23] Justices Hosmer and Williston were both out of the territory at the time, a point of ridicule with Meagher, but Associate Justice Lyman Ezra Munson replied haughtily that the judiciary must pursue an independent course and that it retained the right to pass on the legality of the legislature and its actions. Meagher's rejoinder was neither restrained nor diplomatic and did little to further harmony between the two branches of government. Disclaiming any responsibility on his part to the judicial officers he refused additional correspondence on the matter. "My authority shall be maintained with all the power of the Territory if necessary, to resist and set at naught your very extraordinary and presumptuous interference with my prerogatives," he informed Munson.[24]

Soon Meagher clashed with Munson on another matter. James Daniels was acquitted of murder but sentenced to prison when found guilty of manslaughter—a "grievously unjust charge of the Judge," according to the acting governor. When Meagher pardoned Daniels, whom he deemed a man of excellent character, Munson ordered him rearrested, but before this could occur, Daniels was hanged by vigilantes.[25] Ill feeling from this episode added to tempers already frayed over "Meagher's legislature."

Led by William Chumasero and Wilbur F. Sanders, the latter considered by Meagher as "a bitter personal enemy of mine, and a very vicious politician,"[26] extremist Republicans sought to test the legislature's legality in court, but they found, to their dismay, that talk outran action. "The fact is," Chumasero grumbled, "that the Union lawyers of this Territory are a shabby set of weak kneed persons who are unreliable when any action is involved requiring backbone. . . ."[27]

Eventually, however, in June, Judge Manson handed down a de-

23. *Montana Post*, February 24, 1866; Bruce, comp., *Lectures of Gov. Thomas Francis Meagher*, 45.

24. *Montana Democrat* (Virginia City), March 8, 1866. Republicans interpreted Meagher to mean that he would uphold the acts of the legislature with force if need be against objections of the territorial court. Langford to Hauser (Virginia City, February 27, 1866), Hauser MSS.

25. Meagher to Seward (Virginia City, March 12, 1866); Chumasero to Johnson (Helena, February 26, 1866); Lyman E. Munson to James Speed (Helena, March 6, 1866), all in AG (1864–70).

26. Meagher to Seward (n.p., February 21, 1866), TPS.

27. Chumasero to Sanders (Virginia City, March 4, 1866), Sanders MSS.

cision declaring acts of the legislature illegal,[28] an opinion which brought denunciation of Munson and demands for his recall. Meagher, who had earlier complained that he was the only federal officer in the territory "in full and cordial harmony with the Administration," again reiterated that it would "be a blessing to Montaña were every one of these officials removed, and others of more enlightened minds and more positive hearts sent out here to supersede them."[29] The partisan *Montana Democrat*—the only newspaper in support of President Johnson's policies, according to Meagher—echoed this refrain, urging three new and friendly judges.[30]

Meanwhile, Meagher's legislature threw its weight against the bench by ignoring a plea from the Helena bar that the judges' salaries were "totally inadequate to compensate a lawyer of character and ability for discharging the onerous duties of the office," and repealed the act of the first assembly which allowed extra compensation to the territorial justices.[31] This, in the eyes of the *Montana Post*, showed the adoption of the "Russian principle, of totally insufficient salaries, with the privilege to starve or to steal."[32] Meagher, for his part, in 1866, declined additional pay, but subsequently in 1867, when "utterly-utterly-out of funds," requested them.[33]

The controversy quickly attracted the attention of officials in Washington, where in the Thirty-ninth Congress, the House of Representatives in May, 1866, considered a bill to amend Montana's organic act and to declare the laws of the second legislature null and void. Section two of the proposed measure would have disallowed the payment of any federal funds for expenses of the legislature or for persons claiming to have been members.[34]

This brought howls of protest from Montana's "talking delegate."

28. *Montana Post*, June 9, 1866.

29. Meagher to F. W. Seward (Virginia City, March 22, 1866), TPS; Meagher to Johnson (Virginia City, July 13, 1866), Johnson MSS.

30. *Montana Democrat*, September 6, 1866; Meagher to Seward (n.p., February 21, 1866), TPS.

31. *Council Journal*, 2 Session (1866), 139, 155–56; act of March 26, 1866, *LM*, 2 Session (1866), 3.

32. *Montana Post*, March 10, 1866.

33. Meagher to R. B. Parrott (Virginia City, March 19, 1866); Meagher to J. H. Ming (Benton City, July 1, 1867), both in Thomas Francis Meagher MSS, MHS.

34. *Congressional Globe*, 39 Congress, 1 Session (1865–66), 2368. Staunch Republicans like George Piney urged Congress to annul the laws or the "Union Party of Montana will have—to use a homely phrase—'hard sledding.'" George M. Pinney to Trumbull (Helena, June 10, 1866), TPUS.

Hard-drinking, fun-loving Colonel Samuel McLean—"a gay old Boy"
—dragged his some three hundred pounds erect on the floor of the
House and sharply criticized this bill in particular and federal territorial policy in general:

> You cannot injure the feelings of the honorable gentlemen who are
> members of that body by refusing to pay them the miserable pittance
> allowed by law as a compensation for their services. . . . I speak at
> least for my own Territory in saying that we are almost unanimous in
> the belief that much congressional territorial legislation will be of no
> benefit to the General Government and very injurious to us. . . . We
> do claim to know our own wants, and when it cannot possibly prejudice
> the interests of the nation, we would solicit the privilege of attending
> to our own affairs in our own way. The prejudice arising from political
> bias should not be allowed to operate against us while we remain in a
> territorial capacity.

McLean's concluding remarks were less conciliatory: likening the
territorial cause to that of the American colonists before the Revolutionary War, he noted the proximity of British Canada to his own constituency. "Do not," he pleaded, "by unwise and oppressive legislation
drive us over the border, while our love of country would actuate us
to stand upon its outer edge a living wall of strength in the defense of
our land."[35] Montana Republicans scoffed at this "foolish diatribe,"
rejecting the idea that their people would ever "don the red coat
under the shadow of the British Ensign"; the House, on its part, lis-
tened calmly, then passed the obnoxious bill, only to see it lost in the
Senate, and the situation in Montana unchanged.[36]

All the while, the rakish Meagher continued his slashing attacks on
his adversaries. He challenged Henry Blake to a duel over a "scandalous article" in the *Montana Post*, but it was an invitation which Blake
chose to reject.[37] Soon he issued a proclamation calling for the elec-

35. *Congressional Globe*, 39 Congress, 1 Session (1865–66), Appendix, 202,
203. For an interesting description of the rotund McLean, who kept his trunk
full of whiskey and his clothes on the foot of his bunk, see H. D. Upham to Abner
Wood (June 18, 1865), in Paul C. Phillips, ed., "Upham Letters from the Upper
Missouri, 1865," *The Frontier*, XIII (May, 1933), 315.
36. *Montana Post*, July 7, 1866; *Congressional Globe*, 39 Congress, 1 Session
(1865–66), 2368.
37. *Montana Post*, October 20, 1866. Blake later commented, of Meagher:
"He had an excessive bump of vanity, was fond of seeing his name in a halo of
praise, and his office in Virginia City was thronged with a gang of bibulous
politicians and flatterers who promised to send him to Congress." Paladin, ed.,
"Henry N. Blake: Proper Bostonian, Purposeful Pioneer," *Montana*, XIV (Autumn, 1964), 39, 40.

tion of a third legislative assembly, to meet in the winter of 1866–67, and he urged that no man be elected "who has shown himself weak in the legs and pliant in the back-bone" in the dispute over the second session. Though he declined to "waste his shot upon jack-rabbits," "spoil his hands in squelching skunks," or bother with the "pimps and blackguards of political life," he took time to castigate the judges as the "sublime oracles of law, with all the gravity of Minerva's owl."[38]

Before the assembly was elected, the territory was favored with a new governor, thus relieving "the Acting One" of executive responsibilities for a time. Green Clay Smith, the incoming governor, arrived in October, although Democrats like Sam Hauser had been at work to secure his appointment as early as April of that same year.[39] A Kentucky Union Democrat and an officer in both the Mexican and Civil Wars, Smith was serving his second term in the U.S. House of Representatives when appointed to the territorial post. Montanans like to remember him, whether accurately or not, as the man who came within one-half a vote of becoming president of the United States, having been a strong contender for nomination as Lincoln's running mate in 1864.[40] Described as "a stout, pleasant-looking young man, of about five-and-thirty . . . with 'hail-fellow-well-met' manners," "a very pleasant gentleman," and as "a boy all his days with the best blood of Kentucky in his veins,"[41] the new governor seemed to understand both the northern and southern viewpoints and hopes for a more harmonious administration seemed well grounded.

When the third session—"the Jeff Davis Legislature," one observer

38. *Montana Post*, October 27, 1866; Bruce, comp., *Lectures of Gov. Thomas Francis Meagher*, 52–53.

39. *Montana Post*, October 6, 20, 1866; Walter B. Dance to Hauser (St. Louis, April 4, 1866); James Tufts to Hauser (n.p., April 9, 1866), both in Hauser MSS; Dance et al. to Johnson (St. Louis, April 3, 1866), Green Clay Smith file, TPS.

40. A graduate of Transylvania University, Smith (1826–95) served with the first Kentucky Volunteers in the Mexican campaign and with the 4th Kentucky Volunteer Cavalry during the Civil War. He was elected as a Union candidate to the 38th and 39th Congresses. Leslie contends that Smith came within half a vote of becoming Lincoln's vice-presidential candidate in 1864, but the *Proceedings* of the Union Convention indicate that while Smith was present as a delegate, his name was never placed in nomination. Wold, *Biographical Directory*, 1536; James E. Callaway, "Governor Green Clay Smith, 1866–1868," *Contributions*, V (1904), 108–13; Preston Leslie, "Biographical Sketch of Green Clay Smith," *ibid.*, 179; *Proceedings of the National Union Convention Held in Baltimore, Md., June 7th and 8th, 1864* (New York, 1864), 73, 93.

41. Daniel S. Tuttle, *Reminiscences of a Missionary Bishop* (New York, 1906), 131; Sanders to James E. Callaway (Helena, May 16, 1904), Sanders MSS; entry for October 10, 1866, Diary of Neil Howie.

called it—convened at Virginia City on November 5, 1866, it was soon
apparent that controversy still raged. Chief Justice Hosmer, now returned from the East, sided with Munson as to the illegality of the
second and third sessions and drew down "the vengeance of the
Legislative party," as he put it.[42] Already the country commissioners,
with Meagher's urging, had been "playing a game of freeze-out" with
Hosmer, refusing to provide stationery or wood to heat his courtroom.[43] Now the legislature registered its displeasure by redefining the
territorial judicial districts in such a way as to assign both Hosmer
and Munson to undesirable areas, while the third judge, Williston,
who proved more cooperative, was given the most attractive district.[44]

While territorial Republicans sought to dissolve it, the Democratic
legislature considered but did not adopt a house resolution calling
for Congress to agree that "the laws passed by this and the preceding
legislature should be held and declared to be the laws of the Territory
beyond all question."[45] Presumably such a statement was rejected
because to ask for legislation validating acts already claimed to be
legal would be to destroy the central Democratic argument. Instead,
the legislature sent Governor Smith to Washington to argue this, and
other questions, in person, leaving Meagher again in charge.[46]

But Smith was not alone in the nation's capital. Judge Munson was
on leave between October, 1866, and January, 1867, and evidence
indicates that part of his time was spent lobbying for the nullification
of the acts of the two legislatures.[47] Munson's presence was inciden-

42. Thomas W. Stephens to James Fergus (Virginia City, November 11,
1866), copy, Allis Stuart Collection; Hosmer to Andrew Johnson (Virginia City,
August 13, 1866), copy, Hayes Memorial Library; *Montana Post*, December 22,
1866.

43. *Montana Post*, November 3, 1866. "Stop the supplies, and even a Chief-
Justice would have to collapse," Meagher told an audience in Diamond City on
August 5. Bruce, *Lectures of Gov. Thomas Francis Meagher*, 53.

44. Act of December 15, 1866, LM, 3 Session (1866), 45–49. After the
first assembly met and until Congress modified the law, judicial districting was a
legislative function. The organic act required the judge to reside in the district
he served and the legislature provided a $5 fee to the judge for each case
brought before him. Thus when Hosmer and Munson were banished to thinly
populated wilderness districts, Williston was assigned to civilization where
there were more cases and consequently more income from fees. *Montana Post*,
December 29, 1866; act of May 26, 1864, 13 *USSL*, 88–89, 91.

45. *House Journal*, 3 Session (1866), 89–90.

46. Green Clay Smith to Seward (Virginia City, December 15, 1866; Washington, February 16, 1867), TPS; joint resolution (December 15, 1866), LM, 3
Session (1866), 87.

47. Hosmer to Sanders (Virginia City, January 24, 1867), Sanders MSS;
Senate Executive Document No. 6, 40 Congress, Special Session (1867), 5.

tal: the main arguments of the Unionists would come from Wilbur F. Sanders, long a contemptuous critic of "Meagher's Mob," who, with Robert E. Fisk, was "working for the interests of Montana" in Washington.[48] Part of Sanders's armament was a biting letter from leading Montana Republicans addressed to James Ashley of the House Committee on the Territories, asking aid in Congress "by wiping out the whole proceedings of the said sham legislatures," which after all were composed of "men reeking with treason and boasting their copper head proclivities still. . . ."[49] Sound party politics dictated no less. As Chief Justice Hosmer wrote Sanders late in January, "If our friends in Congress will help us now, there is little doubt that we will send a Republican in the fall. For God's sake give this matter attention, and let us lay out those rebellious disorganizers."[50]

When a bill was introduced to nullify the acts of both legislatures under question, Sanders, Smith, and McLean were all called before the Senate Committee on Territories, and Congress became convinced that the Republican cause was just. Sanders had done his work well and left the impression that only immediate congressional intervention could rescue Montana from the depths of turmoil and confusion. "That Territory is in a state of anarchy," said Ben Wade of Ohio, in explaining the need for the bill.[51]

As it emerged in final form, approved by both houses and by President Johnson, the measure specifically nullified all acts of the second and third legislative bodies and authorized the governor to establish new districts for representation and to call a new election. As further evidence of irritation toward the Democratic populace of this ill-mannered western province, Congress raised the salaries of the judges by $1,000, and took away the power of the legislature to set judicial districts. Hereafter, the justices, as a group, would exercise that prerogative and also determine the dates and sites for holding courts.[52] Thus the judiciary was vindicated, while the legislative branch was sharply rebuked.

48. Robert E. Fisk to Elizabeth Fisk (Washington, February 28, 1867), Fisk family MSS, MHS.

49. A. W. White et al. to James M. Ashley (Helena, December 26, 1866), Sanders MSS.

50. Hezekiah Hosmer to Sanders (Virginia City, January 24, 1867), *ibid.*

51. *Montana Post*, August 17, 1867; *Congressional Globe*, 39 Congress, 2 Session (1866–67), 1816, 1817.

52. To be completed by July 1, 1867, apportionment was to be on the basis of population figures then available; and the number of members of the Council and House would remain as originally provided in the organic act. Act of March 2, 1867, 14 USSL, 426–27.

Reaction in Montana was divided. Republicans were jubilant. The *Montana Post* heralded the action as "merely the refusal of Congress to recognize the validity of the enactments of an illegal assemblage."[53] But the territorial elections of 1867, fought out on the nullification issue, showed the depth of Democratic feelings. In a bitter campaign, Sanders, whom his partisans dubbed "the great war-horse of the Union party," "an intrepid, able, life-long Republican . . . whose record is unimpeachable except in the court of disloyalty,"[54] was pitted against James Michael Cavanaugh, a man of extensive western political experience. A genial Irishman, Cavanaugh has been described as a "born politician," a man of keen wit and great personal magnetism. He was "a wonderfully eloquent man, and in the matter of billingsgate and sarcasm the only peer Sanders had met with up to that time." His opponents thought him the strongest man the Democrats could have nominated, "but a rascal—at heart." He was pilloried as a man of mercurial political affiliations, who had "Belong to Evirry Party that ever Excistet,"[55] as one rustic critic noted a few years later.

> A creature of amphibious nature,
> On land a beast, a fish in water,
> That always preys on grace or sin,
> A Sheep without, a wolf within.[56]

But Cavanaugh—the "congressional acrobat," some called him—swept the polls with more than 55 percent of the vote. Only one Republican was elected to the fourth legislature and he was not seated, for, says Bancroft, "he was not wanted in that body. . . ."[57]

One of the first acts of the new assembly was the adoption of a resolution defending the laws of the two preceding sessions as "just, equitable and beneficial," and condemning congressional invalidation of them as "injurious to the people of this community." The assembly charged both Hosmer and Munson with having "polluted the judicial

---

53. *Montana Post*, March 23, 1867.
54. *Ibid.*, August 10, 1867.
55. Leeson, *History of Montana*, 1197; Alexander K. McClure, *Three Thousand Miles through the Rocky Mountains* (Philadelphia, 1869), 254; "A Partial Sketch of the Civil and Military Service of Major Martin Maginnis," *Contributions*, VIII (1907), 15; entry for July 16, 1867, Andrew J. Fisk Diary; William J. Snavely to U. S. Grant (Helena, March 1, 1870), BIA.
56. *Montana Post*, August 31, 1867.
57. Bancroft, *History of Montana*, 669; the vote was Cavanaugh, 6,004; Sanders, 4,896; for a margin of victory of 1,018 for the Democrat. *Montana Post*, August 31, October 26, 1867; Waldron, *Montana Politics Since 1864*, 18.

ermine of the Supreme Court of this Territory by dabbling in the filthy pool of politics," called them "incompetent and not trustworthy," and requested their resignation on the ground that their part in bringing about nullification of the laws, legal or illegal, had placed property rights and the general welfare of the people of the territory in jeopardy.[58] Hosmer responded in kind but refused to resign, though Munson seems to have acceded.[59]

Annulment created additional work for both the legislature and the judiciary. Most of the work of the fourth assembly was devoted to a reenactment of the laws voided by Congress. The additional labor required extra clerks in each house, and when the forty days allotted by the organic act proved insufficient, Governor Smith was forced to call a special session (December 14–24, 1867) in order that the task might be completed.[60] In Congress, Ashley made an unsuccessful effort to exempt the territorial license and revenue laws and the Sunday laws from the earlier act of repeal,[61] but there was no alternative offered: all laws of the two sessions were repassed, section by section.

The courts were called upon to decide a number of questions arising from the controversy. The nullification act stipulated that no legislation after the adjournment of the first legislature was to be valid until elections had been held for a new and legal fourth assembly. Did this mean actual repeal of the laws of the two "bogus" legislatures, or merely suspension until the election took place? What about the pay of elected and appointed officials during that intervening period?[62] Would portions of the revenue increased in 1866 have to be refunded?

58. *House Journal*, 4 Session (1867), 22, 252, 256; *Council Journal*, 4 Session (1867), 230–31, 233; joint resolution of December 13, 1867; *Montana Post*, December 26, 1867. Hosmer had further alienated the legislature by refusing to accede to a territorial law for change of venue in civil suits, a position which the territorial supreme court ultimately rejected, holding against him. See act of December 6, 1867, *LM*, 3 Session (1867), 139; *Godbe v. McCormick* (December, 1868), 1 *Montana Reports*, 105–10.

59. See Hosmer to legislature (Virginia City, December 25, 1867), *Montana Post*, December 28, 1867; Merrill G. Burlingame and K. Ross Toole (*History of Montana*, New York, 1957, I, 228) say Munson resigned; a petition to the president and the Senate later asked that Munson be removed. *Helena Weekly Herald*, October 22, 1868. See also *Senate Executive Journal*, XVI, 310, 433, and XVII, 31, which in one place says he was removed and in another that he resigned.

60. Council to Smith (Virginia City, December 12, 1867), GEC; *LM*, 4 Extra Session (1867), title page; *Council Journal*, 4 Session (1867), 16; proclamation of February 6, 1867, *Montana Post*, February 23, 1867.

61. *Congressional Globe*, 40 Congress, 1 Session (1867), 333.

62. In one case, the district court upheld the contention of the superintendent

Within the territory, the entire matter was largely a struggle between Democrats and Republicans and between the legislative assembly and Meagher, on the one hand, and the federal judiciary, on the other. Governor Smith managed to steer clear of most of the controversy. While sympathetic with the Democratic position, he seems to have avoided "the political wire pullers," who sought his endorsement, and he managed by being soft-spoken on the subject to keep the Republicans in doubt, although some believed that he would support the Meagher faction "with the hope of coming in on the inside track. . . ." But when sent to Washington to work for the territory during much of 1867, Smith found it easy to maintain this "benevolent neutrality." [63] It was Meagher who led and continued the struggle, even after Smith became governor, until his accidental drowning in the Missouri River in the summer of 1867.

In a sense, the controversy boiled down into the old arguments of local versus federal sovereignty. Residents of Missouri, Georgia, or Louisiana who moved into Montana brought with them typically southern home-rule ideas. Tempered with the independence and individualism of the frontier, these concepts clearly clashed with the political philosophy of the conservative Unionist justices sent out from Washington. Significant, too, as an indication of larger federal policies, was the fact that Congress acted not on the merits of the case itself, but in terms of political expediency. The real issue was never the validity of the two legislative assemblies or their enactments, but rather whether or not these obstreperous Democratic upstarts should be allowed to control the legislatures. Had the territory actually been "in a state of anarchy," as Ben Wade suggested, the action of Congress would have provided little relief. Indeed, had such been the case, practicality would have demanded that the laws of the two assemblies be validated. Congress here legislated not on behalf of Montana Territory, but on behalf of the Republican party.

There were other indications during this period of the same ten-

---

of public instruction that as soon as the election was over, the laws were again in effect and hence he was entitled to his salary from the time of his appointment (March 4, 1867) to the date of the reenactment of the law prescribing the duties and salary of his office (December, 1867). This was reversed by the territorial supreme court on the grounds that the complainant had been appointed two days after the nullifying act. Carpenter *v.* Rogers (December, 1868), 1 *Montana Reports*, 90–98.

63.   *Montana Post*, October 6, 1866; Smith to legislature (November 4, 1867), in *Montana Post*, November 9, 1867; Hosmer to Sanders (Virginia City, January 24, 1867), Sanders MSS.

dency, as well as of carry-over of congressional politics to the territory. As was often done, Congress in early 1867 used the territories as
an experimental field for later national policy, by enacting a law prohibiting any denial of the vote on account of "race, color, or previous
condition of servitude."[64] Montana's legislature recognized the act by
amending the election laws to state that nothing therein might be con-
strued to conflict with or abridge the rights of any person enfranchised
by this particular federal law, but it did not remove the phrase "all
white male citizens" from the statutes which prescribed suffrage requirements in the territory.[65]

It could hardly be expected that such moderate action would carry
favor with the Radicals of the Fortieth Congress. In the House, a resolution was introduced calling for an investigation and the recommendation of "such measures as may be necessary to secure obedience on
the part of the Legislature and Governor of Montana to the laws of
the Congress of the United States." Elihu Washburne suggested that
if the inquiry showed Montana in violation of federal statutes, as reported, then the organic act of the territory should be repealed![66]
Such threats were effective: the fifth territorial assembly made haste
to expunge the obnoxious phrase from its election laws.[67]

Although Wilbur F. Sanders would later liken the administration
of Green Clay Smith in Montana "to the reign of Charles the 1st,"[68]
and although Smith was away from the territory for considerable
lengths of time, he was a man of sound governmental ideas and consistently sought to make improvements. He prodded Washington for
more money, land, and post offices; he urged—and achieved—the
streamlining of the territorial tax law and the adoption of the California civil code; he invited the legislature to curb the governor's excessive military power; he practiced rigorous governmental economy
and saw the need for outside capital to develop Montana's resources.[69]
Regarded as "a brick to travel with," the personable Smith was generally well-liked. With his wife—"a high-spirited Southern belle," according to one observer—he enjoyed "the social whirl," but was not

64. Act of January 24, 1867, 14 *USSL*, 379–80.
65. Acts of November 22 and December 10, 1867, *LM*, 4 Session (1867),
77, 96.
66. *Congressional Globe*, 40 Congress, 2 Session (1867–68), 781.
67. Act of December 30, 1868, *LM*, 5 Session (1868–69), 100.
68. Sanders to Callaway (Helena, May 16, 1904), Sanders MSS.
69. "Second Message of Governor Green Clay Smith," *Contributions*, V
(1904), 133; *Council Journal*, 4 Session (1867), 67; *House Journal*, 4 Extra
Session (1867), 7–8; *Montana Post*, November 9, 1867.

regarded as a dilettante: his clubbing of a drunken Irishman with a fence stake at Fort Benton in early 1867 could only endear him to his constituents.[70] He spoke at political meetings but was not without his antagonists. In 1868, for example, an Indian agent accused him of losing $1,645 of agency funds "at a gambling table"; his accuser quickly withdrew the charges, sheepishly admitting that he had been erroneously informed by "personal and political enemies" of the governor.[71]

Despite the establishment of a series of government forts to guard the east-west line of travel along the Missouri and to protect the Bozeman Trail swinging in from the south and east,[72] the year 1866 brought new Indian tension. Federal garrisons were usually small and some were located as to be almost ineffective in time of greatest need. As James L. Fisk wrote late in 1866, ". . . it confused everybody here, and throughout the territory, with one accord to fathom or devise what earthly object there can be in this present fancied disposition of paid military forces."[73]

Meanwhile, Montanans were thrown largely upon their own devices for protection against an increasing number of depredations, particularly among the Piegans in the north. "We are now organizing a vigilance committee here among the whites," reported the chief clerk of the Blackfoot Agency early in 1866, and the objects of atten-

70. James Stuart to Granville Stuart (St. Louis, January 24, 1867), Stuart MSS; Herman Francis Reinhart, *The Golden Frontier*, ed. by Doyce Nunis (Austin, 1962), 267–68; *Montana Post*, June 29, 1867; Sanders to Callaway (Helena, May 16, 1904), Sanders MSS.

71. *Montana Democrat*, December 26, 1867. Even after the charges had been withdrawn, Green took pains to deny them. See George B. Wright to N. G. Taylor (Fort Benton, June 11, 15, 1867); Smith to Seward (Washington, August 25, 1868), in TPS.

72. Fort Buford was established at the mouth of the Yellowstone and Camp Cook on the south bank of the Missouri, near the mouth of the Judith River, a hundred miles or so below Buford to guard the east-west line. To protect the Bozeman Trail, the government built Fort Phil Kearney on Piney Creek just east of the northern Big Horns; Fort Conner near the upper reaches of the Powder was regarrisoned as Fort Reno; just within the southern bounds of the territory, Fort C. F. Smith was built on the Big Horn at the crossing of the Bozeman Road. In the following year, 1867, Fort Shaw was established on the Sun between the head of navigation of the Missouri and the mining regions to the south and west; and Fort Ellis, a cavalry post, was constructed in the Gallatin Valley. *Annual Report of the Secretary of War, 1867*, 32–49; Protection Across the Continent, *House Executive Document* No. 23, 39 Congress, 2 Session (1866–67), 20–21.

73. James L. Fisk to William R. Marshall (Helena, September 29, 1866), quoted in "Expeditions of Captain Jas. L. Fisk to the Gold Mines of Idaho and Montana, 1864–66," *Collections of the State Historical Society of North Dakota*, II (1908), 460.

tion were the Piegans and the Bloods. "I am afraid but little freighting will be done here next spring, without these gentlemen are whipped during the winter."[74] The killing of half a dozen whites during the spring only intensified feelings; Governor Smith in his annual message to the legislature in November noted the growing restlessness of the various tribes and observed that if federal troops were not made available the territory must necessarily act on its own.[75] At the same time, Smith evidenced further sympathy for his constituents' plight when he recommended that the land allotted to the Flatheads and Kutenais be reduced, though it is conjecture whether he would go as far as the legislature, which in late 1867 urged that Congress put Indian affairs in the hands of the War Department and "abolish the whole system of Indian agencies which has been so fruitful of wrong to the Indians and of war to the whites."[76]

Smith departed for Washington early in 1867, leaving the reins of government once more in the hands of the hard-driving Thomas Francis Meagher. During the Civil War, Meagher had fought under the green flag emblazoned with the golden harp of old Ireland—the banner of the Irish brigade. He was not averse to the use of force and he believed political capital could be made of a successful Indian campaign. Earlier Meagher had joined with Justice Munson and Agent Gad Upson in negotiating an agreement with the Blackfeet in 1865, though one old-timer felt the three "knew as much about an Indian as I did about the inhabitants of Jupiter."[77] And hardly had Meagher set foot on Montana soil when he was calling upon the administration in Washington to send "a competent cavalry force," at the same time voicing his opinion that the savages would never be reduced by friendly relations, but only by "the strong and crushing hand of the military power of the nation."[78] Moreover, he was soon

74. Upham to Gad. E. Upson (January 9, 1866), Report of the Commissioner of Indian Affairs, *Annual Report of the Secretary of the Interior, 1866*, 199.

75. *Ibid.*, 202–3; Smith to legislature (November 6, 1866), in *Contributions*, V (1904), 137.

76. Smith to Orville H. Browning (Virginia City, October 31, 1866), BIA; memorial to Congress (December 24, 1867), *LM*, Extra Session (1867), 273. A similar memorial was sent much later in 1879. See memorial to Congress (n.d.), *LM*, 11 Session (1879), 130–31.

77. Meagher to Johnson (Virginia City, January 20, 1866), Johnson MSS; quoted in George Bird Grinnell, *Beyond the Old Frontier* (New York, 1913), 357.

78. Report of Acting Governor Meagher (December 14, 1865), in Report of the Commissioner of Indian Affairs, *Annual Report of the Secretary of the Interior, 1866*, 196–97. See also Meagher to Gen. F. Wheaton (Virginia City, October 20, 1865); Meagher to Seward (Virginia City, October 20, 1865); Meagher to Seward (Virginia City, December 11, 1865), TPS.

convinced that it was an impossible task for the territorial governor to be both chief executive and superintendent of Indian affairs, and he recommended that the two functions be separated. Noting that he was extremely fond of horseback riding and should enjoy making the rounds of the agencies, Meagher wrote the Commissioner of Indian Affairs, "*I beg respectfully to offer myself, though your friendly recommendations, for the appointment.* I should infinitely prefer it to the Governorship."[79]

But that was not to be, and Meagher believed he saw his chance for glory early in 1867 and grabbed it. In March, John Bozeman wrote the acting governor asking protection for the Bozeman Valley, which he insisted was at the mercy of Red Cloud's Sioux warriors. Meagher promptly requested permission to raise a thousand volunteers. "Danger is imminent & will overpower unless measures for defence are taken," he told General Grant.[80] But specific authorization was withheld, pending further investigation. Soon thereafter, Bozeman was killed by renegade Blackfeet along the Yellowstone, and Meagher seized upon this "Bozeman Massacre" as leverage with the War Department. Cryptically and not wholly accurately he telegraphed: "Citizens murdered, Troops within Territory no use whatever. Forts Phil Kearney & Smith inaccessible, Commanding Officer Camp Cook mouth of Judith declines to move. People of Montana thrown upon themselves ask therefore authority from War Dept. to organize even eight hundred (800) men for military duty in the field until relieved by Regulars. This authority most earnestly asked. Not an hour to be lost."[81]

The War Department hesitated to give Meagher, who was regarded as something of a "stampeder," the requested authority, but when General William Sherman, commanding the District of the Missouri, of which Montana was a part, gave a nebulous and misconstrued permission, Meagher proceeded to recruit his volunteers. To equip and supply the militia, the "Acting One" issued vouchers on the general government, and local merchants, recognizing the risk involved, out-

79. Meagher to D. N. Cooley (Virginia City, July 12, 1866), BIA. To Johnson, he made the same request. "Nothing delights me so much as being on horseback, and taking long, rough, and adventurous journeys, and as the Superintendency would enable me heartily to indulge in this partiality and perform these services, I should be perfectly at home with that appointment. Meagher to Johnson (Virginia City, July 13, 1866), Johnson MSS.

80. Meagher to Grant (Virginia City, April 9, 1867), Johnson MSS.

81. Meagher to E. M. Stanton (n.p., April 28, 1867), War Department Telegrams, quoted in Athearn, *Thomas Francis Meagher*, 159–60. Unless otherwise noted, the author has drawn upon Athearn for the story of the Montana volunteers.

fitted and provisioned the troops at prices considerably above market value.

Meagher's motley legions eventually numbered 150 or 200 and most were attracted by the possibility of regular rations and by their commander's order giving them any property captured from the Indians. Duty was limited largely to the patrolling of lines of communication and local saloons, with very little contact with the Indians. One observer reported that Meagher "kept full of whiskey" and "he and his staff had a merry time in Virginia City," while preparing to take to the field.[82]

Shortly after Meagher's death in July, 1867, Governor Smith returned to the territory and took command of the volunteers. Temporary camps were established at the mouth of the Musselshell and on the Yellowstone, a relief force was sent to Fort C. F. Smith, and a band of stolen horses was recovered from marauding Crows, but real contributions were limited.[83] New difficulties were created when Smith ordered the militia mustered out on October 1: a large number disobeyed the orders and decamped with some 250 horses and mules, as well as a large portion of the quartermaster's and commissary stores; loyal members who waited for proper discharge found no paymaster and no funds and many were compensated so far as possible in horses and rations.[84]

Nor were the merchant outfitters who had accepted vouchers in any better position. At the end of the "campaign," General Sherman was embarrassed to receive warrants totaling $980,313.11. The Montana legislature asked that Congress appropriate $1,100,000 to defray the expense of raising and equipping the volunteers, a figure the Senate Committee on the Territories considered exorbitant, though it recommended paying a "reasonable" sum.[85] The War Department was more demanding, however, and sent Inspector General James Hardie to the territory to make a thorough investigation. He found evidence of heavy overcharging and some of pay asked for goods not delivered. Some Montanans had already labeled Meagher's Indian war "the big-

82. Reinhart, *The Golden Frontier*, 264.

83. Burlingame, *Montana Frontier*, 124; Athearn, *Thomas Francis Meagher*, 161–63.

84. Smith to legislature (November 5, 1867), *Montana Post*, November 9, 1867.

85. Burlingame, *Montana Frontier*, 125; memorial to Congress (December 11, 1867), *LM*, 4 Session (1867), 268; memorial to Congress (January 11, 1869), *LM*, 5 Session (1868–69), 117; Report of the Committee on the Territories on the Payment of Expenses for the Montana Volunteers, *Senate Report* No. 31, 41 Congress, 2 Session (1869–70), 3–4.

gest humbug of the age, got up to advance his political interest, and to enable a lot of bummers who surround and hang on to him to make a big raid on the United States treasury."[86] Another resident of Helena wrote President Grant in 1870 with a good deal more insight than grammatical precision: "I have Beene Reading in the Last Papers that theare has Beene Some Ressolution Offered in Regard to The Montana Indian war that has happent in Sixty Seven And what I Know About it I think It was Got up for A Speculation. . . . The best way to get up an Indian Excitement and let the government pay the Bill the got Govener Meagher to issue A Proclamation to Raise Vollientiers. But it was an uphill Business till the Got up an Excitement. . . ."[87]

Inspector General Hardie recommended the payment of $513,000 as sufficient to cover all expenses; the legislature indicated a willingness to settle for this amount; and in the end slightly more than that was paid out.[88]

This episode, says Meagher's biographer, represents an excellent case study of "an Indian war which never materialized despite the efforts of the troops to produce it, cost the federal government a half million dollars and complicated the job of the regular army by exciting the native tribes."[89] Even so, territorial residents were never completely satisfied. At the end of the period Delegate Joseph K. Toole still spoke sadly of "Millions of dollars of unpaid claims, mildewed by age, growing out of these atrocities . . . while the heroes of these troublesome times, overcome with the weight of years and no longer able to conquer their feelings, have gone to join the silent majority, leaving destitute widows and orphans to keep alive before Congress the memory of their trials and tribulations. Verily the cruelty of Congress cuts as keenly as the scalping-knife or the tomahawk."[90]

Despite the lack of instructions covering the job, Governor Smith undoubtedly took seriously his duties as superintendent of Indian af-

86. Montana Indian War Claims, *House Executive Document* No. 98, 41 Congress, 3 Session (1870–71), 10–11, 12; Report of Flathead Agent August H. Chapman (July 5, 1867), in Report of the Commissioner of Indian Affairs, *Annual Report of the Secretary of the Interior, 1867,* 259.

87. Snavely to Grant (Helena, March 1, 1870), BIA.

88. Testimony in relation to Indian War Claims of the Territory of Montana, *House Miscellaneous Document* No. 215, Pt. 2, 42 Congress, 2 Session (1871–72), 8; memorial to Congress (January 12, 1872), LM, 7 Session (1871–72), 647–48; Letter from the Secretary of War Relating to the Payment of Montana Indian War Claims of 1867, *House Executive Document* No. 9, 43 Congress, 2 Session (1874–75), 5.

89. Robert G. Athearn, "The Montana Volunteers of 1867," *Pacific Historical Review,* XIX (May, 1950), 136.

90. *Congressional Record,* 50 Congress, 2 Session (1888–89), 821.

fairs. He showed compassion and requested aid for the destitute Bannacks and Shoshonis, but urged reduction of the lands of the Flatheads and Kutenais. He visited the various agencies and went on record as a "peace at any price" man. He was, he said in the summer of 1867, committed to securing "peacable and amicable relations with the Indians if I can, (if I have the means) . . . but forcible if I must. . . ."[91]

Smith went east in the summer of 1868 and never returned: late in the year he resigned and turned to the ministry, ultimately in 1876 to become the Prohibition party candidate for president.[92] Until the arrival of his successor in the summer of 1869, Secretary James Tufts, a man of considerable western political experience, served as acting governor. Though a lawyer of some ability and a man who strongly urged certain changes upon the legislature, Tufts later ran into difficulty in handling territorial finances before he "inherited a comfortable fortune" and retired to more seasonable climes.[93]

The years from 1865 to 1867 belonged to Meagher and they were dominated by the "bogus legislature" fiasco, which in turn was a product of both local and national politics. In the seventies, Democratic newspapers still condemned the Congress that "rode roughshod over the people" of Montana, while Republican editors still staunchly defended this action. Forty years after the episode, the voice of old Martin Maginnis, long a Democrat and territorial delegate, still crackled with bitterness as he called the nullification of the laws of both legislatures "the most unjust act ever perpetrated by the Congress of the United States on a Territory." "Indeed," he said, it was "the only one of the kind ever known in the history of government."[94]

91. Smith to O. H. Browning (Virginia City, October 31, 1866); Smith to Taylor (Washington, April 1, 1867; Virginia City, July 29, 1867), BIA.

92. Smith, who for many years was engaged in religious work in Kentucky and in Washington, D.C., polled some 10,000 votes on the Prohibitionist ticket in 1876. Montana Republican newspapers saw him as "a better minister than politician" and cast aspersions on his earlier career as a temperance advocate. "He was one of the most frightful examples in that line, periodically, that ever warned a people of the danger of the excessive use of strong drink," carped editor Fisk. *Helena Daily Herald*, March 24, 1874; October 17, 1876; Wold, *Biographical Directory*, 1536; Leslie, "'Biographical Sketch of Green Clay Smith," 179–80.

93. Born in New Hampshire, Tufts was a graduate of Middlebury College and was admitted to the bar in Iowa. He had served in the Nebraska legislature and had been speaker of the house of the Idaho assembly before moving to Montana. See Tufts to legislature (December 8, 1868), *Council Journal*, 5 Session (1868–69), 15–26; *Herald*, March 24, 1871; September 3, 1884; October 15, 1886.

94. Martin Maginnis, "Thomas Francis Meagher," *Contributions*, VI (1907), 106.

Politically, Meagher had no choice but to side with Montana Democrats. He knew his action would be popular in the territory. Perhaps he did not foresee that one result of stern Republican policy and opposition was a fusion of northern and southern Democrats into a solid voting bloc which would long dominate Montana politics. Only twice in fourteen territorial elections were Republican delegates sent to Congress. Sanders ruined himself politically, not only for the 1867 delegate race, but also for the campaign of 1880, when his role in the affair was again made a matter of moment by the voters.[95] In the short term, animosities generated in the controversy would carry over into the administrations of subsequent governors, compounding their problems and those of the territory in general.

95. *Herald,* October 7, 1880.

"He Is Loser by Coming Here":
A Radical Republican in Charge

Green Clay Smith's resignation late in 1868 was the signal for a number of "missionaries from Helena to Washington" to descend upon
the nation's capital in the hope of influencing that "Knight of the
Cigar," President Ulysses Grant, in the selection of the new governor.
Although the *Montana Post* sarcastically proclaimed that the forty-
man Montana deputation in the Grant inaugural parade was "the
only delegation in the procession in which not a single person aspired
to office," the local hopefuls there seeking the job included Secretary
James Tufts, Samuel Hauser, Nathaniel P. Langford, and Wilbur F.
Sanders.[1] While Sanders and his backers blanched, President Johnson,
in his waning days in office, nominated Langford, who had strong
support, but the election of Grant and the temper of Congress left the
issue in doubt. Langford "hasn't the ghost of a chance," Bob Fisk reported from the Washington scene, and knowing Democrats agreed
with him.[2] Their analysis was correct: Republican Radicals in the

1. *Montana Post*, April 2, 1869.
2. Robert E. Fisk to Elizabeth Fisk (Washington, March 5, 1869), Fisk
family MSS; Walter B. Dance to Samuel Hauser (Deer Lodge, February 22,
1869), Hauser MSS. Langford had solid backing from Roscoe Conkling of New
York and O. P. Morton in Congress. He was the candidate of George Pinney, one
of the territorial political powers, and was fought obliquely by Fisk, who
sought to stop him by attacking Pinney, even accusing him of murder and
of "endorsing notorious and irresponsible men for places of trust and emolument

Senate refused to confirm the appointment, and Sanders, who politically had "been firm all the time from Alpha to Omega," according to his supporters, was given another chance.[3]

Earlier, in assessing his own chances, Langford had sounded a note of caution: "as Ashley and a few other prominent Republican congressmen were defeated, they might be looking for it."[4] He was referring specifically to James M. Ashley, lame duck from Toledo who had failed in his bid for reelection to the House of Representatives in 1868, and who was one of eight or ten non-Montanans who were serious contenders for the governorship. Others included Daniel R. Anthony of Kansas—"the Jayhawker, Red Leg, murderer, and leader of mobs," according to one partisan; young Benjamin Potts of Ohio, who had marched with Sherman; and General J. A. Campbell—"Old Abbatis"—also from the Buckeye State. To the list might be added "about one hundred more candidates," if newspaper correspondents on the Washington scene may be taken literally.[5]

Soon the press reported that efforts to make a Montanan governor had been "knocked into a cocked hat," and that "Sam Hauser has left Washington in deep distress"; Langford, Bob Fisk wrote a little later, was "the most terribly disappointed man I ever saw"; in about two weeks, Fisk's brother Andrew would write in his diary in Helena: "Sanders, Ex 'War-horse' of the Republican party, called at the office this A.M. His usual amount of brass seems to have foresaken him. He acknowledges that he was 'cornered' in Washington."[6]

Sanders had been "cornered," as Fisk put it, by James Mitchell Ashley, whose name Grant sent to the Senate in April, 1869, in nomination to be governor of Montana. A fiery abolitionist and an ardent advocate of Radical Reconstruction, Ashley had packed considerable experience into his forty-five or so years. At various times he had been

in Montana"—both equally heinous crimes in his eyes. Conkling to "whom it may concern" (Washington, March 15, 1869); O. P. Morton to U. S. Grant (Washington, March 19, 1869); George M. Pinney et al. to Grant (n.p., n.d.); Fisk to Hamilton Fish (Washington, March 30, 1869), all in Langford file, APS.

3. William H. Patten to N. B. Banks (Virginia City, January, n.d., 1869), Sanders MSS; *Senate Executive Journal*, XVI, 431; *Weekly Independent*, January 16, 1869.

4. Langford to Hauser (Helena, October 27, 1868), Hauser MSS.

5. *Weekly Rocky Mountain Gazette* (Helena), February 11, 1869; *Montana Democrat*, February 20, 1869; *New North-West* (Deer Lodge), December 24, 1869; Cleveland *Leader*, March 16, 1869. Campbell would be appointed governor of Wyoming. Cleveland *Leader*, April 5, 1869. For Daniel R. Anthony, see *Kansas: A Cyclopedia of State History* (Chicago, 1912), III, 55.

6. *Montana Democrat*, February 20, 1869; Fisk to Elizabeth Fisk (Washington, April 5, 1869), Fisk family MSS; entry for April 20, 1869, Fisk Diary.

a riverboatman, lumberer, newspaper editor, lawyer, and drug store proprietor, and had served ten years in the U.S. House of Representatives, before being turned out by his constituents by an overwhelming margin. In Congress, his leadership in the fight against Andrew Johnson had earned him the epithet of "Ashley the Impeacher" and the scorn of the more liberal factions of both parties.[7]

Ashley's name was known to the public, but it was seldom mentioned in polite terms. Although Rutherford B. Hayes found him "a large, good-natured popular style of man—full of good humor,"[8] others disagreed. Ben Perley Poore, for example, described him as "a man of the lightest mental calibre and most insufficient capacity," with a "large shock of bushy, light hair, which he kept hanging over his forehead like a frowsy bang threatening to obstruct his vision," and who "passed much of his time in perambulating the aisles of the House, holding short conferences with leading Republicans, and casting frequent glances into the ladies' gallery."[9] Gideon Welles, outgoing secretary of the Navy, thought him "a calculating fanatic, weak, fond of notoriety, not of very high-toned moral calibre."[10] A Missouri editor once carried sketches of Radical lawmakers on his front page with the comment: "That bushy headed biped in the back row of seats is Buckeye-impeacher Ashley. He only lacks a tail to convert him into an African ourang outang. . . ."[11]

Ashley's unpopularity was reflected in the columns of the *New York Times* when his nomination became known. The *Times* protested his selection, accused him of "public corruption,—of venality, voluntary and confessed, in high office," and cited his case as a brief for "a proper civil service of trained officials and competitive examina-

7. There are no full-length published biographies of Ashley. Short sketches appear in the *DAB*, I, 389–90, and the *Biographical Directory of the American Congresses*, 793. A two-part article by Maxine Baker Kahn, "Congressman Ashley in the Post-Civil War Years," *Northwest Ohio Quarterly*, XXVI (Summer and Autumn, 1964), 116–33, 194–210, does not deal with his Montana experiences. At least two master's theses cover part of his career. Margaret Ashley Paddock, "An Ohio Congressman in Reconstruction" (Columbia University, 1916) is overly sympathetic and superficial. "The 'Original Impeacher': James M. Ashley in Civil War and Reconstruction," done by Kenneth J. Spencley at the University of Illinois in 1962, is a fine study, but does little with Ashley in Montana. See also the recently completed dissertation on Ashley written by Robert F. Horowitz at the City University of New York.

8. Charles R. Williams, ed., *Diary and Letters of Rutherford Birchard Hayes, Nineteenth President of the United States* (Columbus, 1924), III, 6–7.

9. Ben Perley Poore, *Perley's Reminiscences* (New York and Philadelphia, 1886), II, 201–2.

10. *The Diary of Gideon Welles* (Boston and New York, 1911), III, 12.

11. *Missouri Vindicator*, quoted in *Weekly Independent*, June 5, 1868.

tions."[12] Specifically, the *Times* referred to Ashley's action several years earlier in attempting to use his position as chairman of the Committee on Territories to bring about an appointment in Colorado for his own personal benefit, an action which a House investigation later whitewashed.[13]

But Ashley had strong backing. After his failure to retain his congressional seat, 142 members of the House had supported him for the Montana gubernatorial position. "They have a way of taking care of their dead," one editor put it.[14] Even so, despite aid from Congressional stalwarts like Ben Wade, Zach Chandler, and Charles Sumner, Ashley's confirmation came only after strenuous debate and by the narrow margin of a single vote. According to newspaper reports, the debate was the "fiercest discussion ever had in Executive session by a President in sympathy with Congress," and it was reported that Ashley was "buffeted and cuffed so sadly" that his pride would not permit him to accept the appointment. But he did accept the position, which he preferred, he said, "to any in the gift of the President."[15]

A number of Republican newspapers in the East supported Ashley and thought him entitled to his reward and "'he will administer the duties of office carefully and well," noted the Cleveland *Leader*.[16] But other commentators, including *The Nation*, echoed the *New York Times* in condemning not only the appointment, but the system of patronage which made it possible.[17] Gideon Welles was even more vehement. "The nomination and confirmation of this corrupt wretch," he said, "is further evidence of the total debasement of the Radical Party."[18]

In Montana, reaction at first was drawn largely along party lines. When they first heard rumors that the governorship had been promised to the Ohio Radical, Democrats were incredulous. "Moonshine—and a green cheese moon," scoffed the editor of the Helena *Post*.[19] "Angels and Ministers of grace defend us," pleaded the *Montana Democrat*, when news of the appointment became definite.[20] ". . . the

12. *New York Times*, April 18, 19, 21, 28, 1869.
13. See Cleveland *Leader*, March 13, 1863; "Report on Investigation of Hon. J. M. Ashley," *House Report* No. 47, 37 Congress, 3 Session (1862–63), 1–63.
14. *New North-West*, December 24, 1869.
15. *New York Times*, April 18, 21, 27, 28, 1869.
16. Cleveland *Leader*, April 12, 1869.
17. *The Nation*, VIII (April 15, 22, 29, 1869), 286, 305, 325–26.
18. *Diary of Gideon Welles*, III, 575–76.
19. *Montana Post*, February 26, 1869.
20. *Montana Democrat*, April 10, 1869.

broken down political hack, James M. Ashley, has been appointed Governor of Montana," lamented the editor of the *Weekly Independent*, echoing a common plaint in the territory against officers drawn from outside Montana's boundaries. "How long are the people to be scorned and insulted by being told, by implication at least, that there is not one among the thirty thousand freemen of Montana who is capable of discharging the functions of the Executive office?"[21] Montana Democrats were inclined to agree with the *New York Times* that Ashley's aspirations were political and senatorial—"he has in view a fat office as soon as Montana becomes a State," said the *Independent*.[22]

Democrats were especially incensed over a bill Ashley had co-sponsored as a lame duck, which would give territorial governors broad powers in local elections. Its intent, according to Montanans, was to deprive "almost one-half of our best citizens of the right of suffrage," in order to give control to the Radical minority. That accomplished, it was charged, Montana would become a state acceptable to Congress, with Ashley as one of its senators. "Ye gods! wait till carnival day on the Ashley and Williams bills," shrieked J. H. Rogers of the *Independent*. "Get away, ye mudsills! Don't talk to United States officers of people's rights. . . ."[23]

As chairman of the House Committee on the Territories for several years, Ashley had gained an excellent working knowledge of territorial government—at least from the congressional point of view. In order to reduce proportionately the power of the South in Congress, he adhered to the principle of organizing state governments "at the earliest day practicable in every one of the Territories," but he believed that territories should be consolidated wherever possible in order that "rotton borough" states, as he labeled Nevada, not be created. Ashley hoped new states would be Republican, and he believed in use of the patronage to make every territory Republican as a prelude to statehood. To President Lincoln he had written in 1865, "I am in favor of removing every appointee of the Administration in the Territories who *bolts* the *regularly nominated union ticket* & unites with the opposition."[24]

21. *Weekly Independent*, April 10, 1869.
22. *Ibid.* "If we do not hear of Senator Ashley, of Montana, one of these days, it will not be his fault," predicted the *Times. New York Times*, April 21, 1869.
23. *Montana Democrat*, April 17, 1869; *Weekly Independent*, March 6, 1869. See also *Congressional Globe*, 40 Congress, 3 Session (1868–69), 365–66.
24. J. M. Ashley to William H. Hunt (Toledo, April 28, 1892), single letter in

He had been the most singularly important figure in the creation of Montana Territory, and in 1865, had visited there, along with other parts of the West, showing an interest in speculative mining ventures.[25] Yet because of his Radical proclivities his arrival in Virginia City in 1869 would be greeted with anything but enthusiasm by a majority of territorial residents. Few Republican governors would have been acceptable, for that matter, least of all a "carpetbagger" from the East; but Ashley, with his frank antipathy for all people with Democratic, southern, or anti-Negro leanings, was the most Radical of Radicals, and would hardly have been less welcome in the states below the Mason-Dixon line. Too much of Montana's population was of the "bourbonized" variety; events in the Meagher-Smith administration had pulled both wings of the Democrats closer together. For the ultra-Unionist Ashley, this could ultimately mean political stalemate.

Four months after he accepted the post, Ashley arrived in Montana, already committed to help campaign for the Republican candidate for delegate in the coming election, a contest which would see the Democrat James Cavanaugh reelected over former territorial secretary James Tufts—to the surprise of few.[26] Ashley promptly threw himself into his job, toured the territory, and attempted to learn something of his new constituents and their problems. Republicans received him well: his speech in Helena was applauded, his quarters were serenaded, and his reception ball heralded as "brilliant, numerously attended, and full of the 'tender graces' of other years."[27] Settling his family in Virginia City in the James King mansion on Rodney Street, Ashley found time for a boat cruise on the Jocko, which brought one editor to quip, obviously with Meagher and Green Clay Smith in mind: "One of our Governors was drowned, another was converted, by much water. Wonder what affect it will have on this

MHS; Ashley to Lincoln (Washington, March 15, 1865), Robert Todd Lincoln MSS; *Congressional Globe*, 39 Congress, 1 Session (1865–66), 2373; 40 Congress, 2 Session (1867–68), 433–45.

25. Truman C. Everts to Hezekiah Hosmer (Bannack, January 12, 1865); William H. Miller to Hosmer (Bannack, July 14, 1865), both in Hosmer MSS, Beinecke Library.

26. Ashley accepted the position on April 27, but asked for two or three months to get his affairs in shape; his affairs included some campaigning on behalf of Toledo friends which caused some consternation and criticism. H. Chase to Grant (Toledo, June 25, 1869); Ashley to J. C. B. Davis (Toledo, July 23, 1869), TPS; Robert Fisk to Elizabeth Fisk (Helena, July 3, 1869), Fisk family MSS.

27. *New North-West*, August 20, 1869.

one?"[28] Even before he arrived, Ashley had been interested in promoting immigration to Montana, and had appointed Benno Speyer of New York as official "Commissioner of Emigration" for the territory.[29] Once on the scene, he and several others undertook the promotion of a town on Thompson's River to be settled by easterners, and for several years he would continue to extol the virtues of Montana as a haven for the oppressed from the East.[30]

But the governor's main business was politics. When the sixth session of the territorial legislature convened late in 1869, it was overwhelmingly Democratic, with only three Republicans in the House and one in the Council,[31] a situation which for most minority executives would have called for tact and moderation. But the proud, obstinate Ohioan could be characterized by neither of these terms. No compromiser, he plunged immediately into the maelstrom of political currents, unmindful of possible consequences.

To begin with, he challenged the right of the legislature to convene in 1869 in extraordinary session. In 1868 and 1869 two federal acts had paved the way for biennial, rather than annual sessions of the assembly,[32] but there was disagreement as to when this change was to go into effect. On the one hand, the legislature contended it was to meet in 1869 and in 1870, then in alternate years thereafter. For his part, Ashley insisted that Congress had not contemplated a legislative session in the winter of 1869, and had appropriated no funds for its expenses. After considerable maneuvering, the assembly convened, without being technically proclaimed by the governor, who protested on grounds of unnecessary cost, but expressed himself willing to permit the courts to determine the legality of the matter, an opinion that had already been given unofficially by two of the three justices.[33] While he could find no precedents for withholding recogni-

28. *Ibid.*, October 1, 15, 1869.

29. Benno Speyer to Fish (New York, May 22, 1869), TPS.

30. *New North-West*, November 12, 1869. In 1870 he urged Julia Ward Howe to organize a Boston society to help dependent women reach Montana; at the same time, on stationery of the Montana Pioneer Immigrant Association, he emphasized the disparity of the sexes and the opportunity for more females in the territory, noting that the total population was about 30,000—"Perhaps 5 percent of it *female; not more!*" *Ibid.*, March 11 June 3, 1870; Ashley to "Dr Sir" (Helena, April 16, 1870), single letter in Beinecke Library.

31. Ashley to Fish (Helena, January 23, 1870), TPS; Ashley to J. D. Cox (Virginia City, August 28, 1869), BIA.

32. Acts of July 20, 1868, and March 1, 1869, 15 *USSL*, 109, 281.

33. Ashley to legislature (December 11, 1869), *House Journal*, 6 Session (1869–70), 14–15; *New North-West*, November 19, 1869.

tion, he believed that a majority of the acts passed by the sixth legislature "should never have become laws, and it is my opinion that
Congress ought to disprove most of them."[34] Ultimately Congress
would provide funds for the session, but not before Secretary Wiley
Scribner, who refused to provide legislators with authorization to
purchase stationery, books, and other equipment, was subject to considerable harassment.[35]

Back in September, James H. Mills, editor of the Deer Lodge *New
North-West*, had predicted that "freeze-out" would "be the game," if
a legislature did meet, and that the question of appointments would
be one of the most ticklish topics in what likely would be an impasse.[36]
Time soon bore out the correctness of his prophecy. Ashley charged
that the legislative assembly came together "for the purpose of keeping partisan officials in office who had been adjudged by the Chief
Justice not legally appointed."[37] His political opponents, on the other
hand, insisted that the governor, in essence, had permitted the legislature to convene in order to foist some of his favorites into various
offices and "to exhibit his transcendent ability as a political monte-
bank and juggler." Both parties were referring to a bitter controversy
revolving around the right of the governor to appoint certain officials
and the desire of the legislature to curb that power, a dispute that
was never settled during Ashley's tenure.

The organic act creating the territory in 1864 stipulated "that all
township, district and county officers, not herein otherwise provided
for, shall be appointed or elected, as the case may be, in such manner
as shall be provided by the governor and legislative assembly of the
Territory of Montana. The governor shall nominate, and by and with
the advice and consent of the legislative council, appoint all officers
not herein otherwise provided for. . . ."[38] A subsequent territorial law
of November 1867, provided that the territorial treasurer, auditor, and
superintendent of public instruction should ultimately be elected by
the voters and commissioned by the governor.[39] Ashley challenged

34. Ashley to Fish (Helena, January 23, 1870), TPS.
35. *House Journal*, 6 Session (December 13, 1869), 54; act of July 20, 1868,
15 *USSL*, 109.
36. *New North-West*, September 3, 1869.
37. Ashley to Fish (Helena, January 23, 1870), TPS.
38. Act of May 26, 1864, 13 *USSR*, 88.
39. These officers were to be immediately appointed by a joint session of house
and council, to hold office until the general election of 1869, when the people at
large would select successors. Act of November 16, 1867, *LM*, 4 Session (1867),
73; *House Journal*, 4 Session (1867), 3.

the validity of such an act and refused to issue commissions to men elected to these posts in the election of August, 1869, claiming that the law was in direct contravention of the organic act and therefore illegal. The offices in question, he insisted, were not "township, district and county offices," to be filled as the legislature might decide; rather they were positions "not . . . otherwise provided for," to be filled by nomination of the governor, with the assent of the council. "The present executive having drawn the act for the organization of the territory of Montana, has no question as to the true interpretation this section," he said.[40]

Ashley lost no time in selecting men of his own—unswerving Republicans—to replace those elected by the people under the law of 1867, and proceeded to commission them subject to confirmation by the council at its next regular session. One of Ashley's appointments, James H. Mills, declined the post of superintendent of public instruction, and the other two appointees, Leander Frary as treasurer and James L. Fisk as auditor, were unable to gain possession of the respective offices from the incumbents, William H. Rodgers and William G. Barkley, so the case was taken to the courts.[41]

In the meantime, Ashley's relations with his legislature worsened. When the Democrats demanded some of the fruits of appointed office, he refused to consider any but qualified Republicans, and was lauded by local party stalwarts for his unwillingness to compromise.[42] In retaliation, the legislature refused to vote the governor a refund of $500 for a personal outlay made in New York to his "Commissioner of Emigration"; it then repealed an act it had passed for the benefit of Green Clay Smith in 1867, giving extra compensation to augment the governor's salary; and in addition refused to confirm any executive appointments.[43] When it finally offered Ashley a compromise list of names, part Democratic, part Republican, the shaggy-maned Ohioan

40. Ashley to legislature (December 11, 1869), *House Journal*, 6 Session (1869–70), 14–15.

41. *Ibid.*, 17–18; *New North-West*, September 10, 1869. Frary was a friend of Truman Everts, the first assessor of internal revenue, who some called "the power behind the throne of Ashley." Both Frary and Fisk were controversial and could not carry all of Ashley's party behind them, let alone the Democrats. *New North-West*, December 24, 1869.

42. Wiley S. Scribner et al. to Ashley (Virginia City, December 19, 1869), GEC.

43. Act (n.d.), *LM*, 6 Session (1869–70), 100–101; *House Journal*, 6 Session (1869–70), 28, 30, 173, 179. Ashley wrote the Treasury Department early in 1870 that "as soon as they found that they could not use me as they had

still refused to make any concession. To the end of December, 1869, when Ashley wrote the Council, "This is the last communication of this character, which I will favor you with this year," the governor had proposed and the Council rejected a total of fourteen nominations for the office of superintendent of public instruction, and eighteen each for auditor and treasurer.[44] To add insult, the legislature also took upon itself the selection of commissioners for the insane, and attempted, unsuccessfully, to shift control of federal arms and ammunition in the territory from jurisdiction of the governor to the county commissioners. At one point, in desperation, the Democratically controlled legislature voted to abolish the office of superintendent of public instruction on the grounds that it was "unnecessary" and "expensive," although Ashley's resounding veto of the bill insisted that the real issue was that "a partisan representative of the dominant party in the Legislative Assembly is not to be appointed or receive the emoluments of said office."[45] Of a total of sixty-three laws and resolutions enacted by the sixth assembly, three were passed over the governor's veto, and thirty-eight became law without his signature.

One of the measures enacted over Ashley's veto was designed to curb the governor's appointive powers by stipulating that appointments or removals from any office created by territorial law required the express sanction of the Council. In case of a vacancy, the Governor was to make an ad interim appointment, then call a special session of the Council within twenty days to approve or disapprove of the nomination. Ashley vigorously protested that such a law violated the Constitution and the organic act, not to mention common law, and that it would deprive the governor of the power to suspend or remove even officials committing illegal or fraudulent acts.[46] Later Ashley would use his influence in Washington in an effort to have Congress nullify this particular act, as well as to prohibit the granting of extra compensation to federal officers in Montana, and while this special legislation was never forthcoming, Congress in 1872 and 1873

---

been in the habit of using my predecessors," the legislature repealed his extra compensation. "I am therefore as usual 'Short,' " he complained. Ashley to R. W. Taylor (Virginia City, January 14, 1870), LT, Vol. 10.

44. See Ashley to Council (Virginia City, December 20, 21, 22, 23, 24, 27, 28, 29, 30, 31); Council to Ashley (Virginia City, December 20, 21, 22, 23, 24, 27, 28, 29, 31), all in GEC.

45. Ashley to Fish (Helena, January 23, 1870), TPS; Ashley to legislature (January 4, 1870), *House Journal*, 6 Session (1869–70), 167–68, 174.

46. Act of December 29, 1869, *LM*, 6 Session (1869–70), 86–87; *House Journal*, 6 Session (1869–70), 119–22, 124.

ultimately saw the wisdom of general laws which in effect accomplished these ends in all the territories.[47]

When the legislature adjourned, the issues still unresolved, Ashley issued commissions, as he put it, "to well known Republicans for all the Territorial offices," hoping, he said that the courts would soon resolve the question.[48] Not until August, 1870, did the territorial supreme court hand down a decision—a decision that represented more a compromise than a clear-cut victory for either side. On the one hand, the court held that the questionable act of 1867 did violate the organic act; that the officers were, as Ashley had insisted, territorial offices to be filled by the governor with the approval of the Council; that Rodgers and Barkley therefore had no legal claims. On the other hand, Ashley's appointees, unless confirmed by the Council, were also improperly selected and without valid claim.[49] Meanwhile, Rodgers and Barkley continued in office, and it remained for Ashley's successor, Benjamin Potts, to find an enduring solution to the problem.

It is doubtful if Ashley strengthened his position in Democratic Montana when he selected a Negro named Johnson as a notary public, although Johnson declined to serve.[50] Nor did he increase his popularity when he addressed the legislature in joint session on December 11 and called for modification of the territorial election law, "by copying the exact words of the fifteenth amendment."[51] However, he failed to follow through with this recommendation, thereby lending currency to the charges, already being made, of trimming his sails and of abandoning the Negro in the face of a populace overwhelmingly white and strongly pro-southern.[52]

Ashley's enemies made much of another episode in the same legislative session, when A. J. Smith, a member of the House from Beaverhead County, announced his intent to introduce a bill "prohibiting any person from holding any office in the gift of the people of this territory, or of appointment, unless he can produce a certificate that

47. *Congressional Globe*, 41 Congress, 3 Session (1870–71), 970; acts of June 8, 1872, and January 23, 1873, 17 *USSL*, 335, 416.

48. Ashley to Fish (Helena, January 23, 1870), TPS.

49. Fisk *v.* Rodgers, 1 *Montana Reports* (1870), 258–62.

50. *Daily Rocky Mountain Gazette*, July 21, 1870.

51. Ashley to Legislature (December 11, 1869), *House Journal*, 6 Session (1869–70), 41.

52. Earlier *The Nation* had condemned his about-face on "white man's government" in Montana. *The Nation*, IX (October 7, 1869), 282–83. A Chicago newspaper made the same accusation on November 22. Chicago *Post*, quoted in *New North-West*, December 10, 1869.

he has served at least three years in the Confederate service, or has lived at least five years in Missouri." No such bill was ever introduced and the notice of intent was subsequently expunged from the record.[53] Most likely this was only a bit of humorous horseplay, but Democratic newspapers charged that it was a device brought forth by a "tool" of Ashley in order to make political capital. The *Rocky Mountain Gazette* insisted that Ashley supporters had sent word to Washington that such a bill had actually been passed, but vetoed by the governor, leaving the implication that the chief executive was besieged by a legislative body composed of unreconstructed Rebels.[54]

Sometime in the summer or fall of 1869, a full-time superintendent of Indian affairs was appointed for Montana, relieving Ashley and future governors of those duties. The Indian menace had continued in his administration: in 1868, the Bozeman Trail was closed and its protective posts abandoned, though additional forts were built farther north. When the Bannacks complained that, though friendly, they were destitute and ignored, Ashley urged the federal government to send food and blankets.[55] When there were sporadic depredations by the Piegans in the area between Helena and Fort Benton, General Phil Sheridan had "but little doubt the Governor would like to call out a Regiment of Volunteers." But Ashley resisted citizen pressure to do so and instead urged federal patrols over the route. "I am loudly denounced and condemned by many because I have not called out the militia or authorized irresponsible bodies of men to take the public arms and go after and *punish* the Indians," he complained. "The success of my administration depends in a great measure on peace."[56] Early in the following year, Major Eugene M. Baker, with troops from Fort Ellis, moved against the Piegans with devastating results, and in 1871 ex-governor Ashley could assure easterners that life and property were as safe in Montana as in New York City,[57] a point a fair number of locals might have debated.

In mid-December, 1869, Ashley was arbitrarily removed by President Grant. Grant's motives are not clear. According to the *New*

53. *House Journal*, 6 Session (1869–70), 129–30.

54. *Weekly Rocky Mountain Gazette*, July 25, 1870.

55. Scribner to Eli S. Parker (Virginia City, August 10, 1869); Ashley to Parker (Virginia City, August 12, 1869), BIA.

56. Ashley to Gen. P. De Tobriand (Helena, August 21, 1869), copy; Ashley to Cox (Virginia City, August 28, 1869); ". . . but he will receive no encouragement from me," said Sheridan, referring to volunteers in Montana. "I think the thing will worry through this winter." Gen. Phil Sheridan to Gen. O. O. Greene (Chicago, September 8, 1869), copy, all in BIA.

57. *New York Tribune*, February 9, 1871.

York Tribune, the reason given in Washington was that Ashley had "deserted the Republican party and was using his official position to aid the enemies of the administration," an explanation which made Robert Fisk of the *Herald* bristle as he discussed "The Secret Conspiracy Against Governor Ashley."[58]

Some believed that the cause was a speech at Bozeman, in which the governor reportedly expressed sentiments "calculated to tickle the Democracy," a charge his friends denied emphatically.[59] Some of his supporters insisted that his friendship with Senator Charles Sumner of Massachusetts, with whom Grant was at odds, was a basic factor. Certainly Sumner, as well as Carl Schurz, Bishop Simpson, and others, had argued—to no avail—against Ashley's removal. Others contended that his nomination and subsequent discharge were moves deliberately planned to cripple him financially.[60] Later, when asked by a reporter why he thought he had been dismissed, Ashley attributed it to an impolitic and uncompromising speech he had made in Washington at the time of his confirmation. Angry at Grant's failure to consult "representative" men of the Republican party in forming a cabinet, Ashley had described the party as being "dumb in the presence of a dummy." "I was mad as hell," he recalled.[61]

He felt the same way about his removal, which he called "the most unexpected, and the hardest blow I ever received." Urging the president to give him a fair hearing, he noted that "at an expense greater than I could afford," he had moved his family to "this distant country, and had but just unpacked my furniture" when word of his dismissal arrived.[62] "I came here for the express purpose of making this strong hold of democracy, Republican," he said, "and I staked whatever of political hope or ambition I had for the future, on securing success to the Republican party."[63]

Public reaction was mixed. Montana Republican friends—a dozen

58. See undated clipping, in TPS.

59. Davis Willson to Fish (Bozeman, January 13, 1870), State Department, Miscellaneous letters; Hezekiah Hosmer et al. to Fish (Virginia City, January 18, 1870), Ashley file, APS.

60. *Weekly Rocky Mountain Gazette,* January 16, 1871; Charles S. Ashley, "Governor Ashley's Biography and Messages," *Contributions,* VI (1907), 194; *DAB,* I, 390. Sumner had given Ashley important support in the congressional campaign of 1860. See David Donald, *Charles Sumner and the Coming of the Civil War* (New York, 1961), 363.

61. *Weekly Rocky Mountain Gazette,* January 16, 1871.

62. Ashley to Grant (Virginia City, December 20, 1869), TPS.

63. Ashley to Fish (Helena, January 23, 1870), Hamilton Fish MSS, Library of Congress. See also Ashley to Columbus Delano (Virginia City, December 27, 1869), Ashley file, APS.

strong—made a pilgrimage to Washington to urge his reinstatement; and Republican spokesmen in the territory staunchly defended him, insisting that, given time, Ashley could have brought unity and party triumph in Montana. Former chief justice Hosmer, for whom Ashley had secured the Virginia City postmastership, saw him as "the only Governor we have ever had who stood firmly by Republican principles."[64] Others lauded his battle against the "left wing" in the "hoo-doo" legislature and his courage in taking "the rebel bull by the horns with the will and power of a master."[65] He was, said Bob Fisk, "the best governor we ever had," and by waging bitter and unrelenting warfare against him, President Grant descended "from the dignity of a chief magistrate to the common level of a mere politician, and not a very respectable one at that."[66]

Others were less sympathetic and tended to agree with E. L. Godkin, who applauded Grant's action as removing one of "the two great blots on his administration" (the other was the appointment of General Daniel Sickles as minister to Spain).[67] A number of Montanans wrote to thank the president: Ashley was simply not "the right man in the right place," they insisted.[68] In Virginia City, the *Tri-Weekly Capital Times* cheered Grant and damned the "Ashley-Fisk-Scribner clique," as well as the Montana "bummers" who sought to save Ashley in the nation's capital.[69] The *New North-West* was more temperate. Noting that Ashley was a "pilgrim" appointment from "a distant land," its editor quoted part of the Pilgrim's Hymn:

> Do not detain me for I am going.
> I can tarry, I can tarry, but a night.

Ashley had his good points, admitted the editor,

> But he came with the taint of a bad record upon him, and has never inspired a good feeling among his people, or confidence that his administration would be for the good of the Territory. . . . He has travelled over more of Montana than any other Executive ever did, acquainting himself with the Territory and its people, its resources

64. *New North-West*, December 24, 1869; March 18, 1870; *Herald*, June 9, 1870; *New York Tribune*, February 23, 1870; Hosmer to Fish (Virginia City, December 25, 1869), Ashley file, APS.

65. Israel Gibbs to Grant (Virginia City, January 5, 1870), Ashley file, APS.

66. Fisk to Grant (Washington, March 29, 1870); Fisk to Fish (Helena, December 29, 1869), *ibid.*; *Herald*, June 9, 1870.

67. *The Nation*, IX (December 23, 1869), 554.

68. John How to Grant (Virginia City, January 16, 1870); Neil Howie et al. to Grant (n.p., n.d.), Ashley file, APS.

69. *Tri-Weekly Capital Times* (Virginia City), March 23, 1870.

and their requirements. He possesses some good characteristics, practicality, total abstinence from liquors, industry and energy. He is loser by coming here. . . . we trust that he will be compensated and that his successor will possess all his good qualities and none of the bad.[70]

It remained for Martin Maginnis, editor of the *Rocky Mountain Gazette,* and later territorial delegate, to write one of the most biting indictments of Ashley. When the new governor, Benjamin Potts, was confirmed, Maginnis was elated at the failure of the "twelve Apostles" —"the dirty dozen who went from Montana to save Ashley's bacon" though the group did manage to get a bill introduced into Congress, a bill which would greatly enhance the governor's powers: "This is glory enough for one day. The political trickster who proposed to build up the Republican party of Montana, and divide and destroy the Democratic, is himself demolished—politically dead, and as Shakespeare has it: 'the best act of his whole life is dying,' his best, (politically)."[71] It was Maginnis who suggested an epitaph for Ashley's tomb:

> Here lie the remains of James M. Ashley of Ohio, who bestrode the negro hobby and rode it into Congress, who with Conover and other convicts, conspired to impeach and remove Andrew Johnson from the Presidency. He was chief of all dirty work, not having honesty enough to achieve an honorable fame, aspired to one of infamy. Let no one disturb the ghost of Ashley, unless he does it with a long pole.[72]

Despite Ashley's unpopularity with territorial residents, a memorial from the sixth legislature, the very legislature with which he clashed incessantly, complained of the arbitrary dismissal of federal officers, as well as their appointment. But it was not the loss of the fiery Radical that was deplored, it was the principle of his dictatorial removal, a common territorial complaint: ". . . the appointment and removal of our governors, judges, and territorial officers, without consulting the

70. *New North-West,* December 24, 1869; July 15, 1870.
71. This was the Cullom bill (H.R. 1634), which was referred to the Committee on the Territories on March 29, 1870, and which would apply the Iron Clad Oath of Reconstruction to the Montana legislature and give the governor the right to appoint all territorial and district officers, including probate judges, and to suspend such officers and appoint interim replacements during and after hearings. This would, said newspapers, "virtually disfranchise us, make this Territory an absolutism, and excommunicate us from citizenship." The bill was never brought out of committee. *New North-West,* April 15, 29, 1870; *Weekly Rocky Mountain Gazette,* July 11, 1870; *Congressional Globe,* 41 Congress, 2 Session (1869–70), 2235.
72. *Weekly Rocky Mountain Gazette,* July 11, 18, 1870.

wishes and wants of the people of the territory, at the caprice of executive power, has imposed and will continue to impose upon the
people a system of vassalage which is both offensive and burdensome. . . ."[73]

Ashley himself was through politically, broken on Democratic
rocks in Montana. He continued his efforts to promote immigration
to the territory for a brief time and in 1872 supported Horace Greeley
and the Liberal Republicans. When he came out in support of Tilden
in 1876, his defection to the Democrats caused even more surprise.
"Those former days are passed away," sighed the Cleveland *Leader*.
"Jim is not considered much of a fellow now." Though he ran once
more for the Congress, unsuccessfully in 1892, "the ambrosial Ashley," as someone called him, had no more luck in the national arena
than in Montana.[74]

Inflexible, prone to antagonize rather than compromise, he had
neither the talent, the time, nor the opportunity to weld together the
political organization he so desired in this basically hostile environment. Martin Maginnis touched the heart of the matter as he served
notice on incoming Governor Potts, like Ashley a Republican, in 1870:
"Montana is Democratic, and no governor, clique, faction or 'sore-
head' can make it otherwise."[75]

Technically this was correct but this was the short view. True, as
a result of stern Republicanism, northern and southern Democrats
now stood shoulder to shoulder in the territory. Only twice in fourteen
territorial elections were Republican delegates sent to Congress; every
legislative assembly down to 1889 was Democratic—only in the sixteenth and final territorial session did the Republicans have a majority
in both houses. And this was partially the product of an infusion of
new blood, drawn from the East, the Midwest, and from abroad, and
contributing to a dwindling Democratic margin. Time, too, mellowed
Civil War antipathies. Expanding population mitigated somewhat
the stresses and strains of the frontier environment, as the initial
period of "chaotic factionalism" came to a close. Governor Potts

73. Memorial to Congress (n.d.), *LM*, 6 Session (1869–70), 122.
74. From time to time rumors persisted that Grant had reconciled himself
with Ashley and had offered him appointments, diplomatic and otherwise, which
were rejected. *Herald*, May 8, 1871; April 23, 1877. For Ashley's later career,
see: Cleveland *Leader*, May 2, July 2, 1872; July 26, 1876; Benjamin W. Arnett,
ed., *Duplicate Copy of the Souvenir from the Afro-American League of Tennessee to Hon. James M. Ashley of Ohio* (Philadelphia, 1894), 563–65; Spencley, "The Original Impeacher," 208–9.
75. *Daily Rocky Mountain Gazette*, July 21, 1870.

would display the ability and tact to work harmoniously with Democratically controlled legislatures and win the respect of many in both parties. His willingness to cooperate effectively with Democratic leaders Sam Hauser in the territory and Martin Maginnis in Washington created a no-party system which would prevail even beyond his three terms in the executive office. Spirited political, personal, and factional disagreements continued, but they no longer reflected sectional hatreds, nor in some instances even party feelings.

CHAPTER

5

"We Have Redeemed Montana": The Administrations of Benjamin Potts—I

Ashley's successor was Benjamin Franklin Potts, a fellow Ohioan, friend of both Rutherford B. Hayes and James A. Garfield, and pro- tégé of William T. Sherman. Sherman called him "one of my best young Division Commanders in the closing campaigns of the War" and had pointed him out on review at the head of his brigade before the White House as his "Sample Vandal," an example of a superb fighting man.[1] Born in 1836, Potts had studied at Westminster Col- lege in Pennsylvania (1854–55), but a lack of funds forced him to return to Ohio, where he taught school briefly, then read law and was admitted to the bar in 1859. In 1860 he had been a delegate to the Democratic conventions in Charleston and Baltimore, but the break with the South caused him to switch party allegiance. Following Fort Sumter, Potts raised a company of volunteers for the 32d Ohio In- fantry and entered service as a captain. He was part of a number of campaigns, including Vicksburg and Sherman's march to the sea, and rose to the rank of brigadier general before returning to his law practice in 1866.[2] When selected as governor of Montana in 1869 he

1. John Sherman to Ulysses S. Grant (Washington, March 8, 1869), with endorsement by William T. Sherman, Potts file, API; Whitelaw Reid, *Ohio in the War: Her Statesmen, Her Generals, and Soldiers* (Cincinnati, 1868), I, 900.
2. Born in Carroll County, Ohio, Potts was a Buchanan supporter in 1856. A

was a member of the Ohio Senate; indeed, pending confirmation, Potts refused to resign his Senate seat until that body could be organized and take action on the Fifteenth Amendment.[3]

Confirmation was a slow process, though Potts's supporters were persistent under the floor management of Senator John Sherman. But Senators Sumner, Nye, and Cameron led the fight to retain Ashley and so bitter was the struggle that Potts at one point offered to withdraw his name in order to relieve President Grant of any embarrassment. Grant, however, would not hear of it, and doggedly fought the confirmation through and won.[4]

Montanans approached the new governor gingerly. To the question of whether he might be a "Black Republican," editor Mills of the *New North-West* replied, "Did you ever see any Potts that weren't Black?" In a more serious vein, while lamenting the failure to appoint a resident, Mills regarded Potts as a man of integrity and ability; a solid Republican, but no extremist; and a "right hearty welcome" in his displacement of Ashley. Grant should be thanked, he said, "for correction of the worst appointive blunder of his administration."[5]

Arriving in the territorial capital on August 29, 1870, Potts was met by a "large party 5 miles out and escorted into the city," and on the following evening was honored at a public reception "and a *Grand dance* until morning." The new governor called on appropriate editors and impressed them with his war record and his enormous physical size. To his friend Hayes, back in Ohio, he related with amazement what he saw: "I find as much refinement here among the ladies as you will find in almost any of our country towns in Ohio," he wrote. "I find Churches saloons—Banks gambling houses fine stores good Hotels and in fact everything, that you will find in a well ordered community." A little later at the territorial fair, he saw

---

year later he studied law with E. R. Eckley of Carrollton, who subsequently went to Congress. During the war, Potts was a part of campaigns up the Shenandoah Valley, was captured at Harpers Ferry and paroled, and subsequently helped reorganize the Ohio 32d before joining Grant before Vicksburg. *Ibid.*, 898–900; Leeson, *History of Montana*, 1290; *DAB*, XV, 135–36; *National Cyclopaedia*, XI, 80.

3. His appointment as governor "was a startling surprise" to Potts. Benjamin F. Potts to Rutherford B. Hayes (Carrollton, December 20, 1869), Rutherford B. Hayes MSS, Rutherford B. Hayes Library, Fremont, Ohio. See also Hayes to Potts (Columbus, December 21, 1869), copy, letterbook I, *ibid.*

4. *Senate Executive Journal*, XVII, 317, 539; *New North-West*, June 10, 17, 1870; *Daily Rocky Mountain Gazette*, July 6, 7, 1870.

5. *New North-West*, December 24, 1869.

wheat "as fine as any Ohio wheat and vegetables that surpassed anything I ever expected to see." "The cattle show I think surpassed our Ohio cattle shows, this appears almost incredible but it is true." "The people are very energetic and mean business in everything," he told Hayes.[6]

Potts was reacting positively to some of the obvious progress that had taken place since the territory's creation. With a total population of 20,595, Montana in 1870 boasted six newspapers (total circulation, 12,200), thirteen nonprivate libraries (of which nine were church-related), and fifteen church organizations (though only eleven buildings). About two-thirds of the 139,537 acres of farmland was improved; with machinery and implements it represented a value of $874,631 and an annual production of $1,676,660. Total livestock value for 1870 was listed at $1,818,693; mining product ranged in estimate from $4 million to $12 million.[7]

The outgoing governor Ashley was still in the territory and his presence created problems of protocol. Two months after his arrival, Potts reported that Ashley was heading east "to champion the Civil Service reform, opposition to Chinese, Working mens labor reform, and lastly high wages and low prices. The Democrats here say he is one of them and that he is going to organize a party that will cooperate with them in the next Presidential election." With some feeling, Potts continued:

> When I came here (the Capital) Mr A. was not here but resided in Helena 125 miles distant he did not come to meet me or address me a note of welcome. I assumed the duties of the office, and in a few weeks went to Helena Mr A. refused to call on me and of course I refused to call on him, he came here afterward and refused to call on me. A friend of his to get him out of the awkward dilemma into which his ignorance had placed him invited me to meet Gov. Ashley at dinner. I refused so you see I am even with him and I think one ahead. What

6. Potts to Hayes (Virginia City, August 31, 1870), Hayes MSS; according to a contemporary description, Potts weighed 330 pounds and was six feet one inch tall. *Daily Rocky Mountain Gazette*, September 1, 11, 1870; Potts to Hayes (Virginia City, August 31, October 8, 1870), Hayes MSS.

7. See *Ninth Report of the United States Census Bureau, 1870*, I, 46, 475, 484, 506; *A Compendium of the Ninth Census (June 1, 1870)* (Washington, 1872), 688, 689, 690, 708. The *Compendium of the Ninth Census* gives mineral product as $4,030,435 (p. 940). Commissioner of Mining Statistics Rossiter Raymond estimated it at $9,100,000 for 1870, somewhat lower than the estimate of $12,000,000 given by the governor of the territory in a letter of February 17, 1871. Rossiter W. Raymond, Mining Statistics West of the Rocky Mountains, *House Executive Document* No. 10, 42 Congress, 1 Session (1871), 204.

do you think of my etequette? I care nothing about the matter personally but I mean to make him illbred as he is respect the office, which he dishonored.[8]

Later, Potts's enemies in the territory claimed he "came as a Roman gladiator flushed with victory" with the idea that every Ashley man was an adversary. It was Hosmer who arranged the dinner, recalled the *Herald*, and Ashley "true to the instincts of a gentleman of polite training," agreed to attend, while Potts with "many of the instincts of an uncultured boor," refused.[9]

Clearly, Potts had little use for Ashley or his supporters. Early in 1871, he again wrote Rutherford Hayes: "Ashley's lecture here was a eulogy on sore headed Republicans and leading Democrats but he is demagogue enough to change it in the East."[10] That Potts had the full confidence of the administration in Washington was clear. Territorial Secretary Wiley Scribner was charged with having meddled in Potts's confirmation, and Delegate Cavanaugh in mid-July asked the president to replace him with a local man. Scribner "is exceedingly unpopular," he said, "both to his own party and the people, inimical to your Administration, and utterly unfit from habit and character, for the position he occupies."[11] A day later, Potts recommended that Scribner be replaced with Addison Sanders, a personal friend, newsman from Davenport, Iowa, and former brevet brigadier general; the president endorsed the proposal with alacrity on the very same day.[12] Thus Scribner was ousted, as Secretary of State Hamilton Fish explained it, because Potts "felt that some things had occurred which seemed not to give promise to as cordial relations between him & W. Scribner as seemed advisable between the Gov & Sec of a Territory."[13]

But Addison Sanders stayed only five months. He was appointed

8. Potts to Hayes (Virginia City, November 29, 1870), Hayes MSS. "I have not seen Mr. Ashley yet he resides at Helena and did not come here to turn over his office to me—so—I turned in and commenced work by appointing some Commissioners of Deeds." Potts to Hayes (Virginia City, August 31, 1870), *ibid.*

9. *Herald*, January 27, 1876.

10. Potts to Hayes (Virginia City, February 4, 1871), Hayes MSS.

11. Amassa Cobb to Grant (Washington, April 15, 1870). Scribner flatly denied the accusations. Scribner to Cobb (Chicago, April 15, 1870), telegram; James Cavanaugh to Grant (Washington, July 15, 1870), all in Wiley S. Scribner file, APS.

12. Potts to Grant (Washington, July 16, 1870), with endorsement by Grant's secretary, Horace Porter, Addison H. Sanders file, APS.

13. Grant to Scribner (Washington, July 19, 1870), State Department, Domestic Letters (1784–1906), LXXXV; Hamilton Fish to M. H. Carpenter (n.p., July 29, 1870), letterbook I, Hamilton Fish MSS.

during a Senate recess, and before the Senate convened again, he was appointed as register of the Land Office for Montana and was confirmed in this capacity, rather than as secretary.[14] In the interim, Potts was without a secretary and handled the functions of that office as well as his own. Early in 1871 he noted to the Secretary of State that he had heard unofficially of the appointment and confirmation of a new secretary but that no such officer had yet appeared: "I trust your Department will be able to find the missing one and point him to the Star of the Empire—and if he gets a fair start he will come to Montana."[15] By mid-April the "missing one"—James E. Callaway of Illinois, once a colonel in Grant's old regiment—had arrived and Potts was impressed: he "goes to work as though he meant business," he reported to the president.[16]

Governor Potts from the first indicated an innate common sense and a tact and understanding that would win the confidence of the majority of Montanans. His statements were reasonable. "I do not aim to make Montana a Paradise," he wrote Fish, "but I hope to improve the public service and restore confidence." He was lauded when he reportedly squelched a proposal by several local federal officers, "tolerably heavy feeders at the public crib," to raise funds and buy him a furnished house, as the people of Galena, Illinois, had done for Grant.[17]

But while not a Radical Republican, Potts was nonetheless a Republican, and when he came he shared Ashley's aspiration to bring

14. *New North-West*, August 5, 12, 1870; *The Montanian* (Virginia City), January 26, 1871; Wiley S. Scribner to R. W. Taylor (Helena, July 7, 1871), LT, Vol. XI.

15. Potts to Fish (Virginia City, February 27, 1871), copy, Potts letterbook; see also *The Montanian*, March 16, 1871.

16. Potts to Grant (Virginia City, April 12, 1871), copy, Potts letterbook. The delay, said Callaway, occurred because the State Department had lost his address and did not know how to contact him for several months after his confirmation. James E. Callaway to R. W. Taylor (Virginia City, April 7, 1871), LT, Vol. XI; Llewellyn L. Callaway, "Something About the Territorial Judges," *Montana Law Review*, IV (Spring, 1943), 5. Born in Kentucky in 1834, the son of a Whig preacher, Callaway had attended Eureka College in Illinois and was admitted to the bar after studying law in the office of Richard Yates, Civil War governor of Illinois. During the war Callaway compiled an enviable record, reached the rank of lieutenant colonel, then returned to sit in the Illinois legislature and to practice law until Grant appointed him to the Montana post. *Progressive Men of the State of Montana* (Chicago, n.d.), 84–85.

17. Potts to Fish (Virginia City, November 26, December 27, 1870), TPS; See also Potts to R. W. Taylor (n.p., December 24, 1870), copy, Potts letterbook; *Daily Rocky Mountain Gazette*, October 11, 1870.

Montana into the Republican circle. "We have strong hopes of redeeming the Territory from Democratic misrule this fall," he wrote in April, 1871, "or we will at least reduce the majority so low as to make success certain in a short time."[18] Two months later, he reported a fierce campaign to elect a Republican delegate—"and we hope to send greetings to our Republican friends of the far east, the first gun for the administration in 1871 from the Rocky Mountains—'Montana Redeemed.'"[19]

The new governor plunged himself wholeheartedly into the drive to defeat James Cavanaugh, the Democratic incumbent for delegate, whom he deemed a failure, a do-nothing representative. Stung by Cavanaugh's criticism of him as a carpetbagger, Potts was willing to support any candidate who showed promise of being able to win. "I should shout myself hoarse to beat Cavanaugh," he wrote. "I will devote this summer to the defeat of Cavanaugh in any way I can effect a vote."[20] Pledging himself to do "any honorable thing for party unity," he urged moderation, cautioning editor Fisk of the *Herald* to limit his carping, lest his petty grievances destroy party harmony.[21] Though he privately damned Democratic misrule—even to a monopoly on illicit liquor traffic with the Indians—it was Potts who insisted that the campaign against Cavanaugh be "a peoples movement," with no partisan Republican speeches "to irritate or excite the Democrats. . . ." "I do not believe in an open fight we can make the change of a Single Missourian or Irishman, and without some changes we must fail," he warned.[22]

But it was not Cavanaugh the Republicans had to defeat. Even though he returned early "to pull wires for his re-nomination," the delegate had offended many on the Indian war claims question and on his misuse of the congressional franking privilege, and lost the nomination to Warren Toole, a ruddy-faced lawyer known as an open

18. Potts to Giles A. Smith (Virginia City, April 1, 1871), copy, Potts letterbook. He also wrote Grant of his role in "our present struggle to carry out your wishes expressed to me on my departure from Washington last August Viz: 'Make Montana Republican.'" Potts to Grant (n.p., July 3, 1871), copy, *ibid.*

19. Potts to Columbus Delano (n.p., July 1, 1871), *ibid.*

20. Potts to William Wheeler (Virginia City, March 10, May 26, 1871), Wheeler MSS, MHS.

21. Potts to Robert E. Fisk (n.p., March 20, 1871). See also Potts to S. H. Crounse (n.p., March 27, 1871), copies, both in Potts letterbook.

22. Potts to Wheeler (Virginia City, March 10, 1871), Wheeler MSS; Potts to James A. Garfield (Virginia City, June 3, 1871), Garfield MSS.

fighter with little money sense.[23] The Republican Central Committee—heavily studded with federal officers—worked hard to achieve the nomination of William H. Clagett of Deer Lodge, a bright, if somewhat eccentric, attorney and a "marvelous orator" who had traveled with Mark Twain and had stumped Nevada in 1864 on behalf of William Stewart and the new constitution.[24]

In an exciting campaign, with Potts pretty much in the background and the unequivocal Wilbur F. Sanders under wraps, oratory and song filled the air. The Republican treasury was full and its guardian dispensed funds liberally for a span of bays to haul the Clagett ensemble, for the services of the Helena Brass Band, or even for a "Gallon of Old Valley" from Ben Stickney's Saloon to lubricate the golden vocal chords of campaign tenor Lucius Church, a former beer hall singer from Chicago.[25] Fusion tickets in several counties sought to pull Democrat votes for Clagett, an example of the no-party principle in operation. This seems to have been an effective technique: many of Toole's friends defected or abstained. Shortly before the election, James Stuart a nominal supporter of Toole, cautioned his brother to "keep quiet and not say or do anything to make Clagett lose a vote. . . . maintain a masterly inactivity. . . . The truth is that Clagett at present would suit us better than Toole, but we have tied

23. Entry for September 20, 1870, Fisk Diary; "A Partial Sketch of the Civil and Military Service of Major Martin Maginnis," *Contributions*, VIII (1907), 15; William Wallace, Jr., "E. W. Toole," *ibid.*, 445, 447. Cavanaugh's frank was used —without his knowledge, he insisted—to send out printed advertising circulars of a Washington hotel. *Herald*, April 10, 17, 21, 1871.

24. Born in Maryland, Clagett studied law and was admitted to the bar in Iowa. He campaigned for Douglas in 1860, a year later married, and headed westward to Carson City where he was politically active. Handsome, one of old southern-style manners, he came to Montana in 1866. Samuel Clemens, *Roughing It* (Hartford, 1872), 199–214; W. W. Dixon, "Sketch of Life and Character of William H. Clagett," *Contributions*, IV (1903), 250–55; C. C. Goodwin, *As I Remember Them* (Salt Lake City, 1913), 137. Federal officials on the Republican Central Committee included Superintendent of Indian Affairs Jasper Viall, Surveyor General John E. Blaine, Receiver of the Land Office Addison H. Sanders, U.S. Marshal William F. Wheeler, and U.S. Customs Collector Walter Johnson. *Herald*, May 9, 12, June 29, 1871.

25. For this election see Stanley R. Davison, "1871: Montana's Year of Political Fusion," *Montana*, XXI (April, 1971), 46–55; Walter de Lacy to Fannie de Lacy (Helena, December 20, 1875), de Lacy MSS, MHS. Later, Secretary Callaway charged privately that Indian Bureau funds—some $12,000 in "Indian Ring money"—had been used by Clagett against Toole, "besides $5000 paid to Cavanaugh, for his influences. Hoping to find specific evidence to support these allegations," Callaway confided, "*I am deliberately preparing* to shake up some dry bones." Callaway to Robert E. Fisk (Virginia City, October 5, 1874), "Strictly Confidential," Fisk MSS.

ourselves to Toole in the contest for the nomination consequently we can't assist Clagett—but we can do the next best thing, that is, not work against him where there is any possible show to injure him."[26]

The popular Clagett swept the field. "This has been about the most exciting day that I ever witnessed," Andrew Fisk recorded in his diary on election day. "Satan is bound, the millennium has come, and we enter upon a political future, replete with the brightest promise to our young territory," wrote brother Robert.

> Oh, here's to Billy Clagett
> And the balance of his crew;
> The Star Spangled Banner—
> The Red, White and Blue—
> The Bonny Blue Flag—it will not do,
> For he's a-comin—a comin'—Hail, mighty day![27]

Governor Potts believed that his leadership was partially the key to Clagett's victory. He had never known "a party so well organized as was the Republicans of Montana in the late canvas" and he exulted to Rutherford Hayes: "We have redeemed Montana from the misrule of the left wing of Prices Army and elected a noble specimen of a man to Congress."[28] Hayes was not surprised, except for the timing, for Montana lay "between the Republican parallels—in the radical latitude," he said, "but I did not expect you would get the victory so soon."[29] Potts admitted that he had spent "more money than my means really justified but . . . was willing to stake everything on the result." The new delegate had been worth the effort. "Clagett will stand by you until the pit freezes over," he wrote, "and will be with you on the ice. . . ." And further, he pledged, "no man will be removed here without Clagett's consent. . . ."[30] But despite this auspicious beginning, as Potts would soon learn, congratulations were premature. Clagett's victory was unusual: not until 1888 would another Republican delegate be elected by Montana.

26. See Davison, "1871: Montana's Year of Political Fusion," 46; James Stuart to Granville Stuart (Helena, July 14, 1871), Stuart MSS.

27. Entry for August 7, 1871, Fisk Diary; *Herald*, August 8, 11, 1871.

28. Potts to Hayes (Virginia City, August 17, 1871), Hayes MSS; Potts to Columbus Delano (n.p., August 8, 1871), copy, Potts letterbook.

29. Hayes to Potts (Columbus, August 29, 1871), copy, letterbook 2, Hayes MSS.

30. Potts to C. C. Huntley (n.p., September 4, 1871), copy, Potts letterbook. Potts to Wheeler (Virginia City, April 29, 1872), Wheeler MSS. Records in the papers of Republican treasurer Lewis Hershfield indicate that Potts had been assessed $150 for the campaign. Hershfield and C. C. Huntley were down for $1,000 each. Davison, "1871: Montana's Year of Political Fusion," 50, 55.

Potts made it clear that he intended to run not only the executive office but also the party machinery and patronage, though from the beginning he was sharply challenged and incurred the bitter enmity of such Republican stalwarts as Wilbur F. Sanders and the influential Fisk brothers. Soon Potts was wise enough to realize that support of local Democrats was important, perhaps more so than that of the right wing Republicans in the territory.

Assuming a strong voice in the dispensing of the loaves and fishes, Potts more than once set out to purge officials who were not in his eyes loyal to the party. Late in 1870 he was "busy looking after the politics of some of the federal appointments," for he found that Secretary of the Interior J. D. Cox "in his recommendations to the President did not regard politics at all," and "some of the vilest Missouri rebels have been holding offices here," including two newly appointed Indian agents "who were the worst kind of whiskey Democrats." Potts at once appealed to the president through his friend Secretary of War W. W. Belknap that with such appointments he could not build up the Republican party in Montana and Grant canceled the appointment of the two Indian agents. Vowed Potts, "The Delegate from this territory is a Democrat and he has imposed on Cox and got his friends appointed whenever he asked for it. I do not intend that any Democrat shall hold office here while I can help it. . . . I am surprised that we have any party here in view of the fact that Democrats here held some of the best federal offices—during the last four years."[31] Moreover, Potts urged the attorney general to put the penitentiary under the U.S. marshal, for the superintendent, A. H. Mitchell, he said, was "one of the most inveterate enemies of President Grant's Administration in this Territory and the most active in support of the Democratic party."[32] He early served notice that he, not Delegate Cavanaugh, would handle patronage. When he heard early in 1871 that Cavanaugh had sought to have Superintendent of Indian Affairs Jasper Viall removed, Potts complained to Washing-

31. Potts to Hayes (Virginia City, November 6, 1870), Hayes MSS. These agents were drawn from "the old thieves from Minnesota who have been stealing from the Indians for a quarter of a Century" and "were not only notoriously democratic but Scoundrels of the first water. . . ." Potts to Hayes (Virginia City, November 29, 1870), *ibid.* At one point during the war, Potts had commanded the 1st Brigade of the 4th Division, 17th Army Corps, and Belknap had commanded the 3rd Brigade. *War of the Rebellion*, Series I, Vol. XLIV, 21.

32. Potts to Amos T. Ackerman (Virginia City, April 5, 1871), SCF, Montana, 1871–74; see also Potts to Hayes (Virginia City, November 29, 1870), Hayes MSS.

ton: "I think it is about time that Cavanaugh is stopped abusing good federal officers, and getting them removed for no other reason than their fidelity to duty and the interests of the Republican Party. I protest against his interference with the policy of an Administration that he is continually Maligning. . . ."[33] On the other hand, a year and a half later, when Potts learned that Viall employed an agent to the Lemhi who had opposed Clagett and who was an avowed Greeley man, he insisted that the traitor be removed at once: "No enemy of the administration shall hold office in Montana if I can help it," he wrote Viall. When this drew no response, Potts turned on Viall, writing in confidence to James Garfield that he had no faith in his honesty —"he is in the hands of bad men here—and he can't extricate himself" —and calling the attention of Secretary of the Interior Delano to the episode: "I have no disposition to interfere with the affairs of another officer where he does his duty—but when he employs a political enemy I think it my duty to bring the matter to your notice."[34]

Potts also sought from time to time to purge the judiciary. "The office of Chief-Justice is now filled by a Democrat who is a drunken *Brute*," he wrote Hayes late in 1870, promising to appeal directly to the president for a suitable replacement. Though unsuccessful in getting the man of his choice, Potts at one point felt a little uneasy about meddling in what was essentially a presidential prerogative and apologetically explained to Grant that his sole desire in seeking a new chief justice was to redeem Montana from Democratic misrule. Soon he was arguing for the ouster of Associate Justice John L. Murphy, "in the best interests of the Territory—political and otherwise." Murphy's retention, he contended, "will so damage our party in his district that I fear the result at the August election." Two years later, cooperating with a movement to dismiss Justice Hiram Knowles, Potts again touched on the question of party loyalty, when he wrote the attorney general in Washington: "I think it is bad enough to be abused by our political enemies, but when those who live by the favors of the Administration abuse us, they should be compelled to draw their sustenance from some other quarter."[35]

33. Potts to Giles A. Smith (n.p., January 9, 1871), copy, Potts letterbook. See also Potts to Delano (n.p., January 7, 1871), copy, *ibid.*, and Potts to Ackerman (Virginia City, April 5, 1871) TPS.

34. Potts to Jasper Viall (n.p., September 14, 1872), copy, Potts letterbook; Potts to Garfield (Virginia City, September 23, 1872), Garfield MSS; Potts to Delano (n.p., November 14, 1872), copy, Potts letterbook.

35. Potts to Hayes (Virginia City, November 6, 1870), Hayes MSS; Potts to Grant (Virginia City, April 1, 1871), copy, Potts letterbook; Potts to W. W.

Through a constant stream of letters to the nation's capital, Potts tended party business, expressing opinions on appointments ranging from the lowest postmaster to the chief justice of the territory. He urged his friend Garfield to help reform the Montana civil service, especially the corrupt Indian service, and he bluntly warned aside other political leaders of the territory, as in 1878, when he learned that Samuel Hauser was going to Washington to fight for the retention of U.S. Assayer Charles Rumley. "Now this is my matter and I want you to stand from under," Potts wrote Hauser. ". . . I only want you to let the matter severely alone."[36]

He sought to protect his political friends and intervened on their behalf. In general, a Republican from the East was preferable to a Democrat from Montana, as Potts indicated in 1877 when he urged the president to appoint "a sprightly young atty. from the States" to the vacant United States attorney post in the territory, for if a Montanan were selected the office of practical necessity "must go to a Democrat."[37]

At the time of Billy Clagett's election in 1871, Potts could not have known that Republican ascendancy was to be brief and that party harmony would be as short. Almost immediately the governor was lamenting a breach within Republican ranks and was under fire from leading Republicans as well as Democrats. To William Belknap, Potts wrote in 1872: "We have the old Ashley clique showing its teeth here this summer. It is small but annoying, as the Fisks still hold their paper which two years ago so roundly abused the President about Ashley's removal. . . . The Fisk and Ashley clique are without doubt the most corrupt men I have ever known anywhere and no party can satisfy them, although they get all the patronage in the gift of the President."[38]

There were six Fisk brothers. Four of them, all Civil War veterans, came to Montana with the 1866 expeditions. Together with brother Andrew, Robert Emmett Fisk, the oldest, began publication of the

Belknap (Virginia City, June 6, 1872); Potts to George H. Williams (Washington, March 18, 1872), both in John L. Murphy file, APJ; Potts to George H. Williams (Virginia City, October 20, 1874), SCF, Montana, 1871–84.

36. Potts to Garfield (Virginia City, December 3, 1872), Garfield MSS; Potts to Samuel Hauser (Helena, November 24, 1878) Hauser MSS.

37. Potts to Wheeler (Virginia City, April 29, 1872; Washington, March 5, 1872), Wheeler MSS. "We have no Republican Attorney that should be appointed to the place," Potts explained. Potts to Hayes (Helena, June 2, 1877), general file, APJ, Box 410.

38. Potts to Belknap (Virginia City, June 6, 1872), John L. Murphy file, APJ.

Sidney Edgerton

Thomas Francis Meagher

All illustrations courtesy Montana Historical Society, Helena

Green Clay Smith

James M. Ashley

James E. Callaway

Benjamin F. Potts

Wilbur Fisk Sanders

Robert E. Fisk

Martin Maginnis

Joseph K. Toole

B. Platt Carpenter

John Schuyler Crosby

Samuel T. Hauser

Preston H. Leslie

Benjamin F. White

Decius S. Wade

Helena *Herald* late in 1866. Van Fisk sometimes acted as field representative, and James, who had led the expedition for a time served as a kind of unofficial correspondent in Washington. Soon the *Herald* was the most influential newspaper in the territory, for a generation or more published under the Fisk Brothers imprint.

Ironically, Robert Fisk had met with William T. Sherman and Ulysses Grant ("unquestionably the sphynx of modern times") early in 1869 to urge Potts's appointment, but Ashley received the nod instead.[39] A staunch Grant supporter,[40] Fisk now brought the weight of the *Herald* and his most vitriolic invective against Potts in a running verbal duel that spanned most of Potts's thirteen years in office.

It was Fisk's demand for removal of certain minor officials that touched off the feud in 1871. Potts refused and denied "the right of any Republican to drag his personal grievances into the partie's Councils and thereby destroy the harmony of the same," he told Fisk. The editor had no claim on the party, Potts told a friend, "that justifies in making such insolent demands. . . . If he intends to override the Councils of the party he must be prepared to take the consequence. If we concede his right to dictate, we must concede the same to Tom Dick & Harry and the discipline of the party be destroyed."[41] From this first breach over control of patronage, the struggle would broaden and be enhanced by differences over government printing, control of party machinery, the railroad subsidy question, and the controversy over the location of the territorial capital.

Together with Wilbur F. Sanders—"the most unscrupulous man that ever disgraced the legal profession," according to Potts—[42] the Fisks mounted a determined anti-Potts campaign. They abused him scurrilously in the press, lobbied actively for his removal in Washington, and opposed him on a surprising number of territorial issues. Fisk made much of a letter Potts wrote to a Washington friend early

39. James M. Hamilton, *From Wilderness to Statehood* (Portland, 1957), 484; Davison, "1871: Montana's Year of Political Fusion," 49; Robert E. Fisk to Elizabeth Fisk (Washington, March 17, 18, 1869), Fisk family MSS.

40. ". . . if Grant & his army tools were to put the army in motion & declare Grant emperor of America tomorrow & wipe out any vestige of Republic Govt Bob Fisk would throw up his hat for Ulisus Cesar Grant & despotism." Joseph H. D. Street to Martin Maginnis (Gallatin City, February 5, 1875), Martin Maginnis MSS, MHS.

41. Potts to Robert E. Fisk (Virginia City, March 20, 1871), copy, Potts letterbook; Potts to William Wheeler (Virginia City, March 2, 21, 1871), Wheeler MSS.

42. Potts to Hayes (Helena, December 28, 1878), "personal," Decius S. Wade file, APJ.

in 1871, in which he sought congressional action and ended by saying: "Hoping that you may be pleased to aid an old comrade, now cut off from the genial influences of civilization."[43] The Democratic *Gazette* also took after the Governor for his "genial influences" statement:

> Ohio, no doubt, mourned her great loss,
>   When this Solomon of hers was sent far away;
> But duty told him to take up his cross,
>   Over ignorant Montana his talent must sway.
> Cut off from the influence of civilization,
> A martyr here in the interest of the nation.
>
> Morose and dejected he wrote his friend Grant,
>   To send out companions who were his peers;
> That people out here were as green as a brant,
>   Mostly Missourians with terrible lop ears.
> Grant, believing such people liable to raids,
> Sent him a large number of carpet-bag aides.
> Cut off as he is from all civilization,
> A martyr out here for the good of the nation.[44]

While the *Gazette's* successor, the *Independent*, early damned Potts as "Ashley No. Two," it would ultimately come around; but not so the *Herald*. This "vandal" executive was "imperious, cold, selfish, and calculating"; this "Apotheosis of Avoirdupoise" was grasping, incompetent, and "an utter and miserable failure"; he lacked sympathies or friends in the territory, except a "constituency" of ex-criminals built up by executive pardon. By the middle-seventies Bob Fisk was raging. Montanans, he said, were ashamed of "this gubernatorial specimen of imbecility," this "wild and uncouth kind of Buffalo Bill," this "pensioner on public alms," this "Dunce from Carrollton," whose "intellectual limitations are about those of a Saddle Rock oyster." According to Fisk, Potts was a man with "the statesmanship of a cannibal, the morals of a Kaffir, the diplomacy of an ostrich, the integrity of a pirate, the culture of a Digger, and the sagacity of that famed young horse which was the property of farmer Thompson. . . ." Glowing with each unfounded rumor that Potts was to be replaced or kicked upstairs to a foreign court, Fisk displayed great versatility in belittling the governor on all points, ranging from

43. Potts to unknown (Virginia City, February 18, 1871), quoted in *Montanian*, May 11, 1871; See also *Herald*, January 9, 1872; December 29, 1873; January 26, 1876; entry for February 2, 1871, Fisk Diary.
44. "Lop Ear," *Weekly Rocky Mountain Gazette*, July 17, 1871.

his gumchewing and his meerschaum pipe; his bulk and his money-lending activities; his extravagance, on one hand, and his economies, on the other; his war-record; and his do-nothingism. As the *Herald* saw it in early 1876, Potts considered his duties: "to write an occasional commonplace Message of Thanksgiving Proclamation; to sign commissions of Notaries; electioneer at the top of his voice *in his office*, and *try* to brow-beat his brother officials; to whittle on the sidewalks, and promptly draw his pay!"[45]

Bob Fisk sneered at Potts's redemption of Montana for the Republicans, noting sarcastically in 1873 when Madison County went Democratic: "He has reached bed-rock, and now the new edifice will be reared on foundations broad, deep and secure."[46] On more than one occasion, the editor and Wilbur F. Sanders were known to be "talking loudly—in Washington about who is to be beheaded,"[47] and sometimes they were able to sway appointments, for their hold on the territorial party mechanism could never be ignored. Though James Fisk could inform his brother that they had been "thrown" in the 1876 Republican Territorial Convention by the manipulation of Potts, a supporter of Rutherford B. Hayes, the Montana delegation to the national convention went committed to James G. Blaine.[48] Though insisting that he could have controlled the Deer Lodge convention himself, had he fewer scruples, Potts charged that that convention had been "packed" by Sanders and John E. Blaine, "a brother of J.G. but a mere drunken 'pigmy.' "[49] "Jack" Blaine had served as United States surveyor general for Montana but resigned in 1873 in a storm of charges, only to be named paymaster for the U.S. Army in the territory.[50] He had—according to Potts—promised Sanders dispo-

45. *Weekly Independent*, June 8, 1872; *Herald*, January 9, February 16, 1872; January 2, 10, September 25, October 14, December 24, 1873; October 7, 8, December 10, 23, 1874; February 1, 4, 1875; January 3, May 16, 22, August 18, September 4, 1876.

46. *Herald*, August 9, 1873.

47. Potts to Maginnis (Helena, March 8, 1881) Maginnis MSS.

48. James L. Fisk to Robert E. Fisk (Helena, April 24, 1876), Fisk family MSS; Potts to J. Warren Keifer (Helena, May 12, 1876), copy, Keifer Misc. MSS, Hayes Library, original in the Ohio Historical Society Library.

49. Potts to Hayes (Helena, July 5, 1866), Hayes MSS; Potts to Keifer (Helena, May 12, 1876), copy, Keifer Misc. MSS.

50. "Our former Surveyor Genl. Blaine, was an awful drunkard, came near being convicted of extortion, and had to resign, and *in the course of a few months*, was appointed Paymaster in the Army, with the rank of Major." Walter W. de Lacy to Fannie de Lacy (Helena, December 20, 1875), de Lacy family MSS, copies, MHS. Apparently Blaine had augmented his salary by as much as $10,000 a year by charging each surveyor 20 percent of his contract. When a federal grand jury investigated, deputy surveyors refused to testify for fear of

sition of Montana patronage should his brother become president.[51] Four years later, Montana Republicans split again, over whether to endorse Blaine or Ulysses Grant as the party nominee in the 1880 election. Some were convinced that Blaine's success would bring Robert Fisk to the governor's post, a not too palatable prospect.[52] And Potts again was on the losing side. "The Political caldron is beginning to boil," one constituent wrote the territorial delegate. "The Fisk-Blaine faction cleaned up the Potts-Grant party, so the *Plumed Knight* is the nominee."[53]

On his part, Potts gave us well as he received. "A man has to fight scoundrels from the word go here," he informed a friend in 1877.[54] Bob Fisk he characterized as "a professional blackmailer," who had "destroyed the harmony and efficiency of the party" in Montana, because many feared newspaper abuse if they opposed him. He was, insisted Potts, "totally without character for truth" and "has been an applicant for every federal appointment in the Territory in the last nine years. . . ."[55] Sanders, too, was "a disappointed office seeker and has abused and maligned every man who had ever held office in the territory." He was "bankrupt in morals, purse and reputation," and "unworthy of the confidence of any body." "Any officer who secures his enmity is almost certain to be meritorious," said Potts, "and the officer that he champions is almost certain to be incompetent and venal."[56] Neither of these "bitter opponents of the President & his administration," should be given favors in Washington, he warned, and he went out of his way to see that they were not.[57] When Van Fisk applied for an Indian inspectorship, Potts blocked his chances with a scathing letter to the commissioner of Indian affairs; when Robert

---

incriminating themselves. But when the record was forwarded to the Secretary of the Interior, Speaker of the House Blaine prevailed upon his brother to resign, but soon got him the appointment as paymaster, a lifetime job. Potts to Keifer (Helena, May 12, 1876), copy, Keifer Misc. MSS.

51. Potts to Hayes (Helena, June 20, 1876), Hayes MSS.
52. Charles S. Warren to Maginnis (Butte, April 5, 1880), Maginnis MSS.
53. Perry W. McAdow to Maginnis (Bozeman, May 5, 1880), Maginnis MSS.
54. Potts to W. A. Knapp (Helena, March 9, 1877), James H. Mills file, API.
55. Potts to Zachariah Chandler (Helena, September 1, 1876), Robert E. Fisk file, API; Potts to Carl Schurz (Helena, November 14, 1878), James H. Mills file, API.
56. Potts to Schurz (Helena, June 7, 1877), Benjamin F. Potts file, API; Potts to Hayes (Helena, December 28, 1878), Decius S. Wade file, APJ; Potts to W. Dennison (Helena, June 28, 1876), Hayes MSS.
57. Potts to W. K. Rogers (Helena, December 18, 1877); Potts to John Sherman (Helena, March 30, 1877); both in James H. Mills file, API; Potts to Chandler (Helena, September 1, 1877), Robert E. Fisk file, API.

Fisk sought appointment as surveyor general, Helena postmaster, or as territorial secretary, Potts condemned him to influential figures in Washington.[58] When Sanders pushed a local citizen for the Helena land office receivership, Potts used his influence to prevent the appointment of any "of the tools of Sanders & Fisks," and caused Sanders to deplore "the boors like Potts and the carrion-crows like Ashley whose first interest it has been to try and badger and annoy me."[59] One of Potts's basic political tenets was, as he informed Sam Hauser in 1878, "No satellite of W. F. Sanders shall hold office in Montana if I can prevent it."[60]

At the same time, Potts had to contend with the Democrats—the majority party. Early the *Herald* suggested that Potts might well make a deal with the party of treason and in 1876 proposed, tongue in cheek, that he would make a fine candidate for delegate on the Democratic ticket.[61] And the Bourbons themselves promised to remake their new Governor in their own image:

> Now you need reconstruction me carpet-bag boy,
> But firsht to shmall pieces we'll break ye,
> Thin Shtick ye togither in much bether shape,
> I a Dimocrat oven thin bake ye.[62]

Potts remained a loyal Republican to the end, but he learned to cooperate remarkably well with the Democrats after the first few years, when he became convinced that the Republicans were not likely to control the territory, the 1871 election of Delegate Clagett to the contrary notwithstanding. Democratic support was not at first easily obtained. When Potts arrived he caught the backwash of the struggle between the legislature and Ashley over the executive appointive power.[63] The office of superintendent of public instruction was vacant and the offices of auditor and treasurer held de facto by respectively W. H. Rodgers and William G. Barkley, the Democrats whose election Ashley had voided and who had no legal justification.

58. Potts to J. H. Mills (n.p., November 8, 1872), copy, Potts letterbook; Potts to Edward P. Smith (Virginia City, October 10, 1874), BIA; Potts to Garfield (Virginia City, November 29, 1873), Garfield MSS; Potts to Chandler (Helena, September 1, 1877), Robert E. Fisk file, API.

59. Potts to Garfield (Helena, October 9, 1876); Potts to Francis Servis (Helena, September 30, 1876); Wilbur F. Sanders to Garfield (Helena, December 22, 1876), all in Garfield MSS.

60. Potts to Hauser (Helena, November 24, 1878), Hauser MSS.

61. *Herald*, January 9, 1872; February 10, 1876.

62. "Larry O'Gaff," *Weekly Rocky Mountain Gazette*, July 30, 1871.

63. See Chapter 4.

Soon after Potts reached Virginia City, the territorial supreme court held that Rodgers and Barkley were usurpers but that the governor had no power to fill vacancies without confirmation by the Council—and the legislature was not due to convene until December, 1871.[64] This, complained Potts, "stops the wheels of government here unless the Executive Calls an extra Session of the Legislature every time an appointment is to be made at an expense of $40,000 which the present executive refuses to do." Meanwhile, he informed his superiors in Washington, "The finances of the Territory are at a stand still." When he suggested that as governor he did have the right, "notwithstanding the decision of the Court," to fill such vacancies ad interim, Attorney General Ackerman was not helpful: the question would be brought before the Committees on the Territories at the next session of Congress, but in the meantime, Potts's only alternative was to call the Council if he wanted the vacancies filled.[65]

This Potts declined to do, in part because of the expense of an extraordinary session, in part because he realized that the Democratic Council would not confirm his nominations, which, he said, would be "in political accord with the present Administration"—i.e. Republican.[66] And, while he declined to discuss the business in Fisk's *Herald*, he kept up a running correspondence with federal officers and members of Congress, hoping for relief from that quarter or from the U.S. Supreme Court, to which the case was taken on appeal.[67]

In July, 1871, after it was revealed that Barkley had failed to renew and expand his bond, Potts declared the treasurer's office vacant and appointed Richard O. Hickman in his stead, an action which the district court upheld.[68] But when the legislature convened as scheduled in December, Potts was under fire from two sides. Republicans insisted that his nominations hew to the party line without compromise. When Bob Fisk heard it rumored that the governor, "in his new triple

64. *Daily Rocky Mountain Gazette*, October 30, 1870; Potts to Fish (Virginia City, September 2, 1870), TPS.

65. Potts to Fish (Virginia City, October 11, 1870); S. T. Ackerman to Fish (Washington, October 24, November 17, 1870), TPS; Fish to Potts (Washington, October 26, 1870), GEC.

66. Potts to Fish (Virginia City, November 4, 1870), TPS.

67. Potts to Ackerman (Virginia City, December 1, 10, 1870), AG (1864–70); Potts to Fish (Virginia City, December 30, 1870); Potts to J. W. Nye (Virginia City, February 13, 1871); Potts to Lyman Trumbull (Virginia City, February 17, 1871); Potts to Benjamin Bristow (Virginia City, March 20, 1871), copies, all in Potts letterbook.

68. *Herald*, July 26, August 3, September 25, 1871; James E. Callaway to Potts (Virginia City, July 17, 1871), GEC.

role of jobber, bargainer, and pacificator," would "log-roll with the Democrats" on appointments, he exhorted him to adopt "the pluck, the consistency, the sense and honesty" of his predecessor, Ashley, "to uphold the purity and honesty and fairness of the Republican party against one and all of the malignant political elements combining for its humiliation and overthrow." On the other hand, although confirming Hickman, the Democratic Council steadfastly refused to approve Republican nominees, rejecting in early January, 1872, six different ones for the post of auditor and one for superintendent of public instruction. The latter position was filled in 1873, with Potts's original choice, Cornelius Hedges, finally confirmed, but only after the job had been made a political football and several other names rejected.[69] All the while, at least until early 1874, Rodgers continued to act as auditor, though engaged in a bitter feud with Governor Potts —a feud, which to editor Fisk, not an unbiased observer, illustrated "the boorish treatment of an inferior officer by a superior and the bad taste of the inferior in retorting in kind. . . ."[70]

Meanwhile, Potts still looked toward Washington for relief. There, early in 1871, several bills had been introduced in Congress on the matter, among them one which would not only nullify the tenure of office act passed by Montana's sixth assembly, but also prohibit the granting of extra compensation to officials in the territory.[71] But the governor noted that repeal of the tenure of office act would not relieve the situation, for the court decision against filling vacancies without the Council's consent was based not on that law, but rather on the organic act. With six territorial offices unfilled and several illegally staffed, he contended, what was needed was a positive measure, like those introduced by Shelby Cullom and John Sherman, to amend the organic act to expand the governor's power. ". . . without additional Legislation," said Potts, "we are in the hands of the Philistines and the authority of the United States is set at defiance."[72] Nor was the

69. *Herald*, January 5, 13, 1872; *Council Journal*, 7 Session (1871–72), 121–22; Council to Potts (Virginia City, January 10, 11, 12, 1872), GEC. For the shameful manipulation of this post see *Herald*, April 18, 1873; Council to Potts (Virginia City, April 16, 29; May 2, 1873), GEC; Granville Stuart to James Stuart (Virginia City, December 23, 26, 1871), Stuart MSS.
70. *Herald*, May 26, 1873.
71. *Congressional Globe*, 41 Congress, 3 Session (1870–71), 790; *Daily Rocky Mountain Gazette*, February 13, 1871; Potts to Robert E. Fisk (Virginia City, December 31, 1870), Fisk family MSS.
72. Potts to Nye (Virginia City, February 13, 1871); Potts to Trumbull (Virginia City, February 17, 1871), copies, Potts letterbook; Potts to Garfield (Virginia City, January 26, 1871), Garfield MSS.

suggestion of Delegate Cavanaugh that the offices be made elective, any solution for the Governor. ". . . if that is done," he said, "four out of five of them in this territory would be filled by gamble[r]s and black legs."[73]

But legislation was slow in forthcoming and Potts was on edge. "I have written Clagett that if he will have the Organic Act amended so I can kick old Rodgers out that I will let him name the man for the *place*," he confided to James H. Mills, editor of the Deer Lodge *New North-West*.[74] But the president had already signed a law (in June, 1872) destroying part of the bargaining power of the upper house in all the territories, granting the governor the power to fill vacancies with temporary commissions if the council was not in session.[75] Potts's old friend James A. Garfield of Ohio was retained on behalf of the territory to argue its case before the United States Supreme Court, and late in 1873, the court decided that Rodgers held the auditor's office illegally and ordered him ousted.[76] Thus Potts, by early 1874, could exult to Garfield, "I got the old *rebel* out and put a Republican in."[77]

The appointment controversy continued deep into Potts's administration, but was acute only during the first few years. After that, with federal statutes protecting executive prerogatives, the assembly could do little but protest. It generally cooperated on Potts's nominations, though it did, as Potts had predicted, refuse to pay the legal expense of hiring Garfield in the case to oust Rodgers. In 1874 Potts had written Garfield, "The Legislature I *know* will not pay it—for this question has been their stock in trade to fight Republican Governors . . ." and ultimately the governor paid out $382.95 from his own pockets.[78] A territorial law of 1876 recognized his right to fill vacancies by ad interim appointment, unless otherwise specified,[79] thus in theory preserving Council privilege. But in the following year, the

73. "Some of them are now illegally held by the vilest rebel Bushwhackers that ever disgraced Missouri." Potts to Garfield (Virginia City, January 26, 1871), Garfield MSS.

74. Potts to James H. Mills (n.p., November 8, 1872), copy, Potts letterbook.

75. Act of June 8, 1872, 17 *USSL*, 335.

76. *Herald*, November 4, 1873; Potts to Garfield (Virginia City, August 26, 1873), Garfield MSS.

77. Potts to Garfield (Virginia City, April 20, 1874), Garfield MSS. Dr. George E. Callaway, brother of the territorial secretary, was appointed and confirmed by mid-February, 1874. *Herald*, February 16, 1874.

78. Potts to Garfield (Virginia City, November 27, 1874; Helena, April 15, 1876), Garfield MSS.

79. Act of February 11, 1876, *LM*, 9 Session (1876), 84.

legislature memorialized Congress, asking as Democrats in general had asked for years, that the offices in dispute—territorial treasurer, auditor, and superintendent of public instruction—be made elective.[80] In part, this may have been a reaction to an effort of the Council the previous year to punish Superintendent of Public Instruction Cornelius Hedges for having run for delegate as a Republican, by first seeking to eliminate his office and—that failing—by reducing his salary from $1,200 to $800 a year.[81] In any event, the plea for elected officials fell on deaf ears in Congress, but the assembly in 1879 indicated that it had not forgotten the matter by refusing to vote compensation for ad interim appointments until they had been confirmed by the Council.[82]

The general problem of appointments within the territory, of course, could never be resolved to the satisfaction of all parties: political considerations came first, with the governor and the legislative council often at odds and with the Republicans themselves split. Yet there was government by coalition: in the Potts era there was never the bitter, deep-seated cross-party enmity toward the executive and his prerogatives that had characterized the administrations of his predecessors. After the first few years, Potts moved ahead without stalemate, displaying a commonsensical talent for give-and-take that showed a pragmatic acceptance of the fact that Montana was not a Republican stronghold.

During much of Potts's tenure in office, Montana's territorial delegate in Washington was a Democrat. Because the selection of the delegate was arranged to coincide with the election of the legislature, Billy Clagett came up for reelection in 1872, after only one year in office, and was pitted against Martin Maginnis, a Minnesotan with an impressive war record and proprietor of the *Rocky Mountain Gazette*, one of the leading Democratic newspapers in the territory.[83] While the *Herald* scoffed, the *Gazette* lauded "Martin the Modest" and insisted that Clagett "of the pewter tongue" could not compare with the "Little Giant of Montana."[84] When the votes were counted, Maginnis had won, 4,515 to 4,196, and editor Fisk was prompted to sing a parody of "Home, Sweet Home":

80. Memorial to Congress (n.d.), *LM*, 10 Session (1877), 438; *Herald*, November 23, 1871.
81. *Herald*, February 1, 5, 1876.
82. Act of 1879 (n.d.), *LM*, 11 Session (1879), 40.
83. *DAB*, XIII, 199; Leeson, *History of Montana*, 1234.
84. *Herald*, June 11, 21, 1872.

> In the dark lanes of politics,
>   Where e'er we go,
> Be it ever so sable,
>   There's no meat like crow.[85]

But Fisk took defeat with bad grace. He asserted that Maginnis had been elected by illegal votes—by Indians, half-breeds, teen-age boys and "numerous frauds" at the ballot box. In addition, Sam Hauser, treasurer of the Democratic Territorial Committee, was accused by Fisk of having purchased votes for Maginnis. Granville Stuart, who "by strenuous exertions" helped raise $3,000 to campaign as much for the capital in Deer Lodge as Maginnis, noted that Hauser was "as crazy as ever on elections" and had won $6,000 on the outcome, although Clagett "feels very sore."[86]

In Washington, Martin Maginnis proved an able representative for the territory; at home, he proved a master politician and an irresistible campaigner. Six terms as delegate attest to that. In 1874, running on his already impressive record, he was pitted against Cornelius Hedges—Yale graduate, lawyer, editor, and superintendent of public instruction—who was described by his backers as "A ripe scholar; a sound lawyer; a fluent writer; a ready debater." And, it might be added, a graceful loser, for Maginnis won by a handy majority. Two years later his opponent was Erasmus Darwin Leavitt, a Beaverhead physician, who hardly campaigned, if at all, and whose Republican supporters tried to capitalize on a letter Maginnis wrote in 1874, in which he vowed to step aside after serving two consecutive terms.[87] This letter would give Maginnis and his backers "the jimjams" in subsequent election years.

85. *Ibid.*, October 23, 1872; Waldron, *Montana Politics*, 28.
86. *Herald*, August 9, 13, 1872; Granville Stuart to James Stuart (Deer Lodge, August 14, 1872), Stuart MSS. Nine months later, the defeated delegate still felt pained. "Clagett is coming like a roaring lion seeking whom he may destroy," Maginnis was told. E. S. Wilkinson to Maginnis (Helena, April 5, 1873), Maginnis MSS.
87. *Herald*, July 9, 10, 14, 1874; Waldron, *Montana Politics*, 31. Hedges came to Montana in 1864 and practiced both law and journalism. He stood with the vigilantes and was a leading Mason. Later he would serve as U.S. attorney and as probate judge, prepare several volumes of the *Montana Reports*, and sit in the constitutional convention of 1884 and in the first state senate. Leeson, *History of Montana*, 1217; Wyllys A. Hedges, "Cornelius Hedges," *Contributions*, VII (1910), 181–96.
Leavitt was born in New Hampshire and came to Bannack in 1862. "List of Pioneers Who Have Died During the Years 1907–8–9," *Contributions*, VII (1910), 327. "And in case I am re-elected I shall not again allow my name

—Maginnis swore, in seventy-four,
If his friends could his opponents fix,
He'd pull down his vest and do his best
And be off the track in seventy-six.
But Washington city, the more's the pity,
Has fatal allurements for Martin;
He makes a quick flop, say "I'm public prop.' "
But the folks think he's "mighty onsartin."[88]

In what one editor called "an election by default," Maginnis despatched Leavitt by a wide margin in the lightest voter turnout since 1865; two years later he ran against veteran politician Sample Orr, who campaigned on an Independent ticket, after the Republicans failed to select a nominee. This time, Maginnis took more than 70 percent of the vote—a landslide.[89]

The year 1880 brought a much more interesting contest, matching Maginnis and Wilbur F. Sanders. Sanders came down hard on the territorial printing law, demanded a sharp reduction of Indian lands, made an issue of the incumbent's longevity in office, argued that only a delegate of the party in power in Washington could be successful, and lashed out at Maginnis as the pliant tool of Democratic businessmen, especially Hauser, Charles Broadwater, and millionaire A. H. Wilder of St. Paul, who like Broadwater had benefited greatly from provisioning army posts in Montana. "Sam Hauser has a mortgage on Maginnis and Maginnis has a mortgage on the Democratic party," charged editor Fisk, complaining that "Mr. Hawser and Mr. Broadstream" controlled the territory. Fisk still complained of Price's Left Wing as "a powerful factor in Bourbonizing the Territory," and the Republicans still "waved the Bloody Shirt," damning the Democrats as the party of disunion, at a rally in Ming's Opera House in Helena,

---

to be used but will then stand aside, or rather take my old place in the ranks and give to the newly-chose standard bearer of the party as cordial and I hope successful support as each and all of these gentlemen have given. . . ." Maginnis to Hauser et al. (Washington, June 10, 1874), Hauser MSS.

88. *New North-West*, October 20, 1876.

89. Leavitt apparently did not want the job, believed the cause lost from the beginning and did not campaign. *New North-West*, November 10, 1876. A Tennessean, Orr had run for governor of Missouri in 1860 on the Constitutional Unionist ticket and was prominent in Missouri state government before coming to Montana in 1865. A member of the Montana Council for three legislative sessions, "Judge" Orr, as he was generally known, was a splendid stump speaker. Massena Bullard, "Sample Orr," *Contributions*, VI (1907), 468–74; *Herald*, September 23, 25, 26, November 4, 1878; Waldron, *Montana Politics*, 34, 36.

where Governor Potts opened the festivities with a "brief but stirring and pointed address" and the local Republican glee club sang a number of favorites, including "Tenting on the Old Camp Ground" and "Marching Through Georgia." Maginnis was presented as the only Democrat able to gain Northern Pacific influence and defeat Sanders, who was now an attorney for the company, and while the campaign was an unusually hard one, Maginnis won, as usual and the legislature again went Democratic. "Subtract the Northern Pacific Railroad votes, those of the Mormons on the Utah and Northern, and those of the Wild Cat precincts of Choteau, and Maginnis' majority would make a mighty thin showing in the canvass," said the *Herald* petulantly.[90]

The campaign of 1882 was even more exciting. Maginnis seemingly took himself out of the race and other Democrats—Samuel Word, Warren Toole, and Alexander Woolfolk—began a scramble to don the party mantle, only to be outmaneuvered when the delegate belatedly decided to run again. His supporters argued that with his army comrade General Winfield Scott Hancock the party's choice for the presidency, Maginnis would be in a fine position to control territorial patronage if the national Democrats won. Montana Republicans chose Alexander Botkin, a University of Wisconsin graduate who had worked on the Chicago *Tribune* and the Milwaukee *Sentinel* before coming to Helena as U.S. marshal in 1878. Crippled by paralysis and confined to a wheelchair, Botkin would emphasize mental rather than physical properties in the campaign. "Substitute brains for brass," urged his supporters, scoffing at Maginnis's repeated pledges not to run again: his promises "are like pie-crust—made to be broken." Botkin men damned Hauser's "man Friday" and labeled him a carpetbagger who invested his money in Minnesota instead of Montana, and the Republican glee club roared a "rattling campaign song," titled "Whoa, Martin!" which brought a "perfect storm of applause"—at least from Republican circles:

> With Botkin in the field, with men that never yield
> We'll teach Maginnis that he's aimed too high,
> And on election day, we'll hear Maginnis say,
> Oh! take me home and leave me there to die.
>
> Whoa, Martin! Whoa, Martin!
> Martin, a sixth term is awfully unsartin;

90. *Herald,* January 28, August 13, September 14, October 1, 4, 18, 21, 23, 28, November 1, 5, 1880; September 21, October 18, 1882; *Independent,* October 17, 1880; Waldron, *Montana Politics,* 39.

Whoa, Martin! Whoa, Martin!!
Martin, you'll find that a sixth term's no go.[91]

But when the sound died away and the ballots were counted, Maginnis had "again scooped the proud and vainglorious enemy," as Granville Stuart put it.[92] Botkinites immediately cried "fraud." Illegal votes of soldiers, Mormons, Chinese, or "men in buckskin" who could not meet the residence requirements had swelled the Democratic bandwagon, they charged. Botkin entered an official protest, complaining of irregularities on five different counts.[93] Thomas Carter later insisted that in one precinct a large Democratic majority was recorded by copying 300 names each from the Cleveland and Cincinnati city directories, and Republican tradition has it that Maginnis received 400 and some odd votes from Wilder's Landing on the Missouri River. At the time, there were only about a dozen voters in the area, but the government had 400 mules there used in transporting supplies to Fort Assiniboine—and "those four hundred mules, in sympathy for their ancestor, the Democratic Donkey, cast a solid vote for Martin."[94] But when the dispute went before the Committee on Elections of the national House of Representatives, the committee saw no significant irregularities of a concrete nature, although it did admit that a small number of soldiers had voted illegally and that the heavy balloting in the new towns along the railroad was suspicious. But it recommended unanimously—and the Democratic House concurred—that Maginnis be seated, a "grossly partisan" decision to Montana Republican stalwarts.[95]

91. Leeson, *History of Montana*, 1194; *New North-West*, September 15, 1882; *Herald*, August 22, September 5, 18, 21, 28, 30, October 9, 13, 14, 27, November 3, 4, 1882. See broadsides in Thomas C. Power MSS, political boxes, MHS.

92. Stuart to Maginnis (Fort Maginnis, November 26, 1882), copy, letterbook 2, Stuart MSS.

93. These included 3,000 illegal votes allegedly cast in Custer, Dawson, and Missoula counties; illegal polling places in these same counties; coercion of Northern Pacific employees into voting for Maginnis; an unauthorized precinct for Gallatin County actually located on the Crow reservation; and the counting of votes and canvassing of returns in a manner not prescribed by law. Report of the Committee on Elections on A. C. Botkin vs. Martin Maginnis, *House Report* No. 2138, 48 Congress, 1 Session (1883–84), 1–3.

94. Alva Josiah Noyes, *In the Land of Chinook* (Helena, 1917), 133–34; *Herald*, November 19, 1889; *Semi-Weekly Inter Mountain* (Butte), March 29, 1885.

95. Report of the Committee on Elections on A. C. Botkin vs. Martin Maginnis, *House Report* No. 2138, 48 Congress, 1 Session (1883–84), 1–3; *Herald*, December 10, 1883; July 7, 1884; *Independent*, August 4, 1884.

Maginnis bowed out in 1884, but he left behind an impressive record in Washington. Governor Potts was able to cooperate with him and with Sam Hauser, giving Montana what Kenneth Owens has called "a no-party pattern of territorial politics," management of government by a coalition of interest groups cutting across party lines. How important Hauser was is still not clear: certainly he was a major figure, but whether he was the most important single force of his era, as Owens implies, is perhaps debatable. But Potts lived with the Democrats on excellent terms. Indeed, by 1877, leading Democrats in the territory had reached the conclusion that if Montana had to have a Republican in the governor's chair, "the present one will suit us better than any other." Besides, it would keep the party divided "and we stand a much better chance to defeat them in the Elections." In 1880, Maginnis was accused of being under Potts's influence and of reporting to Republicans what went on in the Democratic caucuses he attended. And in 1882, Democrat Alexander Woolfolk believed Potts would be the "unanimous choice of the Democrats in the Territory with whom he has generally cooperated—as well as a large portion of Republicans. It would be a master stroke of policy for the Democrats to keep him in office as a stalwart governor would be a constant 'thorn in the flesh.' "[96] It is a tribute to Potts that, despite a split in the ranks of his own party and invariably confronted with legislatures dominated by the opposite party, over the long run he survived controversy and fashioned a program that redounded to both his and the territory's credit.

But the intraparty conflict with Sanders and the Fisks continued and was acerbated from time to time by new issues of an economic or political nature that often assumed a personal character. The controversy over territorial printing was typical. By law, the secretary was charged with transmitting copies of the laws and legislative journals to the president; the printing of these items, along with the governor's message, proclamations, and other assorted public papers, was, in Montana as elsewhere during the Gilded Age, regarded as legitimate and lucrative patronage. Typical printing bills included $6,307.60 expended by the first legislature, $9,760.75 by the third, and $6,491.43 by the tenth.[97] In addition, officials in Washington some-

96. Kenneth N. Owens, "Pattern and Structure in Western Territorial Politics," *Western Historical Quarterly*, I (October, 1970), 386, 387; Perry W. McAdow to Maginnis (Bozeman, March 14, 1877; May 5, 1880), Maginnis MSS; Alexander Woolfolk to Maginnis (Helena, March 26, 1882), *ibid.*
97. Accounts of Auditor and Treasurer (April 2, 1866), *Council Journal*, 2

times asked the governor to designate favored local newspapers to carry government advertising, a less grand but still welcome plum.[98]

Delay was the story of public printing in Montana. From the beginning work lagged behind. In 1865, United States Attorney Edward Neally had to prod Wilbur F. Sanders and found him "inclined to be indolent" in preparing the preface to the session laws.[99] In 1869, Delegate James Cavanaugh complained that the journals of the second and third legislatures, both convened in 1866, were still unprinted due to the poor condition of territorial finances.[100] Often delay was a product of sending work east to save costs. One editor in 1869 remarked sarcastically that the laws "could be published cheaper in London than in the United States, and not be so reckless with the peoples money."[101] Part of the story, too, was bound up with petty squabbles over whether the legislature could force the secretary to copy the laws or whether the secretary was obligated to make the index for the printer.[102] But the major cause of trouble was a very simple one: Who was going to get the public printing subsidy and at what rate?

In theory, it was the territorial secretary who dispensed this particular form of largesse, although the governor exerted some influence and the legislature might also have a voice, especially in the printing of materials for itself or for the counties. But that the governor was in no position to control public printing is indicated by the fact that the Fisks' *Herald* received its share and more during the Potts era. Understandably Bob Fisk took an active interest in promoting friends for the territorial secretarial post. From Washington, where he was pushing the candidacy of Wiley Scribner in 1869, he wrote his wife: "You know how important this nomination is to myself and the

Session (1886), 195; James Tufts to R. W. Taylor (Virginia City, March 25, 1868), LT, Vol. VIII; Mills to Maginnis (Helena, January 23, 1879), Maginnis MSS.

98. John Potts to Benjamin Potts (Washington, December 15, 1870; January 4, 1871), GEC.

99. Edward Neally to Thomas F. Meagher (Burlington, Iowa, November 17, 1865), Meagher MSS.

100. Cavanaugh to Hugh McCulloch (Washington, January 22, 1869), LT, Vol. IX. See also Mills to Taylor (Helena, November 27, 1877), LT, Vol. XIV; *Herald*, June 30, 1874.

101. *Weekly Independent*, March 20, 1869.

102. Callaway to Taylor (Helena, January 24, 1876), LT, Vol. XIII. "It is the duty of the Secretary to make the Index for the printer and is therefore deducted from the bill." Taylor to Wiley Scribner (Washington, November 3, 1869), LT, copy, outg., Vol. VIII.

Herald, in the large amount of printing it will bring to the office."[103]

In the Gilded Age printing and politics were intertwined and often hard to separate. For example, how much was political and how much was realistic economy in the 1873 report of the Council Committee on Ways and Means, a report which charged that territorial printing costs were higher than private, that "execessive sums have been paid the *Montanian, Helena Gazette,* and *Herald* for territorial printing," and that the best solution would be to let all public printing by contract to the lowest bidder?[104]

Though Robert Fisk denied in 1871 that there was any rivalry between the *Herald* and James Mills's *New North-West* for the public printing, and contended that, as the leading Republican newspaper in the territory, the *Herald* would get its due, he nonetheless condemned as special legislation a House bill which would have split the publishing of the laws among three papers.[105] Obviously, at this time Fisk had the lion's share, and when Mills approached Secretary Callaway for a portion, he was stalled off, on the grounds that he might soon receive a federal appointment.[106] Callaway's relations with Fisk were excellent but the secretary knew the political explosiveness of the situation. In October, 1873, when he informed Fisk of his appointment as public printer, he cautioned against any announcement of this. "The *devil* will be to pay before long—so watch as well as pray," said Callaway.[107] Some light is thrown upon Callaway's association with Fisk by a letter the secretary wrote early in 1874, asking the editor for funds to bring his family home. ". . . I will deem it a personal and especial favor and will make it all right—*When we dig our potatoes,*" he promised.[108] Until the early seventies, James H. Mills of

103. Robert E. Fisk to Elizabeth Fisk (Washington, March 27, 1869), Fisk family MSS.

104. Report of the Committee on Ways and Means (April 26, 1873), *Council Journal,* Extra Session (1873), 80.

105. *Herald,* November 25, 29, December 23, 27, 1871. James H. Mills was born in Ohio in 1837 and educated there and in Pennsylvania. In 1861, he enlisted in the 11th Pennsylvania Reserves and remained with that outfit through various campaigns—the Peninsula, Mechanicsville, Antietam, Fredericksburg, Gettysburg, and the Wilderness among them—before being mustered out as a brevet lieutenant colonel in 1864. He went into the wholesale leather business and moved to Montana in 1866, eventually to become editor of the *Montana Post* until he founded the *New North-West* at Deer Lodge in July, 1869. *Progressive Men of the State of Montana,* 317–18; J. R. Sypher, *History of the Pennsylvania Reserve Corps* (Lancaster, 1865), 692, 693.

106. Callaway to Robert E. Fisk (Virginia City, December 14, 1871), Fisk family MSS.

107. Callaway to Robert E. Fisk (Virginia City, October 8, 1873), *ibid.*

108. Callaway to Robert E. Fisk (Virginia City, March 12, 1874), *ibid.*

the *New North-West* had "been the recipient of a sweet suck at the public titty-bag and obtained a 'fat take,' in the shape of public printing," according to one critic.[109] But late in 1874, Secretary Callaway confided to the president that he had alienated Mills—that "d—d half-idiotic anti-railroader—and thats all" by not giving him printing for two consecutive terms and distributing the patronage to favor Fisk.[110]

Governor Potts complained to the First Comptroller of the United States about Fisk's handling of the laws and journals, not only because of the tardiness in their printing but because of what he insisted was excessive profit derived by subcontracting the job to a firm in Iowa. ". . . is it just to the government and this people to allow a man to make three or four thousand dollars without investing any money or performing any labor and to the great inconvenience of every citizen in the Territory?" he asked. But Potts's suggestions that Fisk be allowed only the cost of printing in the States, plus freight from Davenport, and that in the future the task be done by the Government Printing Office in Washington, were not accepted. Fisk contended that James A. Garfield, at Potts's insistence, brought the matter to the House Committee on Appropriations, but enough delegates prevailed to persuade them to leave printing to the territories. Potts did put printing of his message of 1875 in the hands of Mills, to be done at government rates, but grew increasingly skeptical of his secretary. "Bob Fisk appears to be running Callaway & is hot of course that he did not get all the printing & additional rates from the Territory," he wrote Martin Maginnis. At the same time, he complained that Callaway refused to give copies of the laws to the *Independent* for publication without payment for copy and for certification. According to the Fisks, the *Independent* was Potts's "official and semi-political organ," and the governor held many "secret conferences" with its "Bourbon editor," that "low-bred political bummer and self-confessed blackguard—Barret."[111]

Believing that the legal rates for public printing were "unreasonably high," Potts in 1876 recommended legislation to let all printing

109. "J.R.W." to editor (Bannack, March 4, 1873), quoted in *Herald*, March 11, 1873).

110. Callaway to Grant (Virginia City, December 29, 1874), Callaway file, TPI; Callaway to Robert E. Fisk (Virginia City, June 15, 1874), Fisk family MSS.

111. Potts to Taylor (Virginia City, October 10, 1874); Robert E. Fisk to Taylor (with endorsement), LT, Vol. XII; *Herald*, January 2, 1875; January 3, 1876; Potts to Maginnis (Helena, December 29, 1875; February 24, 1876); Maginnis MSS.

to the lowest bidder. Ignoring this, the assembly adopted a bill to create a printing board, comprised of the governor and presiding officers of each house, whose function it was to designate a public printer for the territory and for each county except Lewis and Clark—a measure the Fisks saw as "a bold attempt at a robbery, . . . the joint offspring of Governor Potts and the editor of the *Independent*, and is intended as a relief bill for the *Independent* at the expense of the property men and tax-payers of Montana."[112] Republicans opposed the bill and the Democrats supported it and Potts confounded at least the *Herald* editors when he vetoed the measure and was sustained.[113] But another was introduced, this too for the benefit of the *Independent*, complained the Fisks, and it "cantered through the House, and, without halting, galloped over to the Council, where, as immaterially amended, it was put through with a rattling pace" and was signed by the governor as part of a political package.[114] The new law created a board to contract for all printing at a fixed rate—a rate which was at least 50 percent below that previously existing by statute. While it was not ideal, Potts believed it would lower printing costs by some $5,000 per year.[115]

But Secretary Callaway saw it as an example of the extravagance for which the Montana legislature was known—"the offspring of a joint Democratic caucus" of the two houses and a partisan enactment to benefit Democratic journals. Soon Potts announced that the *Independent* had been selected to do the county printing. It was a matter of simple economy, he said, but he knew the political ramifications and was careful to ask Delegate Maginnis to protect his flank in Washington. The news left editor Fisk livid: that "Johnsonized" anti-Republican governor, that Executive "Hippo-Potts-imas" owned stock in the *Independent*, he charged. And fearing that Secretary Callaway would delay in submitting the bill of Mills and Hessler for the printing of the messages, Potts sent a new invoice directly to Maginnis, asking him to present it to the Treasury, "as Callaway will delay the payment to the last hour, if referred to him."[116]

112. *Herald*, January 5, 1876; Potts to Carl Schurz (Helena, June 7, 1877), Potts File, API.

113. *Herald*, January 8, 12, 13, 1876.

114. According to Fisk, Potts signed this measure in exchange for Council confirmation of D. H. Cuthbert, his nominee for treasurer. *Herald*, January 17, 20, 21, 1876.

115. Potts to Schurz (Helena, June 7, 1877), Potts file, API.

116. Callaway to Taylor (Helena, January 24, 1876), LT, Vol. XIII; Potts to Maginnis (Helena, February 6, 1876), Maginnis MSS; *Herald*, January 28,

Potts and Fisk would clash over the application of the law of 1876. In the fall of 1875, the *Herald* had contracted to print the pamphlet edition of the Record for the recorder of marks and brands, as provided by law, and the legislature set aside $225 for this purpose. But Fisk presented his bill for the work after the new printing law went into effect, and Potts refused to approve more than the amount fixed by the latest statute—in this case $137. Charging off the record that Potts had paid 50 percent more when the *Independent* had done the job the year before and that the governor sought merely to delay payment or "defraud us of our money" out of personal animosity, the Fisk brothers brought suit and in the end won their case.[117]

Potts continued his efforts to put printing of the laws and journals in the hands of the Government Printing Office in order to save money "and destroy the corruption fund of the Secretary." When the Fisks and Callaway joined hands in an all-out effort to have Potts removed in 1877, one of their criticisms was that he had created a printing monopoly for a Democratic newspaper. But it was Callaway, not Potts, who was ousted, and Fisk discontent was unallayed, especially in 1879 when, short of money, the new secretary, James H. Mills, accepted the offer of the *Independent*, rather than the *Herald*, to handle the bulk of the printing "and look to Congress for their pay." A year later, the Republican Convention of Lewis and Clark County, in which the Fisk-Sanders influence was strong, adopted resolutions calling for an end of the "odious monopoly of public printing" established by Montana Democrats. Ultimately—three years later—Chief Justice Decius Wade struck down the printing law, and, the Fisks cheered, released "the public treasuries from years of Democratic extortion."[118]

It seems clear that selfish and political motives lay behind the public printing squabble. It seems clear too that Potts used what influence he could to limit the Fisks' patronage and cooperated both with other Republican editors and some Democrats. The issue was one which alienated Callaway and the governor and one which

March 18, June 21, 1876; Potts to Maginnis (Helena, July 26, 1876), LT, Vol. XIII.

117. Potts to Schurz (Helena, June 7, 1877); Wilbur F. Sanders to Schurz (Helena, May 5, 1877), both in Potts file, API; *Herald*, January 17, 20, 1877; Fisk Bros. *v.* Cuthbert, 2 *Montana Reports* (1877), 593–605.

118. Potts to Sherman (Helena, March 30, 1877), James H. Mills file, API; Alexander H. Beattie, Robert E. Fisk, et al. to Rutherford B. Hayes (n.d., n.p., endorsed April 23, 1877), Potts file, API; Mills to Maginnis (Helena, January 23, 1879), Maginnis MSS; *Council Journal*, Extra Session (1879), 36; *Herald*, September 11, 1880; December 12, 1883.

heaped fuel upon the fires of antagonism between Potts on the one hand and the Sanders-Fisk faction on the other.

Potts's financial program generated less opposition, although certain aspects of it had their political implications and engendered partisan feelings. From the beginning, he preached economy and sound business management. "We have a bungling system of finance here and I want to try and remedy it," he wrote in 1871, asking Rutherford Hayes to send him a copy of Governor Chase's 1857 message to the Ohio legislature, "which I think contains some suggestions about the safe keeping of the public funds &c." [119]

Almost as soon as he arrived, Governor Potts complained that government in Montana was shot through with corruption and petty graft. He quickly discerned irregularities in the transactions of the previous secretary, Wiley Scribner, who, although suspended, had been employed as clerk of Judge George Symes's court. According to Potts, Scribner had issued vouchers worth $1,500 for wood, but received less than $200 worth; government furniture was missing. and $150 worth of stamps had never been received. Potts also discovered what he believed were "rent scandals" dating back several years: contracts made by the secretary for executive offices at absurdly high rental rates. Indeed, said Potts, investigation of Scribner's vouchers would indicate "that one fraud after another has been committed here by U.S. officials. . . ." "No man shall steal here by virtue of a Commission signed by U.S. Grant while I am here," he pledged. "The petty stealing of our officials here has lost us the territory to the party—and if honesty will redeem it I will give it a trial." "I mean to clean the Augean Stable," he told Secretary of State Fish. [120]

Whereupon the Governor cancelled the existing rent contract and leased three rooms upstairs in the Patten Building for only $25 a month, "whereas this old barracks costs 90$ per mo. . . ." [121] Thus Potts inaugurated his economy drive with a flair. But his attacks on Scribner may have been largely political. The former secretary was branded "a defaulter" but the government exonerated him of wrong-

119. Potts to Hayes (Virginia City, August 17, 1871), Hayes MSS.
120. Potts to Hayes (Virginia City, November 29, 1870), *ibid.*; Hamilton, *From Wilderness to Statehood*, 312; Potts to George S. Boutwell (Virginia City, October 6, 1870), LT, Vol. X; Potts to Taylor (Virginia City, November 18, 1870), "private," *ibid.*; Potts to Hayes (Virginia City, November 29, 1870), Hayes MSS.; Potts to Fish (n.p., December 26, 1870), copy, Potts letterbook.
121. Potts to Taylor (Virginia City, December 24, 1870), LT, Vol. X; Potts to Robert E. Fisk (Virginia City, December 30, 1870), Fisk family MSS.

doing any greater than extravagance.[122] Still, one of Governor Potts's most substantial contributions to Montana territorial history was a sustained and successful program of financial responsibility and economy of government.

One of his first targets, again for political as well as economic reasons, was the payment of extra compensation by the legislature to its own members and to federal officers. Not only was the practice expensive—to October, 1872, he pointed out, the territory had gone into debt $130,000 to pay out $201,000 for this purpose—Potts resented the use of the purse strings against uncooperative appointed officials, historic as the practice was. In general, Montana Democrats favored extra compensation, and thoughtful men of both parties saw the issue as a political one. Democrat Granville Stuart urged his fellow legislators in 1871 to cut additional compensation by one-half "on purely political grounds." ". . . it gives the Rads a pry on us every election," he explained to his brother. Potts realized this also. Anti-extra compensation was the best possible issue with which to embarrass the Democrats, he argued, "and it should be kept before the people. . . . I can live on 2,500$ and the Judges ought to live on $3,000 and can if they keep out of Saloons and if they don't $4,000 won't keep them. . . . I want the Democrats to oppose & we will go to the people on it next election," he wrote early in 1871.[123]

But when the legislature ignored his recommendations for the repeal of all such laws and indeed enacted another over his objections,[124] Potts took his case to influential Congressmen in Washington. When legislators raised their own per diem stipends from the $4 allowed by federal law to $16, he could "only regard this as robbery," he told his friend Garfield, while to Lyman Trumbull he expressed the hope that "Congress will not permit the Legislature to continue the bribe any longer."[125] Ultimately, early in 1873, Congress passed a Garfield bill prohibiting territorial legislatures from paying extra

122. *Herald*, January 9, 1872.
123. Potts to Garfield (n.p., October 26, 1872), copy, Potts letterbook; Granville Stuart to James Stuart (Virginia City, December 26, 1871), Stuart MSS; Potts to William Wheeler (Virginia City, February 9, 10, 19, 1871), Wheeler MSS.
124. *Herald*, December 9, 1871: *Council Journal*, 7 Session (1871–72), 43, 44, 51, 80.
125. Potts to Garfield (n.p., October 26, 1872); Potts to Trumbull (Virginia City, February 17, 1871); Potts to Nye (Virginia City, February 13, 1871), copies, all in Potts letterbook. See also Potts to Garfield (Virginia City, June 3, 1871), Garfield MSS.

compensation to their own members or to their governors or secretaries,[126] thus removing from the people's representatives what was
both a coercive influence and a political lever. Potts undoubtedly saw
the question in all its dimensions, but economy loomed large in his
mind.

In many ways Potts practiced frugality. In 1873, the warden of the
penitentiary resigned, primarily because of differences over expenditures with the governor. After Warden Adriance had spent a total of
two dollars for a toothbrush for each convict, according to the story,
Potts is supposed to have returned the voucher with the endorsement:
"I consider this item an extravagant and useless expenditure. If the
hotels in Montana can get along with one tooth-brush, I don't see
why the Territorial Penitentiary can't do the same!" All of which sent
editor Fisk into explosions of sarcasm: "Cursed be Canaan unless it
revels in dirt and rejoices in squalor. Whoever is found with soap in
Montana let him be shot as a traitor. If one calls for hot water—or
cold either, unless it be to cool his heated coppers—hunt him down as
disloyal. Hereafter clean no finger nails; nay, more, pick no teeth,
comb no tangled locks, abolish all Chinese wash houses, and bend
every energy to developing 'the genial influences of civilization.'"
A little later, another warden and two of the prison board members
resigned, again over financial problems. According to the *Herald*,
the warden purchased a dozen small-sized washbowls for use as
prisoners soup plates. "But the great Ohio Statesman declined to
allow the bill, and hence there is fresh trouble in the camp."[127]

These are extremes and no doubt overdrawn by Potts's political
enemies, but they indicate that he was a close man with government
monies. Few, if any Montanans, knew that several times he suggested to friends in Congress where appropriations might be cut.
"Most of the people here believe it to be legitimate to get all the
appropriations they can without regard to whether needed or not,"
he wrote Garfield. He then proceeded to detail where funds might
be trimmed from the Montana survey and land office funds.[128] He

126. Garfield to Potts (Washington, December 30, 1872), copy, letterbook
12, Garfield MSS; act of January 23, 1873, 17 *USSL*, 416. Judges were not
included.

127. *Herald*, December 24, 29, 1873; January 17, 1874.

128. Unless the Crow Treaty were ratified, $20,000 would be enough for the
1874 survey, he suggested, and there was no need of the Bozeman land office
unless the treaty were accepted. Not one-tenth of the land surveyed in the
territory was currently taken up, he said. Potts to Garfield (Virginia City, May 1,
1874), "private," Garfield MSS.

urged his friends in Washington to warn the Secretary of the Interior to keep a watchful eye on appropriations for the Sioux, for a number of "human vultures" from Montana were after them.[129] Montanans also accused Potts, unfairly, of opposing payment of the Montana Indian war vouchers, an issue left over from the days of Thomas Francis Meagher; Potts insisted Inspector Hardie's report was a fair one and that he would support it.[130]

Invariably his messages to the legislature stressed governmental economy, and his actions supported his words. "Extravagance must be checked and economy exercised," he told the assembly in 1873. "No people exist so rich and powerful that prodigality and corruption cannot destroy." By this time the territorial debt had reached $158,300, but the governor's thrift campaign had already started a downward trend. With care and proper management, now that extra compensation was forbidden, Potts saw no reason why $20,000 of the debt could not be retired each year. Already he had been responsible for its re-funding at a lower interest rate, and from time to time would prompt the legislature to do so again.[131]

By 1874 Potts believed the corner had been turned. To his friend Hayes, he wrote:

> I have had a severe task here—to keep the Territory from going to ruin my battle has been to prevent expenditure. I had to learn the people that to continue the increase of indebtedness must end in bankruptcy. The debt is now under control and in course of liquidation but I have been abused shamefully by those who had heretofore been in charge of the affairs of the Territory and Counties   I have not even had the support of my own party "Press" but the permanent residents and taxpayers have stood by me and I now have a party that can control the affairs of the Territory.[132]

129. Potts to Garfield (Virginia City, September 23, 1872), Garfield MSS.

130. Because Senator John Sherman had opposed paying the vouchers and Potts was known to be close to him and his brother William, it was charged that the governor was seeking to block payments. Potts to Robert E. Fisk (Virginia City, March 25, 1871), Fisk family MSS.

131. Potts to extra session (April 15, 1873), *Council Journal*, Extra Session (1873), 19, 20, 21; *Herald*, December 15, 1873; act (n.d.), *LM*, 7 Session (1871–72), 578–81; act of May 1, 1873, *LM*, Extra Session (1873), 65–66; act of July 21, 1879, *LM*, Extra Session (1879), 12–14.

132. "You can have no idea of the number of Scoundrels and adventures [*sic*] that are found in a single Territory. They do not intend to remain permanently and they are ready for any steal that will enrich them. I have often almost despaired of being able to defeat their Schemes but a better day has dawned upon us and a few years hence Montana will be free from debt and very prosperous." Potts to Hayes (Virginia City, June 9, 1874), Hayes MSS.

By 1883 Potts could announce that for the first time the territory was free of debt, with a surplus of $14,005.90 in its treasury.[133]

As part of his fiscal reform, Potts preached the need for more efficient tax collection, fewer exemptions, and especially a broader levy on liquor dealers and operators of producing mines. And although mine owners never paid their share, he did improve the tax structure of the territory.[134] No doubt the governor agreed with editor Fisk, who sounded a clarion call for frugality in 1874: "Cut down salaries, abolish sinecures, stop all extravagant and useless expenses. Let the army take care of the Indians, and our navy surround Cuba."[135] In this respect, Potts's cheese-paring nature was manifested in numerous ways. He condemned a bill of the sheriff of Madison County for $222 for conveying a prisoner to Deer Lodge, a trip which two men could make for not more than $80 both ways.[136] He vetoed a bill of the 1874 legislature which authorized the semiannual publication of reports of county commissioners, although they collected taxes only once a year; and he chided that session for having "signally failed to make any considerable reduction in the public expenditures."[137] He urged the combining of certain jobs, and in 1877 returned a bill which would make the clerk of the supreme court ex officio territorial librarian, with additional pay, in lieu of the auditor who performed the task as part of his normal duties. Fisk complained that the veto was the result of Potts's personal animosity toward the clerk and that "the valuable law books of the Territory are consigned to the rats, the mould and mildew of the storehouse,"[138] a charge that was unfounded.

A watchdog of public funds, Potts was quick to veto money bills he thought were excessive. In 1879, for example, he returned a measure to compensate the chief clerk of the Council, Harry R. Comly, for work in codifying the general statutes. Noting that the best lawyers in Helena could perform the job for much less, he rejected it as special legislation. "The bill bears the impress of the

133. Potts to legislature (January 8, 1883), *Council Journal*, 13 Session (1883), 30.
134. See Chapter 11.
135. *Herald*, January 16, 1874.
136. Potts to extra session (April 15, 1873), *Council Journal*, Extra Session (1873), 21.
137. Potts to House (February 11, 1874), *House Journal*, 8 Session (1874), 213.
138. *Herald*, January 5, February 5, 1876; February 12, 1877; Potts to Schurz (Helena, June 7, 1877); Potts to House (February 9, 1877), both in Potts file, API.

personal lobby and the title should be changed so as to read 'A bill for the relief of H. R. Comly.' "[139]

But successful though he was in curbing and eventually eliminating the territorial debt, Potts was never able to limit the county debts, though this was a subject close to his heart. One approach was to reduce the high fees accorded county officers. These, he originally wrote in a call for a special session in 1873, "are so exorbitant as to smack of robbery and amount to a denial of justice to the poor and are daily devouring the substance of the people."[140] And though he deleted the expression, "smack of robbery" in the official proclamation, there was no doubt of the depth of his feeling on the matter. Fees, percentages, and salaries of assessors, county clerks, sheriffs or other lesser officers were unreasonable, he argued, and he cited the auditor's report to show that in 1873, when the territorial governor received a salary of $3,500 and the secretary $2,500, the assessor of Deer Lodge County and the sheriffs of Deer Lodge, Missoula, and Madison counties all received more than either.[141]

The extra session of 1873 attacked the problem with alacrity. The Council Committee on Ways and Means came out four-square behind the governor's program of "economy, retrenchment, and reform," urging sharp reductions in salaries and fees of most county and territorial officers. The result was what the editor of the Helena *Gazette* called "sweeping reform," with stipends for many functionaries— including clerks, sheriffs, treasurers, recorders and probate judges— markedly lowered. Some believed these positions now hardly worth having and the *Herald* thought it detected a tendency to cut fees "of officers who might, from the nature of their tenure be Republicans, and to retain the present exorbitant fees of county officers who are elective. . . ."[142]

This was a beginning, but was far from being a thoroughgoing reform. Too many local officials had not been touched and Potts went before the 1874 assembly asking further salary reductions, although it is doubtful that he would have gone along with the bill J. C.

139. *Herald*, February 22, 1879.
140. Proclamation (Virginia City, March 17, 1873), GEC.
141. For the year ending March 1, 1873, the assessor for Deer Lodge County received $3,843.77 and the sheriff, $5,361.50, while the sheriff of Missoula County was paid $5,072.90 and the sheriff of Madison County, $4,192.60. *Council Journal*, Extra Session (1873), 13, 16, 46–47; *Herald*, April 14, 1873.
142. *Council Journal*, Extra Session (1873), 57; acts of April 28, 29, 30, May 1, 2, 3, 8, 1873, LM, Extra Session (1873), 50–65; *Daily Rocky Mountain Gazette*, May 7, 1873; *Herald*, April 21 1873.

Kerley threatened to introduce, which would abolish all county offices and put their work into the hands of territorial officers—without additional pay. In 1876 Potts complained that district and county fees had been reduced only minimally, while those of the territorial auditor and treasurer had been sharply cut, a fact "so inconsistent and unreasonable that it presented the appearance of political partisanship." His proposals that the positions of probate judge and county clerk and those of sheriff and county treasurer be combined brought only scoffing that Potts was a true reformer: "He would like to reform money out of everybody's pocket except his own."[143]

Fee fixing and reduction gradually expanded, but even in 1881 some county clerks made more than judges of the territorial supreme court; and four years later it could be pointed out that the assessor of Lewis and Clark County had been paid $3,664.40 for only four months work in 1882.[144] And despite Potts's call for legislation to prohibit county debt beyond annual income, cumulative indebtedness continued to climb at the county level, reaching a total of over $658,974 as of March, 1882, with the governor complaining of a lack of action by the legislature and that skeptical cattlemen were taking their herds out of counties which were deeply in the red.[145]

But overall, Potts did much to put the territory on a sound financial basis. Former delegate William Clagett said of Potts in a letter to the president in 1874: "The economy which he has compelled in the management of the territorial finances, has not only caused a steady appreciation of the credit of the Territory, but has probably saved it from the verge of bankruptcy."[146] A debt, increasing at the rate of about $25,000 per year, had been eliminated, and territorial credit restored. In 1870, according to Potts, territorial warrants were "dragging on the market at 60 cents on the dollar," while in 1877 despite "much adverse legislation," they commanded 97.4 cents.[147]

---

143. *Council Journal*, 8 Session (1874), 123; *Herald*, January 8, 1874; January 5, 1876; Potts to legislature (January 3, 1876), *House Journal*, 9 Session (1876), 16–18, 19; A bill to abolish the office of county treasurer was reported out of committee in 1876 but lost. *Herald*, February 5, 1876.

144. Potts to legislature (July 11, 1881), *Council Journal*, 12 Session (1881), 16–17; Potts to legislature (January 8, 1883), *Council Journal* 13 Session (1883), 30, 32.

145. Potts to legislature (January 8, 1884), *Council Journal*, 13 Session (1883), 30, 32; *House Journal*, 13 Session (1883), 3–4.

146. Clagett to U. S. Grant (Deer Lodge, May 30, 1874), Potts file, API.

147. Potts to W. Dennison (Helena, March 14, 1877). See also Andrew J. Smith to Charles Devens (Helena, April 11, 1877); R. O. Hickman to Hayes

Even though the governor had dabbled in the sale of such warrants to eastern associates early in his Montana career,[148] he was largely responsible for their soundness—and for that of the economy of the territorial government in general.

In his fiscal policies, Potts stepped on relatively few toes. The same was true of his relations with the Indians, for in general the governor had the outlook of most of his Montana constituents. By Potts's administration, the chief executive of the territory was no longer superintendent of Indian affairs, but he was concerned with protection, and like Edgerton and Meagher before him, would find occasion to call up the militia against the Indians.

Moreover, Potts took a first-hand interest in any factor which might delay transportation development or settlement. " 'Sitting Bull' the leading War Chief means to fight the N.P.R.R. and no compromise can be affected with him," Potts wrote Garfield in the fall of 1872, at the same time indicating to officers of the Northern Pacific the need to move against the Sioux. "Any delay is prejudicial to the progress of the Road."[149] Several years later, he urged that the policies adopted against the Apaches in Arizona be applied to the Sioux in order to facilitate the completion of the Northern Pacific.[150] In general, his policies were vigorous—to subjugate the Indians, protect settlement, and whittle down reservations, all approaches which would not harm him politically.

When settlers in the Gallatin Valley seemed to be threatened by large numbers of Sioux, the governor urged the Secretary of War to send additional federal troops or to permit him to organize a few companies of volunteers in case of emergency. "My hands are tied now and our whole population might be murdered before I could get any authority and have time to make it available," he said in 1871. But Potts made it clear he had no intention of calling the militia without approval from Washington and in the end he did little more than visit the Gallatin Valley to see for himself and to

---

(Virginia City, March 14, 1877), all in Potts file, API; Potts to Schurz (Helena, November 16, 1878), TPI.

148. For sale of warrants to Carrolton bankers see: Potts to G. A. Baker (n.p., September 21, 1871); Potts to Cummins and Couch (n.p., June 26, October 31, November 9, 1872); also Potts to J. Kountze Brothers (n.p., December 14, 1872, January 14, 1873), copies, all in Potts letterbook.

149. Potts to Garfield (n.p., October 16, 1872); Potts to A. B. Nettleton (n.p., October 21, 1872), copies, Potts letterbook.

150. *Herald*, January 8, 1874.

promote a small-scale lend-lease arrangement bringing 1,000 breech-loading rifles and 200,000 rounds of government ammunition to the settlers there.[151]

But he continued to warn Washington about possible troubles in the Gallatin Valley, not only because of the encroachment of the Sioux, but also because the Crows were dissatisfied over their new agent, the infiltration of wolfers in the Judith Basin and on the Mus-selshell, and the failure of the federal government to protect them from the Sioux. But Potts disparaged the idea that the Yellowstone Wagon-Road and Prospecting Expedition into the Yellowstone Val-ley in 1874 posed any threat to the Crows. Although the governor never explained it officially as such, this was a Montana enterprise to explore the Yellowstone Valley—despite the claims of the Indians to that area—with the objects of (1) locating a site for a trading post whence farm products of the Gallatin Valley might be funneled to proposed military posts along the Northern Pacific route; (2) ac-quiring land for speculative purposes; (3) locating new mines; and (4) possibly provoking the Indians, forcing the army into the field against them, and incidentally providing a market for agricultural goods unsalable after the panic of 1873. Potts continued to assure Washington that Montanans were friendly toward the Crows and that the expedition would cause no trouble, but he expressed alarm at some eight hundred Sioux lodges at the mouth of the Musselshell trading for arms and ammunition. General Philip Sheridan wrote the Secretary of the Interior about the expedition, noting that the Yel-lowstone group was only one such group and it was favored by Potts. But its rival hoped to stop it by shouting "Indian scare." Sheridan gave simple advice to Secretary Delano: "I propose to let these parties fight their own battles, have refused either of them any as-sistance, and if the Interior Department will do the same, we will get rid of a subject which has no public interest in it."[152]

Potts continued to counsel protection of the mountain Crows against the Sioux, who were also a menace to the white settlers of the Gallatin Valley: they were "at the mercy of 'Sitting Bull' and his band of murdering robbers" and a sharp military operation

151. Potts to W. W. Belknap (Virginia City, August 14, 1871), copy, GEC; Potts to Columbus Delano (Virginia City, August 12, 1871), BIA; act of May 21, 1872, 17 USSL, 138.

152. Potts to Delano (Virginia City, May 2, 1873, March 14, 1874), BIA; Burlingame, *Montana Frontier*, 208–9; Potts to Delano (Virginia City, March 14, 17, 25, 1874), BIA; General Philip Sheridan to Delano (Chicago, April 15, 1874), copy, BIA.

against them from Fort Ellis would be most helpful. In 1875 and 1876 he reiterated the need for a campaign against the Sioux. "The opening of the Country from Bozeman to Bismarck I regard as absolutely necessary to the prosperity and growth of Montana. . . . We can have no peace until the Sioux Indians on the Yellowstone are whipped: no other policy will answer the purpose," he wrote Delano. Early in 1876 Potts sought through the War Department, and indirectly through a bill introduced by Maginnis, authority to raise a batallion of Montana volunteers to move under his command to help the regulars protect the Black Hills against the Sioux. These efforts came to naught and the scoffing Fisks hooted. "Governor Potts has returned from the front," they said. "The 'signal fires' were too much for him, and he retreated in masterly style to his base of supplies." [153]

In the following summer, Montanans felt themselves threatened when Chief Joseph and the Nez Percés fled across Montana from the Clearwater in Idaho, heading for Canada with U.S. troops slowly following. ". . . a great excitement prevails" in the Bitterroot Valley, reported Potts, who pledged himself to arm the people of the western counties.[154] He called for volunteers and appointed his new secretary, James Mills, adjutant general of the militia, to report on the situation.[155] At the same time, he sent arms to the settlers and had Flathead agent Peter Ronan confer with the western Montana tribe to urge peace and alliance with the whites.[156] He urged upon President Hayes a harsh policy: the Nez Percés should be "punished or exterminated, . . . they should be treated like the Modocs."[157] William A. Clark of Butte organized several companies of militia and Potts was urged to take personal command; but the War Department turned down his official request to organize three hundred volunteers, and without financing most of the militia disbanded, convinced that the Nez Percés merely wished to pass through the territory peacefully. But Potts urged all armed men to "hold themselves in constant readiness," and regular troops clashed with the Indians at

153. Potts to Edward P. Smith (Virginia City, August 24, 1874), BIA; Potts to Delano (Virginia City, March 27, 1875; Helena, August 6, 1875), BIA; *Herald*, July 20, March 22, August 1, 1876; Belknap to Potts (Washington, July 7, 1876), GEC.

154. Potts to Schurz (Helena, June 1, 1877), BIA.

155. Potts to Schurz (Helena, June 28, 1877), BIA.

156. Potts to Peter Ronan (Helena, June 29, 1877), copy; Ronan to Potts (Missoula, July 10, 1877); Potts to Schurz (Helena, July 2, 1877), BIA.

157. Potts to Hayes (Helena, July 2, 1877), Hayes MSS.

the Battle of the Big Hole. The *Herald*, as usual, regarded Potts's efforts as "opera bouffe."[158]

Clearly Potts was not impressed with Grant's "Peace Policy" toward the Indians. He agreed with W. F. Chadwick that the appointment of "psalm singing Methodist ministers" was no solution. Church selection resulted in agents "without business capacity or knowledge of men and things," he believed.[159] And he made his views known, sometimes writing the Secretary of the Interior urging retention of good men in the Indian service; intervening as an arbitrator in a dispute over furnishing beef to the agent at Fort Belknap; or actively condemning those agents he believed were weak ("Agent Wright is old and timid and ought to be on his farm in Iowa").[160]

He was prone to consider himself "a close observer of Indian affairs"—one whose observations "are worth something to the Administration," and he did sometimes advise Washington on Indian matters and sometimes was empowered to negotiate with the Indians. He urged removal of the Crow agencies from the Yellowstone to the Judith Basin in 1874 and wrote a long letter to President Grant in 1873, as intermediary between the "Great Father" in Washington and Blackfoot, chief of the Crows, because Blackfoot trusted him to present his true sentiments to the president.[161]

Late in 1871 he had visited the remaining Flatheads in the Bitterroot Valley and urged their complete removal to the Jocko Agency.[162] Like most other Montanans, he opposed any proposals to expand the size of Indian land holdings, complaining about a proposal in 1875 to add parts of Gallatin and Big Horn counties to the Crow reservation. ". . . do not force upon [us] any more Indians unless the Country is to be surrendered to them," he wrote the Secretary of the Interior. Throughout his administrations the popular drive continued to reduce and throw open Indian lands to white settlement. Both the

158. *Herald*, July 26, August 7, 1877; Potts proclamation of July 31, 1877, in TPI; for correspondence on this episode see Paul C. Phillips, ed., "The Battle of the Big Hole," *The Frontier*, X (November, 1929), 63–80.

159. W. F. Chadwick to Martin Maginnis (Helena, November 23, 1873), Maginnis MSS; Potts to Delano (Virginia City, July 1, 1873), BIA.

160. Potts to Delano (Virginia City, November 14, 1872; May 2, 1873; July 11, 1874); Potts to B. R. Cowan (Virginia City, June 24, 1874); Potts to John Q. Smith (Helena, May 2, 1876), all in BIA.

161. *Herald*, July 15, 1874; Potts to Dennison (Helena, March 22, 1877), Potts file, API; Potts to Delano (Virginia City, February 20, 1875), Potts file, API; Potts to Grant (Virginia City, December 1873), BIA.

162. Only about 150 remained. Potts to Commissioner of Indian Affairs (Virginia City, September 8, 1871), BIA.

governor and the delegate felt strong pressure, especially from large-scale cattle operators like Granville Stuart, who had pushed Delegate Maginnis for boundary lines he designed himself and who railed at "that idiot Carl Schurz" for his restraints in the Interior Department.[163]

163. Potts to Delano (Helena, July 8, September 27, 1875), BIA; Granville Stuart to Maginnis (Helena, April 5, June 13, 1880), copies, letterbook 1, Stuart MSS.

"The Governor Walked over the Course in Washington": The Administrations of Benjamin Potts—II

Potts's attitude toward the Indians and their land holdings was the standard one of the West and was neither unpopular nor especially controversial. The same was not true, however, of the governor's position on railroad subsidies, an issue which for a decade inflamed public feelings in the territory and often set Potts at odds with his legislature. Most Montanans, Potts included, agreed that Montana's future was wrapped up in the completion of a railroad. But there agreement stopped and the dispute began. Was it desirable and legal for the territory to underwrite the construction of private lines by the issue of public bonds or by tax exemption. If it was, which lines should benefit and to what extent? Beginning in the early 1870s a number of subsidy proposals were considered but in the end none consummated. However, all the while, Potts and members of the legislature were subjected to severe and often dishonest lobbying pressures from parties interested in one enterprise or another.

Much interest was shown in driving a north-south connection with the Union Pacific in Wyoming or Utah. As early as 1868, General Grenville Dodge of that line had assured James Tufts, then acting governor, that with government aid his company could build a track into Montana in eighteen months.[1] But nothing happened. Entre-

1. Grenville Dodge to James Tufts (Salt Lake City, August 17, 1866), GEC.

preneurs like Samuel Hauser sought to build their own rail links with Cheyenne or to gain a congressional charter to construct along the Bozeman Trail, both abortive efforts.[2] Likewise an attempt by Delegate Clagett in 1872 to obtain the approval of Congress for the Helena and North Utah Railroad Company, to tie Helena and Corinne together, was also unsuccessful, although Hauser, Robert Fisk, Cornelius Hedges, and other Helenans conferred with Leland Stanford and other Union Pacific–Central Pacific leaders and embarked on a major campaign to provide a subsidy through the issue of territorial or county bonds for a Helena-to-Corinne link.[3]

Meanwhile, the Northern Pacific was pushing westward to Bismarck, still not having reached the Montana border. Helena was not likely to be a major center on this route, but as terminal of a north-south road might indeed prosper. On the other hand, a town like Deer Lodge—with Helena aspiring in 1872 to become capital—was loath to see any advantage accrue to her rival as result of her favored location at the end of a north-south line. Hence Montanans began to divide into two opposing camps: one supporting the east-west Northern Pacific; the other pushing for tracks to be brought up from Utah.

Potts was one of those who initially put his faith in the Northern Pacific, perhaps not altogether from selfless reasons. Hardly had he arrived in the territory when he was pestering Rutherford Hayes to use his influence with Jay Cooke to secure information about the routing and the schedule of the railroad's construction. "I want that information in advance, so I may be able to profit by it not corruptly but legitimately, . . ." Potts said.[4] Seeking to learn the exact route, he cautioned a Montana friend to avoid publicity: "I trust we can make the knowledge we acquire of some benefit to us personally. I mean to save all the money I can in order to make some investments at an opportune time. . . . I am laboring to get into the secrets of the Co and think I will succeed," he said.[5] "I am now trying to squeeze something more out of Jay Cooke," he confided a few months later,

2. *Herald,* November 21, 1870; February 13, 1871.
3. John E. Blaine et al. to William H. Clagett (Helena, April 3, 1872); Clagett to Samuel T. Hauser (Washington, April 13, May 23, 1872); Stanford to Hauser et al. (San Francisco, June 24, 1872); Alfred A. Cohen to Hauser (San Francisco, August 12, 1872), all in Hauser MSS; *Herald,* April 25, June 18, October 31, November 14, 1872.
4. Benjamin F. Potts to Rutherford B. Hayes (Virginia City, October 8, 1870), Hayes MSS.
5. Potts to William Wheeler (Virginia City, December 8, 1870), Wheeler MSS.

"and hope to succeed in a short time. Keep this quiet for we don't want too much known until we get our grab."[6]

Whether Potts ever got his "grab" is doubtful. But at the same time, he was actively seeking favors from the Northern Pacific. Early in November, 1870, he asked Hayes "to secure for me if possible the Attorneyship of the RR—for this territory. . . ." Once work began in Montana, the road would need legal aid "and in fact will before that —for they are now anxious that their land in this Territory should be exempt from tax for a certain number of years by the Legislature."[7] "I trust Mr. Cooke will accede to my request," he wrote later. "I think I can in an honest way promote the interests of the Company."[8] Subsequently, not having received an appointment as resident attorney in Montana, he suggested to Cooke that the company "ought to have some person to watch your land as some pretend to claim prior rights to that of the R.R. when such rights don't exist." He would be pleased to offer his own services, charging "*only* my *personal* expenses. . . ."[9] When Northern Pacific officials questioned the propriety of his proposed "quasi-connection" with the railroad, Potts saw no conflict. "My official duties are light and I can devote a large portion of my time to the interests of your company," he wrote. And should his two loyalties conflict, he would abandon one, though he was careful not to say which.[10]

Along with personal motivation, which seems not to have been rewarded, Potts no doubt sincerely believed, that, as he wrote Hayes two months after he arrived in Montana, "The only hope of this Country is in the Northern Pacific R.R. . . ."[11] The railroad was a panacea for bad times. "Our grain and stock market is exhausted or *glutted* and many of our people are ready to grasp at anything that promises early relief," he wrote even before the financial crisis took hold in 1873.[12] Not only was the railroad the key to territorial economic prosperity—"the Great Enterprise that is to break our insolation and set us free"[13]—it was indirectly a means of bringing

6. Potts to Wheeler (Virginia City, February 10, 1871), *ibid.*
7. Potts to Hayes (Virginia City, November 6, 1870), Hayes MSS.
8. Potts to Hayes (Virginia City, November 29, 1870), *ibid.*
9. Potts to Jay Cooke (n.p., January 7, 1871; July 23, 1872), copies, Potts letterbook.
10. Potts to A. B. Nettleton (n.p., September 3, 1872), *ibid.*
11. Potts to Hayes (Virginia City, October 8, 1870), Hayes MSS.
12. Potts to G. W. Cass (n.p., January 16, 1873), copy, Potts letterbook.
13. Potts to William Belknap (n.p., November 2, 1872), copy, Potts letterbook. See also Potts to Cooke (n.p., January 7, 1871; July 23, 1872), *ibid.*

Montana into the Republican camp. "Republicans have a hard road to travel here," he wrote Hayes in 1870. "My hope for redemption from this rule is in the N.P.R.R. which will bring new emigration."[14] With this in mind, Potts sought to encourage migration by various devices. In 1871 he was trying to induce several "colonies" to settle en masse in Montana. Several, including the Ohio Soldiers Colony, were from the Buckeye State and one from Pennsylvania. "If we can get one or more of them farewell to Democratic Supremacy in Montana," he told U.S. Marshal Wheeler.[15] Potts was also active in writing promotional literature. One of his letters of praise for the territory, originally appearing in the *Philadelphia Inquirer*, appeared in James R. Boyce, *Facts about Montana*; another piece, "Climate and Resources of Montana," was published in *The New Northwest*, a Northern Pacific pamphlet edited by William Darrah Kelley; and a contemporary noted early in 1872 that the governor was "getting up a book on Montana to be published in various languages by the N.P.R.R. Co."[16] Through emigration, Montana would prosper and become Republican: the railroad would be the instrument of this change.

In the fall and winter of 1872 Samuel Hauser and the Committee of One Hundred launched a campaign to persuade Potts to call a special legislative session to consider a subsidy for a north-south line. This was a major drive, for possible subsidies of $4 million were concerned, and it involved paid newspaper propagandists, numerous town meetings, "some misrepresentations, a few Greenbacks, & considerable bad whiskey."[17] The Fisks were in the middle of it, categorizing Potts along with the Deer Lodge faction, "bristling and swelling like horned toads in antagonism to the projected North and South railroad," and threatening to oust Potts unless he convened the legislature.[18] Wilbur F. Sanders, too, was working "out among the 'brethring' on the R.R. subject," and the issue was important in the ter-

14. Potts to Hayes (Virginia City, November 6, 1870), Hayes MSS.
15. Potts to Wheeler (Virginia City, February 27, 1871), Wheeler MSS; *Herald*, March 3, 1871.
16. *Philadelphia Inquirer*, April 22, 1872, in James R. Boyce, *Facts about Montana Territory and the Way to Get There* (Helena, 1872), 22–24; William Darrah Kelley, *The New Northwest* (Philadelphia, 1871?), 31–32; Granville Stuart to James Stuart (Deer Lodge, February 14, 1872), Stuart MSS.
17. Edward Stone to Potts (Missoula, December 23, 1872), Potts MSS.
18. *Herald*, November 15, 1872. In October, Potts wrote: "Van Fisk on a recent visit publicly announced that unless I called an Extra Session of the Legislature Helena would get a man who would." Potts to Seth Bullock (n.p., October 28, 1872), copy, Potts letterbook.

ritorial election of August, 1872, when the Democrats, led by Sam Hauser, defeated the Republican organization.[19]

Potts "positively declined" to call an extra session. ". . . while I am Governor," he vowed, "I shall resist it at every step—and think I can defeat it. . . . We have a Co. and territorial debt now sufficient to keep our noses to the grindstone."[20] The north-south advocates he labeled "selfish croakers." Subsidy he saw as "destructive of the interests of our people and unfriendly legislation to the N.P.R.R. Co."[21] When he heard that Sanders, Fisk, and Hauser—all spokesmen for a link with the Union Pacific—were seeking to have him removed in Washington, Potts sought to enlist the aid of Jay Cooke to "meet this Crusade against me with Counter influences: I want to remain in the Executive Chair of Montana until the N.P.R.R. is completed that I may be able to aid it and thereby aid the growth of the Territory. I regard the interest of your road and Montana identical and shall therefore exert myself to serve both."[22]

At the same time, Potts explored the legal avenues. He wrote the governor of Colorado to see what that territory had done by way of railroad subsidies and he solicited an opinion from the U.S. attorney general on the legality of issuance of bonds by a territory to underwrite a private railroad venture. This, replied Attorney General Williams, was "a matter of purely local concern, and involves nothing that affects the general government in any way."[23]

While the *Herald* ranted against the "Deer Lodge Ring," it also damned Delegate Clagett, who early in 1873 sought, without success, to get through Congress a "railroad squelcher"—a bill to forbid the territories to give or loan credit to railroad companies and to restrict towns and counties under stringent terms. Potts praised the Clagett bill and predicted that ultimately three-fourths of the population would endorse it.[24]

19. Wilbur F. Sanders to James A. Garfield (Helena, November 27, 1872), Garfield MSS; Granville Stuart to James Stuart (n.p., August 14, 1872), Stuart MSS.

20. Potts to Nettleton (Virginia City, October 1, 1872) copy, Potts letterbook.

21. Potts to Nettleton (n.p., October 1, November 6, 1872), *ibid.*

22. Potts to Cooke (n.p., November 23, 25, 1872), *ibid.*

23. Edward McCook to Potts (Denver, November 14, 1872); George H. Williams to Hamilton Fish (Washington, February 27, 1873), copy; Fish to Potts (Washington, March 1, 1873), all in GEC.

24. *Herald*, January 18, 30, 31, February 1, 13, 14, March 1, 8, 11, 1873. Counties or towns might give credit only if authorized by the legislature and by two-thirds of their own voters. Potts to Wheeler (Virginia City, March 5, 1873), Wheeler MSS.

"Limber Jim" Mills of the Deer Lodge *New North-West* was certain that the governor would stand firm. ". . . I know they will not get an Extra Session from Potts," he wrote Clagett late in 1872.[25] But the pressure began to intensify: the move for a legislative session and for a north-south subsidy seemed growing in popularity and even some of the Deer Lodge stalwarts defected. As early as November, Potts had privately begun to waver, admitting that he might have to convene a special session, "but I want to be able to meet and overwhelm them with arguments. . . ."[26] Finally, after Northern Pacific officers proposed speeding up construction if the Montana assembly would offer tax exemption benefits, the governor, on March 17, 1873, called a special session to meet on April 14. But his proclamation did not mention railroad subsidy; instead, it emphasized the need for laws to cut the high fees collected by public officials, to straighten out contradictory statutes, or to govern the control of the penitentiary, soon to be turned over to the territory.[27]

It was clear that Potts hoped to block the north-south backers in the assembly and realists like Charles Broadwater were not optimistic. The subsidy movement was doomed, he thought. "Twill be a failure." Even if carried through the legislature, key counties were opposed and would block it when it came to a vote. "Gallatin is bucking about as heavy as Deer Lodge," Broadwater informed Maginnis two weeks before the legislature was scheduled to meet.[28]

To the assembly, Potts emphasized that the Northern Pacific line would soon be completed into Montana, that the territory was already deeply in debt, and that there was no authority "vested in the law making power of the Territory to legalize the issue of Bonds" to private corporations.[29] His message, mumbled the *Herald*, merely "recovered from obscurity" and "shook out and aired . . . like second-hand garments rescued from the mould and mildew of an old clothes store" the arguments of "the Deer Lodge coterie," and it generated suspicion that the "Governor of the Northern Pacific," as one called

25. James H. Mills to Clagett (Deer Lodge, December 3, 1872), LT, Vol. XI.
26. Potts to Nettleton (n.p., November 6, 1872), copy, Potts letterbook.
27. Potts to Clagett (n.p., January 13, 1873); Potts to Nettleton (n.p., December 14, 1872); Potts to Cass (n.p., January 16, 1873), copies, all in Potts letterbook; Potts to Wheeler (Virginia City, March 13, 1873), Wheeler MSS; Proclamation for extra session (Virginia City, March 17, 1873), GEC.
28. Charles Broadwater to Martin Maginnis (Helena, April 1, 1873), Maginnis MSS.
29. Potts to legislature (April 14, 1873), in *Herald*, April 14, 1873; Potts to Wheeler (Virginia City, March 13, 1873), Wheeler MSS.

him, would veto any measure to aid the north and south road.[30] But
his position was not clear: one confidant of Sam Hauser thought that
the Deer Lodge and Missoula delegations were relying on Potts's veto
of such a bill. "If that is his position why in hell did he call the
legislature?"[31]

Sam Hauser was in Virginia City leading the north-south lobby,
and Judge Rice, vice president of the Northern Pacific, by chance
"dropped into" the capital "quite unheralded" on the first day of the
session.[32] The assembly ignored the Northern Pacific tax exemption
proposal, but gave close attention to a bill introduced by Wilbur F.
Sanders authorizing counties—with approval of a majority of their
voters—to float bonds for stock subscription to the north-south railroad up to the extent of 20 percent of their taxable property. Though
this was short of the $4 million sought by many, it meant that up to a
total of $2.3 million might be subscribed. And though at one point in
the bitter debate, the bill seemed lost, it was revived and passed by
both houses, with "joy unbounded in the hearts of all our citizens
save the score of sore heads" from Deer Lodge, according to the
Herald.[33]

But Potts "put his foot on it," as the Deer Lodge legislators urged
him to do, and handed down a ringing veto which questioned the
legality of the measure, the wisdom of accruing additional county
debt, and the inflated basis for issuing bonds. "The bill appears to
have been framed in the interest of the railroad corporations, rather
than that of the people," he insisted.[34] But he was overridden and
Bob Fisk and the people of Helena got the joyous news by telegram:
"Railroad bill has climbed the veto. The people of Montana have won
a victory over the Northern Pacific. Glory to God in the highest and
whoop em up on the north and south plenty."[35]

The *Herald* pilloried Potts unmercifully for his veto, but many

30. *Herald,* April 14, 22, 1873.
31. A. J. Simmons to Hauser (Helena, April 16, 1873), Hauser MSS.
32. *Herald,* April 21, 1873.
33. *Ibid.,* April 25, 28, May 1, 6, 1873; act of May 7, 1873, LM, Extra Session
(1873), 110–15. For the general history of the Utah and Northern, the north-
south endeavor, see Robert G. Athearn: *Union Pacific Country* (Chicago, 1971),
237–63, and "Railroad to a Far Off Country: The Utah & Northern," *Montana,*
XVIII (October, 1968), 3–23.
34. Potts to Council (May 7, 1873), *Council Journal,* Extra Session, (1873),
144–45, 146–47.
35. Seth Bullock to Robert Fisk (Virginia City, May 7, 1873), telegram, Fisk
MSS.

agreed and did "not think it a good bill for the Counties."[36] The struggle now shifted to that arena and county voters. "Local politics here are red hot," Martin Maginnis's former partner wrote him from Helena in June, 1873.[37] Sam Hauser, who had paid the editor of the *Montanian* $100 a month to boom the subsidy and who was rumored to have had a fund of $30,000 to distribute judiciously in the legislature, again took the lead.[38] But providence and the depression of 1873 intervened, halting all railroad construction, making county voters wary, and curbing the sale of bonds throughout the country. The crash, and especially the failure of the Northern Pacific, "greatly retards the growth of Montana," wrote Potts, "but I am here—and must make the best of it." But he did not despair: "Our only hope is in the building of the N.P.R.R. and I still have faith it will be built."[39]

The north-south subsidy came up again in the eighth legislature, which convened early in 1874 but was rejected. As Potts explained, "An effort has been made a few men with Sanders sandwitched between them to get the Legislature to issue bonds to some imaginary R.R. I have fought the scheme from its inception and have frustrated their plans—the most recent Legislature having killed their scheme."[40] And by mid-1874 it was clear that county action was not forthcoming. "The railroad bills, which engaged so much time, have already come to naught, and stand only as tomb-stones over buried hopes," lamented the *Herald*.[41]

But the Sanders-Fisk-Hauser coalition was persistent. Sanders hoped to get authorization for another special session from Washington, a move which Potts sought to forestall. Four-fifths of the population were opposed to an extra session, the Governor insisted. "Montana has had enough—too much—legislation such as it is. . . ."[42] Subsidy bills were introduced into Congress in 1875, and while Congress granted the right of way to railroads organized in the territories, the subsidy did not "stand a ghost of a show," according to Delegate Maginnis. But he believed that if too much attention were

36. *Herald*, May 14, 16, 17, 29, 1873; J. Rice to Charles Dahler (n.p.), letter-book II, Charles Dahler MSS, Bancroft Library.
37. Peter Ronan to Maginnis (Helena, July 30, 1873), Maginnis MSS.
38. *Ibid.*; George F. Cope to Hauser (Virginia City, September 1, 1873), Hauser MSS.
39. Potts to Hayes (Virginia City, June 9, July 3, 1874), Hayes MSS.
40. Potts to Garfield (Virginia City, February 17, 1874), Garfield MSS.
41. *Herald*, June 24, 1874.
42. Potts to Garfield (Virginia City, February 17, 1874), Garfield MSS.

focused on the question, Congress might prohibit all territorial subsidies. The best approach, counseled Maginnis, was to keep the issue
away from Washington and "make it right at the polls."[43]

Meanwhile, Hauser kept the issue alive in the territory with continued local meetings in 1875 and 1876; however, there seemed to be
some shift in favor of the Northern Pacific. A territorial convention
held in Helena expressed a preference for the N.P. route, though it
insisted that it kept an open mind. Helenans were unsuccessful in
obtaining a congressional land grant to build a line to the Union
Pacific, but Northern Pacific directors unofficially promised to build
into Montana if they received a subsidy.[44] Early in 1876, the Northern Pacific sent its chief engineer and its vice-president to present its
case to the public and to the legislature, asking the assembly to consider "a plan under which you can extend a helping hand to this great
enterprise, and put its wheels in motion *without* giving a subsidy
and without taxation, either for interest or principal." The proposal
was for the company to build at least two hundred miles into Montana, with the territory to issue two million dollars worth of 8 percent bonds maturing in twenty-five years, and the N.P. to pay the
interest out of gross receipts.[45]

After much acrid debate and over the opposition of Potts, who
stressed economy, the legislature offered the Northern Pacific a loan
through the issue of bonds of up to $3,000,000, pending approval by
the electorate. At the same time, it would sanction subsidization to
the tune of $1,150,000 of a north-south line to run from the Utah
Northern terminal at Franklin, Idaho, to a point on the Jefferson
River; and at the same time would permit county aid, voters approv-
ing, of $750,000 for a line linking Fort Benton and Helena.[46] Though
apprehensive, Potts signed the bills, probably because he still hoped
to ease the path of the Northern Pacific and would have found it
embarrassing to veto one but not the others.[47]

43. Maginnis to Hauser (Washington, January 8, 1875; March 25, 1876),
Hauser MSS; *Herald*, March 17, 1875; act of March 3, 1875, 18 *USSL*, (1873–
75), 482–83.

44. *Herald*, March 11, 20, April 22, 24, 1875; Maginnis to Hauser (Washington, January 8, 14, 1876), Hauser MSS; Cass to Potts (New York, March 25,
1875), GEC.

45. W. Milnor Roberts and George Stark to legislature (January 17, 1876),
Council Journal, 9 Session (1876), 72–76; *Herald*, January 21, 1876.

46. Potts to legislature (January 3, 1876), *House Journal*, 9 Session (1876),
40–41; acts of February 11, 1876, *LM*, 9 Session (1876), 128–36, 136–38, 139–
47; Stark to Potts (New York, March 9, 1876), Potts MSS.

47. The *Herald* charged that Potts signed the Northern Pacific aid bill on the

Two counties—Chouteau and Lewis and Clark—approved bond issues totalling $430,000 for construction of a narrow-gauge Fort Benton to Helena line. The Northern Pacific quickly accepted its subsidy proposal and settled back to wait for the verdict of the voters. But the Utah Northern, skeptical that the territory could support three different subsidy measures, viewed its own proposal without enthusiasm, its officers urging Hauser to "do all you can to defeat the adoption of the bonds for the Northern Pacific," and ultimately giving up.[48]

And Hauser worked diligently since the railroad subsidy issue was a warm campaign issue in the spring of 1876. Newspapers were full of the question. Budding poets waxed enthusiastic:

We want quick transit for our ores!
Quick transit for our bullion!
Quick transit for our farmer's yield!
Quick transit for the million

Hardy settlers who will rush into
Our broad and fertile vales,
To make their homes of comfort
In our mountain-sheltered dales.

And though we have but "Hobson's choice"
(Better than *none*, by far!)
On Monday choose, as Hobson chose,
And vote for the N.P.R.![49]

But Montanans were not so easily convinced. "When the election comes the People will make clogs of themselves and stop both roads," predicted one Helena advocate of free enterprise.[50] And the voters did reject the Northern Pacific subsidy, in part because Helena feared being bypassed.[51]

promise of appointment as auditor of the railroad's land department, but presented no real evidence. *Herald*, February 12, 1876.

48. Chouteau County approved a bond issue of $80,000; Lewis and Clark, $350,000. Act of February 16, 1877, *LM*, 10 Session (1877), 369–72; Potts to legislature (January 8, 1877), *Council Journal*, 10 Session (1877), 35; *Herald*, March 16, 1876; Maginnis to Hauser (Washington, March 25, 1876), S. or J. Richardson to Hauser (New York, March 11, 1876), both Hauser MSS; Samuel Wilkeson to Potts (New York, March 7, 1876), telegram, GEC; George Stark to Potts (New York, March 9, 1876), GEC.

49. "Old Subsidy" in *Herald*, March 30, 1876.

50. "I am looking every day for some one to come and buy me a railroad, set me up in business and so on." S. G. Gilpatrick to James Fergus (Helena, March 26, 1876), copy, Allis Stuart Collection.

51. Potts to Legislature (January 8, 1877), *Council Journal*, 10 Session (1877), 35; Stuart, *Forty Years on the Frontier*, II, 38.

However, thanks to Samuel Hauser and his cohorts, the railroad issue continued to hold a dominant place in local political thought.[52] After conferring with Union Pacific officials, Hauser formed a group to run the Utah Northern from Franklin to the mouth of the Big Hole, and Potts, still cautious but more cooperative, brought before the 1877 legislature a proposal from Jay Gould and associates who backed the Hauser enterprise.[53] Soon there were four subsidy bills in the legislature and the interest was great, though not the "fierce and un-reasoning enthusiasm" of previous years. In his lobbying, Hauser was accused of bribery by the Council sergeant at arms, but charges never went beyond the newspaper stage.[54] In the end, the assembly passed and Potts accepted a subsidy to the Utah and Northern of $1,700,000 in territorial bonds, subject to voter approval.[55]

At the same time, hoping to liquidate the interest and principal of territorial and county investments more quickly, the legislature asked the federal government for land grants along the routes of the Utah and Northern and the Helena and Fort Benton, but were ignored. Jay Gould and his cohorts rejected the bond proposal because of a pro-vision that provided monthly royalties to the territory from revenues of the entire line, with no expiration date.[56]

By 1879, Potts had business connections with Hauser and seemed more favorably inclined toward the Utah and Northern, though the issue in the legislature that year was of exemption of railroad prop-erty from taxation, rather than subsidy by bond. "The exemption question is meeting with bitter opposition & I doubt its success," Potts wrote in midsession. "Housel of Omaha is a poor manager & is the wrong man to work up a R.R. feeling." Wilbur F. Sanders, whom Potts called "a positive injury to Legislation," proposed a tax exemp-tion bill which packed the galleries and brought crowds outside the open windows to hear debates.[57] But the measure was defeated in the

52. See *Herald*, August 16, December 11, 1876; January 5, 15, 1877.
53. This asked a subsidy of $1,500,000 in 8 percent bonds, with construction to begin within sixty days of their deposit in New York and with at least a hundred miles to be built annually. Jay Gould et al. to legislature (New York, October 23, 1876); Potts to legislature (January 8, 1877), both in *Council Journal*, 10 Session (1877), 30–31, 61; *Herald*, January 18, 1877.
54. *Herald*, January 26, 1877; *New North-West*, March 2, 1877.
55. One and a half million dollars was for pushing the line to the Big Hole River; $200,000 would be for building on to Helena. Act of February 17, 1877, *LM*, 10 Session (1877), 380–81; *Herald*, February 13, 14, 1877.
56. Memorial to Congress (n.d.), *LM*, 10 Session (1877), 438–40; Gould et al. to Potts (New York, March 24, 1877), telegram, Hauser MSS.
57. Potts to Maginnis (Helena, February 5, 1879), Maginnis MSS; *Herald*, February 19, 20, 1879.

Council, some thought by the "devilish fraud" concealed within the bill itself, while others blamed the Council, "'certainly the thinnest body of the kind that ever got together in the Territory,'" which contained nine members "who subscribed to a written pledge to vote against any and all rail road measures."[58] Chief Justice Decius Wade could grumble about the achievements of lawmakers at this session who seemed to have little to do except block railroad bills: "The only measure of consequence to the territory (exemption of rail roads from taxation for 12 years) was, much to my regret, after having passed the House, defeated in the Council by a vote of 10 to 3, a record that some day those who made it will be ashamed of."[59]

Undaunted, Sam Hauser kept up his behind-the-scenes activity, now with the support of Governor Potts. In May, the two met with Union Pacific officials in Omaha, and Potts meditated about a possible special session of the legislature to again consider furtherance of a north-south line. Hauser, said a sarcastic Helena lawyer, was "working bravely" for an extra session and for "relief in some shape for the Utah & Northern—or more especially for his poor destitute friend Jay Gould." And Potts and Hauser had their heads together, as Hauser put it, "to make sure the Legislature will do what is right after they get together."[60]

With the approval of the president, Potts called the extra session for July, 1879, and urged it, among other matters, to consider a proposal from Sidney Dillon of the Union Pacific to build at least 130 miles of track in Montana in 1879–80 if the territory would exempt the Utah and Northern from all taxation for fifteen years.[61] A county bond subsidy was also introduced and assemblymen were subjected to royal treatment, including the offering of bribes. But both measures were lost, to the chagrin of their supporters.[62] A friend wrote

58. W. F. Chadwick to Maginnis (Helena, March 3, 1879); W. E. Cullen to Maginnis (Helena, February 23, 1879), both in Maginnis MSS.

59. Wade to Maginnis (Helena, February 21, 1879), *ibid*. See also Martin Barrett, "Holding Up a Territorial Legislature," *Contributions*, VIII (1917), 93; James Fergus to Andrew Fergus (Helena, July 11, 1879), copy, Allis Stuart Collection.

60. Potts to Hauser (Helena, May 8, 1879); Hauser to Sidney Dillon (Helena, June 7, 1879); both in Hauser MSS; Chadwick to Maginnis (Helena, June 17, 1879), Maginnis MSS.

61. *Herald*, June 23, 1879; proclamation (June 4, 1879), in TPI; Potts to legislature (July 1, 1879), *Council Journal*, Extra Session (1879), 13–15.

62. Lifetime passes were offered and one member was reportedly offered free shipment of a car load of livestock from Canada. Barrett, "Holding Up a Territorial Legislature," 93–96.

Hauser, ". . . in this day of 'Champions' of various kinds for champion jackasses commend me to the 'Majority' of the members of the Montana legislature."[63] Probably most Montanans, in the legislature and out, by this time felt that the railroad was on its way, subsidy or none, and they were undoubtedly right.

The Northern Pacific crossed into the territory in November, 1880, though completion was still several years away; the Utah and Northern would build into Butte in 1880, with a branch to Garrison the next year which would ultimately link with the Northern Pacific.[64] As these lines neared completion, a change of attitude came over the Montana legislature and its constituents. No longer were railroad companies benevolent corporations operating for the good of the territory; now they were vehicles of greed and corruption. The legislature's effort to repeal the 1876 laws which permitted the various counties to support the Helena and Fort Benton was blocked in 1881 by Governor Potts's veto, but two years later the thirteenth assembly accomplished that end.[65] Where Potts in 1879 had favored tax exemption for the Utah and Northern, by 1883 he now believed that "property of the railroad corporation should be made to share the burden of taxation the same as that of the individual citizen.[66] Control by a foreign corporation now seemed obnoxious and the remainder of the territorial period was filled with efforts to bring about the forfeiture of much federal land originally granted to the Northern Pacific.[67]

Where railroads were concerned, Potts displayed a certain amount of flexibility and complex motivation. Early in his governorship, he undoubtedly hoped to benefit personally from speculation in or employment by the Northern Pacific, and for economic as well as political reasons, he put his faith in this enterprise and for half a dozen years fought subsidies to opposing companies. Concerned with high county debts and working hard to eradicate the territorial deficit, he was never strong for any subsidy, yet would ultimately support aid for the north-south endeavor of Samuel Hauser. But the subsidy battle was never, strictly speaking, a party one; rather it was regional

63. D. C. Corbin to Hauser (New York, August 22, 1879), Hauser MSS.
64. Stuart, *Forty Years on the Frontier*, II, 38; *Herald*, November 11, 1880.
65. *Herald*, February 24, 1881; act of February 23, 1883, *LM*, 13 Session (1883), 137–38.
66. Potts to legislature (January 8, 1883), *Council Journal*, 13 Session (1883), 32.
67. See Chapter 11.

and a matter of special interest groups. Undoubtedly Potts's association with some of these railroad leaders would make it easier for his critics to condemn him for faithlessness to his own party and friendship with the Democrats. And the whole prolonged struggle helped create additional enemies.

Paralleling the subsidy controversy for part of the era was a bitter dispute over location of the capital, an issue which had been boiling steadily since the inception of territory but which now boiled over, scalding more than one federal official. And it was so tied to other disputes, including the Fisk-Sanders feud with Potts, that it is difficult to separate personal, political, regional, or other strands.

The organic act permitted the governor to select the seat of government for the first assembly and stipulated that thereafter the site was to be determined by the legislature, but once fixed in this fashion, no future change might be made without consent of the majority of the voters in the territory. Governor Edgerton chose Bannack as the first capital and the first legislature moved it to Virginia City.[68] But with new gold discoveries elsewhere, Virginia dwindled and other competitors, notably Helena and Deer Lodge became strong contenders. The third legislature in 1866 brought the question of a permanent capital before the electorate, giving a choice between Helena or Virginia City, and the results indicated that Madison County still retained enough voting power to block any move at that time. Efforts were no more effective to change the capital by congressional action, but each session of the territorial assembly saw renewed attempts and much secretive maneuvering by local partisans.[69] Governor Smith twice vetoed bills passed by the fourth assembly to throw the question into the hands of the voters again, but even then the hoary perennial would not die: early in 1869 the legislature provided for relocation of the capital at Helena, pending approval by the electorate in August of that year. The election was spirited but inconclusive: both Helena and Virginia City seemed to return more votes than their populations warranted. The returns were sent to the secretary at Virginia City but before they could be officially canvassed the office and all its contents burned and the seat of government remained at

68. Act of May 26, 1864, 13 *USSL*, 91; act of February 7, 1865, *LM*, 1 Session (1864–65), 432.

69. Act of December 14, 1866, *LM*, 3 Session (1866), 78–79; Burlingame, *Montana Frontier*, 170; *Congressional Globe*, 40 Congress, 1 Session (1867), 333, 429; William H. Edwards to Granville and James Stuart (Virginia City, November 28, 1867), Stuart MSS.

Virginia, though unofficially the ballots seemed to have favored Helena.[70]

Behind the scenes, the politicians kept busy. Sam Hauser was doing what he could on behalf of Helena, to the distress of Granville Stuart, who sat in the Council and kept free of political alignments which might interfere with the all-important capital question. "I am disgusted to think that Sam always will keep on spending money in trying to keep every thing at Helena when he knows how important for *us poor devils* it is for Deer Lodge to take the lead."[71] Early in 1872, Stuart could write his brother from the Council Chambers in Virginia: "That d—d drunken fool Smith of Lincoln Gulch has been bought by Helena, for he has just introduced a bill in the House to move the Capital to Helena, but they can't get it through the Council unless some of our Councilmen throw in & I don't think they will—if we can keep it from Helena we are sure of it either now or next session."[72] Two weeks later, Stuart was even more pleased. "By good management we got the bill locating the Capital here passed and it was done so cleverly as to leave everybody our friends & consequently we will carry it at the Election," he wrote.[73]

Governor Potts apparently took no strong position. He expressed a willingness to sign a bill either for Helena or for Deer Lodge, but he did not enjoy being pushed on the subject by Robert Fisk. "I don't profess to be courageous but I can't be driven or bluffed," he wrote a Lewis and Clark County legislator. "I care not for the ravings of an ass like Fisk but he assumes to speak for your people. . . ."[74] In August, when the question of removal to Deer Lodge was placed before the voters, Virginia City still retained the advantage by a substantial margin.[75]

Deer Lodge and Gallatin were now but mock pretenders: the real struggle was between Virginia and Helena and in 1874 it reached its

70. *House Journal*, 4 Session (1867), 84–88; *Montana Post*, November 30, December 7, 1867; act of January 2, 1869, *LM*, 5 Session (1868–69), 106; Barsness, *Gold Camp*, 131–32. According to Waldron the vote was Helena, 4,769; Virginia City, 4,677; and "other locations," 139. Waldron, *Montana Politics*, 22.

71. Granville Stuart to James Stuart (Virginia City, December 26, 1871), Stuart MSS.

72. Granville Stuart to James Stuart (Virginia City, January 4, 1872), *ibid.* H. D. Smith was a representative from Deer Lodge County.

73. Granville Stuart to James Stuart (Deer Lodge, January 24, 1872), *ibid.*

74. Potts to Bullock (n.p., October 27, 1872), copy, Potts letterbook.

75. Bancroft, *History of Washington, Idaho, and Montana*, 670. The count was Virginia City, 4,963; Deer Lodge, 3,228; and "other," 197. Waldron, *Montana Politics*, 28.

climax, when for the fourth time the legislature set the question before the electorate. Local partisans, like the fun-loving editor of the
Helena *Independent*, had their sport:

> Our Hugh McQuaid
> Has been waylaid,
> And we know not where to find him;
> But let him alone,
> And he'll come home
> With the Capital close behind him.[76]

An unidentified Councilman expressed disgust at the rumor that Potts
might veto the capital bill: ". . . the idea of the sentiments and best
interests of a young, intelligent, progressive and enterprising community being 'squelched' by such a *mush-head* is humiliating indeed."[77] But despite strong pressure, Potts signed the measure and
Hauser wrote a charitable word on Potts's behalf to the Fisks: "Helena
can afford to rejoice that we have a Governor who will do his duty,
even if he does get off wrong on railroads."[78] But the air crackled.
The *Montanian* charged that Helena had procured the capital bill at
the expense of the north-south railway; it was reported that James
Stuart had been offered $1,500 to oppose the measure; unhappy Vir-
ginians presented Walter Dance, who had supported the bill, with a
"tin-headed pine cane," as a token of their displeasure; and editors
flayed each other mercilessly.[79]

On August 3, 1874, voters went to the polls to mark ballots "Capital
law approved" (for Helena) or "Capital law disapproved" (for Virginia City). In order to forestall any overexuberance on the part of
champions on either side, a supplemental act imposed drastic penalties for illicit voting or for fraudulent or dishonest handling of returns by election officials; and it was stipulated that the votes of each

76. Quoted in *Herald*, February 9, 1874. McQuaid was the "junior" of the
Independent. The Virginia City *Madisonian* responded: (February 14, 1874):

> This same McQuaid
> That you have said
> Would bring the Capital with him,
> Is still in town,
> Scooting aroun',
> Being unable to tote the Capital on
> his back—and expects to leave it at
> a way-station, or at its present location.

77. Quoted in *Herald*, January 24, 1874.
78. Hauser to D. W. Fisk (Virginia City, February 11, 1874), quoted in
Herald, February 11, 1874.
79. *Herald*, February 10, 12, 16, July 29, 30, 1874.

county were to be counted by the commissioners, then sent to the territorial secretary, who, together with the United States marshal and in the presence of the governor, was to canvass and proclaim the results.[80]

In spite of—or perhaps because of—such precautions, a serious imbroglio ensued and the whole smacked of corruption. Unofficial tabulation of the returns indicated approval of the move to Helena and on August 8 residents there gave themselves a Saturday night victory "jollification," with bonfires, Chinese lanterns, fireworks, and a torch procession headed by the Helena Silver Coronet Band, all culminating in a grand rally in front of the St. Louis Hotel, presided over by Sam Hauser and addressed impromptu by Wilbur F. Sanders and Chief Justice Wade among others.[81]

But the celebration was premature. The vote of Gallatin County, heavily anti-Helena, was discounted as not being in the proper form. The unofficial tabulation of the Meagher County returns showed a vote of 561 to 29 in favor of Helena; but when the returns were brought officially before the canvassing board, the figures were transposed, giving 561 for Virginia, enough to retain the capital there. "A great crime has been committed," cried the *Herald*, "a bold piece of villany. . . . The time has come for action."[82] At a public indignation meeting at the Court House in Helena, words like "crime," "conspiracy," and "outrage" were used with abandon, and a committee of thirty-one was formed to raise funds and apprehend the culprits. Ultimately more than seven thousand dollars was raised by public subscription as a reward for the apprehension of those responsible.[83]

Meanwhile, the clerk and recorder of Meagher County proclaimed the returns forged. United States Marshal William Wheeler agreed and sought to postpone the official canvass in order to get a true, verified return. But after "much investigation, hard work, thought, perplexity—and doubt" and lying awake "most all night reasoning on the *cussed* subject,"[84] Secretary Callaway refused, arguing that by law the count must be completed within thirty days or the results

80. Acts of February 11, 12, 1874, *LM*, 8 Session (1874), 43–44, 61–62.

81. The affair broke up "only with the warning of the approaching Sabbath, when the people, their wives and children, with joy in their hearts, dispersed and repaired to their homes." *Herald*, August 10, 1874.

82. *Herald*, September 3, 4, 5, 1874.

83. *Ibid.*, September 7, December 31, 1874.

84. *Ibid.*, September 4, 10, 21, 1874; Callaway to Robert Fisk (Virginia City, September 26, 1874), Fisk family MSS.

were void. The canvassing board held a hearing before interested witnesses, but Callaway held firm, holding that the board's function ceased with its first canvass. Because of contradictory statements, it is not clear whether fraud was nor was not committed.[85]

Marshal Wheeler protested to the governor, made private inquiry on his own which indicated that the Meagher County returns were forged, and certified to Potts that Helena had carried the election by more than nine hundred votes. With Callaway refusing to concur, both Wheeler and Potts solicited a ruling from U.S. Attorney General Williams, who responded that Wheeler's unilateral re-canvass, made without the other board members, had no validity, but that the issue in general was one of "purely local concern, in which the general government is not interested. . . ."[86]

Though he maintained that he was a mere bystander, only a witness to the canvassing of the vote by the marshal and secretary, Governor Potts came under heavy fire from Helenans, especially the Fisks. He should have called a delay to investigate; he should have offered a reward for the culprits; he should have accepted Wheeler's canvass on behalf of Helena. Instead, "this gubernatorial specimen of imbecility," this "Disciple, Apologist, and Apostle of Fraud," turned out to be a "eunuch on the Canvassing Board. . . ."[87] On the other hand, Callaway received the same kind of treatment from other newspapers, especially Democratic, and described them to Bob Fisk at the height of the controversy: "The Deer Lodge paper is run by a low bred bully whose meanness is equalled only by his malice. The Independent is run by a set of fellows who should yet be wearing pinafores in a school of feeble minded children and the Missoula & Bozeman outfits possess all the meanness of the Deer Lodge prostitute and the feebleness of the Independent idiots."[88] No wonder Wilbur F. Sanders could write to James Garfield "We are having war in Mon-

---

85. *Herald*, September 4, 10, 1874. In a statement printed in the *Herald* on September 21, Callaway acknowledged that there had been fraud but argued that the courts were the proper vehicle to handle the matter. In a private and personal letter five days later, he doubted that the returns had been forged or tampered with, but if they were it was before they reached Virginia City. James E. Callaway to Fisk (Virginia City, September 26, 1874), Fisk family MSS.

86. Wheeler to George H. Williams (Helena, September 29, 1874), SCF, 1874–77; Williams to B. R. Cowan (Washington, October 8, 1874), copy, GEC; Cowan to Potts (Washington, October 9, 1874), GEC.

87. Potts to Schurz (Helena, June 7, 1877), Potts file, API; *Herald*, September 5, 29, October 3, 5, November 17, December 10, 1874.

88. Callaway to Fisk (Virginia City, September 26, 1874), Fisk family MSS.

tana at least a condition of feeling exists here not different from that feeling which civil war evolves. . . ."[89]

Meanwhile, the dispute was being handed over to the courts, an action in mandamus having been brought against the canvassing board. In mid-December, in a report Callaway called "infamous," a grand jury in Lewis and Clark County called the return "a glaring and palpable forgery in every particular." Since all the returns stood exposed on the shelves of the Virginia express office for more than two weeks, though Callaway had been informed of their arrival, evidence "creates a grave suspicion of complicity in the crime" and "exhibit a reckless and criminal disregard of his official responsibility and of the rights of the people, and prove him to be in sympathy with the fraud if not a party to it."[90]

Potts was absent when the Montana courts heard the case, though Sanders and others had sought to prevent his leaving the territory.[91] The basic question before the bench was whether the canvassing board, composed of the marshal and the secretary, had the power merely to count the returns and pass on the result to the governor for proclamation, or whether it also had the power to determine the correctness of the returns and compel the governor to proclaim the results on that basis. In written testimony Potts disclaimed any responsibility, arguing that the law requiring the three officers to canvass the election violated the organic act, which prohibited federal officials from holding any territorial position. The court, however, ruled otherwise, and emphatically supported the right of the legislature to require federal appointees to perform duties not specifically enumerated in the organic act. It then ordered a recanvassing on the basis of the true vote, with the governor instructed to proclaim the results accordingly.[92] The decision was subsequently appealed, with James A. Garfield handling the case for the territory, but the United States Supreme Court refused to hear it for want of jurisdiction.[93]

89. Sanders to Garfield (Helena, November 14, 1874), Garfield MSS.
90. Callaway to Fisk (Virginia City, December 21, 1874), Fisk family MSS; *Herald*, December 19, 1874.
91. A. J. Simmons et al. to Columbus Delano (Helena, November 30, 1874), Potts file, API.
92. William Chumasero et al. *v.* Potts et al., 2 *Montana Reports* (1875), 247, 256–57; *Herald*, January 11, 1875.
93. *Herald*, February 2, 1876; transcript of record (U.S. Supreme Court No. 545) and other papers are found in the Garfield MSS. See Law Cases, Vol. VI, Series 12, Garfield MSS.

Apparently with Potts still absent, Callaway conducted the re-canvassing and issued a proclamation transferring the capital to Helena, an action, he said, which "cooled many Virginians in their admiration of the *little Secretary*."[94] Helenans received the news with "great enthusiasm and rejoicing," and, according to Bancroft, thus "ended a long struggle, in which all the dishonest practices of unscrupulous politicians were exhausted to defeat the choice of the people."[95]

True, the capital location was for all practical purposes settled,[96] but the controversy merely set the stage for the next act, in which differences between Potts and Callaway over moving the capital, and probably the printing and the railroad subsidy questions, were exacerbated to the point where Potts would seek Callaway's removal, and the latter's defenders, taking the initiative, would in turn attempt to block the governor's reappointment. And in the process, the long-standing feud between Potts and the Fisk-Sanders faction would be brought to a head.

Callaway came up for reappointment early in 1875. He wrote President Grant late in 1874 that having located in Virginia City "with my wife and little ones," he felt like a permanent resident. He had, he said, "invested my money here and such investment has proven unprofitable, in the present gloomy and depressed condition of affairs in the territory, I feel greatly the need of the salary of said office, and a second term is very desirable."[97] But the capital dispute brought forth an anti-Callaway opposition, which circulated petitions charging him with neglect of duty, overcharging for his services,

94. Callaway to Fisk (Virginia City, January 19, 1875), Fisk family MSS.

95. *Herald*, January 14, 1875; Bancroft, *History of Washington, Idaho, and Montana*, 670.

96. Occasionally thereafter a legislator would make a futile effort to promote change, as did Lee Mantle in 1883, when he served notice of a bill to move the capital to Butte or Bozeman. "To B or not to B; that is the question," quipped one editor. *New North-West*, March 2, 1883. And in the 1889 constitutional convention, with every whistle-stop vying for the honor, two full days of exasperating debate on this subject left members with frayed nerves and upset stomachs. A typical voice from Gallatin County was heard to plead: "Let it remain in Helena if you like. Name Missoula; name Anaconda; name Wilder's Landing or any other place, but for Heaven's sake name something. . . ." Perhaps, as had been suggested on several occasions, only a perambulating capital on wheels could please everyone! *Proceedings and Debates of the Constitutional Convention Held in the City of Helena, Montana, July 4th, 1889, August 17, 1889* (Helena, 1921), 769; *Herald*, March 6, 1874.

97. Callaway to Ulysses S. Grant (Virginia City, December 29, 1874), Callaway file, API.

and refusing "to certify to known facts" in the fraudulent election returns "for pretended technical reasons."[98] Maginnis passed these petitions along to the president, and to Senator Boreman, noting that they represented a majority sentiment of the territory, and he also enclosed a copy of the grand jury report charging Callaway with possible complicity in the forged returns.[99]

Callaway fought like a tiger in his own defense. In a "strictly confidential" letter to Robert Fisk, he saw Maginnis as the arch villain, to be fought to the finish: "The weapons Maginnis is using against me (and he is doing me *dirt*) are that lying grand jury report, my letter on fees and Petitions sent him asking my removal. I am now going to beat the *dirty scrub* if it leaves me a pauper."[100] He urged Fisk to use his influence with those friendly with Maginnis "to call off 'the *dogs of war*'" and he mounted a counter-offensive of petitions and letters.[101] To the president, he explained that opposition stemmed from "embittered local prejudices," growing out of the capital election, "a state of affairs, we were wholly irresponsible for, were powerless to control and a fatality we could not foretell." He went on to explain: "Every man and especially every United States official, must bear the load of suspicion and envy, of the rival locality in which he does not happen to reside. . . . It is the settled policy of many residents of the *most prominent locality* in the Territory, that if they can not run a Federal officer while *in* office they will endeavor to run him *out*."[102] His friends, notably Bob Fisk, also wrote President Grant, emphasizing that Callaway had complied with the law on the capital question and that public favor had now swung in his favor. Potts, too, supported him, noting that most opposition was being withdrawn. Callaway, he said, was "a good officer," "a brave soldier." "I will vouch for his good conduct as an officer," Potts wrote.[103]

In the end, Callaway was reappointed, to the distress of Helenans

98. See undated petitions, marked "Received, December 22, 1874," in *ibid.*
99. Maginnis to Grant (Washington, January 5, 1875), *ibid.*; Maginnis to A. J. Boreman (Washington, January 20, 1875), Callaway file, Papers of the U.S. Senate re Nominations, 43B–A5, National Archives.
100. Callaway to Fisk (Virginia City, February 8, 1875), Fisk family MSS.
101. Callaway to Fisk (Virginia City, January 19, February 5, 1875), *ibid.*
102. Callaway to Grant (Virginia City, December 29, 1874), Callaway file, API.
103. Fisk to Grant (Helena, January 27, 1875), telegram, SCF, 1874–77; Potts to Boreman (Washington, January 25, 1875; Crestline, Ohio, February 5, 1875), Callaway file, Papers of the U.S. Senate re Nominations, 43B–A5. For other expressions of support, see Hiram Knowles to Delano (Virginia City, January 16, 1875), Callaway file, API; Garfield to Francis Servis (n.p., January 13, 1875), copy, letterbook 17, Garfield MSS.

like W. E. Cullen who called the renomination "a terrible bitter blow for the people of the Territory." "I hope you may be able to prevent his confirmation by the Senate," he told Maginnis.[104] But Maginnis could not or would not.

Meanwhile, Callaway made arrangements for moving the capital to Helena, and the *Madisonian* described the transfer in the fall of 1875: "Yesterday. . . to the jingle of a string of bells on a mule team the last remains and remnants of the moving Capital of Montana Territory passed down Wallace Street on a couple of Murphy freight wagons. It was an indifferent lot of old second-hand chairs, tables and three-legged stools, and might, if exposed at public auction, find a purchaser in some poor devil about to commit premature matrimony. Not another soul in the wide world would dream of buying it."[105]

But Callaway was reluctant to move his residence from Virginia City and at one point even attempted to return the official records of his office to that place. By the end of 1875, Potts was beginning to have second thoughts. "I confess *now* that I fear that I made a mistake last winter in assisting Callaway," he confided to Maginnis. "He has no gratitude & is under the control of scoundrels wherever he goes. I may be compelled to ask his removal."[106] A few months later, irked at the rumor that Callaway wanted the governorship, Potts had made his decision. "I just received proof of his complicity in the capital fraud," he said. "I am going to 'burn him up' as they say in Montana." To this end, he solicited Maginnis's support and promised: "I will not remain in this office if the President does not remove Callaway."[107]

In 1873, Potts and Callaway had differed over the railroad subsidy question. Callaway opposed Potts's veto and could "heartily applaud" the legislature in overriding it, but he also resisted Bob Fisk's efforts to bring an open clash between him and the governor.[108] But the fuel

104. W. E. Cullen to Maginnis (Helena, February 24, 1875), Maginnis MSS.

105. *Madisonian*, October 9, 1875. See also issue for September 4, 1875; *Herald*, March 15, August 30, 1875.

106. Potts to Maginnis (Helena, February 6, 1876). See also Potts to Maginnis (Helena, December 29, 1875), both in Maginnis MSS.

107. Potts to Maginnis (Helena, February 6, 24, 1876), *ibid.*

108. Callaway wrote Fisk: "I shall stand by my guns and marshal under the banner of the Railroad party. The Governor can train with any crowd or faction to his taste, and as long as he observes the rules of civilized warfare, I shall not fall out with him. . . . If he opens his batteries on me surely he will hear my guns and he will certainly see the *black flag* floating uncomfortably near his headquarters." Callaway to Fisk (Virginia City, May 30, 1873), "confidential," Fisk family MSS.

of the capital controversy and of Callaway's handling of printing contracts brought the smouldering feud into open flame, and Potts began
a campaign to oust the secretary.

In mid-1876, he lamented to Rutherford B. Hayes, the Republican
nominee for President, that his secretary was "a drunken little scrub
& I can't well leave the Territory."[109] After the election, he indicated
to an aide of Hayes that he would come east for the inauguration
were it not for Callaway, "a low drunken fellow who would sell out
the whole territory if he was left to discharge the duty of Governor."[110] To Hayes's friends and to the new president directly, Potts
urged Callaway's removal, "as a personal favor," and replacement by
James H. Mills, an Ohio soldier and "a good square man."[111] The
governor also carried his campaign to other important Washington
officials—to Secretary of State William Evarts, Secretary of the Interior Carl Schurz, Secretary of the Treasury John Sherman, and
Postmaster General W. A. Knapp, dwelling at length on Callaway's
nonresidence in the capital, his intoxication and "drunken street
fights," and "his consequent association with the worst element that
can be found about one of our Western towns"—and in this category
Potts included the Fisks. Potts said Callaway sadly neglected the
duties of his office, which he made "the home for three or four loafers
who have no visible means of support," and there was question of
his honesty. Potts had challenged Callaway's claim to exclusive cus-
todianship of the territorial seal and his right to collect a three-dollar
fee each time he used the seal, and when the secretary locked the seal
in his safe, Potts had a duplicate made, an action which brought
charges of "counterfeiting" from Robert Fisk and a grand jury as
well as legislative investigation.[112] "The fellow is getting lower every
day if such a thing could be," Potts complained when matters had
reached the point where he and Callaway were no longer speaking.[113]

109. Potts to Hayes (Helena, July 5, 1876), Hayes MSS.

110. Potts to N. E. Lee (Helena, February 10, 1877), *ibid.*

111. Potts to W. A. Knapp (Helena, February 22, 1877), James H. Mills file,
API; Potts to Hayes (Helena, March 6, 1877), Potts file, API.

112. Potts to William Evarts (Helena, March 20, 1877); Potts to Carl Schurz
(Helena, March 22, 1877), both in Callaway file, API; Potts to John Sherman
(Helena, March 30, 1877); Potts to W. A. Knapp (Helena, March 9, 1877), both
in James H. Mills file, API. For the bitter dispute over the duplicate seal, see:
Potts to Hayes (Helena, April 24, 1877); Sanders to Schurz (Helena, April 27
[?], 1877); J. C. Robinson to Schurz (Deer Lodge, April 27, 1877), all in Potts
file, API; Zachariah Chandler to Potts (Washington, April 12, 1876), GEC; Potts
to Maginnis (Helena, February 23, 1876), Maginnis MSS; *Council Journal*, 10
Session (1877), 161–62, 181; *Herald*, February 5, 8, 1877.

113. Potts to Maginnis (Helena, March 30, 1877), Maginnis MSS.

Behind him, Callaway had the support of Robert Fisk and W. F. Sanders. Early in April, 1877, it seemed as if Potts had won, for news dispatches announced the appointment of Mills to the secretarial post. But Robert Fisk arrived in Washington about that time, Callaway's resignation in his pocket to be used at his discretion, and he succeeded in getting Mills's name withdrawn pending clarification of charges against Callaway.[114] By this time, the struggle had broadened: Potts was seeking Callaway's head, and supporters of the latter now sought to remove Potts or to prevent his reappointment in 1878, when his term expired.

When seeking his second term in 1874, Potts had claimed support of "the great mass of both parties" in the territory, with a few exceptions. "Some decapitated Indian Agents, and the Greely men like Sanders will oppose me because I adhere too strongly to the party & because they can't use me officially," he said, with the added note: "I am like the South was in 1861, 'I want to be let alone. . . .' "[115] But despite efforts of Sanders and the "'Fisk clique" to prevent it, Potts was reappointed in 1874 without difficulty and continued on, even though his enemies tried again in 1876 to get rid of him.[116]

Potts had made it clear early in 1877 that despite its disadvantages, the governorship was desirable to him. "The reduction in the salary does not make it a desirable office for a man to hold but I have been pressing many measures of economy with a good degree of success and desire to remain until I can consumate them," he explained.[117] "I have at least 4/5 of the entire people for me and none against me but Ashley's old 'Ring' that could not use me & hence have abused me," he wrote John Sherman. "The list is a short one—to wit W. F. Sanders, R. E. Fisk, J. A. Viall, J. E. Callaway—& a few of their hangers-on."[118] The governor noted that "one of the Fisk's has gone to Washington to make a fight against me," but with solid backing in

114. Callaway gave Fisk his resignation and authority to present it to the president anytime after April 5 (in order to collect his salary for the current quarter) and only after Fisk was *"first absolutely certain* that you would be appointed in my stead." Callaway to Fisk (Helena, March 6, 1877), Fisk family MSS. See also: *Herald*, April 6, 16, 1877; Potts to Maginnis (Helena, April 6, 1877), Maginnis MSS; Maginnis to Hayes (Washington, April 4, 1877); Callaway to Fisk (Virginia City, April 6, 1877), telegram, both in Callaway file, API.
115. Potts to Garfield (Virginia City, April 20, 1874), Garfield MSS.
116. Sanders et al. to Delano (Helena, June 4, 1874), Potts file, API; Potts to Maginnis (Helena, May 17, 1876), Maginnis MSS; Potts to Garfield (Helena, May 17, 1876), Garfield MSS.
117. Potts to W. Dennison (Helena, March 14, 1877), Potts file, API.
118. Potts to John Sherman (Helena, February 28, 1877), *ibid.*

Montana, he was unafraid of anything this group of "corrupt political adventurers" might be able to accomplish.[119]

Soon Potts realized that he had a fight on his hands. Callaway
itemized a list of grievances against him and Robert Fisk brought
these charges to Secretary of the Interior Carl Schurz, as an all-out
effort got under way to save the territorial secretary and oust the
governor. This official attack on Potts was built around several points.
"By his arrogant manners, petty malices, disreputable associations
and persistent interferences in other peoples' business," he had lost
the respect of his people and especially "the great body of the Republican party." He had forged the territorial seal and with it had
illegally sealed more than $90,000 worth of territorial bonds in the
refunding of the debt. He had, it was charged, given his influence to
secure lucrative mail contracts for C. C. Huntley and Company, and
had received in exchange furniture and a horse and buggy. He had
"coarsely and profanely abused" and interfered with the judiciary,
threatening that when Hayes took office he would have all three
judges removed. His office was headquarters of the "Indian Ring";
he had misused territorial funds in hiring Garfield as attorney in
appeal of the capital case; and had by "malicious and tyrannical acts"
defrauded private citizens. Worse yet, according to his detractors,
Potts had split the party, by "his clanishness and petty scheming."
Most of his friends were Democrats, and was "so fully identified
with the Democratic party," that he had adopted a Democratic newspaper as "his official and personal organ."[120]

With the "gallant 'Capting Bob,'" as the *Independent* called Fisk,
in Washington with "blood in his eye," longing "to sever the gubernatorial head from the shoulders where it had so long been a prov-
ocation and an offense to him," Potts's political enemies stepped up
their fire, amplifying their charges against the governor, and labeling
his accusations against Callaway "manifestly and conspicuously untrue"—the rantings of a "thoroughly malicious and vindictive man"
who was a natural obstructionist and breeder of discord.[121] Potts

119. Potts to Hayes (Helena, March 6, 1877), *ibid.*; Potts to Knapp (Helena,
March 9, 1877), Mills file, API.
    120. Callaway to Schurz (n.p., n.d., stamped "Received," April 4, 1877);
Potts file, API; Fisk to Schurz (Washington, April 9, 1877), Callaway file, API;
New York Times, April 7, 23, 1877.
    121. *Weekly Independent*, May 10, 24, 1877; Alexander H. Beattie et al. to
Hayes (n.p., n.d., stamped "received April 23, 1877"); Potts file, API; Fisk to
Hayes (Washington, April 6, 1877); Fisk to Schurz (Washington, April 9,
1877), both in Callaway file, API.

believed that even Chief Justice Wade was a party in the movement to oust him, and certainly Hiram Knowles, an old enemy, and still a member of the bench, joined Fisk and Sanders. Sanders wrote Knowles that his object was "in seeing this arrogant piece of executive stupidity humiliated. . . ." "All his lickspittles are searching the country for names," said Sanders, while the anti-Potts faction was willing to let the record speak for itself. He admitted "Bob F is of course a damage to some but he has made this a good fight—and I enjoin caution & prudence on him daily." And Potts would know he had been in a fight. "He may not learn decent deference," Sanders said, "but the comb is badly cut & he will hereafter conceal his arrogance."[122]

Although such questions as printing patronage, railroad subsidies, personal animosities, and the capital dispute were all important ingredients, both in motives and in arguments, the struggle was basically political. Writing to Washington as chairman of the Territorial Republican Committee, Fisk blamed Potts for the factionalism that permeated the party in the territory and argued the retention of Callaway to "spare the Republicans of Montana the visitation of additional calamities."[123] Fisk joined with Sanders, Callaway, and a number of other Republicans in a round-robin letter which pointed out to the president that Potts had "abandoned substantial interest in or identification with our party, and has identified himself with the Democratic element." Not only had he warred against Republicans and their newspapers, he was to blame for Madison County going Democratic, while Lewis and Clark County "acknowledges his presence by decreasing Republican majorities. . . ." "A betrayal of political and official integrity so bold has heretofore not been our experience." Party harmony and good government dictated Potts's removal, argued Fisk; though behind the scenes, Callaway and perhaps even the editor himself, considered Fisk the logical successor to the executive chair.[124]

That Potts drew support from both parties was quickly evident when his defense machine rolled into gear. Along with support from Republicans like Richard Hickman, Potts had the endorsement of

122. Potts to Garfield (Helena, June 14, 1877), Garfield MSS; Sanders to Knowles (Helena, May 2, 1877), Hiram Knowles MSS, MHS.
123. Fisk to W. K. Rogers (Washington, April 7, 1877), Callaway file, API.
124. Alexander H. Beattie et al. to Hayes (n.p., n.d., stamped "received, April 23, 1877"), Potts file, API; Fisk to Hayes (Washington, April 23, 1877); Callaway to Fisk (Virginia City, April 6, 1877), telegram, both in Callaway file, API.

Democrats Samuel Word and William A. Clark. Perry McAdow, also a Democrat, thought him fair, impartial, and responsible; Word labeled him the best governor Montana had ever had.[125] Others, Republicans such as John Potter of the Gallatin County Republican Committee and Surveyor General Andrew J. Smith, denied that Fisk had the right to speak for Montana Republicans. His position as chairman of the Territorial Republican Committee came "by default" and "by sheer accident," and he "no more reflects the true feelings of the Republicans of the Territory than does Wendell Philipps or Benjamin Wade those of Massachusetts and Ohio—concerning your excellent policy toward the South," President Hayes was told.[126]

Both Potts and his advocates pointed out the long history of the feud with Fisk and Sanders, and labeled Fisk with the tarbrush of invective, calling him "thoroughly unscrupulous"; Sanders was even worse, he was represented to Hayes as "a rampant Blaine man."[127] Potts, a pillar in the church, enlisted the support of the Methodist ministers in Montana, who took pride that the governor "holds himself aloof from the bar-rooms and gambling saloons . . . and arrays himself upon the side of morality, temperance, and truth. . . ."[128] Potts now claimed the support of "at least 49/50 of the people," and his "lickspittles," as Sanders had called them, collected from 3,000 to 4,000 signatures on petitions urging his retention.[129]

To offset Callaway's sworn deposition that Potts had taken gifts in exchange for his aid in gaining mail contracts for C. C. Huntley and Company, Delegate Maginnis forwarded to the president the report of the grand jury, together with statements from its foreman and clerk, and a letter from Chief Justice Wade, completely exonerating Potts on these charges. This must have been especially damaging because Fisk, Sanders and Callaway had all appeared as witnesses before the grand jury, where they had been forced to admit that

125. Richard O. Hickman to Hayes (Virginia City, March 14, 1877); Samuel Word to Hayes (Virginia City, March 14, 1877); Potts to Dennison (Helena, March 22, 1877), all in Potts file, API; Perry McAdow to Maginnis (Bozeman, March 14, 1877), Maginnis MSS.

126. John Potter to Hayes (Hamilton, May 4, 1877); Andrew J. Smith to Charles Devens (Helena, April 11, 1877), both in Potts file, API.

127. Potts to Hayes (Helena, April 24, 1877); Smith to Devens (Helena, April 11, 1877), both in *ibid.*

128. W. W. Van Arsdell et al. to B. Peyton Brown (Helena, May 3, 1877), *ibid.*

129. Potts to Knapp (Helena, April 28, 1877); Potts to Dennison (Helena, April 27, 1877), both in *ibid.*; W. E. Cullen certification of signatures against Callaway, with endorsement (Helena April 28, 1877), Callaway file, API.

they had no personal knowledge of the matter.[130] A legislator, a Democrat, explained the "bogus" territorial seal dispute in the governor's favor, and Potts, labeling the charges against him as "maliciously false" and arguing that he could "sustain every charge" against Callaway, "and others of great turpitude," defended himself at length to the White House, maintaining that he wanted his name cleared so that he might retire with honor at the end of his term.[131]

He rebutted the accusations against him point by point, paying special attention to those with political implications. He ran through intricacies of the territorial seal squabble, dismissed the mail-contract bribe charge as nonsense, condemned Callaway for absenteeism and partiality in awarding printing contracts, and denied he had ever sought to interfere with the judges or the prosecution of their cases. If he had sought to oust Justice Knowles in 1874 on charges of drunkenness, it was Sanders who provided the information and instituted the move, he insisted. He had paid Garfield's attorney's fees out of his own pocket, and he was a mere bystander in the capital fraud case. As an added fillip, he denounced Sanders for using the title "Colonel," when he had never held rank above first lieutnant and that only nine months.[132]

But it was the political climate on which he dwelled most lovingly, beginning with the situation when he arrived, when two warring Republican factions, one headed by Fisk and one by Sanders, strove for supremacy. By refusing to support either, or to remove several postmasters, he had alienated both, but most of all Fisk. "Almost every measure that I have advocated, no matter how heartily the people approved it, nor how necessary the adoption of it was for the welfare of the people, this man has opposed it, with an insane malignity, that would disgrace the lowest journalism," he told the president. Despite such opposition, the legislature had adopted far more of his recommendations than was expected. If he had not contributed campaign funds for E. D. Leavitt's delegateship race in 1876, it was because Leavitt did not campaign and Potts had "paid all I felt able

130. See Callaway depostion (April 18, 1877); Report of the Grand Jury (n.d.; W. M. Jack and Benjamin Ezekial to Hayes (Helena, April 7, 1877), telegram; D. S. Wade to Potts (Helena, April 7, 1877); Maginnis to Hayes (Washington, April 28, 1877), all in Potts file, API.

131. J. C. Robinson to Schurz (Deer Lodge, April 27, 1877); Potts to Hayes (Helena, April 30, 1877); Potts to Hayes (Helena, April 6, 1877), telegram; Potts to Sherman (Helena, April 6, 1877), telegram, *ibid.*

132. Potts to Dennison (Helena, April 27, 1877); Potts to Knapp (Helena, April 28, 1877); Potts to Hayes (Helena, April 24, 30, 1877); Potts to Schurz (Helena, June 7, 1877), all *ibid.*

to pay" to the National Republican Committee in September of that year. Except for a few, his territorial appointments had been Republican; he had consistently supported party nominees who were not dishonest or incompetent; and he had contributed five times as much money to party expenses as Callaway and Fisk had. But basically, contended Potts, "I have endeavored to be the Governor of the whole people." "I have refrained from taking an active part in politics," he said, pledging however to do his best to carry out the president's policy, "even at the risk of incurring the enmity of the clique of political tricksters that have followed me for the last six years."[133]

Then, having alerted his friends in the nation's capital, Potts wired the president early in May that he was leaving for Washington.[134] In that city, Robert Fisk had wangled several interviews with President Hayes and at one, in April, had tendered Callaway's formal resignation, assuming that the secretary would be vindicated. But after another meeting with Hayes, Fisk was surprised to learn otherwise and quickly withdrew the resignation while charges were pending.[135] Potts's coming to Washington would prolong his stay, he wrote his wife, but he could not "for a moment think that the President will consent to take the responsibility of holding him in place."[136] But ten days later, when he learned that the accusations against Potts had been dismissed, Fisk saw Callaway's removal as "the necessary sequel" to the governor's vindication and promptly resubmitted the secretary's resignation.[137]

Potts had been exonerated. As Delegate Maginnis put it, "The Governor walked over the course in Washington. The President took him to his bosom and sent him home happy."[138] But the malcontents

133. Potts to Hayes (Helena, April 24, 1877); Potts to Schurz (Helena, August 24, 1877), *ibid.*

134. Potts to Garfield (Helena, April 22, 1877, April 30, 1877), Garfield MSS; Potts to Hayes (Helena, May 3, 1877), telegram, Hayes MSS.

135. Fisk to Hayes (Washington, April 24, May 8, 1877) Callaway file, API. For Fisk-Sanders correspondence to officials on the matter see: Fisk to Hayes (Washington, April 6, 9, May 17, 18); Fisk to Schurz (Washington, April 9, 1877), all in *ibid*; Sanders to Schurz (Helena, May 5, 1877), Potts file, API.

136. Robert Fisk to Elizabeth Fisk (Washington, May 8, 1877, Fisk family MSS.

137. Fisk to Hayes (Washington, May 18, 1877), Callaway file, API; *New York Times*, May 20, 1877. Callaway's resignation gave no indication of the upheaval in Montana. His reason was simple: "The salary allowed the Secretary is inadequate for the services required to be performed." Callaway to Hayes (Helena, March 5, 1877), Callaway file, API.

138. Maginnis to Hauser (Redwing, Minnesota, June 5, 1877), Hauser MSS.

in Montana were "still grumbling" and the Fisk's *Herald* announced
sarcastically,

> And where the mighty Sultan rules
> The greatest of despots,
> We'll send to "skin" his army mules,
> Our "vindicated" Potts.

Whereupon the *Independent* responded in kind,

> Montana could not her Governor spare,
> She cannot take such risks;
> But for all her people care
> The Sultan can take the Fisks.[139]

Thus ended what one historian calls "Montana's greatest political
upheaval of the territorial period,"[140] a controversy stemming not
from deep-rooted grievances or political ideologies, but from the
pettiness of men and local political strife. Nor was it a battle drawn
along party lines. Many Democrats supported Potts against the extremists of his own party and many others undoubtedly chuckled
with glee to see the Republicans fighting among themselves.

But vestiges of controversy lived on. Callaway's successor as secretary was James H. Mills, editor of the Deer Lodge *New North-West*
and a veteran of twenty-seven engagements of the Army of the Po-
tomac.[141] Though commissioned in June, 1877, Mills was still not in
control of his office three months later. "Callaway by absence and
evasion delays transfer of Secretary's office and government property," he complained to his superiors in Washington.[142] But once in
possession of the office, Secretary Mills continued to live in Deer
Lodge, although the physical facilities were now in Helena. Several
times Potts wrote to President Hayes, through his private secretary,
lauding Mills and indicating that unless Deer Lodge was acceptable
as a residence, the new secretary would resign.[143] Apparently Hayes

139. Potts to Hayes (Helena, July 2, 1877), Hayes MSS; *Weekly Independent*,
May 31, 1877.
140. W. Turrentine Jackson, "Territorial Papers in the Department of the
Interior Archives, 1873–1890—Washington, Idaho, and Montana," *Pacific North-
west Quarterly*, XXXV (October, 1944), 338.
141. *Progressive Men of the State of Montana*, 317–18; Potts to W. K. Rogers
(Helena, December 18, 1877), Mills file, API.
142. Mills to R. W. Taylor (Helena, September 17, 1877), telegram; Mills to
Schurz (Helena, September 22, 1877), telegram, both in Callaway file, API.
143. Potts to W. K. Rogers (Helena, October 18, 1877), Mills file, API;
Potts to W. K. Rogers (Helena, November 14, 1877), Hayes MSS.

did not respond, but later in the year Mills began to come under fire for nonresidence, although Potts asserted that he "had put the office in the most orderly condition it has ever been & no person has been inconvenienced by Mills' absence."[144]

Ironically, in 1874 Potts had denounced Mills, the recipient of federal largess in the form of printing patronage who "now for nearly a year . . . has been throwing mud at the Administration." "Mills is run by Hiram Knowles," insisted Potts at that point.[145] In 1877, he admitted having had differences with Mills, but believed him an "honest man" who "will make a most acceptable officer."[146] And in late 1877 and early 1878, Potts would be defending Mills for his residence in absentia, though only shortly before he had condemned Callaway for the same shortcoming.

Mills argued that Deer Lodge was but forty-three miles from Helena, with telegraph and daily mail coaches. Leaving the office in charge of a "business associate," he was in daily communications and made frequent trips himself. The income of his newspaper and ranch was necessary, Mills contended, "on account of the inadequacy of the Salary of the cost of maintaining my family," and in December, 1877, he sent the administration his resignation, to be accepted if residence in Helena was required.[147]

But this was unnecessary. Potts used his influence on his secretary's behalf, pointing out that the complaint "no doubt comes from R. E. Fisk or W. F. Sanders, the bitter opponents of the President & his administration."[148] Late in 1878, Fisk reopened the question both in the columns of the *Herald* and in correspondence to Washington. Except for rare intervals, Mills "has become an alien to his office," having made three brief visits to the Capital in six months—no more," while the actual work was "jobbed out to cheap understrappers. . . . Brother Mills, come home, The clock in the steeple strikes one." Obviously, Fisk suggested, this was "a virtual abandonment of his office," and "a Secretary should be appointed who will reside where the

144. Potts to Maginnis (Helena, December 16, 1877), Maginnis MSS.
145. Potts to G. H. Williams (Virginia City, October 24, 1874), SCF, Box 517.
146. Potts to Hayes (Helena, April 30, 1877), Potts file, API. Fisk also was quick to seize upon the earlier differences. Fisk to Hayes (Washington, April 18, 1877), *ibid.*; *Herald*, June 8, 1877.
147. Mills to Schurz (Helena, December 17, 1877); Mills to Hayes (Helena, December 17, 1877), both in Mills file, API.
148. Potts to Schurz (Helena, December 17, 1877), copy, TPI; Potts to W. K. Rogers (Helena, December 18, 1877), Mills file, API.

office is located and give to its duties his personal attention."[149] But Potts assured his superiors that Mills was doing a superb job and that his critics were men "totally without character for truth" who had urged the retention of Callaway, who resided 140 miles from the capital and 25 miles from a post office, and who came in once in four months, leaving his office in charge of a drunken incompetent.[150] Mills was retained until his commission expired and was not an applicant for reappointment in 1882.[151]

The fight for survival had left Potts tired and discouraged and in October, 1877, he confided to his friends that he contemplated giving up political office and concentrating on the sheep business. "My enemies here keep up the fight against me but I will soon let them out by retiring to private life." A little later, he wrote Garfield, "I certainly will not ask or accept a reappointment & may resign this winter. I am thoroughly tired of public life."[152] But the governor soon changed his mind and actively sought reappointment in 1878. "The president told me that I could be Governor & attend to my stock just as well, but I did not ask him about reappointment," he told Charlie Broadwater. If not reappointed, he argued, an easterner would be sent out "and the Lord only knows who we will get." To the president he wrote, "I am free to confess the salary of the office will aid me very much in my venture in the sheep business."[153] And in June, 1878, the president's private secretary directed the Secretary of the Interior to prepare papers for Potts's renomination.[154]

Relationships with Fisk and Sanders did not improve, though the the feud proceeded on low key. Potts charged Sanders with using coercion in an effort to get his brother an appointment as teacher at the Blackfoot Agency, and the *Herald* continued to harass this "very behemoth of beef and bones," this "executive incumbent that has long hung like a mill stone dragging Montana down to the depths of

149. *Herald,* October 21, November 12, 1878; Fisk to Schurz (Helena, October 21, 25, 1878); Fisk to Hayes (October 21, 1878), all in Mills file, API.
150. Potts to Schurz (Helena, November 14, 1878), *ibid.*
151. *New North-West,* December 16, 1881.
152. Potts to Garfield (Helena, October 15, November 12, 1877), Garfield MSS; Potts to W. K. Rogers (Helena, October 8, 1877), Mills file, API. Sanders, too, threatened to retire from Montana, which was too "far from the madding crowd's ignoble strife." Sanders to Garfield (Helena, November 11, 1877), Garfield MSS.
153. Potts to Broadwater (Helena, March 30, 1878), Maginnis MSS; Potts to Hayes (Helena, January 2, June 1, 1878), Potts file, API.
154. Rogers to Schurz (Washington, June 11, 1878), Potts file, API.

despair."[155] Early in 1881, the anti-Potts drive in the territory had picked up enough momentum that Potts felt compelled to ask President Garfield "as a special favor" for his own retention until his term expired in July, 1882. Through Russell Harrison, his ranching partner and son of the senator from Indiana, he made it clear that he would resign if Garfield wanted him replaced. "I do not want to embarrass him nor do I want to be removed," he wrote.[156] Informed politicians foresaw a stubborn fight between Potts and local candidates, but were convinced that as long as Garfield was in the White House, Potts was safe, even for a fourth term if he wanted it.[157] Robert Fisk, however, believed that Potts would not be retained and early in 1881 was in Washington working hard for Sanders, who, he told his wife, "stands the best show to get the office."[158] Potts's enemies reminded the president of the governor's promise four years earlier not to seek reappointment; they portrayed him as corrupt and partisan, "faithless to the Republican party in Montana, friendly to the Democratic party therein, a servant of dishonorable public plunderers and an enemy to the best interests of the civil service."[159] With Garfield gone, Potts was no longer a realistic contender. One of his Democratic friends wrote Delegate Maginnis in Washington that the governor wished to be satisfied that he would be nominated before committing himself. "He will consequently not be an applicant unless the coast is clear." Maginnis was asked to sound out President Arthur as to Potts's chances. If they appeared hopeless, "he prefers to retire

155. Potts to Schurz (Helena, June 30, 1877); John S. Wood to Potts (Blackfoot Agency, July 19, 1877), Potts file, API; *Herald*, March 12, 1878. "Let the incumbent out with his sheep, to ruminate upon the mutton-making properties of bunch-grass, to watch the cavourting antics of sportive lambs, to study the motherly instincts of twinbearing ewes, and laugh at the cajoleries of lordly bucks." *Herald*, June 11, 1878. Fisk was particularly incensed when Potts was reappointed, and John C. Frémont went to Arizona, and he was even more unhappy in 1881, when, on hearing of the death of President Garfield, Potts left his office for his ranch, leaving underlings to drape the executive offices in mourning. *Herald*, June 12, 15, 1878; September 21, 1881.

156. Potts to Garfield (Helena, March 17, 1881), Garfield MSS; Potts to Russell B. Harrison (Helena, February 19, 1881), Russell B. Harrison MSS, Lilly Library, Indiana University.

157. Oliver M. Wilson to Robert E. Fisk (Indianapolis, January 25, 1881), Fisk family MSS.

158. Robert E. Fisk to Elizabeth Fisk (Washington, May 2, 1881), *ibid.*

159. L. M. Black to Garfield (Washington, May 4, 1881); Alexander Beattie et al. to Chester Arthur (Helena, July 4, 1882); Henry Blake et al. to Arthur (n.p., June 22, 1882), all in Potts file, API.

gracefully and with the appearance of resignation."[160] This, apparently, was the course of events. Potts served out his third term but was not reappointed.

But his administrations had spanned more than half of the territorial era and he had presided over striking development in Montana. By 1880, population in the territory had grown to 39,159, an increase of 90.1 percent over 1870, although a population density of only .3 persons per square mile indicated that plenty of room for expansion still existed.[161] Montana farms had quadrupled in value during that decade; livestock was worth $15,151,554, up from $1,800,000 while in precious metals, the territory ranked second in production per capita in the nation and fifth in actual output and in production per square mile.[162]

Despite the controversies with which he was beset, Benjamin Potts brought a more stable economy and a more effective functioning of government than any of his predecessors—or probably his successors. But he did not unify the Republican party: he depended as much on Democratic support as upon his own party but was still adroit enough and popular enough to gain a seat in the legislature in 1885. For the rest of the territorial period, little of political note would occur, except that as Ross Toole has indicated, men were beginning to come to the fore in Montana, as elsewhere, whose concern in political life stemmed from their desire to protect business interests, be they mining, cattle or banking—thus setting the stage for a new era.[163]

160. A. M. Woolfolk to Maginnis (Helena, March 26, 1882), "confidential," Maginnis MSS.

161. Overall population included 28,177 males and 10,982 females. *Tenth Report of the United States Census Bureau, 1880* (Washington, 1883), I, xxxiv, 5, 70.

162. *A Compendium of the Tenth Census* (Washington, 1883), 715, 991, 1230–31, 1235.

163. K. Ross Toole, *Montana: An Uncommon Land* (Norman, 1959), 111.

"The Dawdling Dandy
from the Bank of the Arno":
Governor Crosby
and Subsequent Administrations

In the winter of 1883, Montana's new governor arrived in Helena, that city described architecturally by another visitor that year as "Queen Anne in front and Crazy Jane behind."[1] He was forty-two-year-old John Schuyler Crosby, scion of an old aristocratic New York family, grandson of a signer of the Declaration of Independence, and later one of Ward McAllister's Four Hundred and vice-president in charge of the eastern offices of the "Cody Military College and International Academy of Rough Riders (incorporated)."[2] A man of charm and culture, Crosby was a personal friend of President Arthur, a veteran of the Civil War and of subsequent Indian campaigns with Sheridan. A lawyer of ability and "a Republican of the Republicans," he came to Montana with "the stuff in him our people will like," promised Robert Fisk. Was he not considered by a New York man of the world as "among the handsomest young men, or boys, I ever saw?" Had not Congress awarded him a medal for lifesaving when the yacht *Mohawk* capsized a few years earlier? And did he not come fresh from an Italian consulate, where he had distinguished himself by aiding in the capture of a band of Tuscan criminals?[3]

1. Almon Gunnison, *Rambles Overland* (Boston, 1891, 4 ed.), 87.
2. *DAB*, IV, 568; Dixon Wecter, *Saga of American Society* (New York, 1937), 219; see advertisement in *Buffalo Bill's Wild West and Congress of Rough Riders of the World* (Buffalo, 1901), n.p.
3. *Herald*, July 20, 29, 1882; entry for November 11, 1867, Allan Nevins and

It was reported that Crosby's appointment had had the support of both Potts and Maginnis, but it was the more conservative Republicans who now took new hope. A number of them, including Charles Warren, met him at the Idaho line and escorted him into the territory with a flourish. "Thank God we have at last got a Governor who is both a Republican and a Gentleman," Warren could write a friend in Washington.[4] Others were also impressed with this "gentleman of magnificent face and head" who had "seen enough of the world to be at home anywhere" and who promised to give the territory "an honest energetic and capable Executive."[5] And there were also the eternal scoffers, anti-carpetbaggers like the Democratic editor of the Butte *Miner*, who referred caustically to Crosby as "Our affable Governor—the gentleman who came to Montana with twenty-six trunks, a three hundred dollar dog, and two private secretaries. . . ."[6]

The new governor seemed pleasant enough. When he arrived the thirteenth session of the legislature was already convened and it received two messages—one from the outgoing Potts and one from the incoming Crosby, who with an "easy and effective" delivery discussed a number of problems—voter qualifications, railroad taxation, enforcement of game laws, and Indian policy—as if he had been in the territory ten years instead of a few days.[7]

Crosby quickly settled in, making the Cannon residence at Broadway and Ewing the executive mansion, and showing all the earmarks of a permanent resident. He bought the Diamond Springs ranch, ten miles out of Helena, and stocked it with brood mares. He purchased shares in several of Sam Hauser's banks and, with Hauser and Charles Broadwater, launched the first steamer on the upper Missouri—the "Little Phil," a pleasure craft. By December, 1883, he had invested

Milton H. Thomas, eds., *The Diary of George Templeton Strong* (New York, 1952), IV, 165. Crosby (1839–1914) left the University of the City of New York after a year (1856) for a grand tour which took him to the Far East and on a rarely attempted crossing of South America from Valparaiso to Montevideo. During the Civil War he served under McClellan and was breveted lieutenant colonel; subsequently he was aide-de-camp to General Philip Sheridan in the West, resigning from the regular army in 1871. Wed to Harriet Van Rensselaer, Crosby was U.S. Consul in Florence from 1876 to 1882. *DAB*, IV, 568–69; *National Cyclopaedia*, XI, 80.

4. *Herald*, July 20, 1882; *New North-West*, September 1, 1882; Warren to Harper Orahood (Butte, February 6, 1883), William J. Galbraith file, APJ.

5. Quoted in *Herald*, January 12, 1883.

6. *Semi-Weekly Miner* (Butte), March 28, 1883. Crosby brought with him a nephew, Edward F. Crosby, and Gen. H. B. Sergeant as private secretary. *Herald*, January 12, 1883.

7. Crosby to legislature (January 25, 1883), in *Herald*, January 25, 26, 1883.

more than $20,000 in the territory, according to Robert Fisk, who defended the governor against the "incendiary creeds about carpet baggers" hurled by "our socialistic neighbor," the *Independent*.[8]

It was soon apparent, too, that Crosby was a man of independent mind. As James Fergus said, "his forwardness for a pilgrim attracted my attention soon after his arrival."[9] And not all Montanans were enchanted with his brash approach. "Governor John Schuyler Crosby has made more noise in the sixty days he has been in Montana than did plain, unassuming B. F. Potts in the twelve years of his gubernatorial career," wrote an unidentified journalist. "And yet the people are already longing for the old governor and getting heartily sick of the new."[10]

Part of the complaint was undoubtedly a matter of party politics, the natural reaction of a Democratic majority governed by an executive, who, like Potts and Ashley before him, aspired to create a Republican stronghold in Montana. "I am having a hard fight out here between a lot of thieves, drunkards & vicious democrats," Crosby wrote the Attorney General in mid-April, 1883, "but I feel thoroughly confident that if I have the support of the administration I can make this Territory thoroughly Republican."[11] In attempting to assume leadership of the party, Crosby ran afoul of Wilbur F. Sanders on matters of appointment, a fact which only indicated to Robert Fisk, whose relations with the governor were excellent, that the Republican party was "not carried in the pocket of any one man or set of men, officers or citizens, as the Democratic party has been for ten years carried in the pocket of Major Maginnis and Samuel T. Hauser, Esq."[12] That Sanders still retained considerable influence was indicated when he wrote back from the party's national convention in Chicago in 1884, "Our Republican Platform leaves Crosby a 'drawn chicken.' It is not, however, the last gun but the 'first. . . .'"[13]

Some problems Crosby inherited, political implications and all. For example, before Potts left office, he became aware that at least one of the county commissioners of Custer County lived outside the

8. *Herald*, April 3, August 4, September 14, 17, 24, December 12, 1883; Crosby-Hauser agreement (Helena, February 21, 1883), letterbook, 1881–85, Hauser MSS.

9. James Fergus to Wilbur F. Sanders (n.p., n.d.), copy, Allis Stuart Collection.

10. Unidentified clipping (n.d.), Granville Stuart scrapbooks, MHS.

11. John Schuyler Crosby to Benjamin H. Brewster (Helena, April 15, 1883), SCF (1861–84).

12. *Herald*, April 3, 1884.

13. Sanders to Samuel T. Hauser (Chicago, June 5, 1884), Hauser MSS.

territory, and he was asked by residents there to remove the commissioners "to protect the county from inexcusable extravagance and even shameless plunder." But the governor lacked such power and Crosby appealed to the legislature for some remedy.[14] That body enacted a law early in 1883, vacating the Custer County offices in question, appointing three ad interim commissioners, and providing for a new election.[15] Partisan sources saw this as a political maneuver designed to control the county, to discard its votes, purportedly cast illegally in the 1882 election, and to elect Alexander Botkin, Republican, as delegate. "Sanders is at the bottom of the deviltry, & they have united all the sore heads, political and otherwise in bringing this pressure," one resident of Miles City complained.[16] And Crosby, "His Excellency, the Veto," was condemned for his urging of action and in signing the bill.[17] Is was also charged—without real foundation—that "His Royal Nibbs" came into office "with the determination of ruling the Roost," and that he was behind the ouster of Justice Everton Conger, because Conger was a friend of the Custer County commissioners.[18]

One evidence of Crosby's unfettered political spirit was his use of the executive powers, "very freely, to veto legislative bills," to use the words of Granville Stuart.[19] Some admitted simply that he "slightly overdid the matter," but others were much less objective in their analysis, sorely resenting the unwarranted effort to dominate legislation by one who had not been in the territory long enough to vote and who came "fresh from a long sojourn among the effete monarchies of Europe."[20] The editor of the *Independent*, with whom Crosby constantly battled, had little use for the new chief executive:

Dazzled by the giddy height to which he had been elevated by federal appointment this son of Apollo and "grandson of a signer" evidently imagined himself President of the United States delivering his first message to congress. All this might have been excused and forgotten, but when the new governor began the free exercise of the

14. Crosby to legislature (February 23, 1883), *Council Journal*, 13 Session (1883), 154–55.

15. Act of March 8, 1883, *LM*, 13 Session (1883), 140–41.

16. J. B. Hubbell to Martin Maginnis (Miles City, March 11, 1883), Maginnis MSS.

17. Unidentified clipping (n.d.), Stuart scrapbooks.

18. *Semi-Weekly Miner*, March 28, 1883, clipping, *ibid*. See also Chapter 10.

19. Stuart, *Forty Years on the Frontier*, II, 168.

20. *Avant Courier* (Bozeman), March 15, 1883, clipping, Stuart scrapbooks; unidentified clipping (n.d.), *ibid*.

veto power, and turned all the artillery of the Executive upon the Legislative branch of the government, the people's representatives, without regard to party, began to murmur at the unusual interference.[21]

Crosby vetoed eleven bills of the thirteenth assembly, of which only three were passed over his head. Vetoed were measures on convict labor, on water rights, on the care of the insane and of deaf-blind children, on the refunding of the Dawson County debt, on formation of building associations, on the costs of public printing, and most important of all, on creation of a territorial system of cattle commissioners and inspectors designed to protect Montana herds from depredating Indians and renegade whites.[22] This latter the governor scored heavily, calling it a "grave menace to personal liberty. . . . a step backward from the spirit of the free north-west, to the dangerous days of the star-chamber and the Stuarts"[23] and thereby earning the enmity of territorial stockmen.

On the other hand, Crosby stopped the importation of cattle with Texas fever, adopted a hard line on pardoning criminals, urged a fourth judge for the territory, called for reduction of Indian lands (though arguing "It is cheaper to feed the Indian than to fight him"), and proposed to "treat polygamy as a social leprosy and establish effectual social, political and legal quarantine all around it"—all of which were popular positions.[24] An ardent outdoorsman, he sought joint action with the governors of Wyoming, Idaho, and Dakota to prevent wholesale game destruction, especially on the fringes of Yellowstone Park, and he complained to the chairman of the Senate Committee on the Territories that private parties sought to lease parts of the park for cattle grazing.[25]

21. *Weekly Independent,* March 15, 1883.
22. *House Journal,* 13 Session (1883), 150–51, 272, 305, 318–19, 339; *Council Journal,* 13 Session (1883), 166, 173, 210, 211–12, 221, 222; *Semi-Weekly Miner,* March 28, 1883, clipping; *Avant Courier,* March 15, 1883, clipping, both in Stuart scrapbooks.
23. Crosby to legislature (March 8, 1883), *House Journal,* 13 Session (1883), 338–39.
24. *Herald,* January 25, February 10, May 28, November 15, 1883; August 16, 1884; Crosby to Maginnis (Helena, March 8, 1884), Maginnis MSS. The thirteenth session considered an anti-polygamy bill, and heard a "sharp, witty, prolonged, effectual and bestial" speech on the subject by Councilman Charles Cox. "The like of it is not often heard in civilized assemblies, . . ." commented the *Herald,* noting that the bill was defeated by a strictly party vote—Republicans for and Democrats against. *Herald,* March 3, 1883.
25. Crosby to Governors Hale, Neil, and Ordway (Helena, February 7, 1883), *Council Journal,* 13 Session (1883), 240; Crosby to Chairman, Senate Committee on the Territories (Helena, January 17, 1883), unidentified clipping (n.d.), in Stuart scrapbooks.

But there was about him a certain imperiousness and impulsiveness that kept him constantly at war with many of his constituents. One example was his too flippant reference to a tragedy at Greenhorn, when he reported to the Department of Interior that vigilantes there "have removed the Democratic postmaster by hanging. Government fuel must be scarce as he was caught barn-burning."[26] In another letter to Washington, he referred to Montana as the "Territory I govern," a major blunder, which at least one legislator compared to Potts's "genial influences of civilization" remark.[27] Woolfolk of the *Independent* was constantly haranguing him. Crosby "should not magnify his office, but amuse himself with hunting, fishing, or even letters on the National Park and leave Montana to her exalted destiny. She only asks of her federal officials to keep their hands from her throat and out of her pockets."[28] If Crosby insisted on fighting with the press, said Woolfolk, he need not complain if the papers "did not constantly bathe his tender body with pomatum and cologne perfumed with fulsome praise."[29]

And the governor was something of a moralist. Late in 1883, having traveled to West Point, he escorted Chester Arthur and the presidential party through Yellowstone National Park on his return. Once back in Helena, he found a scandal, an unsavory divorce business involving Secretary Isaac McCutcheon, a hot-headed lawyer from Charlotte, Michigan, who had replaced Mills in 1882. McCutcheon had come to Montana in the company of a woman "relative," while his wife remained in Michigan. Early in March, 1883, he filed for divorce before the chief justice of the territory, on grounds of desertion, charging that his wife had not lived with him for nearly nine years and had refused to accompany him to Montana. The decree quickly granted, he married the woman he had brought with him.[30]

Immediately there were repercussions. Because of the divorce, "a trivial affair," McCutcheon called it, his bondsmen abandoned him, and he was in trouble with the Treasury Department, to whom he presented himself as an industrious, if maligned, public official. ". . . I am sober, do not consort with abandoned women, nor gamble,"

26. *Weekly Independent*, April 12, 1883.
27. James Fergus to Sanders (n.p., n.d.), copy, Allis Stuart Collection.
28. *Weekly Independent*, March 15, 1883.
29. *Daily Independent*, January 9, 1884.
30. *Weekly Inter Mountain*, November 1, 1883; *Herald*, July 23, August 3, 4, 1883; A. M. Esler to Hauser (Junction, August 28, 1883), Hauser MSS; *New North-West*, June 9, 1882; "Col. Isaac D. McCutcheon" (Helena, August 9, 1889), MS dictation, Bancroft Library.

he wrote the First Comptroller.[31] And the *Independent's* handling of the story brought him into a street brawl with editor Woolfolk. After an exchange of words, McCutcheon cracked Woolfolk across the head with his walking stick, the two "ending with a roll into the gutter, the editor beneath, the Secretary on top."[32]

After calling for a statement of facts from McCutcheon, Governor Crosby, convinced that the secretary had impaired his usefulness, forced his resignation, "because in his domestic relations he had offended against public morality."[33] McCutcheon remained in Montana, stepping "into a very active law practice, worth several times the salary derived from his Federal position,"[34] but it is clear that his feelings toward Crosby were deep and dark. At an election in 1884, when the governor arrived to vote, McCutcheon was supposed to have shouted, "Make way there for a New York ward politician."[35] And a few years later, when Crosby, no longer governor, was suing the *Montana Live Stock Journal* for libel, the *Journal* having accused him of being a social leper in Montana, of the theft of jewelry, and of patronizing prostitutes "selected for his majesty by the chief pimp of the household," it was McCutcheon who was reported as having prepared the libelous material.[36]

While on leave in Washington, Crosby resigned on November 11, 1884, effective that very day, to become first assistant postmaster general, writing his resignation on official Post Office Department stationery.[37] His stay in Montana had been brief and his contemporaries, as well as later writers, would belittle his contributions, and members of the legislature would disdainfully refer to him as "the dawdling dandy from the bank of the Arno."[38] Yet despite the com-

31. Isaac McCutcheon to William Lawrence (Helena, August 9, 1883); McCutcheon to Henry M. Teller (Helena, July 23, 1883), McCutcheon file, API.

32. *Herald*, July 17, 1883.

33. *Weekly Inter Mountain*, November 1, 1883. In September, under heavy pressure, McCutcheon resigned, then several weeks later tried unsuccessfully to withdraw his resignation. McCutcheon to Arthur (Helena, September 2, 1883; October 10, 1883), McCutcheon file, API.

34. *Herald*, December 6, 1883.

35. *Ibid.*, April 21, 1884.

36. For this affair: see, *Montana Live Stock Journal* (Helena), April 30, 1887; *Weekly Independent*, April 18, 1889; *Herald*, April 11, 12, 1889; *New York Herald*, April 12, 1889; unidentified clipping (n.d.), Political Scrapbook, T. C. Power MSS.

37. Crosby to Teller (Washington, November 11, 1884), Crosby file, API; *Herald*, November 11, 1884.

38. Robert B. Smith, "Executive Department," *Contributions*, IV (1903), 101; Sanders, "Hundred Governors Rule Montana in Two Centuries," *ibid.*, IX (1923), 363.

plaints brought forth by his ringing vetoes, his personal airs and independence, the territory might have done worse. Though he made enemies, his ideas were sound and he constantly kept the welfare of Montana in mind. Perhaps the *Missoulian* was not far off when it called him "a pretty good Governor, notwithstanding the fact that everybody can't boss him."[39]

When Crosby resigned, McCutcheon, who later took the credit for his going, assured the Secretary of the Interior that "At least nine tenths of the Republicans of Montana desire the appointment of Wilbur F. Sanders for Gove," and that Montanans had some reason to expect one of their own, for both national parties that year had in effect pledged themselves to resident appointments in the territories.[40] Thus it was with considerable surprise that they learned that their new chief executive was B. Platt Carpenter, a portly New Yorker whose credentials easily met the test demanded for the office: he was a lawyer, he had been chairman of the New York State Republican party, and he had been defeated for the position of lieutenant governor of New York in the election of 1882.[41] The *New York Times* saw the nomination as indicating, "not for the first time," that President Arthur's views "concerning what is good for the Territories do not agree with those of the party at large as expressed in the last convention."[42] A Minneapolis editor thought it "vicious," an "insult to the people of Montana" to send out "a petty New York politician to play viceroy over them," and predicted that Carpenter would not stay long. ". . . he will not need to bring out his trunk; and of course his family will not make a winter journey to the bleak and frozen pro-consulate of Montana."[43]

39. *Missoulian,* quoted in *Herald,* August 16, 1884. See also *Herald,* September 10, 1884.

40. McCutcheon to Teller (Helena, November 21, 1884), telegram, Wilbur F. Sanders file, API. In 1889, McCutcheon wrote a friend: "If I were to live one thousand years, I should point with pride to my success in driving Crosby out of the territory and with unbounded hatred to the sneaking wretches, who today find fault with that action." McCutcheon to Russell B. Harrison (Helena, March 7, 1889), Russell B. Harrison MSS.

41. Born in New York in 1837, Carpenter was a graduate of Union College, had served in various political posts, including district attorney, assessor of internal revenue, county judge and state senator. He was a delegate to both national Republican conventions that nominated Grant, a member of the New York Constitutional Convention of 1867, and chairman of the Republican State Committee of New York. *Herald,* December 23, 1884; January 10, 1885; Leeson, *History of Montana,* 1196; *Progressive Men of the State of Montana,* 1319–20.

42. New York *Times,* December 17, 1884. The sister *Tribune* believed it was "a movement in the senatorship matter." *New York Tribune,* December 17, 1884.

43. Quoted in *Semi-Weekly Miner,* December 27, 1884.

Carpenter arrived early in January, 1885, "a robust-looking man with a clear-cut face and blue eyes which sparkle in conversation." He was "plain and unassuming," "affable and agreeable," "large, healthy-looking, well preserved." But as usual, the *Herald* and the *Independent* disagreed—this time by nearly twenty years as to his age.[44] Leasing executive offices in the St. Louis block on Main, the governor went to work on his message to the legislature, which dwelled briefly but forcefully on the need for better penal facilities, tightening of election laws, reduction of fees for public officials, and curtailment of territorial expenses, which in the previous year, he noted, had exceeded income by $28,558.77.[45]

He rented the Holton house on Benton Avenue, where Sam Hauser had lived for several years, and brought his family to Helena, as well as his law library of at least two thousand volumes, the largest in the territory.[46] But his administration was largely as uneventful as it was short. Carpenter took a keen interest in seeking a solution to the housing of convicts, looking for "boarding" arrangements with other states or territories, but reached no agreements.[47] He stepped on a few toes with his pocket veto of a bill to exempt a railroad from taxation, but it was clear from the beginning that he was biding his time, for with the Democrat Grover Cleveland elected president in November, 1884, there seemed little doubt but that the territorial board would soon be swept clean of Republicans, although the Fisks discounted the idea that a purge was immediate.[48]

But as soon as the new president was inaugurated, the move to oust Carpenter was begun. With the administration in the hands of friends, Montana Democrats subscribed to a policy of "turn the rascals out." One wrote Maginnis: "This last Governor is the worst pill we have had yet. I do hope the President will remove every Republican office holder if they should be retained it would be a bitter disappointment to the party." Complained another, "We are tired of our Carpenter and want a mountain man."[49]

44. The *Independent* thought he was about "65 years of age"; the *Herald* estimated 54, then revised it down to 47, which was correct. *Weekly Independent*, January 8, 1885; *Herald*, January 7, 1885.
45. *Herald*, January 9, 14, 1885; Carpenter to legislature (January 14, 1885), *Council Journal*, 14 Session (1885), 14–15.
46. *Herald*, April 29, May 5, June 2, 1885.
47. *Herald*, June 5, July 6, August 17, 1885.
48. *Ibid.*, March 19, 24, 27, 1885.
49. Perry W. McAdow to Maginnis (Billings, March 20, 1885); W. H. Suther-

Even before this they had begun to discuss the logical successor. Former delegate Martin Maginnis, who had remained in Washington after his replacement by Joseph K. Toole, was a strong contender, supported not only by Democrats, but even by stalwart Republicans like Charles S. Warren of Butte, who thought he "would make as good a Governor as I care to live under" and promised a telegram "signed by 50 square toed Republicans" within three hours if it would be useful.[50] As early as February, Sam Hauser was also being boomed for the position,[51] and if his past political record were taken into consideration, his supporters had every reason to believe he had earned the appointment.

Born in Kentucky, Hauser by 1854 was working as a civil engineer and railroad surveyor in Missouri. When the Civil War came, he pushed west, perhaps because of pro-southern sympathies, perhaps to escape military service. In 1862 he trekked across to the Columbia River to prospect, and swung back to the Bannack diggings later in the same year. In Montana he rapidly built up large holdings in mining, milling, banking, and transportation. In the words of John Hakola, Hauser "was probably the most important single individual in Montana's economic life for at least two decades before 1890."[52]

The same might almost be said of the political arena, for he was from the beginning a major influence in the politics of the territory. Perhaps Kenneth Owens's statement that Hauser "not only had a voice in selecting a majority of the governors sent out to his territory, but he did more to direct territorial policy for Montana under Republican and Democratic administrations alike than any official in Washington"[53] is a bit strong, but clearly he was one of the most important political manipulators in Montana for nearly thirty years.

Hauser had been one of those working actively for the creation of the territory in 1864; he had supported Edgerton for governor and later Green Clay Smith; and his relations with Potts were excellent.

---

lin to Maginnis (White Sulphur Springs, March 22, 1885), both in Maginnis file, API.

50. Charles S. Warren to Maginnis (Butte, December 16, 1884), Maginnis MSS.

51. William B. Hundley to Hauser (Helena, February 20, 1885), Hauser MSS.

52. Hakola, "Samuel T. Hauser," 309. For his background see *ibid.*, 1–7; Leeson, *History of Montana*, 1217; *Progressive Men of the State of Montana*, 202–3; *DAB*, VIII, 402–3.

53. Kenneth N. Owens, "Research Opportunities in Western Territorial History," *Arizona and the West*, VIII (Spring, 1966), 15.

As the local level, he was a kingmaker and a stringpuller par excellence. If an associate saw an opportunity to elect a Hauser man as delegate in 1870, it was Hauser he asked to secure the nomination for him.[54] If an important figure like Charles Broadwater had to be away at the time of the 1874 Democratic territorial convention, it was Hauser he asked to "arrange to delay matters."[55] It was Hauser who led the campaign for a subsidy of the north-south railroad throughout most of the seventies and who was said to have "accomplished a heap of log-rolling" on behalf of Helena. When the editor of the Butte *Miner* wanted the presiding officer of the Council defeated, it was Hauser he asked to interfere to that end.[56] When cattlemen had problems with depredating Indians, more than one turned to Hauser. "Cannot you & Maginnis have these alien Indians removed north of the line where they belong?" asked Granville Stuart in 1881, almost as if Hauser were commander of the Army of the West, rather than a private citizen.[57]

Hauser had extensive Washington connections. He had met Senator George G. Vest of Missouri as a young man and subsequently the two were involved together in a copper enterprise, while Senator John Sherman of Ohio held at least a few shares in Hauser's First National Bank of Montana.[58] He was one of those entertaining Secretary of War Belknap and his party when they visited Montana in 1875, and he was introduced to President Chester Arthur in 1882 as "one of the prominent men of Montana."[59]

Because of his power within the territorial party and the range of his influence outside, Hauser's endorsement was important to any office-seeker and most men in the territory knew it. In 1869, when James Stuart, who had placer holdings in Central America, decided he "would like to go and prospect the country at Uncle Sam's expense," he sought Hauser's help in getting a consulship to Hon-

54. James Stuart to Hauser (Deer Lodge, February 8, 1869), Hauser MSS.

55. Charles Broadwater to Hauser (Washington, April 6, 1874), *ibid.*

56. *Herald,* February 16, 1874; see Chapter 6. H. T. Brown to Hauser (Butte, December 30, 1880), Hauser MSS.

57. Stuart to Hauser (Fort Maginnis, February 5, 1881), *ibid.*

58. George G. Vest to Hauser (Hot Springs, Arkansas, April 30, 1883); John Sherman to Hauser (Mansfield, Ohio, August 16, 26, 1883) both in Hauser MSS; Vest to Grover Cleveland (Washington, May 15, 1885), Hauser file, API.

59. Entry for August 16, 1875, in Gen. W. E. Strong, *A Trip to the Yellowstone National Park in July, August, and September, 1875* (Norman, 1968), 118–19; William Arthur to Chester Arthur (Governor's Island, April 4, 1882), Hauser MSS.

duras.[60] Hauser would run into the wrath of Governor Potts over appointments in 1878[61] but smoothed matters over and still retained his influence. Several months before he became governor in 1885, Hauser was approached by M. A. Myendorff, who sought a government post. ". . . I know & everybody else does that one good word from you can do more good than the spontaneous cry of the whole Territory of Montana & much from elsewhere," wrote Myendorff.[62]

By the mid-1880s other important Montana Democrats included Charles Broadwater, William A. Clark, and Marc Daly. The careers of Clark and Daly were on the rise, while that of Broadwater, having risen steadily in the seventies and early eighties, was on a plateau. Probably Hauser played a more consistently influential role in territorial politics than any other of these "Big Four," though until 1885–86, his and "Broad's" political fortunes were often closely allied.

Broadwater and Co., which included A. H. Wilder of St. Paul, had greatly expanded the scope of its trading at army posts, sometimes even to the Indians, as distressed competitors like Tom Power were quick to point out.[63] In 1881, one of Hauser's associates wrote from Fort Maginnis: "Broadwater got away with the tradership here. I may remark confidentially that he is fast becoming a power in this land. He now runs Forts Assiniboine, Keogh, Custer & Maginnis, besides summer Camps such as Coal Banks, Rocky Point, &c."[64]

In economic matters and in political matters both, Hauser and Broadwater often worked together and both contributed liberally to the Democratic party. And both apparently were not averse to betting on election results.[65] Delegate Maginnis was widely regarded as a Hauser-Broadwater man and neither of them was shy about making demands upon him. Perhaps with tongue in cheek, Broadwater could inform Maginnis in 1881 of reservation boundary changes and appropriations for completion of Fort Assiniboine that he desired. "Both I must have or damned if I don't go back on you next election."[66] In twelve years in Congress, contended the Butte *Inter*

60. Stuart to Hauser (Deer Lodge, December 5, 1869), Hauser MSS.

61. Benjamin F. Potts to Hauser (Helena, November 24, 1878), *ibid.*

62. M. A. Myendorff to Hauser (Helena, February 18, 1885), *ibid.*

63. Broadwater to John Q. Smith (St. Paul, October 26, 1876); Thomas Power to E. A. Hayt (Helena, November 20, 1879), both in BIA.

64. Granville Stuart to Hauser (Fort Maginnis, June 18, 1881), Hauser MSS.

65. Broadwater to Hauser (Washington, January 29, 1874; Fort Assiniboine, October 17, 1880), *ibid.*

66. Broadwater to Maginnis (Fort Assiniboine, December 6, 1881), Maginnis MSS.

Mountain, Maginnis accomplished nothing "except for Broadwater, Hauser, Wilder & Co."[67]

In summing up Democratic power in Montana late in 1880, the editor of the Bozeman *Avant Courier* had a party stalwart saying facetiously: "My ballot will be fired at the banker and crafty politician from Helena, the cunning Indian trader of the Yellowstone, and that wonderful military genius who sprang at once jump from being a bovine thumper to a colonelcy (on paper) Broadwater."[68] Hauser was "the banker and crafty politician of Helena," and presumably "the cunning Indian trader of the Yellowstone" was Tom Power, merchant prince from Fort Benton; but most Republicans would have been willing to admit that Hauser was the dominant figure: he was the "autocratic boss who carries the Democratic party of Montana in his pocket," according to the *New North-West* in 1882.[69] Here, then, were two leading candidates for the governorship in 1885: Hauser, the successful, behind-the-scenes political manager, and Maginnis, who was regarded by many as his puppet, but who had acquired a great deal of political know-how in many years in Washington.

In the nation's capital at this time, where in the words of Senator Vest, "The office seekers are thick, and as hungry as Snake River trout," both Vest and Delegate Toole were urging Hauser to throw his hat in the ring and both promised their aid on his behalf. Together they had gone to see Maginnis and found, as Vest put it, "Maginnis is for Maginnis."[70] At first Hauser was coy, as was William A. Clark, who declined to be a candidate, but he was bothered more than a little by the thought of Maginnis in the governor's chair. Soon he quietly let it be known to friends that he was available. Toole sought to persuade Maginnis to step aside, reminding him that Hauser, "his old friend who had fought six battles for him and each time furnished the sinews of war wanted the place. . . ." But Maginnis remained "ugly disposed and makes no overtures," arguing that his own appointment would unify the Democratic party in Montana,

67. *Semi-Weekly Inter Mountain* (Butte), March 29, 1885.
68. *Avant Courier*, October 28, 1880.
69. *New North-West*, September 15, 1882. A shrewd and highly successful pioneer in freighting, Power made a fortune supplying federal troops, the Northwest Mounted Police, and reservation Indians. His economic endeavors and those of Charles Broadwater and Hauser touched at many points. See Paul Sharp, *Whoop-Up Country* (Minneapois, 1955), 40–41, 184–85, 213–16, 221, 225–26.
70. Vest to Hauser (Washington, March 30, 1885), Hauser MSS.

while Hauser's would split it. "He talks like a dynamitor, and it is amusing to me to see what a high opinion the little fellow has of himself," Toole reported.[71]

In Washington, Hauser, Toole, Vest, and others disagreed, believing—to the contrary—that Maginnis's selection would rupture the party, but they did not settle upon a candidate. Instead they simply agreed not to support Maginnis, and would give Toole free reign to consult party leaders in the territory and allow leading Democrats there "to cooperate and control the appointment if we could." When Hauser returned to Helena, he found Edward W. Knight, his brother-in-law and cashier of his First National Bank, was now a candidate, though not a very active one. Hauser was convinced, as he told William A. Clark, "that a great *majority* of Democrats there would stand me, but wouldn't stand Knight," and he instructed his brother-in-law to withdraw, giving at the same time a lukewarm endorsement of Samuel Word. But when Toole and Vest made it clear that unless he entered the race, Maginnis could not be stopped, Hauser openly became a candidate.[72] Yet from the beginning, he left no doubt in his supporters' minds that it was not the office he was seeking so much as the opportunity to block Maginnis. Most of the governors "have been a lot of broken down politicians that could not make a living at home" and had created "the general feeling that to be governor was no great shakes," he said. "And I am vain enough to think that it would not elevate my position & standing, and I know the office would be a bore."[73]

Already, early in April, Toole had approached the president on Hauser's behalf, emphasizing the party's commitment to appoint residents. A veteran of twenty years in Montana, Hauser was "thoroughly conversant with the interests and necessities of the Territory" and had "contributed more than any other individual to the establishment and maintenance of democratic supremacy in Montana."[74]

71. Joseph K. Toole to Hauser (Washington, March 30, 1885), *ibid.*

72. Hauser to William A. Clark (Helena, April 16, 1885), *ibid.* While asking support from the Secretary of the Interior in March, Knight admitted, "I am not making a very earnest struggle for the appointment," because he understood that Maginnis had strong congressional backing. By mid-April, however, he was pushing for Hauser. Edward W. Knight to L. Q. C. Lamar (Helena, March 4, 30, 1885), Knight file, API; Knight to Lamar (Helena, April 16, 1885), Hauser file, API.

73. Hauser to Vest (n.p., April 13, 1885), copy, letterbook (1885–87), Hauser MSS.

74. Toole to Cleveland (Washington, April 6, 1885), Grover Cleveland MSS, Library of Congress.

Maginnis and his backers cried treachery. "The action of your Democratic friends here has been contemptible," Charles Warren wrote him.[75] And a number of Montanans, when they discovered Hauser in the race, dropped Maginnis quickly. As one expressed it, he "has received from the democratic party of Montana all he is entitled to and more really than he had any right to expect."[76] Maginnis himself claimed duplicity, that he had been double-crossed by Hauser. In urging friends to present his case to the president, he explained that of the 16,000 Democratic voters in Montana, probably 1,500 were Missourians and of southern outlook. "They are good citizens and generally well-to-do," he said, "but you know that it would not do to put them in supreme control, by the influence of Sen. Vest and others in a northern community." This group, he continued, had supported him "under some sort of protest" and he had backed their man, Toole, as delegate in the 1884 race. "I made such a canvass for him as I never made for myself and barely pulled him through, . . . although during his canvass, and since, indeed until recently it was understood that I was the choice of the party for Governor, as much so as if [I] had been nominated." Why, he asked, should Vest control affairs "in a Territory that I redeemed from the Republicans and have held steady for twelve years . . ."?[77]

Most of the Irish wing in Montana was for Maginnis, reported the pro-Hauser *Herald*; and the former delegate was supported by many local petitions and by public figures like James J. Hill, General Nelson Miles, William Rosecrans, and former governor John Crosby, not to mention a substantial group of congressmen from both parties. "If we don't win it will be because Maginnis has Republican Senators legging it for him," predicted Toole at one point.[78] Relations in Washington rapidly deteriorated. Maginnis and Toole were reported to "seldom speak" when they met and it was charged that Senator Vest

75. Warren to Maginnis (Butte, April 20, 1885), Maginnis MSS.

76. Joseph E. Marion to Toole (Frenchtown, April 15, 1885), Hauser file, API.

77. Maginnis to Samuel J. Randall (Washington, May 22, 1885), Cleveland MSS. Randall presented these arguments, with less enthusiasm, to Colonel Lamont, Cleveland's aide. Randall to D. S. Lamont (Washington, May 23, 1885), *ibid.*

78. *Herald*, April 25, 1885; Nelson Miles to Cleveland (Vancouver Barracks, March 29, 1885); Crosby to Lamont (n.d., n.p.); James J. Hill and P. H. Kelly to Cleveland (n.p., April 7, 1885), telegram; Abram Hewitt to Cleveland (New York, March 17, 1885), telegram; Abram Hewitt to Cleveland (New York, March 17, 1885), all in Maginnis file, API. See also numerous petitions, *ibid.*; Toole to Hauser (Washington, May 30, 1885), Hauser MSS.

had to take over the task of introducing the new delegate, Toole, in the nation's capital. "Maginnis is still here and working like a beaver," Vest reported on May Day. "He has about quit speaking to me and I am glad of it, for I think he is about as coarsehaired as a Mexican mustang."[79]

But Hauser also had a broad and significant backing, with territorial support even from stalwart Republicans like the Fisks, Wilbur F. Sanders, and former justice Hiram Knowles (beaten badly by Toole in the 1884 delegate election), who all gave solid endorsement to Hauser, " 'The Warwick' of his party in this Territory," as Knowles called him.[80] At the same time, Democrats swung behind him and deluged the president with letters and petitions.[81] Toole worked industriously, and Senator Vest, who called Hauser "one of the noblest men living," directed the campaign in Washington personally, calling on the president and convincing others of his colleagues that they should do likewise. Secretary of the Interior Lamar was persuaded, despite his initial objection that failure to select Maginnis might offend the Irish and Catholic vote.[82]

Meanwhile, another element was introduced. The breach in Montana Democratic ranks was even more apparent when Charles Broadwater jumped into the fray against Hauser, branding him an opportunist. In the summer of 1884, "Broad" claimed, when prospects for Cleveland seemed bleak, Hauser was negotiating "with a party who stood close to Blaine and who offered him the control of the Federal patronage in the Territory in exchange for the payment of $5,000 in cash, half of which he flatly asked me to subscribe." Hauser was unfit and in a monetary sense "and otherwise" had contributed less than many others in Montana "who have had no axe to grind." On the other hand, Maginnis was "a life long Democrat and his course has been a consistent one throughout." His appointment "would command fully ninety percent of the total Democratic vote as against any other Democrat in the Territory."[83]

79. *Semi-Weekly Inter Mountain*, May 17, 1885; Vest to Hauser (Washington, May 1, 1885), Hauser MSS.
80. Sanders to Cleveland (Helena, May 2, 1885); Hiram Knowles to L. Q. C. Lamar (Butte, April 9, 1885), copy, both in Hauser file, API; *Herald*, April 20, 21, 1885.
81. See Hauser file, API.
82. Toole to Cleveland (Washington, April 22, 1885); Vest to Cleveland (Washington, May 15, 1885), both *ibid.*; Toole to Hauser (Washington, May 30, 1885); Vest to Hauser (Washington, June 19, 1885), both in Hauser MSS.
83. These reached the president through James J. Hill, with whom Broadwater

Such charges required a response. "Telegraph me at once," ordered Vest. "Fight very hot."[84] Hauser vigorously denied the accusations as flagrantly untrue: together, he and William Clark had given more than $5,000 to help defeat Blaine, he said. "I have expended over twenty thousand dollars to maintain the supremacy of the democracy in this Territory, and contributed three thousand dollars to defeat Blaine and never offered or gave any thing to elect him."[85] Vest took Hauser's statement to President Cleveland, who rejected the Broadwater charges. Senator Gorman was there, too, "and stood by me like a thoroughbred," Vest wrote, even telling Cleveland, "Mr. President, if Sam Hauser is not a Democrat, there is not one living." With support from Senator Preston Plumb, Vest was convinced by the end of June that the battle was won. "We have *spiked* the gun and that's enough. . . ."[86]

For Cleveland, the entire episode must have been a little embarrassing. Committed to civil service reform and pledged not to remove officials without cause, he was under great pressure to reward faithful Democrats. Late in May, Toole had written that Cleveland would require some basis for ousting Carpenter. ". . . He must have charges," he told Hauser. "Can't you get them up there? Of course you must not do it yourself. I think Sanders would do it." Of Carpenter, Toole continued. "His reputation for character in N.Y. was notoriously bad —and it preceeded him to Montana. We must fix him. He is certainly vulnerable."[87]

Sanders had already damned Carpenter to the president, describing him as ignorant and confused, "well treated but terrified at the responsibilities thrust upon him. . . ."[88] Now, two days after Toole's request for a statement of cause against Carpenter, such new charges were forthcoming over the signature of five Helenans, including William E. Cullen, who was chairman of the Democratic Territorial Committee and also Sanders's law partner. The specifications were flimsy. Carpenter's selection had violated both 1884 party platforms. Carpenter had vetoed good and needed laws and had refused to pay rewards offered by his predecessor. ". . . he has manifested in the

had business dealings. Broadwater to Hill (Helena, May 20, 1885), Cleveland MSS.

84. Vest to Hauser (Washington, June 25, 1885), Hauser MSS.
85. Hauser to Vest (one letter n.p., n.d.; another letter, n.p., June 25, 1885), copies, letterbook (1885–87), *ibid.*
86. Vest to Hauser (Washington, June 29, 1885), *ibid.*
87. Toole to Hauser (Washington, May 27, 1885), *ibid.*
88. Sanders to Cleveland (Helena, May 2, 1885), Hauser file, API.

conduct of the grave affairs of a great territory the spirit of a trifler, lacking the courage to do what his duty required."[89] Unimportant though the charges were, when added to earlier accusations of absenteeism, equally as trivial, they provided an excuse to suspend a Republican in a Democratic administration, as was done on July 3.[90]

When simultaneously Hauser's appointment was announced, Toole gave the credit to Vest, who "had moved 'heaven and earth'" to accomplish it. "I do not believe that any other man could have overcome the strong pressure in favor of Maginnis," the delegate confided.[91] Though Charles Broadwater made another attempt, through Senator Benjamin Harrison of Indiana, to block Hauser, this time in the Senate,[92] there was no real question of confirmation. In the territory, newspapers applauded and the Dillon *Tribune* wrote a political obituary.

> MAGINNIS.—In Washington City, U.S.A., on Friday July 3, 1885, and of the Declaration of Independence the 108th year, at the hands of Sam T. Hauser, assisted by Joe K. Toole, Major Martin Maginnis, lately an aspirant for Governor of Montana, aged (politically) six consecutive terms in Congress. . . . Devoted to the Hauser-Broadwater ring of manipulators of Government contracts, Maginnis was ever faithful to the clique that run the Democratic machine of Montana. . . . Tired of Maginnis, the hand that gave him political birth dealt him political death, and the grand, gloomy and all-powerful Democratic boss scooped him for governor.[93]

89. William E. Cullen et al. to Cleveland (Helena, May 29, 1885), Carpenter file, Charges, API.

90. Who charged absenteeism is not clear. See Jacob Carpenter to Cleveland (Poughkeepsie, March 18, 1885), *ibid.* A memo in Carpenter's file says "Suspend him and date suspension July 3, 1885." A further note says "Done July 3, 1885," *ibid.* Carpenter later acknowledged the letter written four days later by the Secretary of the Interior, acompanying the president's suspension order. Carpenter to Lamar (Helena, July 13, 1885), *ibid.*

91. Toole to Hauser (Washington, July 5, 1885), Hauser MSS.

92. Harrison was conducting a campaign against Cleveland's removal of Republicans. Broadwater reiterated his earlier charges that Hauser had played both sides in the Blaine-Cleveland election. Really an "Independent," he had for years "been sailing under false colors," and was "adept in 'stealing other men's thunder,'" but was no leader of his party and could never be elected to an office. Cleveland, insisted Broadwater, now realized his error in naming Hauser and needed help out of his dilemma. Broadwater to Benjamin Harrison (Helena, March 7, 1886), Benjamin Harrison MSS, Library of Congress. Harrison's response included the comment that "some of the matters you suggest are interesting; but as long as they rest only in suggestions and not in charges or evidence we can make nothing of them." Besides, this was a political office. Harrison to Broadwater (Washington, March 15, 1886), *ibid.*

93. *Dillon Tribune*, July 11, 1885.

Hauser was serenaded at his Helena home, his visitors withdrawing after a speech and refreshments, "shouting hearty cheers for the first Territorial resident appointed Governor of Montana."[94] Congratulations poured in. Some saw in his appointment the death knell of carpetbaggism, as the prelude to a seat in the U.S. Senate for Hauser. From Sun City, the new governor-select was assured that "even here among the border ruffians and Republican barbarians" friends rejoiced in his "elevation to the proudest office in Montana." Wrote another, "We deplore your politics," but "know your administration will be a vast improvement on the one run by the imported article from Italy."[95]

When he was appointed, some expressed the fear that with many irons in the fire, Hauser would find the job "an obstruction and an annoyance," but his champions argued that with an able private secretary he need not interrupt his business affairs.[96] Apparently, this was Hauser's point of view also, for immediately after being sworn in on July 14 in his private office in the First National Bank, he chose J. A. Johnson to handle the details of the post, and headed east, returning by early August long enough to entertain a party of distinguished visitors, which included Senators Vest and Harrison.[97] As Hauser viewed it, probably the job was not too strenuous and he devoted little time to it. In response to a request for an extended leave of absence, Toole could write him: "I saw the Secretary of the Interior today, told him that the Governor of Montana didn't have to do anything except to pardon a few criminals now and then and occasionally appoint a Notary Public."[98] Hauser spent a good deal of time in New York and Washington, mostly on private affairs, although when Toole requested leave on his behalf—usually after the governor had already left the territory—it was "upon business of importance to the Territory. . . ."[99] Records indicate that Hauser spent nearly four months in the East during the winter of 1885–86 and was afterward absent a good deal as well.[100] Unquestionably he was head

94. *Herald*, July 6, 1885.

95. John H. Curtis to Hauser (Butte, July 4, 1885); R. S. Ford to Hauser (Sun City, July 11, 1885); H. R. Horr to Hauser (Gardiner, July 7, 1885), all in Hauser MSS.

96. *Herald*, July 13, 1885.

97. Hauser to Cleveland (Helena, July 14, 1885), Cleveland MSS; *Herald*, July 14, 1885. Official confirmation would not come for another ten months. *Herald*, July 15, August 7, 1885; May 14, 28, 1886.

98. Toole to Hauser (Washington, February 5, 1886), Hauser MSS.

99. Toole to Lamar (Washington, February 4, 1886), Hauser file, API.

100. *Herald*, March 29, 1886; memo (n.d.), Hauser file, API.

of his party, but at least one supporter was disappointed that he did not emerge in Washington as the territory's spokesman; William A. Clark had shown well there, but Maginnis seemed to be the central figure in the Montana group on Capitol Hill. "It is about time that the feathers of this Bantam were clipped," wrote Washington McCormick, ten months after Hauser took office.[101]

To be sure, Hauser kept a hand in on all appointments, sometimes to his regret. At Toole's request, he endorsed a young Democrat, William B. Webb, for secretary, over Horace Buck of Benton. One of his constituents had warned him against Buck, "this Hermorphradite for any position within the gift of President or Governor." "Mr. Hor-*ass* R. Buck has one foot in the Republican kitchen, the other in the backyard of Democracy and stands ready and willing to jump either way for an office." Hauser was also warned against Webb, but too late. Webb had helped split the party already, Perry McAdow wrote, and if appointed, "will not only be a detriment to our future success but will be a great source of annoyance and mortification to you."[102] This prediction proved accurate: Webb, who became territorial secretary, ultimately was ousted for malfeasance in office. But nonetheless, even after he had left the governorship, Hauser would continue to play an important role in territorial appointments.[103]

Though a resident, it is doubtful if Hauser met more fully the needs and aspirations of the territory than other governors, especially Potts. His frequent absences indicated his view of the office, and while his party maintained numerical superiority, its margin was never a particularly safe one. In addition, the limitations of the territorial "system" helped make his administration no radical departure from those of his "foreign" predecessors. If Hauser was an advocate of Free Silver and of statehood under conditions friendly to large mine operators, he was not the first executive with these ideas.[104]

His role in legislative affairs was not great. Pestered by a "brigade

101. W. J. McCormick to Hauser (Missoula, May 4, 1886) Hauser MSS.
102. Horace Buck to L. Q. C. Lamar (Helena, September 28, 1885); Hauser to Buck (Helena, September 17, 1885), both in Horace Buck file, API; Toole to Hauser (Washington, July 5, 1885); McAdow to Hauser (Billings, August 21, 1885); Ford to Hauser (Sun River, June 2, 1886), all in Hauser MSS.
103. See, for example: Vest to Hauser (Washington, March 26, 1887); Marcus Daly to Hauser (Anaconda, November 11, 1887), *ibid.*; Hauser to Vest (n.p., April, 1887 [no other date]), copy, telegram, letterbook (1885–87), *ibid.*
104. Vest to Hauser (Washington, February 20, 1885) Hauser MSS; Report of the Governor of Montana (1885), 1002–3; Joseph A. Brown to Hauser (Glendale, December 21, 1885); William A. Clark to Hauser (Butte, January 15, 1886), both in Hauser MSS.

of Democratic patriots" clamoring for territorial appointments, he gave in in making nominations for auditor and treasurer and the Council accepted them "without a grimace."[105] His message to the fifteenth legislature, was, in the words of the *Herald*, "a document full of fruits of long experience and intimate knowledge of the history and wants of Montana." It urged strengthening the territorial militia, memorialized Congress for laws to provide for the sale of federal timberlands or for a stumpage tax on timber cut from U.S. lands, and condemned the defects in existing territorial statutes.[106] That he was for economy was indicated in his veto of an insane asylum bill; that he was sympathetic to cattlemen and to settlers in general was shown by his proclamation of a quarantine, his appointment of a territorial veterinary surgeon backed by the Montana Stock Growers' Association, and his insistence that Montana's Indians were better off in Indian Territory (Oklahoma) in a climate more conducive to agriculture.[107] But indications are that his official reports and messages were written by a Helena lawyer—a Republican at that—and how much is Hauser and how much is his ghost writer, is hard to say.

A few months after Hauser became governor, Commissioner of the Land Office William Andrew Jackson Sparks issued his circular cracking down on the cutting of timber on public lands and instituted suit against the Montana Improvement Company, in which Hauser was an important figure.[108] "If we are not allowed to cut timber on public lands it will stop all mining & set this Territory back ten years," Hauser telegraphed Vest. Vest went to work on Secretary Lamar and Toole managed to gain a stay of suits against the company pending a hearing, but the situation was grim. As to timber depredations, said Toole, Sparks "is crazy on the subject and is giving the newspapers a horrible Statement about 'Montana Timber Thieves'

105. *Herald*, January 25, February 2, 7, 1887.

106. *Ibid.*, January 12, 1887.

107. *Herald*, February 7, March 11, 1887. In 1885, Hauser complained that millions of acres of "the finest agricultural and grazing lands to be found on the continent" were included in Montana reservations. A year later he had decided: "If the Indians are to subsist by agriculture and become civilized and self-sustaining, a country further south, and with more natural rainfall, would suit them better." Report of the Governor of Montana (1885), 1000; Report of the Governor of Montana (1886), 833 (This is my own abbreviation for the document which was annually a part of the Report of the Secretary of the Interior).

108. Report of the Commissioner of the General Land Office in *Annual Report of the Secretary of the Interior, 1885,* 463–66; Report of the Commissioner of the General Land Office, in *Annual Report of the Secretary of the Interior, 1886,* 447–53.

every day or two."[109] Former governor Crosby offered his lobbying services and Marc Daly and other mining men petitioned Lamar and suggested that Hauser appoint a commission to meet with him in Washington. Hauser went in person; Toole also did yeoman work, and ultimately Lamar reversed himself, asking Toole to prepare something legal for the Montana case, an action which gave time and which Hauser believed would solve the problem.[110]

About a month before the legislature convened and after persistently denying rumors to the contrary, in December, 1886, Hauser tendered his resignation, in his words, because of the "absolute necessity of giving my entire attention to private business."[111] Newspapers in Montana and in the Midwest carried the story that his action had not been voluntary, and that he had been "practically forced" to resign because of his extreme criticism of Sparks. "We predicted Hauser's removal when he had the courage and fidelity to speak the truth in his report regarding the Sparks policy in Montana," said the *New North-West* grimly. "No official head can wag its tongue against that policy and stay on."[112] Governor Francis E. Warren of Wyoming later reiterated the same point of view—that Sparks had been responsible for his own suspension and for Hauser's "compelled" resignation.[113] Others, more magnanimous, insisted that Hauser had resigned to avoid conflict of interest when the legislature considered benefits to railroads in which he was interested.[114]

But Hauser denied these stories, contending that the press of private business and that alone was responsible. Likely his version is accurate. He was not without influence in Washington. There is no

109. Hauser to Vest (n.p., September 17, 1885), telegram, letterbook (1885–87); Vest to Hauser (Washington, September 20, 27, 1885); Toole to Hauser (Washington, September 20, 27, October 8, 1885), Hauser MSS.

110. Crosby to Hauser (New York, November 16, 1885), telegram; Daly to Hauser (Butte, November 13, 1885); Toole to Hauser (Washington, November 17, 1885; May 29, 1886); all in Hauser MSS; Hauser to Toole (Helena, October 27, 1885); Hauser to Daly (Helena, November 20, 1885), telegram, both in letterbook (1885–87), Hauser MSS.

111. Hauser to Cleveland (Washington, December 13, 1886), Hauser file, API.

112. *New North-West*, December 17, 1886. See Minneapolis *Tribune*, quoted in *Herald*, December 23, 1886; Chicago *Tribune*, quoted in *Herald*, December 28, 1886.

113. Francis Emory Warren MS dictation, 34, Bancroft Library. Sparks had recommended in October, 1886, that Warren be removed for dubious and probably fraudulent personal land entries. William Andrew Jackson Sparks to Cleveland (Washington, October 23, 1886), Cleveland MSS.

114. *Semi-Weekly Inter Mountain*, December 19, 1886.

indication that he was forced out: indeed, Cleveland waited nearly a month and a half before accepting his resignation.[115] He did not like the executive job and was simply too busy to do it justice. His own business was showing financial problems about this time and Hauser was the kind of man to look after his own affairs.

Whatever the reason for his decision, it was regretted by many Montanans, regardless of party. Hauser had assumed the position as a sacrifice, only out of pride in Montana and its interests, according to the *Herald*, and was "the most popular and satisfactory Governor Montana has ever had. . . ." A fellow editor at Great Falls agreed and believed his administration only demonstrated further "the utter folly and diabolism of importing some superannuated politician to govern this Territory."[116]

According to Hauser, when he resigned he recommended Martin Maginnis as his successor. Apparently this was part of a horse trade arranged by party leaders in Helena. In exchange for the support of Maginnis and Broadwater behind the reelection of Toole to Congress in 1886 and Hauser for the United States Senate after statehood, Hauser, who wanted out anyway, would resign after the 1886 campaign and he and Toole would back Maginnis for the governorship and support a bill that Toole had previously helped block for right of way across a reservation. In that canvass the "Bloody Shirt" still waved, as Wilbur F. Sanders, the old war stallion, made his fourth bid for the delegateship.

> The Bourbon yell sounds just as loudly,
>   'Tis the same old yell we heard of old,
> And the Bourbon rag flaunts just as proudly
>   With treason stamped, from every fold.
>
> On every fold, my fair Montana,
>   But for the future have no fears,
> For God and people both have said it
>   That Sanders wins the next two years.[117]

But God and the people spoke too softly and in addition failed to get out the vote: Toole's margin of victory was a substantial one.

115. *Herald*, December 23, 1886; *Semi-Weekly Miner*, January 5, 1887; Hauser to Cleveland (Washington, December 13, 1886), Hauser file, API. This is endorsed as accepted, January 27, 1887.

116. *Herald*, December 18, 1886; February 7, 1887; March 18, 1889; Great Falls *Tribune*, quoted in *Herald*, February 10, 1887.

117. Quoted in *Herald*, October 28, 1886. See also September 16, 21; December 18, 1886; February 7, 10, 1887, March 18, 1889.

Broadwater had "marshalled his Central Montana graders and voted them like sheep for Toole," and Sam Hauser had used his influence with the Northern Pacific, according to the press.[118]

Even so, the gubernatorial mantle somehow did not descend on Maginnis. Possibly Hauser and Toole did all they could but "simply couldn't deliver the goods"; the Minneapolis *Tribune* believed Cleveland turned thumbs down on Maginnis because he was attorney for the St. Paul and Manitoba Railroad.[119] Maginnis, and Broadwater too, had reason to suspect that Hauser had done nothing to carry out his end of the bargain and might even have scuttled Maginnis's chance for the appointment. ". . . Broad thinks that Hauser 'threw the lash' to him pretty lively in the governorship deal. . . . Hereafter when Broadwater and the ex-Governor meet it will require a spirit thermometer to determine how coldly they will gaze on each other."[120]

And though the impending vacancy was to be a guarded secret, open only to those friendly to Maginnis, the word got out and soon it was announced that ". . . a Kentucky colonel, by gad, suh, has been chosen by that patriotic statesman, Cleveland, to rattle around in Hauser's seat. . . ."[121] The "Kentucky colonel" who "scooped the persimmons," as the *Inter Mountain* put it, was Preston H. Leslie, whose selection came as "a grievous surprise. . . . Leslie wanted an office. He asked for a judgeship. The President plugged the first hole with him that was empty," was the Fisks' explanation.[122]

A Democrat, a temperance advocate, and a man of varied political experience, Leslie had served four years as the "Coldwater Governor" of the Blue Grass State.[123] When he was sworn in early in February, 1887, in Hauser's own office in the bank, which he used temporarily until his own was ready, he was described as sixtyish and vigorous: "He is tall and spare with a well shaped head covered by a thick suit of grey hair. His whiskers, which he wears Abraham Lincoln style, are

118. *Herald*, November 2, 13, December 15, 16, 1886; *Semi-Weekly Inter Mountain*, December 19, 1886; January 5, 1887; Waldron, *Montana Politics*, 46.
119. Herald, December 16, 17, 20, 1886.
120. *Ibid.*, December 16, 1886; *Semi-Weekly Inter Mountain*, December 19, 1886.
121. *Semi-Weekly Inter Mountain*, December 19, 1886.
122. *Ibid.*; *Weekly Independent*, December 16, 1886; *Herald*, December 18, 20, 1886.
123. Born in Kentucky in 1819, Leslie was a lawyer by profession. He had served as circuit judge, state senator, lieutenant governor, and finally in 1871 as governor of his native state. *Progressive Men of the State of Montana*, 176; *Herald*, December 18, 1886; *Weekly Independent*, December 16, 1886.

also grey. . . . His manner is frank and cordial and marked by the courtesy of his class."[124]

A hard-working executive, but never a real leader, Leslie rarely took a holiday, except for the Sabbath, working even on Washington's Birthday. And although he verbally prodded the legislature, urging a Sunday law, revenue reforms, and improved prisons and facilities for the insane, he was largely ignored.[125] Behind the scenes, men like Hauser, Broadwater, Tom Power, W. A. Clark and Marc Daly called the tunes. But Leslie served two years and bothered few people, though in the beginning there were the usual "carpetbag" complaints. Some thought his position in favor of free wool was realistic; others raised their eyebrows when he pardoned a Helena courtesan convicted of grand larceny, on the grounds that the territorial penitentiary was not equipped to accommodate female prisoners. Early in 1899 with the pocket veto of an appointment bill, he incurred the wrath of prominent Republicans, Wilbur F. Sanders among them. "Republican party demands his removal," was the message disgruntled party leaders sent to their delegate in Washington.[126]

Meanwhile, Delegate Toole had declined a third term. His decision not to run again in 1888 set the stage for a bitter, scandal-ridden contest, the beginning of open feud between two of Montana's most powerful figures, William A. Clark and Marcus Daly. The fastidious and aloof Clark, "millionaire banker, monopolist and member of the great foreign copper trust," as someone labeled him, was the Democratic nominee and was looking beyond the delegateship to the United States Senate. His Republican opponent, Thomas H. Carter, a Silver Bow lawyer, was described as "a son of an Irish exile, illustrating in his person the consequences of the blighting and expatriating consequences of British Free Trade," a position that fitted neatly with the Republican damnation of Cleveland, England, and free trade.[127]

In a campaign stressing personalities and national issues, Carter was the candidate of statehood: ". . . I believe I can do as much in

124. *Herald*, February 7, 8, 1887; *Weekly Independent*, December 16, 1886; Preston H. Leslie to L. Q. C. Lamar (Glasgow, Kentucky, January 28, 1887), Leslie file, API.

125. Leslie to legislature (January 14, 1889), *Council Journal*, 16 Session (1889), 7–15; *Herald*, August 29, 1887; February 22, 1889.

126. *Herald*, December 23, 1886; February 9, 1887; January 4, October 31, 1888; Sanders et al. to Thomas Carter (Helena, March 15, 1889), telegram, Benjamin F. White file, API.

127. *Herald*, September 18, 1888.

the next six months for Montana's admission as the Democrats have done in the last six years," he told his audiences."[128] With a Democratic administration in Washington, the local Republicans condemned Cleveland's failure to appoint resident officials, and Carter argued for the tariff, with support of former governor Carpenter. Former chief justice Wade gave his endorsement, while several territorial officers, including Secretary "Sweet William" Webb, took an active role on behalf of Clark.[129] Clark embraced the Cleveland position in favor of more moderate duties, but the tariff issue was a warm one, for wool-growers and copper interests were both sensitive. Another issue was much more personal: "Yeastpowder Bill," as opponents called Clark, was accused of trying to buy his way into office with his "boodle bar'l," a weapon of some importance.[130]

The result of the election was surprising. Carter won handily and the *Herald* chortled with glee: "Brainy Tom Carter Goes to Congress With a Majority of 3000 or More to Back Him"; "Montana is Redeemed From Bourbon Rule and Will Enter the Union a Republican State"; "The Boodle Candidate Given a Back-Set."[131]

> Here's to Montana,
> Which will now be admitted,
>   Good-bye, Old Grover, good-bye;
> In people and wealth
> None are better fitted,
>   Good-bye, Old Grover, good-bye.[132]

No one was more stunned than Clark supporters. Maginnis saw a number of contributing factors: Cleveland's nonresident appointments, the administration's tariff position; but above all, "a powerful personal combination against him of men whose support he expected."[133] Clark was bright enough to look behind the scenes, and he wrote Maginnis: "The conspiracy was a gigantic one, well planned, and well carried out, even though it did involve the violation of some

128. *Ibid.*, October 8, November 3, 1888.

129. *Ibid.*, October 19, 24, November 1, 2, 1888; *Weekly Independent*, October 25, November 1, 1888.

130. *Herald*, September 11, October 5, 10, 18, 19, November 5, 1888. A Missoula politician wrote Thomas Power, Republican territorial treasurer, a few weeks before the election: "In this County for the next ten days anyway 'silence is golden' as we don't want Mr. Clark's barrel turned loose on us." Alvin Lent to Thomas C. Power (Missoula, October 22, 1888), Power MSS, political box.

131. *Herald*, November 7, 1888.

132. *Ibid.*, November 16, 1888.

133. *Pioneer Press* (St. Paul), November 17, 1888, quoted in *Herald*, November 20, 1888.

of the most sacred confidences. This was necessary, or deemed necessary, at least in order to insure success. However as you suggest the day of retribution may come when treason may be considered odious." [134] Maginnis to the contrary, Clark saw that the tariff had not beaten him—the largest wool-producing counties went strongly for him; but he was beaten in Butte, Anaconda and the western mining counties where Marc Daly's influence was strong and where the Northern Pacific Railroad and the Montana Improvement Company employed large numbers of men. Charles Broadwater held Daly and Hauser responsible for "the late Democratic smash-up" and Clark was inclined to agree. His defeat, he said years later, was caused by "an envious and diabolical desire" by Daly "to forever destroy my political influence in the Territory." [135]

Careful analyses indicate that the vote against Clark was controlled. Some coercion was evident, along with liberal use of whiskey and cigars. Employees of the Anaconda mine, the Montana Improvement Company, and the Northern Pacific Railroad were instructed how to vote and intimidated. Daly, Hauser, and others connected with the Montana Improvement Company were under indictment for trespass on public timber lands and Daly was convinced that to extricate himself would require political aid in Washington and that a Republican delegate in a Congress likely to go Republican was vital. [136]

Delegate Carter was only partly successful in getting the suits quashed—his most notable achievement in the six months he bore that status—but the election of 1888 signaled the beginning of a twelve-year feud, which, says Ross Toole, "in turn, was the fulcrum on which the entire political structure was precariously balanced for more than a decade." [137] As Table 1[138] indicates, it signaled a shattering of Democratic ranks, the election of the first Republican delegate in seventeen years. The "big four" were no longer acting in unison. Broadwater and Hauser were already at odds; now Daly and

134. Clark to Maginnis (Butte, November 10, 1888), Maginnis MSS.

135. *Congressional Record*, 56 Congress, 1 Session (1900), 5532. See K. Ross Toole, "The Genesis of the Clark-Daly Feud," *Montana*, I (April, 1951), 21–33, for a detailed analysis of this episode.

136. Toole, "The Genesis of the Clark-Daly Feud," 31–32; Toole, *Montana*, 181–82.

137. Toole, *Montana*, 174; K. Ross Toole and Edward Butcher, "Timber Depredations on the Montana Public Domain, 1885–1918," *Journal of the West*, VII (July, 1968), 351–62.

138. Compiled from Waldron, *Montana Politics Since 1864*.

TABLE 1. ELECTIONS OF MONTANA DELEGATES TO CONGRESS, 1864–89

Year	Winning Candidate	Number of Votes	Losing Candidate	Number of Votes
1864	Samuel McLean (D)	3,898	Wilbur F. Sanders (R)	2,666
1865	Samuel McLean (D)	3,808	Gad E. Upson (R)	2,422
1867	James E. Cavanaugh (D)	6,004	Wilbur F. Sanders (R)	4,923
1869	James E. Cavanaugh (D)	5,805	James Tufts (R)	3,745
1871	William H. Clagett (R)	5,274	E. Warren Toole (D)	4,861
1872	Martin Maginnis (D)	4,515	William H. Clagett (R)	4,196
1874	Martin Maginnis (D)	4,144	Cornelius Hedges (R)	3,313
1876	Martin Maginnis (D)	3,827	Erasmus D. Leavitt (R)	2,980
1878	Martin Maginnis (D)	6,485	Sample Orr (R)	2,757
1880	Martin Maginnis (D)	7,779	Wilbur F. Sanders (R)	6,381
1882	Martin Maginnis (D)	12,398	Alexander Botkin (R)	10,914
1884	Joseph K. Toole (D)	13,584	Hiram Knowles (R)	13,385
1886	Joseph K. Toole (D)	17,990	Wilbur F. Sanders (R)	14,272
1888	Thomas H. Carter (R)	22,486	William A. Clark (D)	17,360

Hauser deserted Clark. Lee Mantle, of the Butte *Inter Mountain,* put his finger on a basic fault when he noted that these men, Daly, Clark, Hauser, and Broadwater, were "not leaders in their party," but "autocrats of the strongest type," who unfortunately subscribed to the pernicious "theory of the millionaire employer that he can command the suffrage as well as the services of the unemployed. . . ."[139]

By this time, that good Republican Presbyterian elder Benjamin Harrison had been installed in the White House, and the search for a deserving replacement for Governor Leslie was under way. Now the leading contenders were all Montanans and the squabble over who would get the honor would be strictly at the territorial level. In the race was Isaac McCutcheon, now something of a power in the orthodox Montana Republican apparatus and who believed that he was entitled to the governorship. His appointment, he asserted would be "perfectly satisfactory to ninety-nine per cent of the Republicans."[140] Thomas C. Power was mentioned, as was Lee Mantle of Butte; Charles S. Warren was the "unanimous" choice of Silver Bow; but the most popular candidate was Lewis H. Hershfield, successful banker and head of the territorial Republican organization.[141]

139. Quoted in Toole, *Montana,* 179.
140. Petty jealousies were depriving him of "that which properly belongs to me"—the gubernatorial office—McCutcheon insisted. McCutcheon to Russell B. Harrison (Helena, March 6, 7, 1889), Russell B. Harrison MSS.
141. Louis A. Walker to Russell B. Harrison (Helena, March 6, 1889), *ibid.*;

A nasty intraparty fight soon developed, however, which not only menaced Republican harmony but threatened to offer a "splendid opportunity" to the Democrats unless resolved.[142] McCutcheon's supporters believed that his "family relations," like "Mantle's Gambling & Wh---ng," were insurmountable liabilities, and unknown to them, McCutcheon had been ruled out early: penciled across his application, dated March 9, 1889, were the words "Not desirable—abandoned his wife—street fights."[143] Reluctantly, McCutcheon withdrew from the race in favor of Charles K. Cole, Helena physician, former legislator, and vice-president of the National Bank, who was then pledged to push the former secretary for the post of attorney general.[144] Apparently with Broadwater's support, McCutcheon and Louis Walker, another would-be kingmaker, made an all-out effort to block Lewis Hershfield, using smear tactics that were both personal and anti-Semitic. Tom Carter's victory of 1888 was no tribute to Hershfield, they argued, but rather to the strong party organization he had inherited and to the support of the Northern Pacific Railroad. Hershfield's "family relations" were little better than McCutcheon's, Walker insisted, and his nomination could only be detrimental to the Montana Republican party. Already Montanans, Walker said, were asking "Haven't we plenty of Christians in the country without having to select a Jew?"[145]

On the other hand, Tom Power urged Delegate Carter to "Stand pat or the party ruined." Success depended upon Hershfield's appointment. Others saw the struggle as having a "demoralizing effect" on the Republican organization and urged the administration to "shake" the deadlocked contestants before irreparable harm was done.[146]

Working with McCutcheon and Walker was Russell B. Harrison,

A. Fred Wey and S. W. Graves to Russell B. Harrison (Butte, March 20, 1889), telegram, Charles S. Warren file, API; *Herald*, March 11, 18, 1889.

142. Lee Mantle to Thomas Carter (Butte, March 22, 1889), telegram, Benjamin F. White file, API.

143. McCutcheon application, with endorsement, McCutcheon file, API.

144. Cole application, with endorsements, dated March 15, 1889, Charles K. Cole file, API; Walker to Russell B. Harrison (Helena, March 10, 1889), Russell B. Harrison MSS.

145. Walker to Russell B. Harrison (March 6, 10, 14, 1889); McCutcheon to Harrison (Helena, March 7, 13, 1889), *ibid.*

146. Power to Carter (Helena, March 9, 16, 1889); George Irwin to Carter (Butte, March 20, 1889); Mantle to Carter (Butte, March 22, 1889), all telegrams, Benjamin F. White file, API.

son of the new president, whose opinions, even if not always accepted, had to be taken into account. Some believed that young Harrison— whom they called McCutcheon's "stand by advisor & only friend for years," was "out for Senator & bald headed at that." [147] But together, the Walker-McCutcheon-Harrison opposition was so persistent that Hershfield withdrew and party leaders settled upon a compromise candidate, Benjamin F. White, veteran merchant, banker, and the first mayor of Dillon. [148]

As Carter and Hershfield pointed out to the president, White was "a life long Republican, and a Republican from principle," and was not linked with any railroad group nor to any party rivalry. His selection "would prove a victory for all, and a humiliation to none of those candidates." [149] And perhaps they might have mentioned two other factors in favor of White: First, he was not Jewish; and second, "no senatorial bee buzzes in his bonnet," as the *Herald* expressed it. [150]

So White was the man. Governor Leslie received a letter of removal signed by the president and sent registered mail on March 26, [151] a letter that could not have been unexpected. "The Gubernatorial agony is over, at last," noted the *Miner*. White was perfectly acceptable—"a first-class man," to the *Herald*, but it was generally conceded that McCutcheon and Russell Harrison had not distinguished themselves. Many resented the "unwarranted and unwise action of the President's son, . . . the uncalled-for interference and the undue influence exerted" by him in the affair. [152]

White's administration was brief and undistinguished. His was a caretaker arrangement. Statehood came just a few months later and his role was to steer the territory through the organizational period. Commuting between Dillon and Helena, he was a governor in tran-

147. A. J. Seligman to Power (n.p., March 21, 1889), Power MSS.

148. Carter and Lewis Hershfield to Benjamin F. White (Washington, March 21, 1889), copy, telegram; White to Carter (Dillon, March 22, 1889), telegram, both in White file, API. Born in Massachusetts in 1838, White was educated at Pearce Academy in Middlebury, shipped out to Australia, then came to California where he raised fruit and read law in the Napa Valley from 1857–66, when he moved to Idaho and was clerk of the United States district court until 1878. One of the organizers of Dillon, he sat in the Montana legislature and made a fortune in mercantile and banking trade. *Progressive Men of the State of Montana*, 96–98; Benjamin White MS dictation (Dillon, 1889), Bancroft Library.

149. Carter to Benjamin Harrison (Washington, March 22, 1889); Hershfield to Harrison (Washington, March 22, 1889), White file, API.

150. *Herald*, March 18, 22, 1889; *Semi-Weekly Miner*, March 30, 1889.

151. Memo (n.d.), Leslie file, API.

152. *Semi-Weekly Miner*, March 30, 1889; *Herald*, March 25, 26, 1889.

sition for a people in transition.[153] Though he had not sought the job and probably did not want it, he took it as a service at a time when political stalemate threatened his party's ambitions; he took it, he said, in order "to increase our chances for making Montana a solid and reliable Republican state."[154]

In general, the post Potts era—1883 to 1889—was one of small men and small executive government. During this period the governors did not exert great influence by virtue of their office. Hauser was a potent force, as he was before and after his stint in the gubernatorial chair, but his strength had little to do with the governorship, which he tended to ignore. Legislative government was undoubtedly strengthened during these years, even despite Crosby's parade of vetoes.

153. *Herald,* April 10, September 14, 1889; Walker to Russell B. Harrison (Helena, April 19, 1889), Russell B. Harrison MSS.
154. White to Russell B. Harrison (Dillon, April 2, 1889), *ibid.*

8

"One of the Standard Amusements
of the City":
The Legislative Branch of Government

In many ways the most influential of the three branches of government in the territory was the legislative. Limitations imposed by the
organic act were few, the assembly could override the executive veto
by a two-thirds majority, and the legislature clearly represented local
feelings, as apart from federal. Inherently, however, Congress retained supreme authority: the power to declare acts of the assembly
null and void. The organic act was merely an enactment of the national law-making body, subject to amendment at will or even revocation if Washington's wise men saw fit. In the case of Montana,
Congress used its power to nullify sparingly; actually the disavowal
of the acts of the second and third legislatures in 1867 was the only
real invocation of this federal prerogative.[1] For the most part, obnoxious territorial laws were either undetected in Washington or
they were erased from the statute books before Congress could act.

But used infrequently though it was, the federal veto power provided a strong argument against the territorial system and would be
criticized repeatedly in the struggle for statehood. "The enactments
of the legislature are as the merest chaff before the breath of its

1. For a few examples of this rarely used federal veto power as it pertained
to areas outside Montana after the Civil War see: act of July 27, 1868, 15 USSL,
239; acts of July 1 and 15, 1870, 16 USSL, 183, 366.

master," said Chief Justice Wade in 1879. "They represent in mere mockery the shadow of self-government"—a sentiment reflected by the territorial assembly in the same year.[2]

The taint of the "bogus" legislature experience was never completely scrubbed from the minds of Montanans, but it was the principle, rather than the fact of federal veto, that kept alive suspicious resentment. On the other hand, the more positive aspects of congressional legislation for the territories also aroused apprehensions based on tangible evidence. Congress could and sometimes did enact laws for its western provinces that it could not have applied to the states. Perhaps Delegate Toole exaggerated when he charged that the territories were made "the dumping ground for all the experimental legislation that the whims and caprices of Congress can invent,"[3] but his constituents understood his point. In their minds, the question was basically very similar to that of the eighteenth-century American colonies: Wherein lay governmental power? Was there to be local or federal autonomy? For a quarter of a century Montanans sought to enhance their prerogatives of self-government, as they saw them, at the expense of controls from Washington.

In a number of ways, congressional policy tended to restrict the powers of the territorial legislature. Washington too often regarded members of the assemblies as mere adventurers, who were interested only in immediate and selfish ends, and whose activities should be sharply scrutinized. Legislators did either too much or too little; congressmen were not always sure which. While some argued that too many territorial laws were passed, other complained that legislatures "meet time and time again, and have nothing to do but simply receive their pay."[4]

One area in which congress limited territorial legislators was the passage of private acts. As noted, the first Montana session enacted more than a hundred special laws, mainly grants of charters and incorporations, and the second and third assemblies were only slightly less generous.[5] Some laws gave virtual monopolies to individuals or small groups which included Governor Edgerton and Chief Justice Hosmer; a few, like the chartering of the Upper Missouri River

---

2. Decius S. Wade, "Self-Government in the Territories," *International Review*, VI (March, 1879), 304; memorial to Congress (n.d.), *LM*, 11 Session (1879), 139.

3. *Congressional Record*, 50 Congress, 2 Session (1888–89), 822.

4. *Congressional Globe*, 40 Congress, 2 Session (1867–68), 4452.

5. The third assembly, for example, adopted thirty-two general laws, eleven resolutions, and fifty-eight private acts. *Montana Post*, January 5, 1866.

Steamboat Navigation Company, conferred privileges clearly outside of territorial jurisdiction.[6] To be sure, without potentially lucrative franchises to private concerns, few roads, bridges, or ferries would have been built during the early years. From the beginning, too, the assembly retained a measure of control of these concessions, regulating their lifespan, the rate of tolls to be collected, or the proper repair of equipment.[7]

But the spectre of exclusive wagon-road rights over routes which had for years been free public thoroughfares quickly brought complaints. Secretary Meagher officially protested in late 1865 the "illegal monopoly" and "damaging fraud" perpetrated in turning over some hundred miles of the Mullan Road to private companies.[8] Meagher rejected some of the private legislation of the second session, but that body nonetheless gained a reputation as the agent of privilege. "They have made their mark on every man's purse," remarked the *Post*.[9]

Soon complaints reached Congress. In April, 1866, James Ashley introduced a bill in the House which would forbid special or private legislation in the territories but would permit the granting of charters under general incorporation laws. The measure failed and late the same year Montana enacted legislation designed to achieve the same end.[10] Continued protests that Montana legislators tended to "overload the endurance of good nature or public safety" with charters to "partisan friends who use the emoluments of said privileges for political purposes," showed the act to be unworkable.[11] Early in 1867, Congress took positive action, prohibiting "private charters or special privileges," but allowing general incorporation laws to permit associations for "mining, manufacturing or other industrial pursuits."[12]

6. Acts of January 24, 1865, *LM*, 1 Session (1864–65), 569–70, 590–92, 595–98, 659.

7. *Council Journal*, 3 Session (1866), 121–22; act of January 14, 1869, *LM*, 5 Session (1868–69), 97; act of February 14, 1874, 8 Session (1874), 143.

8. Act of January 9, 1865, *LM*, 1 Session (1864–65), 561–63; Owen, *Journals and Letters*, II, 294–95; Thomas F. Meagher to William H. Seward (Virginia City, December 11, 1865), TPS; Meagher to Democratic Convention of Madison County (n.d.), in Bruce, *Lectures of Gov. Thomas Francis Meagher*, 44.

9. Meagher Executive Order (Virginia City, March 30, 1866), TPS; *Montana Post*, May 12, 1866.

10. *Congressional Globe*, 39 Congress, 1 Session (1865–66), 2148, 2600–2601; act of December 10, 1866, *LM*, 3 Session (1866), 3–6.

11. A. W. White et al. to James M. Ashley (Helena, December 26, 1866), Sanders MSS.

12. Act of March 2, 1867, 14 *USSL*, 426.

Montana tailored its statutes to fit these requirements,[13] but the new federal law was not retroactive. Special acts of the first three sessions remained on the books: when those of the second and third assemblies were expunged in the "bogus" legislature episode, many were reenacted by subsequent sessions. Because of loopholes, the problem remained, and Governor Ashley in 1869 could vigorously attack the vestiges of private laws still in effect. The more than forty dollars in tolls exacted on a team and wagon between Helena and Corinne, Utah, was "legalized highway robbery," he insisted; and in response to his urging and a petition to congress, the legislature did rescind a large number of franchises and charters.[14]

Another type of special legislation was the granting of divorces by the assembly's action, a common approach. "Charters were the strong suits, and divorces next in order," said a skeptical onlooker in 1866. "All the streams and roads throughout the Territory were spanned with charters for a ferry or a toll gate, and grass widows grew so thick that you could mow 'em down with a shingle, by swaths of scores in every section!"[15] Lacking general divorce laws, complainants were forced to appeal to the legislature for individual treatment. In returning two divorce bills unapproved in 1866, Acting Governor Meagher argued that they gave no grounds and that the courts were a more appropriate place for redress. ". . . these divorce bills," he lamented, "are multiplying in such a measure to bring our social condition into grave disrepute, and give to strangers the impression that Montana is a paradise for all belligerent wives and husbands. . . ."[16] Nullification of the laws of the second and third legislatures created a number of technical and temporary bigamists in the territory, but with time the number of divorce measures tapered off, although as late as 1874 the assembly still wrestled with them occasionally.[17]

13. Act of December 13, 1867, *LM*, 4 Session (1867), 25–39.
14. Ashley to legislature (December 11, 1869), *House Journal*, 6 Session (1869–70), 37–8, 39. For reenactment of a number of private laws see acts of November 25, December 2, 3, 6, 10, 12, 20, 25, *LM*, 4 Session (1867), 108–18, 120, 125–28.
15. "Goldrick," "Montana As It Is," unidentified clipping (May 25, 1866), Bancroft Scrapbook, 75. See also McClure, *Three Thousand Miles through the Rocky Mountains*, 371–72.
16. Meagher to legislature (April 4, 1866), *Council Journal*, 2 Session (1866), 217–18.
17. See *Madisonian*, quoted in *Herald*, November 1, 1872; *Herald*, February 6, 1874.

In 1872 and again in 1878 Congress clarified its general incorporation laws for the territories, specifically including railroads, irrigation ditches, wagon roads, colonization schemes, land improvement projects, municipal corporations, colleges, churches, libraries, or "any benevolent, charitable or scientific association."[18] Yet as late as 1886, when suggesting more stringent limitations, the House Committee on Territories went out of its way to condemn the "corrupting and demoralizing influences of local and class legislation" which still persisted.[19]

In response, Congress adopted a measure sponsored by Benjamin Harrison, then senator from Indiana, which among other restrictions, listed specific subjects on which territorial legislation was forbidden, except under general acts. These included divorces, the granting of special franchises, changing names of persons or places, assessment of taxes, protection of fish or game, regulation of court practices, remission of fines or penalties, changing the law of descent or interest rates, and the removal of county seats.[20]

Even while the bill was pending, Montanans protested; once it became law Governor Hauser complained that a great many Montana statutes would have to be reenacted. The Council debated formal petitions to Washington, but decided on silence, after it was pointed out that the states operated under the same limitations and that Montanans themselves had written such a provision into their proposed constitution of 1884.[21]

Probably the most onerous aspect of the Harrison law was that it limited the total indebtedness of a territory or a municipality to an amount equal to 4 percent of the taxable property therein. Senator Harrison had seen this provision as being "very important," but Governor Hauser saw it as "unjust and oppressive," and Delegate

18. Act of June 10, 1872, 17 *USSL*, 390–91; act of June 9, 1878, 20 *USSL*, 101.

19. Report of the Committee on the Territories on H.R. 5179 to prohibit passage of local or special laws in the territories, *House Report* No. 1477, 49 Congress, 1 Session (1885–86), 1.

20. Act of July 30, 1886, 24 *USSL*, 170–71. The creation of new counties and the location of county seats was excluded by a subsequent act. Act of July 19, 1888, 25 *USSL*, 366.

21. *Herald*, June 23, July 7, 21, 1886; January 27, 1887; Report of the Governor of Montana, 1886, 834; Constitution of 1884, *Senate Miscellaneous Document* No. 39, 49 Congress, 1 Session (1885–86), 7; Constitution of 1889, in Francis N. Thorpe, *The Federal and State Constitutions, Colonial Charters, and Other Organic Laws of the States, Territories, and Colonies* (Washington, 1909), IV, 2307.

Toole believed it "bound the legislature hand and foot" and would retard economic development.[22] Although the courts did interpret the act to prevent Helena from incurring further bonded indebtedness to build its own water plant, actually the 1884 constitution would have put comparable limitations on counties and cities and it is doubtful if the territory—now debt-free—contemplated further debt for fear of jeopardizing its chances for statehood.[23] Opposition seems to have stemmed primarily from a fear of the principle of such federal controls. This was the case also when Montanans grumbled about a national law (1886) which stipulated that study of the effects of alcohol and narcotics must be included in the public school curriculum in the territories. Some residents thought the school curricula already too burdensome; others believed manual training more important; while still others suggested that the new subject might "stimulate the youthful mind to greater activity," only if "attended by the science of cards and other concomitants" as was the case outside school.[24]

If Congress was not likely to exert much control over personal drinking habits, it was in a position to provide a check on the territorial legislative assembly. It had the power to set the number and pay of the members of each chamber, the time of meeting, and the length of sessions, and to regulate the governor in calling extraordinary sessions to meet special problems. But congressmen and Montanans rarely saw eye to eye on most of these questions and territorials spent much time, without great success, trying to change them.

As indicated earlier, a lack of agreement over the number of legislators was one of the causes of the great debacle of 1866–67. After the first two assemblies had met with seven members of the Council and thirteen of the House, by a territorial law of early 1866, the third session convened with a membership of thirteen in the Council and

22. Act of July 30, 1886, 24 *USSL*, 171; Benjamin Harrison to George Edmunds (Washington, May 27, 1886), Harrison MSS; Report of the Governor of Montana, 1886, 834–35; *Congressional Record*, 50 Congress, 2 Session (1888–89), 821; *Herald*, January 17, 1887.

23. Constitution of 1884, *Senate Miscellaneous Document* No. 39, 49 Congress, 1 Session (1885–86), 26; *Herald*, December 14, 15, 1886.

24. Act of May 20, 1886, 24 *USSL*, 69. For the movement to dry up Montana by congressional action, see: *Herald*, February 11, 1873; January 17, 1887; *Daily Independent*, May 22, 1886; *Congressional Record*, 46 Congress, 2 Session (1879–80), 1069; 49 Congress, 2 Session (1886–87), 420; 50 Congress, 1 Session (1887–88), 2242; Report of the Select Committee on Alcoholic Liquor Traffic on Sale of Intoxicating Liquors in the Territories, *House Report* No. 2586, 48 Congress, 2 Session (1884–85), 1; Report of the Committee on the Territories on the manufacture and sale of intoxicating liquors in the Territories, *House Report* No. 2444, 49 Congress,, 1 Session (1885–86), 1.

twenty-six in the lower chamber, and prescribed these numbers for future legislatures.[25] By nullifying the acts of the second and third assemblies, Congress reduced them to the original seven and thirteen respectively, but the legislature immediately boosted the figures to thirteen and twenty-four, and with the addition of two more representatives again reached the maximum total in 1872. Six years later, Congress standardized the legislatures of all the territories, limiting them to twelve members in the Council and twenty-four in the House and requiring that redistricting and reapportionment be carried out in the next session of the assemblies.[26] Shorn of one of its councilmen and two representatives, Montana, like Idaho and Wyoming, failed to agree on a new apportionment, and Governor Potts was compelled to call a special legislative session in the summer of 1879. But Potts vetoed a reapportionment bill set up along county lines instead of population distribution, and it appeared that once more, for the second time in Montana history, there could be no legal convention of the legislature without federal intervention. Consequently Congress took special action, by a law empowering a "board of apportionment," consisting of the governor, the speaker of the House and the president of the Council, to redistrict the territory on the basis of the 1878 guidelines and the population figures of 1880.[27] Even so, with population steadily increasing, Montanans were never content with a legislature made up of but thirty-six members: they constantly complained of "inadequate representation" and urged a larger assembly, without success.[28]

25. *House Journal*, 3 Session (1866), 3; *Council Journal*, 3 Session (1866); 4; act of December 13, 1866, *LM*, 3 Session (1866), 56–57.

26. Act of March 2, 1867, 14 *USSL*, 426; act of December 13, 1867, *LM*, 4 Session (1867), 87; act of January 10, 1872, *LM*, 7 Session (1871–72), 561–62; act of June 19, 1878, 20 *USSL*, 193; act of June 27, 1879, 21 *USSL*, 35; *Herald*, May 31, 1878.

27. Potts Proclamation (June 4, 1878); Potts to Council (July 21, 1879), both in *Council Journal*, Extra Session (1879), 8, 83–84; *Herald*, July 22, 23, 1879; August 17, September 11, November 4, 1880; February 20, July 18, 1882; *Congressional Record*, 46 Congress, 1 Session (1879), 2011; 47 Congress, 1 Session (1881–82), 3705; Report of the Committee on the Territories on the reapportionment of the members of the Legislatures in the Territories of Montana, Idaho, and Wyoming, *Senate Report* No. 538, 46 Congress, 2 Session (1879–80), 1; act of June 3, 1880, 21 *USSL*, 154.

28. Memorial to Congress (n.d.), *LM*, 11 Session (1879), 139; memorial to Congress (n.d.), *LM*, 15 Extra Session (1887), 112–13; *Billings Herald*, June 1, 1882; *Congressional Record*, 47 Congress, 1 Session (1881–82), 3705; 48 Congress, 1 Session (1883–84), 121. The constitution of 1884 provided a 45-member house and a 21-member senate; that of 1889 stipulated 16 members for the senate and 45 for the house at the first session. Constitution of 1884, *Senate Miscel-*

Congress also determined the rate of compensation for legislators. The organic act of 1864 allowed each member four dollars a day during attendance and twenty cents a mile for travel to and from sessions, with additional stipends for presiding officers and lesser functionaries in both houses. Especially when paid in depreciated greenbacks, legislators deemed these allowances unrealistic and at the first session voted themselves and their successors supplemental compensation from the territorial treasury. In addition to federal fees, each member would receive a per diem of twelve dollars, plus twenty-five cents a mile for travel, and Congress was asked to assume this additional expense, an action that body refused.[29]

With nullification of the laws of the first two sessions, compensation reverted to the unvarnished level of the organic act. While Governor Potts condemned the principle of legislators voting themselves extra stipends "as robbery" and called upon Congress to prohibit it, the legislators asked Congress to raise their salaries by at least 100 percent.[30] Congress responded in 1873 by increasing per diem payments to six dollars, and by banning supplemental pay to officials or assemblymen; five years later it frugally reduced per diem payments to the 1864 level, just retribution for the "folly and wickedness" of the Democratic legislature, according to Republican stalwarts in Lewis and Clark County.[31] But even Republican Bob Fisk agreed that the fiscal limitations on the legislature were humiliating "Wood sawyers or choppers can make more than the government allows legislators," he complained early in 1879.[32] Yet despite protests and despite positive recommendations by the House Committee on the Territories for realistic increases, travel and per diem expenses remained unchanged after 1878.[33]

laneous Document No. 39, 49 Congress, 1 Session (1885–86), 5; Constitution of 1889, Thorpe, *Federal and State Constitutions*, IV, 2305.

29. Act of May 26, 1864, 13 *USSL*, 90; act of January 24, 1865, *LM*, 1 Session (1864–65), 391–92; memorial to Congress (n.d.), *LM*, 718–19; joint resolution, April 4, 1866, *LM*, 2 Session (1866), 50; joint resolution, November 30, 1866, *LM*, 3 Session (1866), 3.

30. Benjamin F. Potts to James A. Garfield (n.p., October 26, 1872), copy, Potts letterbook; memorial to Congress (n.d.), *LM*, 7 Session (1871–72), 645–46; *Weekly Independent*, January 6, 1872.

31. Act of January 23, 1873, 17 *USSL*, 416; act of June 19, 1878, 20 *USSL*, 193; Official Opinions of the Attorneys-General of the United States, *House Miscellaneous Document* No. 238, 51 Congress, 1 Session (1889–90), 540–42; *Herald*, July 7, 1873.

32. *Herald*, January 13, 1879.

33. Memorial to Congress (n.d.), *LM*, 11 Session (1879), 139; *Congressional Record*, 47 Congress, 1 Session (1881–82), 2531; 48 Congress, 1 Session (1883–

Congress also determined how often the legislature should meet and for how long. The organic act called for annual sessions, with House members holding their seats for one year and Councilmen elected for two. As part of an economy drive, Congress tacked a rider on the annual territorial appropriations bill in 1868 stipulating that thereafter funds for legislative expenses would be distributed for biennial sessions only.[34] Although there was no express authorization to carry this amendment into effect, Montana's legislature on its own provided for sessions every two years, only to have to adjust its meetings to coincide with the even numbered years after Congress enacted specific legislation in 1869.[35]

During the territorial period, the Montana legislature was called into extraordinary sessions on four separate occasions: in December, 1867, after the fourth assembly failed complete reenactment of the laws nullified by Congress earlier in the year; in the spring of 1873, ostensibly to assume control of the federal penitentiary and to reconcile conflicting statutes, but actually to consider railroad subsidies; in 1879, when the regular session could not agree on redistricting; and in 1887 when a bad bounty law threatened to bankrupt the territory.[36] In each case—and when the legislature made the switch from meeting in even to odd years in 1877—the federal government was asked to provide additional funds for legislative expenses. And in each instance, Congress responded, albeit sometimes late and begrudgingly. In 1874, when it appropriated $16,395 for costs of the 1873 special session, it stipulated that thereafter no extra session might be called in any territory without explicit prior approval of the president.[37] Montanans chafed under this restriction and blamed Delegate Martin Maginnis, but in 1879 and 1887 when emergencies required special sessions, both presidential approval and congressional money were readily available.[38]

---

84), 121; Report of the Committee on the Territories on Additional Members of Territorial Legislatures, *House Report* No. 1322, 48 Congress, 1 Session (1883–84), 1; *Semi-Weekly Miner*, March 9, 1887.

34. Act of May 26, 1864, 13 *USSL*, 87; act of July 20, 1868, 15 *USSL*, 109; *Congressional Globe*, 40 Congress, 2 Session (1867–68), 4502–3.

35. Act of January 15, 1869, and memorial to Congress, January 15, 1869, *LM*, 5 Session (1868–69), 95, 116–17; act of December 24, 1869, *LM*, 6 Session (1869–70), 92; act of February 11, 1876, *LM*, (1876), 70; James Tufts to Legislature (December 8, 1868), *Council Journal*, 5 Session (1868–69), 23; act of March 1, 1869, 15 *USSL*, 281; act of May 30, 1872, 17 *USSL*, 29.

36. See Chapters 3, 6, and 11.

37. Act of June 22, 1874, 18 *USSL*, 135–36.

38. Act of June 16, 1880, 21 *USSL*, 240; act of March 30, 1888, 25 *USSL*,

One of the reasons usually given for the calling of extraordinary sessions was that the limit of forty days set by the organic act was too short, although Governor Potts in 1871 expressed pleasure that legislators were proscribed in time "so they can't devil me very long."[39] But after pleas from the territory, Congress in 1880 extended the limit to sixty days and this stilled complaints. Indeed, the proposed constitution of 1884 would have reestablished the forty-day maximum, while that of 1889 allowed sixty.[40]

Like the judiciary, Montana's territorial legislatures met in make-shift quarters, ranging from the old People's Theater in Virginia City, to Taylor's Broadway Hall, the Grand Street Church, and, for the last session, the new Lewis and Clark County Courthouse in Helena.[41] Usually the two houses met in different buildings; in at least one instance, because committees convened separately, they used three.[42] Alexander McClure was intrigued with the meeting of the House in Con Orem's Melodeon Saloon late in 1867, especially after adjournment, when Con rolled up the rug, spread sawdust on the floor, and treated fans to fifty rounds of fisticuffs.[43]

It was the secretary of the territory who leased the facilities and saw to their outfitting for the assembly's convenience. It was the secretary who sought to shave legislative costs when funds for extra sessions were in doubt; who received the blame when physical problems developed— when hat and coat racks fell off the wall, when heat was inadequate, when smoke from the stoves caused "great inconvenience and suffering" in the House, or when melting snow dripped through the ceiling and left the Council chambers "flooded with the prohibition element."[44]

49; memorial to Congress (n.d.), *LM*, 9 Session (1876), 198–99; *Herald*, April 21, August 3, 1874.

39. Potts to Rutherford B. Hayes (Virginia City, January 10, 1871), Hayes MSS.

40. Memorial to Congress (n.d.), *LM*, 11 Session (1879), 139–40; *Herald*, December 23, 1880; act of December 23, 1880, 21 *USSL*, 312; Constitution of 1884, *Senate Miscellaneous Document* No. 39, 49 Congress, 1 Session (1885–86), 5; Constitution of 1889, Thorpe, *Federal and State Constitutions*, IV, 2305.

41. *Montana Post*, November 3, 1866; *Weekly Independent*, November 4, 1871; *Herald*, October 30, 1875; November 21, 1876; June 27, 1879; November 13, 1880; January 5, 1883; November 23, 1886; June 9, 1887; January 2, 1889.

42. *Herald*, November 21, 1876.

43. McClure, *Three Thousand Miles*, 384–85, 422–23.

44. James E. Callaway to R. W. Taylor (n.p., April 26, 1873), LT, Vol. 12; House Resolution, January 21, 1876, *House Journal*, 9 Session (1876), 145; *House Journal*, 13 Session (1883), 62, 68; *Herald*, January 13, 1885; February 5, 1887.

The convening of the legislature was an occasion of interest and pleasure, a source of much excitement to the public. Sometimes it was paralleled by a "Third House," a burlesque of the real thing accompanied by much wit and sarcasm.[45] So too was the legal assembly. McClure regarded that of 1867 as "one of the standard amusements of the city." The *Montana Post* had earlier echoed Charles II, who is supposed to have remarked of Parliament, "This is better than a play."[46] On opening day, at least, good will radiated throughout the capital, loudly expressed in oratory, blaring bands and the firing of salutes.[47] No doubt a majority of legislators were serious and reasonably sober citizens, but a few at least gave an alcoholic aroma to the entire body. "Whisky will suffer when those fellows gets here," a Virginia City resident wrote of the 1867 legislators; "about all they do is drink whiskey and play Billiards."[48] Councilman Granville Stuart named at least four legislators on a drunken spree one night during the 1872 session and a little later he described another as "in his glory legislating & drinking, hasn't been sober for six months. . . ."[49] How much of the reputation was earned is difficult to say, although it is significant that one observer thought the closing scenes of the final territorial assembly of 1889 "the most quiet and orderly" he had ever witnessed, and that no one had seen any of its members drunk or "in any disreputable place or company."[50]

What ever their reputation, saints or sinners, or most likely somewhere on the spectrum in between, Montana legislators do warrant some generalizations, though to characterize a "typical" assemblyman might be difficult. They were generally Democrats. After the first legislature, in which the Council was Unionist by a single vote, until 1885 the Republicans did not hold a majority in either house. Only once—in the sixteenth and final session—did the Republicans command both houses.[51] Generally the Democratic margin was

45. See entry for March 15, 1866, James Knox Polk Miller, *The Road to Virginia City: The Diary of James Knox Polk Miller*, ed. by Andrew Rolle (Norman, 1960), 98; McClure, *Three Thousand Miles*, 411; *Herald*, May 14, 1873.

46. McClure, *Three Thousand Miles*, 410; *Montana Post*, November 3, 1866.

47. *Montana Democrat*, March 8, 1866; *Herald*, January 10, 1881.

48. "Jack" [no other name] to James Fergus (Virginia City, February 23, 1867), copy, Allis Stuart Collection.

49. Granville Stuart to James Stuart (Virginia City, January 4, 1872), Stuart MSS; Granville Stuart to James Stuart (Deer Lodge, April 24, 1873), in Anne McDonnell, ed., "Letter to a Brother," *Montana*, III (Summer, 1953), 6. See also Granville Stuart to James Stuart (Virginia City, December 23 1871; Deer Lodge, February 14, 1872), Stuart MSS; *Herald*, May 17, 1873.

50. *Herald*, March 15, 1889.

51. In 1885 the House was Republican by a margin of 15 to 9, while the

clear cut: the fourth session (1867), labeled by some Republicans the "Missouri Admiration Society," had but one Republican and he was ruled ineligible; in the fifth assembly (1868–69), the make-up was thirteen to zero for the Democrats in the Council and twenty-two to two in the House; while in the thirteenth session (1883), the score stood fourteen to ten in favor of the Bourbons in the House and a close six to five margin in the Council, with one independent in the balance.[52]

In occupation, the average legislator was most likely to be a lawyer, a rancher, or a mining man, if a breakdown of three legislatures—the fifth, the thirteenth and the fifteenth—are fair representations.[53] Next in numbers came merchants and farmers. In background, a legislator was most likely to have been born in one of the eastern-seaboard states or in Kentucky or Missouri. In age, he was comparatively young. "Most of the members are young and vigorous, and but few grey hairs are seen in either House," remarked editor Fisk in 1881, after death had invaded the legislative halls for the first time in Montana's history.[54] In the fifth session the median age in the Council was forty-one and in the House thirty-four; in the thirteenth assembly, forty-eight in the Council and forty in the House; while in the fifteenth session the median was forty-five in the Council and thirty-nine in the House.

If observers noticed the absence of gray locks in the legislature, they also noticed a lack of political experience in the formative years. None of the first assembly had ever sat in a legislature before and the legislators' knowledge of parliamentary usage was limited. The governor knew even less, apparently, for after signing his first bill, he returned it to the house whence it originated.[55] In 1867, reacting as a good Republican should to an assembly that was predominantly Democratic, Alexander McClure saw only one member of either house "who had left a State reputation behind him when he came to Montana"—Sample Orr, who had once been a serious contender for the governorship of Missouri. "Taken as a body," said McClure,

Council remained Democratic. In the last legislature the Republicans controlled the House 19 to 5 and the Council 7 to 5. *Herald*, January 6, 12, 1885; November 23, 27, 1888.

52. McClure, *Three Thousand Miles*, 378; Barsness, *Gold Camp*, 128; *Montana Democrat*, August 29, 1868; *Herald*, December 2, 1882.

53. Compiled from data in *Montana Democrat*, January 16, 1869; *Herald*, January 9, 10, 1883; January 11, 12, 1887.

54. *Herald*, February 14, 1881.

55. N. J. Bond, "Early History of Colorado, Montana, and Idaho" (Denver, 1884), 59–69, MS, Bancroft Library.

"the legislature falls below mediocrity, although every county in the Territory has first-class men who would serve the forty days if called upon."[56]

But gradually men of experience emerged. Of the twelve councilmen and twenty-four representatives seated in 1883, nine of the upper house and seven of the lower had previously served; in the last session (1889) the figures were six in each house.[57] Individuals were reelected many times. In 1884 Granville Stuart could point with pride to his five terms; William E. Bass of Missoula served at least as many, and Alexander Mayhew of Deer Lodge sat as speaker of the House no fewer than six times.[58]

Early inexperience was reflected in the ambiguities and confusion of legislation and in occasional lapses which left glaring loopholes in the law. The original civil practice act was notoriously poor, until superseded by one adapted from that of California in 1867.[59] The basic school law left much to be desired and in 1872 was replaced with one copied almost verbatim from the statutes of California, the main features of which came originally from New York.[60] A year later, when Governor Potts rejected a new measure on grand juries, he did so with the comment that two conflicting sections on that subject were already in the statutes, hence there was no need for a third.[61] The probate law was notoriously bad. As a result of "mixing and comingling in an unintelligent, careless manner, portions of the laws of several states," it was "the blindest, most indefinite and ill-adjusted piece of legislation ever devised," according to the *Herald*; even after it was replaced in 1877 with one on the California model, it remained "a perfect morass of confusion."[62]

Laws quickly became outmoded or lacking in perspective. The theft of a week-old calf or of a herd worth $100,000 was grand larceny in 1880; the estray law was antiquated and "as dead as Pharoah";

56. McClure, *Three Thousand Miles*, 380, 385, 410; *Montana Post*, November 17, 1866.

57. *Herald*, January 9, 10, 1883; January 14, 1889.

58. Stuart to James H. Mills (Fort Maginnis, June 13, 1884), copy, letterbook 2, Stuart MSS; *Herald*, January 9, 10, 1883; Waldron, *Montana Politics*, 10–50.

59. Green Clay Smith to Legislature (December 14, 1867), *House Journal*, Extra Session (1867), 7; James Tufts to Legislature (December 8, 1868), *Council Journal*, 5 Session (1868–69), 15; act of December 23, 1867, LM, Extra Session (1867), 135–233.

60. Tufts to Legislature (December 8, 1868), *Council Journal*, 5 Session (1868–69), 17; act of January 12, 1872, LM, 7 Session (1871–72), 618–34; *Weekly Independent*, February 10, 1872; *Herald*, January 22, 1872.

61. Potts to House (May 3, 1873), *House Journal*, Extra Session (1873), 137.

62. *Herald*, January 3, 1876; February 15, 1877; December 19, 1888.

Governor Hauser believed in 1887 that "our road laws need repairing as much as our roads"; the mechanics lien law, even after modification that same year, was considered "wretched," "unjust," and "injurious."[63] Many laws were imperfectly drawn and not until 1887 did the territory authorize an attorney general, part of whose job was to draft bills when they left the hands of legislative committees.[64]

Poor codification of the laws was another persistent headache. Compilation of the statutes of the first session by a commission headed by Wilbur F. Sanders cost $9,053.42 and was flagrantly bad.[65] The codification begun in 1872 under former Judge George Symes was "a bundle of incongruities and contradictions," according to Governor Potts, with gross errors, including the complete omission of the law against adultery, an oversight not rectified until 1876. "As a matter of business and of public good," reported the Council Committee on Ways and Means, "it would have been far better had the six thousand dollars been given to the commission *to let the law alone.*"[66] Even as the final legislature convened in 1889, it was clear that the problem was unresolved. "Considering the fact that Montana has had so many codifications of her laws, each succeeding one worse than its predecessor, it requires considerable courage to still recommend another," complained the *Herald.*[67]

Montana's legislatures displayed the same strengths and weaknesses of their counterparts elsewhere, whether state or territorial. They began slowly, and frequently lost much time in organizational disputes or in political manoeuvering. The usual horseplay was there to break the monotony, and assemblies spent too much time memorializing Congress.[68] Individual members sometimes provided roadblocks to legislation, as in 1873, when the special session believed it had completed its work, only to find "a large number" of Council

63. *Ibid.,* November 8, 1880; January 12, 1887; December 19, 1888; January 2, 1889; *New North-West,* January 12, 1883.

64. Act of September 14, 1887, *LM,* Extra Session (1887), 60–61; *Herald,* January 18, September 15, 1887.

65. Smith to Legislature (November 5, 1867), *Montana Post,* November 9, 1867; Accounts of Auditor and Treasurer (April 2, 1866), *Council Journal,* 2 Session (1866), 197.

66. *Herald,* November 7, 1874; act of January 28, 1876, *LM,* 9 Session (1876), 60; Potts to Legislature (April 15, 1873), *Council Journal,* Extra Session (1873), 15, 57; Potts to William Clagett (n.p., January 13, 1873), copy, Potts letterbook.

67. *Herald,* January 11, 1889.

68. See Barsness, *Gold Camp,* 128; *New North-West,* December 31, 1869; *House Journal,* 13 Session (1883), 261; W. F. Chadwick to Maginnis (Helena, January 29, 1879), Maginnis MSS.

bills, yet to be acted upon, in the desk of a member who had already departed for home.[69] Both houses were lax in the granting of leaves of absence, failed to budget their time, and usually had to close with all-night sittings.[70]

Politics and personal animosities frequently hampered the functioning of the legislative branch, as might be expected with a usually Democratic assembly and a Republican executive. The bitter struggle between the legislature on the one hand and Justices Hosmer and Munson on the other in 1866–67 and the efforts to stifle the appointive power of Governor Ashley were cases in point. As one legislator wrote Sam Hauser near the end of the 1869 session, "We are getting along slowly, stand the Ashley & Fisk party off."[71]

Governor Potts, too, would have his differences, although from time to time both he and the legislature made gestures which implied better relations. The Council in 1873 invited the governor and the secretary "to occupy seats within the Rail" at any time they wished, and Potts was convinced, as he told an assemblyman in 1875 that "I go more than half way to meet you law makers in your efforts to legislate for the public good."[72] But, at the same time, Potts was aware of the independence of the legislature and clashed with them on more than one occasion. In 1879, when archenemy Wilbur F. Sanders was a member of the House, some members sought to censure the governor for his calling of the extra session, but the Committee on the Judiciary, to whom the censure resolution was referred, rejected it. A legislature "is not a political convention," said the Committee. "It is its business to legislate, to memorialize, but not to scold."[73] At the 1881 session, Democrats in the House took exception to statements in the governor's message, conducted a "long strike" of nearly a week, refusing to hear the message or have communication with Potts. Ultimately the governor "fetched 'em"; the Democratic majority gave in and the message was read—by a strict party vote and after the loss of much time.[74]

But sometimes the difficulties were wholly within the assembly

69. *Herald,* May 10, 1873.

70. *Ibid.,* January 9, February 16, 1877; January 15, February 25, March 7, 1887; *Semi-Weekly Miner,* February 13, March 16, 1889.

71. Walter B. Dance to Hauser (Virginia City, December 29, 1869), Hauser MSS.

72. Council to Potts (Virginia City, April 16, 1873), GEC; Potts to S. W. Langhorne (Helena, December 14, 1875), copy, Potts letterbook.

73. *Herald,* February 20, 1879; *House Journal,* Extra Session (1879), 155–56, 186.

74. *Herald,* January 5, February 1, 1876; January 17, February 1, 1881.

itself. Perhaps they combined personal and political issues, as in 1872, when Councilman Granville Stuart clashed with the president of the Council, who was well into his cups. Despite apologies, Stuart pledged undying political opposition.[75] Stuart also figured in the thirteenth session (1883), in which intralegislative antagonism reached the ridiculous. It all began in the Council—"this race of circumvention, hocus-pocus collusion, jockeyship, sleight-of-hand imposture, or whatever it is called in the books"—and Bob Fisk naturally blamed "our Democratic brethren."[76] First came a seating controversy over the Council seat from Dawson and Chouteau counties, but no quorum was present for five days, until Democrat Charles Cox finally arrived, having been snowbound for forty-eight hours. Next developed a deadlock over the selection of a president, a stalemate in which neither party would budge. In the midst of this impasse, Granville Stuart wrote a friend: "When Democrat meets Republican in the Legislature, then doth the fur fly. Nine days have we met, without either party scoring a single scalp—six & six, counting Mr. Back of Glendive, who acts with the '8 to 7' fellers & declines to take a back seat. . . ."[77] Some sought to adjourn the legislature for fear rustic local poets might be right when they wrote:

> The sages are all on their ears,
> To a man up a tree it appears,
> And unless they come down
> And take drinks all aroun',
> The session will last for ten years.[78]

Finally, on the seventeenth day and after eighty ballots, the Council agreed on a special selection committee and Stuart was chosen presiding officer.[79] But nearly a third of the term had been wasted, and even when the president was seated and the nineteen standing committees organized, the Council faced a continuing absenteeism problem which it attempted to solve by fining truant members two dollars for each offense.[80]

75. Granville Stuart to James Stuart (Deer Lodge, January 24, 1872), Stuart MSS.

76. *Herald*, January 10, 1883.

77. Granville Stuart to Thomas H. Irvine (n.p., January 16, 1883), letterbook 3, Stuart MSS; *Herald*, January 11, 12, 16, 1883; *Council Journal*, 13 Session (1883), 16–21.

78. *House Journal*, 13 Session (1883), 69; *Daily Inter Mountain*, January 24, 1883.

79. *House Journal*, 13 Session (1883), 69; *Council Journal*, 13 Session (1883), 22–27, 28.

80. *Council Journal*, 40–41; *House Journal*, 13 Session (1883), 285.

The difficulties of the thirteenth session were exceptions, just as they were largely the product of petty local politics. These same politics also determined how Montanans evaluated their various legislatures and their members. To a partisan like W. F. Chadwick, the 1876 assembly was "the most incomprehensible body that every assembled." It was made up, he said "of some good sensible & well-informed men; also, of a small lot of most *damned* rascals; also a lot of honest *damned* fools & the balance of damned fool rascals."[81] Secretary James Mills thought the eleventh "a very temperate, respectable body," "of fair average ability," and "in fact exemplary in all the moralities so far as I observe. . . ."[82] Butte editors believed the 1889 session was a failure; the *Herald* thought it "one of the best that Montana has had."[83]

There were those in the territory who argued that the legislature met too frequently and undertook too much. Men like Samuel Hauser contended that laws ought to be revised as infrequently as possible, to give people an opportunity to get to know them, a complaint reiterated in the constitutional convention of 1889. For this reason, some opposed extra sessions and urged that the legislature convene only every four or even six years and that a law must be passed by two successive assemblies before becoming final.[84]

Probably most sessions did attempt too much. In the second legislature, 138 measures were introduced, of which 64 survived debate. Of these, Acting Governor Meagher vetoed 16, 8 of which became law over his veto. The famous (or infamous) thirteenth saw 124 bills introduced in the House and 68 in the Council, with 80 House measures and 28 Council ones approved. The fifteenth legislature approved a total of 85 out of 175 introduced.[85] Invariably there was a flurry of action at the session's end, with the passage of badly drawn and hastily considered bills, and numerous pocket vetoes.[86]

81. W. F. Chadwick to Martin Maginnis (Helena, February 16, 1876), Maginnis MSS.

82. James H. Mills to Maginnis (Helena, January 23, 1878), *ibid.*

83. *Semi-Weekly Miner*, February 13, March 16, 1889; *Herald*, March 14, 1889.

84. *Herald*, January 12, 1887; February 6, September 13, 1883; *Proceedings, Constitutional Convention, 1889*, 447.

85. Thane, "An Active Acting-Governor," *Journal of the West*, IX (October, 1970), 544; unidentified clipping (n.d.), Stuart Scrapbook; *Herald* March 24, 1885; *Semi-Weekly Miner*, March 23, 1887.

86. In 1885, having been presented with fifty-eight bills only minutes before the session adjourned, Governor Carpenter used the pocket veto liberally. *Herald*, March 19, 24, 1885.

The governor's veto was exercised with reasonable frequency and sometimes overridden by a two-thirds majority. So often did this happen to Ben Potts that in 1879, after a measure had cleared the legislature, the *Herald* could jeer: "This bill shall, as is usual, become a law just as soon as the Governor vetoes it." But when Governor Crosby used the veto eleven times (and was overridden three times) in one session, the *Herald* saw this as a healthy action which "served as a warning to other schemers who had axes to grind."[87]

Within the framework established and modified slightly from time to time by Congress and within the abilities of its collective membership, the legislative branch in Montana functioned about as efficiently as its counterparts elsewhere. Largely an imitator, occasionally an innovator, it patterned most of its laws after those of older regions, but had to adapt them to the Montana environment. Legislation was a blend of tradition, trial and error, local politics, and the pressures of different groups and circumstances. In this Montana was normal.

On the one hand, early legislation reflected at least a desire on the part of the inhabitants to portray themselves as God-fearing, civilized Americans. From the first assembly on, statutes concerned themselves with conservation of natural resources: regulation of fish and game, limitation of careless burning, or prohibition against the defacing of scenery by gaudy advertising.[88] Other laws sought to prove that Montana was as refined as eastern America by restricting gambling, hurdy gurdy or dancing houses, prize fighting, and opium dens.[89] And although Governor Potts and blue-nosed Governor Leslie urged Sunday Blue Laws, and Leslie supported the temperance advocates, neither movement achieved much success in the territory.[90] As else-

87. *Ibid.*, February 22, 1879; March 9, 1883.
88. See act of February 2, 1865, *LM* 1 Session (1864–65), 407; act of December 4, 1867, *LM*, 4 Session (1867), 91; act (n.d.), *LM*, 6 Session (1869–70), 65; act (n.d.), *LM*, 11 Session (1879), 33–34; act of February 20, 1889, *LM*, 16 Session (1889), 157–58; *House Journal*, 16 Session (1889), 55; *Herald*, February 20, 1877; January 15, December 24, 1883.
89. See acts of November 21 and December 13, 1866, *LM*, 3 Session (1866), 49–51, 67–68; act of April 28, 1873, *LM*, Extra Session (1873), 69; Revised Statutes (n.d.), *LM*, 11 Session (1879), 578; act of June 22, 1879, *LM*, Extra Session (1879), 11; act of February 22, 1881, *LM*, 12 Session (1881), 65; acts of March 10 and 12, 1885, *LM*, 14 Session (1885), 108–9, act of March 9, 1887, *Compiled Statutes of Montana*, 15 Session (1887), 558–59; act of September 14, 1887, *LM*, Extra Session (1887), 75–76; act of February 20, 1889, *LM*, 16 Session (1889), 153–57; William B. Hundley to Hauser (Helena, February 20, 1885), Hauser MSS; *Herald*, January 25, 1875; December 21, 1880; January 13, March 16, 1885; August 31, 1886; January 26, 1887; *Weekly Independent*, December 20, 1888; *Billings Gazette*, February 21, 1889.
90. See *House Journal*, 6 Session (1869–70), 139; *ibid.*, 9 Session (1876), 27,

where, the Montana legislature regulated a few time-honored sectors of society, limiting milling charges or establishing rules for the medical profession, for example. Lawmakers sought to subsidize by tax exemption the first blast furnace, sugar beet refinery, and paper and woolen mills, but were quick to tax roller skating rinks and telephone and gas and electric companies. They created the offices of steam-boiler inspector and inspector of mines and passed at least token measures to involve government in labor disputes, although such statutes were weak and hard to enforce.[91]

If Montana did not lead in modern social legislation, some of its laws clearly overstepped the limits of legislative authority. One of 1866 gave Deer Lodge County commissioners jurisdiction over grazing lands, clearly a federal function; another a few years later disfranchised aliens who had declared their intent to become citizens, an unwarranted interference with federal naturalization laws; others would tax the right-of-way of the Northern Pacific Railroad and the personal property attached to it in direct disregard of national statutes.[92]

Legislation pertaining to the civil rights of minorities, especially the Chinese, sometimes reflected the same tendencies, as well as the basic racism of territorial residents. By 1870, the Chinese in Montana numbered 1,949 and congregated mainly in the mining towns of Madison, Deer Lodge, and Lewis and Clark counties; by 1880, the number had dropped to 1,165. Unwanted and regarded almost universally as "unmitigated heathens of the lowest social and moral

28; *ibid.*, Extra Session (1879), 171; *ibid.*, 13 Session (1883), 135–37; *Council Journal*, Extra Session (1873), 17; *ibid.*, 10 Session (1877), 34, 39; *ibid.*, 12 Session (1881), 22; *ibid.*, 13 Session (1883), 33; *ibid.*, 16 Session (1889), 9–10; act of February 11, 1876, *LM*, 9 Session (1876), 108; act of March 3, 1883, *LM*, 13 Session (1883), 51; act of March 10, 1887, *Compiled Statutes*, 15 Session (1887), 1035–38; Granville Stuart to T. C. Leland (Fort Maginnis, March 27, 1883), letterbook 2, Stuart MSS; *Herald*, January 8, 1874; March 19, 1875; February 8, 15, 1883; March 11, 1887; April 20, 1888; January 5, 15, 1889.

91. Act of January 15, 1869, *LM*, 5 Session (1868–69), 62; act of February 3, 1876, *LM*, 9 Session (1876), 113–14; act of February 21, 1879, *LM*, 11 Session (1879), 72; act of March 8, 1883, *LM*, 13 Session (1883), 58; *Compiled Statutes*, 15 Session (1887), 614–15; act of September 14, 1887, *LM*, Extra Session (1887), 76–77; acts of March 14, 1889, *LM*, 16 Session (1889), 101–8, 160–64; *Proceedings, Constitutional Convention, 1889*, 210, 213; *Herald*, March 11, 1887; *Semi-Weekly Miner*, March 16, 1889.

92. Act of April 12, 1866, *LM*, 2 Session (1866), 35; act of November 14, 1866, *LM*, 3 Session (1866), 83; act of January 12, 1872, *LM*, 7 Session (1871–72), 460; act of February 13, 1874, *LM*, 8 Session (1874), 76–77; Northern Pacific Railroad Company *v.* Garland, 5 *Montana Reports* (1884), 199; *Herald*, July 17, 1872; February 28, 1884.

type," to use Governor Crosby's words, the Chinese were restricted and harassed legally, as Montanans reacted very much like Anglo-Saxons elsewhere in the West.[93] Although the second legislature rejected a bill to prohibit marriage and cohabitation of whites with Chinese and blacks, in the next year (1867) it levied a discriminatory license fee of ten dollars per quarter on all males "now or who may hereafter be engaged in the laundry business," and subsequently the fee was boosted to fifteen dollars a quarter, then to twenty, despite the protests of Governor Ashley who believed the tax "utterly indefensible."[94] Another law, this one in 1872, forbade aliens from obtaining title or profits from mining property. Outsiders, including James A. Garfield, who served as legal advisor on the issue, saw this as "rank dishonesty" and as "outrageous" legislation aimed at the Chinese, but soon Chief Justice Wade, in a ringing exaltation of federal supremacy, declared it a violation of federal control of the public domain and this "blot upon our statute books," as one Montanan called it, was repealed.[95]

The legislature sometimes revealed an anti-black bias as well. In 1866, the Council adopted a bill to prohibit Negroes and mulattos from testifying in cases involving white parties, but apparently thought better of its action and reversed its decision a day later. Apparently blacks were able to vote, though an unfounded rumor to the contrary touched off inquiry on the floor of Congress in 1868 and later accusations of challenges to black voters in Helena proved without base.[96] But the school law of 1872 opened the way for clear-cut

93. *Ninth Report of the United States Census Bureau, 1870,* I, 46, 363; *Tenth Report of the United States Census Bureau, 1880,* I, 3; Report of the Governor of Montana (1883), 546.

94. Act of December 13, 1867, *LM,* 4 Session (1867), 240; act of January 15, 1869, *LM,* 5 Session (1868–69), 61; act (n.d.), *LM,* Extra Session (1873), 74; *Council Journal,* 2 Session (1866), 127, 129; Ashley to Legislature (December 11, 1869), *House Journal,* 6 Session (1869–70), 27.

95. See act of January 12, 1872, *LM,* 7 Session (1871–72), 494–97; act of January 15, 1873, *LM,* 8 Session (1874), 97; entry for September 26, 1873, in Harry J. Brown and Frederick D. Williams, eds., *The Diary of James A. Garfield* (East Lansing, 1967), II, 226; Territory of Montana *v.* Lee, 2 *Montana Reports* (1874), 137–38; *Weekly Independent,* January 6, 1872; *Engineering and Mining Journal,* XIII (March 19, 1872), 185; *Herald,* April 28, 1873. Even after repeal, Montana courts interpreted federal mining laws to bar aliens from location and purchase and anti-Chinese discrimination was still evident in 1889 when efforts were made to write drastic limitations into the new constitution. See Tibbetts *v.* Ah Tong, 4 *Montana Reports* (1883), 436; *Proceedings, Constitutional Convention,* 1889, 214, 215.

96. *Montana Post,* December 8, 1866; February 29, 1868; *Herald,* November 16, 17, 1876; *Weekly Independent,* March 9, 1872.

discrimination by prescribing separate schools for "children of African descent" at the discretion of school trustees.[97] Deer Lodge closed its doors to a black pupil in 1873 and three years later, in spite of the protests of the superintendent of public instruction, the Helena school board sanctioned a separate school for "the little bevy of colored children in town." There and at Benton the issue was a warm one until 1882, when Helena voters rejected separate schools, and 1883 when the legislature repealed "this relic of a past age, this burdensome and invidious distinction."[98]

Where the assembly was concerned, slow progress was made in changing the status of women. Until 1887, when it was advanced to fifteen, the age of consent remained at ten. Although married women were in 1874 granted the right as sole traders to transact business in their own names, property-rights legislation continued to be "five hundred years behind the demands of the age." Not until 1887, after Mrs. E. P. W. Packard of Chicago had lobbied in the capitol at Helena was this "useless, insulting and humiliating" law, this "relic of feudalism and barbarism" amended to give married women their full rights.[99]

These rights did not include the franchise, although in the 1880s female taxpayers became eligible to vote in school elections or to sit on school boards or serve as county superintendents of schools.[100] When it modified the election laws in 1873 giving the right to vote to all male citizens over the age of twenty-one and "all persons of the same age, who shall have declared their intention of becoming such citizens," the legislature unintentionally left the way open for women

97. Separate schools were to be established upon the application by parents or guardians of ten such children or by other means for a lesser number, the schools to be governed by the same rules as those for whites. Act of January 12, 1872, *LM*, 7 Session (1871–72), 627–28.

98. See *Herald*, August 19, 1873; March 4, 14, 27, April 25, August 19, 26, 1876; January 21, February 4, May 15, 1882; March 10, 1883; September 17, 1889; *House Journal*, 9 Session (1876), 339–40; act of March 7, 1883, *LM*, 13 Session (1883), 57. The 1880 Census indicated that of 159 public schools in the territory, only one was separate and for "colored," a term inclusive of Chinese and Indians as well as blacks. Of 4,667 students, 46 were "colored." *Tenth Report of the United States Census Bureau, 1880*, I, 916, 918.

99. Act (n.d.), *LM*, 1 Session (1864–65), 184; act of February 4, 1874, *LM*, 8 Session (1874), 93–94; acts of March 5, 7, 1887, *Compiled Statutes of Montana*, 15 Session (1887), 380, 509; *Herald*, January 3, 1876; February 10, 1883; January 12, 13, 21, February 11, March 3, 11, 1887.

100. Act of March 8, 1883, *LM*, 13 Session (1883), 53, 55; act of February 13, 1889, *LM*, 16 Session (1889), 100–101; act of March 10, 1887, *Compiled Statutes of Montana*, 15 Session (1887), 1180, 1191; *Herald*, March 10, 1883; *Semi-Weekly Miner*, February 16, 1889.

who had declared their intent, but quickly plugged the loophole when it met again.[101] Attempts to enfranchise women failed in 1876, and in the 1884 and 1889 constitutional conventions, where the opponents (who styled themselves opposed to "old maids and non-breeders") rejected the broader suffragette goals in favor of more limited rights.[102]

Territorial legislation was molded by a number of factors, including the makeup of the Montana population, the environment, and powerful interest groups. Because originally many of Montana's inhabitants came with experience from Missouri, California, or Colorado, laws often reflected those backgrounds. In the 1870s came a shift and larger migrations from the Midwest and the East. "These successive moves of population brought their peculiar and differing views of legislation and have left their foot-prints on the statutes," noted the *Herald*.[103] Environmental conditions prompted the legalizing of gold dust as an exchange medium, just as proximity to Canada brought the legal use of Canadian and English money.[104] A sparse population scattered over a large area resulted in legislative efforts to modify the court structure to take into consideration the distance factor.[105] Certainly Montana's geologic, geographic, and climatological features would have much to do with the determination of legislation, both directly and indirectly, through the important interest groups arising out of them.

Try as it might, the legislature was never successful in completely eliminating fraud and corruption at the ballot box or in curbing undue influence brought on its own members.[106] Some of the lobbyists in the territorial capital were minor—like the swarm of textbook agents who descended upon Helena after the assembly in 1881 took

101. Act of April 25, 1873, *LM*, Extra Session (1873), 48–49; act of February 13, 1874, *LM*, 8 Session (1874), 76–77.

102. See *House Journal*, 9 Session (1876), 255, 257; entry for January 14, 1884, Minute Book, 58. MHS film; D. M. Durfee, "Sidelights on the Making of the Constitution of Montana," unpublished typescript (July 26, 1940), 3–4, 8, MHS; *Proceedings and Debates of the Constitutional Convention . . . 1889*, 347–51, 363–75, 453–60.

103. *Herald*, December 23, 1880.

104. Act of January 27, 1879, *LM*, 11 Session (1879), 37.

105. See Chapter 9.

106. See Ashley to Legislature (December 11, 1869), *House Journal*, 6 Session (1869–70), 18–20; act of February 12, 1874, *LM*, 8 Session (1874), 61–62; act of February 8, 1876, *LM*, 9 Session (1876), 90–92; act of March 8, 1889, *LM*, 16 Session (1889), 124–35; *Herald*, March 5, 8, 1889; *Semi-Weekly Miner*, March 16, 1889.

it upon itself to prescribe texts for the territorial school system; or the horde of drummers who urged repeal of the commercial license law in 1887.[107] Newspaper editors commonly lobbied for printing contracts and railroad interests were well known for their efforts to promote subsidization in the seventies.[108] But in the long run, the most important influences were the mineral industry and the cattlemen. Mining was likely the most singularly powerful force over the full quarter of a century: mining brought the territory into existence and remained its life blood; miners dominated the assembly during its early years and legislation long favored the mineral interests. Yet at the same time, livestock growers invariably provided a challenge and a check upon rampant and unfettered lawmaking. Together the two groups had much to do with the shaping of Montana territorial statutes. And both benefited in the process.

In 1864 the Bannack assembly swiftly repealed the obnoxious Idaho mineral laws and substituted legislation which gave the broad sanction of territorial government to local mining regulations now integrated into a comprehensive code, and at the same time clarified the legal status of claims taken up under earlier local rules.[109] Subsequent laws hastened the transfer of records from local to county recorders and, in 1867, specifically approved the right of bodies of miners to make mining regulations not in conflict with existing laws.[110] But some citizens thought this statute too complex, that the legislature circumscribed mining communities too much and "assumed a ridiculous superiority in knowledge over the law makers and judges of California" whence came most local mining regulations.[111]

Through the legislature, Montanans early expressed a sharp opposition to a proposal in Congress to include mineral lands in the general survey, but when the mineral act of 1866 became law, the outcry subsided somewhat. This law threw open mineral lands of the public domain, both surveyed and unsurveyed, and recognized the "force of local mining-customs, or rules of miners wherever not conflicting

107. See act of February 23, 1881, *LM*, 12 Session (1881), 78–81; *Herald*, January 22, 1881; March 8, July 12, 1887; January 24, 1889.

108. See Chapters 5 and 6. See also *Herald*, December 23, 1871; "Reminiscenses of Isaac I. Lewis" (typescript), 155, Western History Research Center, University of Wyoming.

109. Act of December 26, 1864, *LM*, 1 Session (1864–65), 327–29.

110. Act of January 9, 1865, *LM*, 1 Session (1864–65), 274–75; act of December 11, 1867, *LM*, 4 Session (1867), 82.

111. *Weekly Independent*, April 24, 1868.

with the laws of the United States," but imposed certain limitations of size and procedure for claims acquisition.[112] Though Delegate Mc-Lean was roundly castigated for saying "it will suit our folks," and there were complaints about the $1,000 worth of labor required before final title was validated, the legislature merely discussed the matter and was not even concerned enough to memorialize Congress.[113]

In 1870 Congress extended the same principles to placer, as well as quartz mining property. Two years later, it enacted new legislation which would stand as the basis of mineral land policy for the rest of the nineteenth century. Local customs and rules were upheld, but now claims were not to exceed fifteen hundred feet in length nor three hundred feet on each side of the lead in width. As before, possessory title became complete with location and recording, but had to be maintained from year to year by annual labor requirements of at least $100 value, until $500 had been thus expended, at which time final patent could be issued upon proof of citizenship and purchase at $5 per acre.[114] Montanans were openly critical and believed that leaders in Washington, including Delegate Clagett, "have dug themselves a political grave deeper than any prospect hole yet sunk." Asking a speedy repeal of the law, the ninth session of the legislature insisted in 1876 that most entries in Montana had been made by outsiders and that the act discouraged mine development by residents and was responsible for the then depressed state of the industry.[115] But to no avail: rather than restrict its mineral policy, Congress in general displayed some tendency to broaden it.

One exception was the so-called Alien Land Law of 1887, which made it unlawful for noncitizens or those who had not declared their intent, or for any corporation not chartered under federal, state, or territorial law, to "hereafter acquire, hold, or own real estate so hereafter acquired, or any interest therein in any of the Territories of the United States or in the District of Columbia." The new law further stipulated that no corporation more than 20 percent of the stock of

112. Memorial to Congress (April 15, 1866), *LM*, 2 Session (1866), 48; *Montana Post*, December 16, 1865; act of July 26, 1866, 14 *USSL*, 251, 252–53.
113. *Montana Post*, August 18, 1866; *House Journal*, 3 Session (1866), 70; Liberal interpretations in favor of the claimant no doubt made the law more palatable. See Robertson et al. *v.* Smith et al., 1 *Montana Reports* (1871), 413–19.
114. Act of July 9, 1870, 16 *USSL*, 217–18; act of May 10, 1872, 17 *USSL*, 91–94.
115. *Herald*, May 20, July 18, 1872; memorial to Congress (n.d.), *LM*, 9 Session (1876), 219.

which was owned by noncitizens or alien corporations could acquire or hold real estate in the same areas.[116]

The law did not mention mineral lands: it was designed to protect grazing lands from foreign control. But by this time, Montanans were much more concerned about attracting outside capital to the mineral industry than with the fear of foreign domination. When the attorney general held that mines were real estate and as such covered by the act, the legislature began to complain, arguing that "several million dollars of foreign capital" had been prevented by its restrictions from coming into Montana. But it was not retroactive and did not affect those foreign concerns already there; moreover it might be circumvented by forming subsidiary American companies to hold title or by taking long-term leases on mining property instead of purchasing. But it represented an unwonted restriction handed down from above, one not applying equally to states.[117]

With mining depressed in the early 1870s, friends proposed that public credit be used to build smelting works to help the industry back onto its feet. The legislature was asked to empower county commissioners to issue bonds for such purposes. If ranchers resisted, insisted one supporter of the idea, they should think of the implications. ". . . unless they want to hawk their yearling 'critters' at from $6 to $8 per head, they had better acquiesce without a murmur in paying a little additional taxes." Apparently authorization was considered but not granted early in 1874, to empower the Beaverhead County commissioners to submit a $30,000 bond proposal to the voters to aid in erecting a smelter.[118]

Nowhere was the impact of the mineral interests more apparent than in the tax structure of the territory. If mining property was taxed at all, it was over spirited opposition—and levies were most advantageous to mine owners. The revenue act of 1867 taxed the net proceeds of all mines or mining claims, but left the owners to determine the value of their own ores.[119] Subsequently mineral claims were exempted, except those held under federal patent, but bullion and sur-

116. Act of March 3, 1887, 24 *USSL*, 476–77.

117. See Clark C. Spence, *British Investments and the American Mining Frontier, 1860–1901* (Ithaca, 1958), 204–13.

118. *Herald*, December 23, 1873; February 16, 1874.

119. This was a quarterly levy of one mill for each dollar value of ore extracted. From the assessed value per ton, $25 was deducted to cover extraction and reduction costs, with 75 percent of the remainder taxable. Act of December 23, 1867, *LM*, 4 Session (1867), 45.

face structures were to remain taxed. With Sam Hauser's aid, the Hope Mining Company fought levies of $2,026.53 on its $88,112 worth of bullion produced in 1875, but lost the case in the courts.[120] Lobbyists like William F. Chadwick early in 1879 brought to a head the campaign to modify the law, and in that year the eleventh legislative assembly laid down a hard and fast tax rule: an assessment on the net proceeds of all mines, plus a direct levy on patented claims in an amount equal to the original purchase price from the United States.[121] This lenient arrangement prevailed for the rest of the territorial period, though not without opposition.

Other interests, especially cattlemen, repeatedly sought in the eighties to tax mining property, not merely on the annual outtake, but on its full value. But only heated arguments resulted, and rancher James Fergus put his finger on the reason when he told his colleagues in the legislature: "The great trouble is, Sir, that capital and mining agents and bankers are in our lobbies and in our anteroom lobbying our members and magnetizing us with their wealth and their influence, and it is humiliating to say that all our members from outside of our mining districts do not have backbone enough to stand up like men and vote against such measures as this, that they believe to be wrong."[122]

In the Constitutional Convention of 1884, where mine taxation was one of the major issues, arguments were clearly mining versus livestock. Mining men saw their interests as paramount in the territory. Mines were "the goose that lays the golden egg" and in a practical sense mining support was essential to get any constitution adopted. Moreover, they argued, a mine was a wasting asset; every ounce taken out lessened its value, while livestock increased naturally. James Fergus, though, was not convinced. "An old cow is capable of having so many calves," he said. "You can't fool a poor old man. Our cattle are just like your mines and horses and cattle get worn out just

120. See act of January 15, 1869, *LM*, 5 Session (1868–69), 41–42; act of January 12, 1872, *LM*, 7 Session (1871–72), 601–2; Hope Mining Company *v.* Kennon, 3 *Montana Reports* (1877), 43–44; L. W. O'Bannon to Samuel Gaty (Phillipsburg, March 21, 1877); Gaty to O'Bannon (St. Louis, April 13, 1877); Gaty to Hauser (St. Louis, April 14, 1877), all Hauser MSS; Hakola, "Samuel T. Hauser," 63–66.

121. Chadwick to Maginnis (Helena, January 29, 1879), Maginnis MSS; act of February 21, 1879, *LM*, 11 Session (1879), 65–68.

122. Copy of speech (n.d.), Allis Stuart Collection. See also *House Journal*, 13 Session (1883), 54.

like your mines do." [123] In the end, the proposed constitution exempted mines, except for net proceeds and the value of the surface ground—and as a sop to the cattle interests, livestock under six months old would also be excluded. [124]

The same controversy raged at the Constitutional Convention of 1889. An effort to tax mines as ordinary property was blocked; an attempt to tax the gross proceeds, rather than the net outtake, failed; and a third proposal, which would have left the question for the new state legislature, was also unsuccessful. At the same time, cattlemen sought to apply the principle of taxation of net proceeds of livestock. [125] But the new constitution departed little from the prevailing territorial tax program: net proceeds of mines were taxable, along with patented claims at the price paid when title was originally acquired from the government—a modest figure. [126] Close investigation of the issue would generally discard the idea that there was a conspiracy to exempt mining from its fair share of the tax burden in 1889: men interested in mining were merely acting like other businessmen, seeking whatever advantage they could get for themselves. [127] This they did throughout the territorial years as well.

Although they had their way on taxation, the mineral interests from the beginning were challenged by the cattlemen, who also exerted considerable pressure upon the assembly and were responsible for some basic legislation. The first lien law noticeably favored farmers, ranchmen, herders, and livery stable keepers, to assure them of pay due for feeding, pasturing, or herding animals. [128] The importance of the cattle interests was seen in early acts to encourage the importation of blooded stock and to record bands and handle estrays. [129] Cattlemen played a decisive role in formulating water law, with early laws broadened to give rights to others not located on the streams. [130] The

123. Discussion of February 4, 1884, Proceedings of the Constitutional Convention, MHS film copy.

124. Constitution of 1884, *Senate Miscellaneous Document* No. 39, 49 Congress, 1 Session (1885–86), 23.

125. *Proceedings, Constitutional Convention*, 1889, 470–71, 472, 475, 591–92.

126. Constitution of 1889, Thorpe, *Federal and State Constitutions*, IV, 2324–25.

127. See John W. Smurr, "Tax 'Conspiracy,'" *Montana*, V (Spring-Summer, 1955), 47–56.

128. Acts of December 28 and 30, *LM*, 1 Session (1864–65), 331, 332–38.

129. Act of December 30, 1868, *LM*, 5 Session (1868–69), 101; acts of December 30, 1871, and January 10, 1872, *LM*, 7 Session (1871–72), 563–64, 636; act of February 2, 1874, *LM*, 8 Session (1874), 91–92.

130. Act of January 12, 1865, *LM*, 1 Session (1864–65), 367–69; act (n.d.),

1870s saw an expanding cattle industry, with legislation to match: movement of diseased animals was restricted by law, more stringent penalties were imposed for theft of stock, and butchers were ordered to keep a "true and accurate record" of all marks and brands of cattle slaughtered.[131] The principle of "customary range" was established in the statutes in 1877, making it a misdemeanor to drive animals from their customary range. This measure set forth a basic concept which would stand well into the twentieth century; it attempted to establish a priority right on public property.[132] But the burden of proof and the task of enforcement were left to the civil courts, which weakened the law, and contributed to the cattlemen's impatience and resort to vigilantes.

By an act of 1881, the legislature compelled railroad companies to compensate for livestock injured or killed by trains, leaving the claimant to determine the value of damage. Montanans soon became aware of the adage that nothing improved the blood of a steer so much as crossing it with a locomotive. But the courts soon nullified a portion of this statute and its replacement went to the other extreme. Later, when the court stipulated that "malicious negligence" by the railroads must be proven, the pressure was on for a law to compel the fencing of railroad lands.[133]

By the early eighties, it was apparent that cattle was big business, second in value only to mining, and that cattlemen were seriously disputing the supremacy of legislators from mining districts.[134] Although the *Herald* saw no sign of a lobby group at work, the thirteenth session met early in 1883, with a heavy sprinkling of stockmen among its members. A number of them met with Granville Stuart, veteran legislator, "to discuss what Legislation is necessary to protect our interests."[135] One result was an effective bounty law on predators;

LM, 6 Session (1869–70), 57–59; act of February 6, 1877, *LM*, 10 Session, (1877), 221–25; act of February 21, 1879, *LM*, 11 Session (1879), 52–53; act of March 12, 1885, *LM*, 4 Session (1885), 130–33.

131. Act of February 11, 1876, *LM*, 9 Session (1876), 61–62; acts of February 19, 20, 1879, *LM*, 11 Session (1879), 35–36, 43–44.

132. Act of February 8, 1877, *LM*, 10 Session (1877), 236–37.

133. Act of February 23, 1881, *LM*, 12 Session (1881), 67–71; act of March 2, 1883, *LM*, 13 Session (1883), 52–53; *Herald*, March 6, 1889; Graves *v.* Northern Pacific Railroad Company, 5 *Montana Reports* (1885), 560–62.

134. Total gross value of exports for 1885 was $26,400,000, of which silver, gold, copper and lead accounted for $20,250,000; beef cattle only $4,000,000. Report of the Governor of Montana (1885), 1001.

135. *Herald*, February 6, 1883; Granville Stuart to R. S. Ford (n.p., February 4, 1883), copy, letterbook 2, Stuart MSS.

another was a bill to protect stockgrowers against depredations of northern Indians and renegade whites by establishing a Board of Livestock Commissioners with broad powers to appoint inspectors in turn empowered to make arrests without warrants and call upon bystanders for aid, with enforcement to be financed by an annual levy of one-third of a mill on all taxable property in the territory.[136] The clash of interests over the inspectors' bill was readily apparent in the legislature and out. Taxpayers protested levies on all to benefit a special group; editor Fisk thought that the machinery cumbersome and believed that "a self-constituted vigilance committeee, inspired by self-interest, without written commissions, legal restraints or the necessity of making written reports, supplied with good repeaters and plenty of rope, could do better work and furnish greater protection." Representative Lee Mantle of Butte suggested a rewording of the bill's title to "An Act to create the office of Head Gamekeeper, Chief Fire Warden and Boss Cow-Boy in the Territory of Montana, in the interest of, and for the sole use and benefit of the impoverished cattle owners of said Territory." But Gran Stuart complained that the "majority of miners in the House were generally disposed to be 'penny wise, and pound foolish,' at least in reference to stock matters."[137] The bill passed both houses, but was returned by Governor Crosby without his signature.[138] Unable to override the veto, stockmen turned to their own organizations for relief, and through the Montana Stock Growers' Association and spontaneous vigilante groups, began to mete out a harsh, swift justice in accordance with time-honored western principles.

Spokesmen like Stuart did not give up. Arousing his fellow ranchers to the dangers of hoof and mouth disease being brought into the territory from other areas in 1884, he wrote Conrad Kohrs, "I think the Govr. ought to get permission from the President to call an extra Session of the Legislature, so we could protect ourselves. I had it in that stock law that was defeated a year ago & done all I could then but the miners beat it."[139] A little later Stuart continued to Kohrs: "I am glad you are stirring up the stock men. Keep your lick up, for

136. Act of March 8, 1883, *LM*, 13 Session (1883), 109–10; *Herald*, February 24, 1883; *House Journal*, 13 Session (1883), 243.

137. *Ibid.*, 243, 244; *Herald*, February 24, March 9, 1883.

138. Crosby insisted that the bill delegated arbitrary powers to functionaries not legally sworn, thus menacing personal liberties. Crosby to Legislature (March 8, 1883), *House Journal*, 13 Session (1883), 338–39.

139. Granville Stuart to Conrad Kohrs (Fort Maginnis, March 24, 1884), copy, letterbook 2, Stuart MSS.

we *must have some legislation so we can protect ourselves*. As it now stands we are liable to have some disease imported onto our ranges that would ruin us all. And the only way to do is to elect a majority of the Legislature that are favorable to stock interests, for the miners have always shown a very narrow & unjust prejudice against us."[140]

Unsuccessful in gaining a special session, the cattlemen were nevertheless heavily represented in the fourteenth assembly—the "cowboy legislature" of 1885. There were four stockmen in the Council and eight in the House—one-third of the membership—and cattlemen in general chose Granville Stuart and Russell B. Harrison, son of Senator Benjamin Harrison of Indiana, to draft the appropriate bills and fight them through. "After an all season struggle," according to Stuart, some success was achieved. Restricting branding operations to specified times of the year in the main cattle-raising counties, the legislature created a more restricted system of stock commissioners and inspectors than that proposed in 1883. Powers of the inspectors were limited and the whole would be financed by a tax on livestock in the major cattle-producing areas only.[141] Already the governor had halted the importation of cattle infected with Texas fever, and the assembly now appealed to Congress to help check the spread of this and the dread pleuro-pneumonia.[142] Stuart later took exception to charges that stockmen had dominated the session and had legislated almost exclusively in their own behalf, denying that they had a majority and noting that only five of the eighty-five laws enacted "had any reference whatever to the livestock interests."[143]

But clearly it was a good session and marked the acme of the cattleman's power in Montana territorial government. The Montana Stock Growers' Association remained a potent organization, but was hard put to offset the influence of the mineral interests and of a few powerful and exceedingly wealthy capitalists. After the elections of 1886, Granville Stuart was discouraged. To Russell Harrison, secretary of the Stock Growers' Association, he wrote: "There will be a determined attempt to repeal the bit & Inspection laws at the coming session and as so few stock men have been elected, they will succeed unless we can make a very good showing of what we have done, for

140. Granville Stuart to Kohrs (Fort Maginnis, May 2, 1884), *ibid.*

141. Granville Stuart to editor of *Fergus County Argus* (Fort Maginnis, October 11, 1886), copy, letterbook 4, *ibid.*; Stuart, *Forty Years*, II, 210; acts of March 10, 12, 1885, *LM*, 14 Session (1885), 53, 91–95.

142. Memorial to Congress (n.d.), *LM*, 231–33; *Herald*, August 16, 1884.

143. Granville Stuart to editor of *Fergus County Argus* (Fort Maginnis, October 11, 1886), copy, letterbook 4, Stuart MSS.

every d—d thief & their sympathizers (who are legion) are very active in working up public opinion against us."[144]

The legislation was not undone: cattle interests continued important, but not predominant. Through control of the Democratic party, the territorial "big four"—Sam Hauser, William A. Clark, Marc Daly, and Charles A. Broadwater—wielded an influence fully as strong as the machine bosses in more eastern regions. For all practical purposes, argued contemporaries, these four men were the Democratic party in Montana;[145] and save for the first and the final sessions, control of the party meant also control of the legislature. Perhaps this was why the *Herald* believed the sixteenth and last assembly was "one of the best" and that it was held in an absence of lobbying and partisan legislation"—something unusual in the territory.[146]

Restricted to an extent by congressional limitations, the legislature was no mere puppet of the territorial executive or judicial officers. Above the few restraints placed on special legislation, contraction of debts, time and length of sessions, and pay of its members, its powers were extensive and real. Congressional inhibitions aroused criticism, but seldom hampered the action of the assembly.

The hundreds of laws enacted during Montana's quarter of a century as a territory were no better and no worse than those of other territories of the same era. Often borrowed from elsewhere, those proving unsatisfactory in the new environment were replaced or modified. But good and bad alike, they reflected the needs and desires of some part of the population, and often, as was so common throughout the nation in the Gilded Age, influential interest groups. In their response to such pressures, Montana legislatures differed only in degree from their counterparts.

144. Granville Stuart to Russell Harrison (n.p., December 7, 1886), *ibid.*
145. Bancroft, *History of Washington, Idaho, and Montana,* 797–98.
146. *Herald,* March 14, 1889.

CHAPTER

9

"The Courthouses . . . Were Not Imposing Temples of Justice": The Judicial Branch of Government

In any frontier area, no matter was more important than the interpretation and enforcement of the law. Invariably, in the absence of effective court or protective machinery, extralegal organizations sprang up to assume these functions. In Montana, the miners' courts and the vigilantes played a significant role in bridging the gap between the first great influx of miners and the creation of a viable working government. But these were temporary devices with obvious weaknesses, and though they would die hard, they soon gave way to the typical western court system, in which appointive judges owed allegiance to the federal government and to political parties, yet at the same time were not insensitive to pressures within the territory itself. Such jurists were at first of necessity concerned with the pragmatic establishment of order, but as settlement progressed and they came more clearly to understand the needs of their environment, they made a lasting impression. They were "agents of acculturation," as John Guice calls them: "civilizers, builders, and makers of law who contributed substantially to the territories and to the nation as a whole."[1]

As outlined in the organic act, the judicial structure of Montana was simple. Patterned on the Wisconsin act of 1836 and the theory in

1. John D. W. Guice, *The Rocky Mountain Bench* (New Haven, 1972), 4, 152.

the Northwest Ordinance, it provided a supreme court comprised of three justices. Each of these same three judges presided over one of the territory's three districts, holding court at times and places prescribed by the legislature. Appeals from the territorial supreme court might be taken to the United States Supreme Court in the same manner as those from U.S. circuit courts in the states, provided that personal freedom was involved or property in controversy above the value of $1,000. In like fashion, appeals from the district courts were to be taken to the supreme court of the territory under rules to be laid down by territorial law. Thus the same justices who rendered decisions at the district level heard the same cases when appeals to the higher court were allowed. Both district and supreme courts were vested with chancery and common law jurisdiction; in addition to exercising both original and appellate authority, each performed another dual function, acting as territorial courts in cases arising under local and territorial law and as United States courts in cases originating under federal statutes. Although as early as 1828 they had been dubbed "legislative courts" by Chief Justice John Marshall,[2] as late as the 1870s these hybrids still had not answered all the questions relating to definition and procedure. But they, together with the probate courts and justices of the peace authorized by the organic act, constituted the judicial structure of the territory.[3]

Governor Sidney Edgerton set up the original judicial districts in the summer of 1864. Chief Justice Hosmer and Justice Williston arrived that same autumn before the legislature had convened. Since the organic act—"hardly more than a right to exist"—ignored procedure or practice, they improvised, using as guides the common law and the Idaho practices act. Already a number of actions had been entered in probate courts established by Edgerton a few months earlier and these were transferred to the district court as soon as Hosmer had completed the preliminary organization.[4] In its first session, the legislature then proceeded to adopt laws governing civil, criminal, and probate actions, and in addition, to write English common law into the books.[5]

2. American Insurance Company et al. *v.* Canter, 1 *Peters* (1828), 545.

3. Jurisdiction of probate courts and justices of the peace was to be set by Montana law, but justices of the peace were to have no authority in controversies over land title or where the sum or debt in question exceeded $100. Act of May 26, 1864, 13 *USSL*, 88–89.

4. "Biographical Sketch of Hezekiah L. Hosmer," *Contributions*, III (1900), 290–93; Helen F. Sanders, *A History of Montana*, 3 vols. (Chicago, 1913), I, 586.

5. The legislature defined the authority of the district courts and gave the

Proper physical facilities were at first lacking. "The courthouses . . . were not imposing temples of justice," recalled Decius Wade, who had held his first court in Chouteau County in an adobe building erected in 1837 inside the Fort Benton stockade by the Northwest Fur Company.[6] Hosmer's first district court convened in the dining room of Virginia City's leading hotel, the Planter's House, after guests had finished breakfast, but soon was switched to the Union League room, with sawdust-covered floor and access only through a rear alley. A few years later, Hosmer's courtroom was "the loft of a store and . . . devoted promiscuously to justice, dances, sermons, itinerant shows, and other useful and ornamental institutions."[7] Rentals were outrageously high—in the late 1860s the federal government paid $4,500 a year for jail, courtroom, and custom house accomodations in a building valued at only $3,500,[8] yet facilities remained inadequate. One session was held in a mosquito-ridden Gallatin City quarters "in the midst of dense smoke created by burning pine boughs, which dispersed the mosquitoes and well nigh dispersed the court," and as late as 1884 there were complaints about the court room at Helena, where attorneys strode back and forth "eloquent in argument and dimly visible through the dust," with the chief justice at times seen "as through a glass dimly."[9]

Not only were court facilities poor, they were often isolated. As a Miles City editor saw it in 1883, because of the grave and important duties before him and the great distances he must travel, "the district judge needs to be a man of powerful physical as well as mental organization."[10] Districts were large and county seats far apart. One judge complained in 1883 that his district included "fully one half of the area of the territory," and that he must travel 3,000 miles a year to hold a total of twelve terms.[11]

probate courts concurrent jurisdiction in cases involving amounts up to $2,500, an action which was probably illegal because of the high figure. Act (n.d.), *LM*, 1 Session (1864–65), 137–39; Wilbur F. Sanders, "Notes on the Judiciary of Montana" (Helena, 1885), 1–4, 8–9, MS, Bancroft Library.

6. Joaquin Miller, *An Illustrated History of the State of Montana* (Chicago, 1894), 385–86; *Semi-Weekly Inter Mountain*, March 24, 1886.

7. McClure, *Three Thousand Miles*, 332–33; "Biographical Sketch of Hezekiah L. Hosmer," 291, 296; *Montana Democrat*, April 11, 1868.

8. R. W. Taylor to W. T. Otto (Washington, February 26, 1869), SCF, 1871–84.

9. "Biographical Sketch of Hezekiah L. Hosmer," 296; *Herald*, December 5, 1884.

10. Miles City *Press*, quoted in *Herald*, April 24, 1883.

11. Conger Statement (July 5, 1883), Everton J. Conger file, APJ.

Stagecoach travel was bad enough at best, but in inclement weather, as Chief Justice Wade once noted, its success usually depended upon several factors, including "a rail fence, a strong constitution and implicit confidence in Divine Providence. . . ."[12] On one occasion Wade was lost for six hours in thirty-below-zero weather; more than once court was postponed because of impassable road conditions or because the judge "got froze coming over."[13] One justice rode horseback 110 miles, crossing the Rockies in midwinter, to hold court at Bannack; another descended the Yellowstone in a thirty-foot mackinaw, covering several hundred miles, to convene a term at Miles City.[14] And once in 1884, en route to hold court at Boulder City, Chief Justice Wade found himself "on a lonely mountain top" with other legal officers "with their empty hands high over their heads, in front of a dozen or more angry looking Winchester rifles pointed at their heads, in the hands of masked men not twenty feet away."[15]

The hardships of travel occasionally caused hostility between judges, with some distrust and jockeying for the best districts, as in 1864, when Hosmer expressed fear that he would be maneuvered out of the district he had carved out for himself but was assured by a member of the legislature that his detractors "might as well try to change the pages of sacred history and place the thief on the cross in the centre, as to change the position for a chief justice. . . ."[16] For the most part, however, the problems of distance and transportation prompted cooperation among judges and flexibility in setting court terms. When one justice went "to the states," or was absent because of his or family illness, a colleague usually held court for him.[17]

Judges made it a point to schedule spring term so that bunch grass would have sprouted and litigants could picket their horses and save

12. *Semi-Weekly Inter Mountain*, March 24, 1886.

13. James Fergus to Andrew Fergus (Helena, December 5, 1880), Allis Stuart Collection; *Herald*, April 5, 1875; December 3, 1880; January 3, 1881.

14. Hiram Knowles to E. R. Hoar (Deer Lodge, March 6, 1870), Hiram G. Knowles file, APJ; Paladin, ed., "'Henry N. Blake," *Montana*, XIV (Autumn, 1964), 51. See also Thomas Carter to Ellen Carter (White Sulphur Springs, September 12, 1887), Thomas Carter MSS, Library of Congress.

15. Decius Wade to Joseph K. Toole (Washington, May 22, 1905), Edward Warren Toole MSS, MHS. A year later, the U.S. marshal sought special funds to protect Wade en route to court. Alexander C. Botkin to Augustus Garland (Helena, April 14, 1885), Dept. of Justice Year File, 1861–85.

16. Charles S. Bagg to Hosmer (Bannack, December 3, 1864), Hosmer MSS, Beinecke Library.

17. Hosmer to James Speed (Washington, January 20, 1866), AG, 1861–70; *Weekly Independent*, August 14, 1868; Conger statement (July 5, 1883); Wade testimony (n.d.), both in Conger file, APJ.

stable expenses, and they were willing for a variety of reasons to curtail, reschedule, or relocate proceedings. Court might be postponed if participants were unprepared or if a new appointee had not yet arrived; they might be moved to save costs in transporting witnesses and prisoners.[18]

As was the case with the legislature, the holding of court was entertainment as well as necessity. In isolated areas, retired chief justice Wade recalled later, it "was the event of the year; the harvest time; and with beer or whisky at twenty-five cents per drink, and other things in proportion, the expectations were never disappointed." Fall term of district court at Virginia City was expected to attract about five hundred people in 1867; "court week" at Deer Lodge was "about the same as the Fourth of July is in some of the Western States," with a rich harvest for hotels, saloons, and restaurants.[19]

Partisan onlookers heard "some splendid speeches," on the part of their favorites, while the opposition "puffed—sweated and black-guarded" and generally looked ridiculous.[20] Some thought that the early judges, were too lenient in permitting oratory without limitation, and sessions which should have been concluded in a few days dragged on several weeks:

> Half a dozen lawyers will speak at once, wrangling over silly technicalities, hurl disgraceful personalities at each other, play a stupid badinage to bring down the house, and talk almost endlessly, with boundless latitude, in advocating causes before juries. The judge tolerates it complacently, and usually lets the show go on in its own way, unless they undertake, as they do once in a while, to explain away the court itself, when he bristles up, clears the board and lets them take a fresh start.[21]

If the court might be diverting for the spectators and uncertain for the litigants, it could be strenuous for the participants including the judges. A "fall round-up in criminal business," in which the judge "branded eleven—for the penitentiary" in 1881 meant long hours on the bench.[22] Moreover, after the daily rounds of the supreme court

18. J. A. Johnston to Martin Maginnis (Helena, January 28, 1884), Maginnis MSS; James Callaway et al. to Benjamin Brewster (Virginia City, March 23, 1883), telegram, Conger file, APJ; *Herald*, June 11, 1873; September 17, 1881; September 21, 1883; May 14, 1886; January 6, 1887.

19. Miller, *An Illustrated History*, 385–86; *Weekly Independent*, October 19, 26; November 9, 1867.

20. Entry for November 20, 1866, Fisk Diary.

21. McClure, *Three Thousand Miles*, 332–33, 334–35.

22. *Herald*, November 18, 1881.

sessions, the justices often found themselves "working like Trojans" far into the night preparing their decisions.[23]

During the early period especially they were hampered by a lack of printed laws and decisions, and, like the public, were dependent upon handwritten drafts and newspaper accounts. No territorial statutes were printed until 1867 and few of the court decisions were delivered in writing before December of 1868.[24] Not until 1871 did Congress provide a law library worthy of the name and it was far from "reasonably complete." As late as 1886, Judge Thomas C. Bach doubted that there was a set of *United States Reports* anywhere in his new district, which centered at Miles City.[25]

With little written material at their disposal, the early Montana courts spent a good deal of time wrangling over what the laws actually were. According to Chief Justice Hosmer, who some thought was much too lax in such matters, the first two weeks of his initial term "were little else than a legal debating school...."[26] With limited background the justices were called upon to handle such ticklish questions as the legal status of gold dust and of Civil War greenbacks; the legality of written contracts without the new Internal Revenue stamps when such stamps were unavailable; and a host of bewildering mining issues stemming from prior rights of discovery; appropriation of water; transfer of title; convergence of lodes; and the interpretation of local custom, territorial, and, after 1866, federal mining laws. Such doctrines as prior appropriation of water might be transferred from placer mining to agriculture, in itself a complex body of interpretations.[27]

23. At the close of each supreme court term, the chief justice assigned opinions to be written by each member on a roughly equivalent basis. *Herald*, January 19, 1887; Wade testimony (n.d.), Conger file, APJ.

24. *Montana Democrat*, April 11, 1868; *Montana Post*, June 29, 1867; Charles Shaft to Thomas F. Meagher (Hell Gate, October 20, 1865), Meagher MSS; Meagher to Andrew Johnson (Virginia City, January 20, 1866), Johnson MSS; Meagher to Speaker of the House (November 9, 1866), *House Journal*, 3 Session (1866), 49; *Montana Reports* (1873), preface, 15.

25. For problems of the library see Meagher to legislature (March 6, 1866), TPS; John L. Murphy to Columbus Delano (Virginia City, March 22, 1871), TPS; Thomas C. Bach to William A. Murray (Helena, August 20, 1886), Thomas C. Bach file, APJ; *Council Journal*, 13 Session (1883), 201–2; *Herald*, January 6, 1887.

26. *Montana Democrat*, April 11, 1868.

27. Miller, *An Illustrated History*, 315–16, 387; Robertson et al. *v.* Smith et al., 1 *Montana Reports* (1871), 410; *Montana Democrat*, November 9, 1867; *Montana Post*, October 20, 1867; John Hakola, "Currency in Montana," in J. W. Smurr and K. Ross Toole, eds., *Historical Essays on Montana and the Northwest* (Helena, 1957), 125–29; "Biographical Sketch of Hezekiah L. Hosmer," 293–94.

Although no industry in the world involved a greater amount of litigation than mining, not until the appointment of Hiram Knowles in 1868 was there a man appointed to the Montana bench with any practical familiarity with mineral law. Most judges learned on the job, and one of the consistent complaints of Montanans was this deficiency and the need of local attorneys to spend time " 'breaking in' pilgrim Judges from Eastern States who have known nothing of our people, laws and customs."[28]

Yet early judges like Hiram Knowles and Henry L. Warren built as well as borrowed precedence. They devised rules for handling cases in sparsely settled districts which remained in force for much of the territorial period. Over a sixteen-year span as chief justice, Decius Wade would be responsible for establishing far-reaching court procedures fitted to Montana's peculiar circumstances. "New Justices do not readily comprehend the reasons which lie at the foundation of these rules," said Knowles in 1882. "They know but little of the history of the Territory or of its jurisprudence and some of them seem to care but little for them."[29]

Since Montana's laws were often based upon those of older states and territories, especially California, so were her court decisions. In an opinion of 1880, Chief Justice Wade explained; "Our habit is to follow the supreme court of California when applicable, having taken our code from that state." A few years later, the Montana court was even more explicit, holding that when a legislature adopted a statute from elsewhere, it was presumed also to have adopted that law's interpretations as set down by the courts of the area whence it came.[30]

In the early years and upon occasion even as late as the eighties, the Montana bench would meet competition in administering justice. When Judge Munson arrived in 1865, one of the first sights he saw was a body suspended by vigilantes from Helena's famous hangman's tree, "the eighth specimen of similar fruit encased in leather boots that tree had borne in so many months."[31] From the beginning,

28. C. P. Connolly and W. H. Maguire, "Three Men of Helena," *Magazine of Western History*, XIV (July, 1891), 261–62; Miller, *An Illustrated History*, 315; William H. DeWitt to Joseph K. Toole (Butte, July 15, 1886), Bach file, APJ; *Weekly Independent*, July 3, 1879; *The Montanian*, July 24, 1873.

29. Knowles to Brewster (Butte, January 2, 1882), Decius Wade file, APJ; *Herald*, January 6, 1887.

30. Hershfield v. Aiken, 3 *Montana Reports* (1880), 449; Lindley v. Davis, 6 *Montana Reports* (1887), 445.

31. Lyman E. Munson, "Pioneer Life in Montana," *Contributions*, V (1904), 208–9. For sketches putting an undue emphasis, perhaps, on the early vigilantes in Montana, see E. W. Carpenter, "A Glimpse of Montana," *Overland Monthly*,

territorial officers condemned the erection of "impromptu scaffolds," deplored "midnight executions," and urged extralegal citizens' committees to "stand at ease."[32] But they noted "the utter contempt" for United States laws and the "growing conviction" in the sixties "that the civil law is a failure and insufficient for the protection of our people." "The crying evil of our time," said one judge in 1873, "is that offenders against our criminal laws so often escape punishment. The truth is the law favors too much the criminal."[33]

And in the beginning, these arguments did have validity. Of the four capital cases tried in Judge Hosmer's first court, none brought conviction, largely due to disagreement over the law's interpretation and the charge to the jury. Early juries were reluctant to apply the death penalty; and when they did, the condemned might be reprieved by higher officials or freed on technical grounds. In 1866, for example, a man sentenced to hang for murder had his penalty commuted to life imprisonment by President Johnson, then escaped while en route to the federal penetentiary at Detroit. In another instance, a prisoner convicted by the courts but released temporarily by the impetuous Thomas Francis Meagher, was strung up by vigilantes, his reprieve in his pocket and a warning on his back: "If our acting governor does this again, we will hang him too."[34]

No doubt the lack of proper prison facilities was a contributing factor. In 1866, citizens of Virginia City petitioned for the release of a man convicted of assault with intent to kill, on the grounds that confinement would create an unnecessarily heavy expense on taxpayers. At the same time, Meagher called attention to the absence of space for federal prisoners at Helena, citing the case of a prisoner who was handcuffed to the U.S. marshal's bed every night during his

II (April, 1869), 382; Albert D. Richardson, *Beyond the Mississippi: From the Great River to the Great Ocean* (Hartford, 1867), 487.

32. Munson, "Pioneer Life in Montana," 236; Meagher to General F. Wheaton (Virginia City, October 20, 1865), TPS; Meagher to Johnson (Virginia City, January 20, 1866), Johnson MSS; *Montana Post*, December 9, 1865; August 11, 1866; Decius Wade, "Charge to Grand Jury" (1885), handwritten, Decius S. Wade MSS, MHS.

33. Edward B. Neally to Speed (Virginia City, September 27, 1865), AG, 1864–70; George W. Pinney to James Harlan (Washington, January 3, 1866), SCF, Accounts, 1865–71; Benjamin F. Potts to Garfield (Virginia City, June 3, 1871), Garfield MSS; Knowles to George H. Williams (Deer Lodge, February 12, 1873), SCF, 1871–84.

34. Bancroft, *History of Washington, Idaho, and Montana*, 658; Munson, "Pioneer Life in Montana," 212; Athearn, *Thomas Francis Meagher*, 151; Lyman Munson to James Speed (Helena, February 26, 1866); William Chumasero to Andrew Johnson (Helena, February 26, 1866), both in AG, 1861–70.

trial because there was no place to keep him.[35] With the construction of a federally financed penitentiary, completed for occupancy in 1871, conditions improved, but that structure remained overcrowded. Governor Crosby pointed out in 1884 that inadequate cell space "has been largely used as an argument for seeking and evercising executive clemency in years past, and the frequency of escapes is an undoubted cause of the growing tendency to resort to lynch law, and the infliction of extreme penalties for offenses of inferior magnitude." Until the government was able to protect Montanans—in this instance cattlemen, said Crosby it would be "useless to complain of these violations of the form of law, as our people feel that self-protection is the older and stronger law."[36] This is not to imply that Montana was dominated by extracurricular justice in the territorial era: rather, such justice came as a sporadic response to the breakdown of formal legal machinery in specific cases, and as the court organization was completed and gained experience, "lynch law" waned.[37]

The judicial structure was also weakened by inadequate federal funds, not only for penal improvements, but for compensation to jurors, witnesses, and court officials as well. After the first few years, payment to jurors and witnesses in cases arising under territorial law was three dollars a day, plus twenty cents a mile for travel to and from court. But jurors and witnesses in federal cases, their stipends set by Congress, received much less: prior to 1879 the amount varied some, but thereafter remained at two dollars a day and five cents a mile for travel.[38]

35. Bancroft, *History of Washington, Idaho, and Montana*, 653; Meagher to legislature (March 6, 1866), in TPS.

36. Report of the Governor of Montana, 1884, 559, 564–65; Report of W. L. Lincoln (August 22, 1884), in *Annual Report of the Commissioner of Indian Affairs, 1884*, 158. See also Oscar O. Mueller, "The Central Montana Vigilante Raids of 1884," *Montana*, I (January, 1951), 33–35.

37. For warnings generated by isolated instances of vigilante action, see Potts to legislature (April 15, 1873), *Council Journal*, Extra Session (1873), 18; Preston H. Leslie to legislature (January 14, 1889), *Council Journal*, 16 Session (1889), 15.

38. The legislature at first paid four dollars a day, plus forty cents a mile for travel, but soon arrived at the reduced figure. An old law of 1853 set a fee of two dollars a day for federal jurors and a dollar and a half for witnesses. In 1870 the allowance for jurors alone went to three dollars per day, and in 1879, at the urging of the attorney general, Congress reduced the per diem to two dollars. Act of February 9, 1865, *LM*, 1 Session (1864–65), 473; Revised Statutes (n.d.), *ibid.*, 11 Session (1879), 716–17; act of February 26, 1853, 10 *USSL*, 167, 168; act of July 15, 1870, 16 *USSL*, 363; act of January 30, 1879, 21 *USSL*, 43; Annual Report of the Attorney General of the United States for the Year 1877, *House Executive Document* No. 7, Vol. X, 45 Congress, 2 Session (1877–78), 7.

Petitions, newspapers, governors, congressmen, even the attorney general and the president of the United States deplored this low compensation. They pointed out the discrepancies between territorial and federal fees given for essentially the same duties; they noted that travel costs in Montana were twice those of New York, which provided the base for federal rates; and they attributed to the inadequate payment of jurors and witnesses the "scandalous disproportion" between violation and conviction under United States laws. Until these matters were remedied, said Governor Crosby in 1884, "it is little more than a farce to attempt to run United States courts. Either suspend their functions or furnish reasonable facilities for their exercise."[39]

But Congress did neither; it made no further changes in the rates of compensation during the territorial period.[40] Indeed, there were times when even the low pay was not available. On the jacket of a letter written by the outgoing U.S. marshal early in 1878 was the notation: "Condition of courts: no funds; no juries; the new marshal not there."[41] A year later, for some inexplicable reason, Congress neglected to appropriate funds for federal marshals and their deputies, an oversight which in Montana brought legal machinery momentarily to a halt.[42]

United states marshals and attorneys in the territory were underpaid. Their remuneration came primarily from fees collected for specific services, not annual salaries, and such fees, set by Congress,

39. Report of the Governor of Montana, 1884, 565. See also: *Herald,* December 3, 1878; *Congressional Record,* 46 Congress, 1 Session (1879), 1906; *ibid.,* 46 Congress, 2 Session (1879–80), 821, 1392; *ibid.,* 47 Congress, 2 Session (1882–83), 711; memorial to Congress (n.d.), *LM,* 13 Session (1883), 206–7; Report of the Committee on the Territories on Jurors and Witnesses in the Territories, *House Report* No. 1288, 46 Congress, 2 Session (1879–80), 1; Annual Report of the Attorney General of the United States for the Year 1883, *House Executive Document* No. 8, Vol. XIII, 48 Congress, 1 Session (1883–84), 13; Chester Arthur to Congress (December 4, 1883), in James D. Richardson (comp.), *A Compilation of the Messages and Papers of the Presidents* (New York, n.d.), XI, 2770; Knowles to Edwards Pierrepont (n.p., April 13, 1876), SCF, 1871–84; Benjamin Harrison to John Coburn (Washington, January 2, 1885), Harrison MSS.

40. Changes came in 1892 and 1902. Act of August 3, 1892, 27 *USSL,* 347; act of June 21, 1902, 32 *USSL,* 396.

41. William F. Wheeler to Charles Devens (Helena, April 6, 1878), SCF, 1871–84.

42. United States *v.* Fox, 3 *Montana Reports* (1880), 519–20; Annual Report of the Attorney General of the United States for the Year 1879, *House Executive Document* No. 8, Vol. XII, 46 Congress, 2 Session (1879–80), 15; *Herald,* March 8, 11; April 29, 1880.

were in Montana, Idaho, and Wyoming only half as large as those in Arizona and New Mexico, although living costs were not proportionately lower.[43] Threatening to resign in 1887, one marshal complained that only personal funds kept him going and expressed the hope that as his successor the president would be able to find "a worthy victim with a very long purse."[44] Low compensation meant less competent men, greater turnover, and criticism of a system that sent federal attorneys and marshals from the East "because they have failed to earn a living at home. . . ."[45]

Perhaps the most damning indictment of the judicial structure in Montana was not a lack of funds nor a dearth of competent personnel as such, but rather the basic inflexibility which prevented the system from keeping pace with the growth of the territory over a quarter of a century. To be sure, the structure was modified, but such changes were always too few and too late, and were often agreed upon by Congress only under pressure and with reluctance. In general the major modifications were designed to meet more fully the requirements of an expanding population widely dispersed over a large geographic area, and they included an enlargement of the jurisdiction of the lower courts, procedural changes to expedite the handling of cases, and an increase in the number of district judges.

In response to legislative petition, Congress in 1867 expanded jurisdiction of the probate courts in civil actions where the amount in question was $500, instead of the $100 limit of the organic act.[46] But despite repeated requests, the nation's lawmakers until 1883 refused to increase authority of Montana justices of the peace to the level of those of other territories.[47] Despite congressional limitations

43. Grover Cleveland to Congress (December 8, 1885), Richardson, *Messages and Papers*, XI, 4939; Annual Report of the Attorney General of the United States for the Year 1885, *House Executive Document* No. 7, Vol. XX, 49 Congress, 1 Session (1885–86), 11.

44. Robert S. Kelley to R. B. Smith (Deer Lodge, September 22, 1887), in Annual Report of the Attorney General of the United States for the Year 1887, *House Executive Document* No. 7, Vol. XVIII, 50 Congress, 1 Session (1887–88), 237.

45. Wade, "Self-Government in the Territories," *International Review*, VI (March, 1879), 304.

46. Memorial to Congress (n.d.), *LM*, 3 Session (1866), 94; act of March 2, 1867, 14 *USSL*, 426.

47. Act of January 19, 1883, 22 *USSL*, 407; *Congressional Record*, 46 Congress, 1 Session (1879), 1763; *ibid.*, 47 Congress, 1 Session (1881–82), 2878; Report of the Committee on the Territories on Justices of the Peace in the Territories, *House Report* No. 472, 46 Congress, 2 Session (1879–80), 1; Report of the Committee on the Territories on extending the jurisdiction of Justices of the

aimed at infidel Utah, Montana probate courts, perhaps illegally, did handle real estate questions, at least down to 1887, and citizens argued that further extension of jurisdiction at this level would take some of the pressure off overworked district judges.[48]

Other minor changes in the lower court structure sought to guard against any stoppage or slowing down of local government or judicial process depending upon a few men. A federal law of 1880, for example, permitted the ad interim appointment of justices of the peace when an unexpected vacancy occurred; territorial statute authorized probate judges to issue writs in the absence or disability of a territorial judge under certain conditions; probate judges had broad authority to regulate the time and place of their courts and were empowered to fill vacant county-commissioner posts on an interim basis.[49]

Montana led the way in abolishing the old distinction between law and equity practices in favor of procedures which combined the two. In an effort to cope with the problems of distance and delay, the legislature in 1869 endeavored to retain some of the old common law principles by substituting a majority of three-fourths of the jurors for a unanimous verdict in civil actions. Jurors were difficult to assemble, especially in the winter, and one "foolish or dishonest" panelist could effect a stalemate and prolong litigation for months, it was argued.[50] While the approach was no innovation in western mining regions, the territorial supreme court rejected the three-quarters principle; the United States supreme court did not pass upon the validity of that aspect, but held that the law in question did in certain cases deprive the supreme and district courts of the territory of their chancery jurisdiction—in effect making it mandatory for them to follow established U.S. court chancery practices, even where territorial laws were involved. But in 1874, Congress gave legal sanction to Mon-

Peace in certain territories, *House Report* No. 1166, 47 Congress, 1 Session (1881–82), 1.

48. *Herald*, February 14, March 7, November 9, 1887.

49. Act of April 16, 1880, 21 *USSL*, 74–75. Prior to this time, all justices of the peace were elected, by special election if necessary. Report of the Committee on the Territories on Justices of the Peace in the Territories, *Senate Report* No. 455, 46 Congress, 2 Session (1879–80), 1–2. See also act of January 12, 1869, *LM*, 5 Session (1868–69), 73; act of March 14, 1889, *LM*, 16 Session (1889), 120; Meagher to Council (March 29, 1866), *Council Journal*, 2 Session (1866), 173; People *ex. rel.* Robinson *v.* Van Gaskin et al., 5 *Montana Reports* (1885), 362.

50. Act of January 15, 1869, *LM*, 5 Session (1868–69), 66; Report of Judiciary Committee, *House Journal*, 5 Session (1868–69), 78.

tana's mingling of common law and chancery jurisdiction and the national supreme court specifically upheld the principle.[51]

From an early date it was apparent more territorial judges were needed. In 1865 three justices were deemed sufficient to handle the district and appellate requirements of an estimated 20,000 people; twenty years later, the same number were still expected to meet the needs of a population increased more than five fold. As early as 1868, according to Chief Justice Hosmer, the courts were unable to keep pace with demands: 656 cases had been handled by the first district court to that date, he noted, and 106 more were still on the docket. In later years, the backlog of civil cases was estimated to be as high as 300.[52] Miles City, the county seat of thriving Custer County, was 433 miles from Virginia City, the base of its judicial district, and the judge serving it had to travel 1,700 miles and spend four weeks on the road to hold two terms there in 1879.[53]

In addition, Congress added to the burden from time to time by enlarging the jurisdiction of the district and supreme courts. In 1867, for example, it gave the territorial supreme court jurisdiction in bankruptcy actions; later it threw cases involving enclosure of public lands into the federal side of the Montana courts; and by stipulating that appeals might not be taken to the United States Supreme Court unless the matter in controversy exceeded $5,000 rather than the $1,000 minimum prescribed in the organic act, it added to the work of the Montana bench, just at a time when the coming of the railroad, the expanding mineral and range cattle industry, and the throwing open of lands of all kinds were producing record numbers of legal disputes.[54]

51. *Weekly Rocky Mountain Gazette*, December 17, 1868; Kleinschmidt *v.* Dunphy, 1 *Montana Reports* (1869), 118; Aylesworth *v.* Reese et al., *ibid.* (1870), 200–201; Dunphy *v.* Kleinschmidt, 11 *Wallace* (1870), 614–15, 616; act of April 7, 1874, 18 *USSL*, 27–28; Hornbuckle *v.* Toombs, 85 *U.S. Reports* (1874), 648; *Congressional Globe*, 42 Congress, 2 Session (1871–72), 1732–33. The constitution proposed in 1884 and that adopted in 1889 provided for verdicts by fewer than twelve men in civil cases; that of 1889 included criminal cases below the grade of felony. Constitution of 1884, in *Senate Miscellaneous Document* No. 39, 49 Congress, 1 Session (1885–86), 4; Constitution of 1889, in Thorpe, *Federal and State Constitutions*, IV, 2303.

52. *Montana Democrat*, April 11, 1868; *Proceedings, Constitutional Convention, 1889*, 286–87.

53. Henry N. Blake to Charles Devens (Virginia City, January 23, 1880), SCF, 1871–84.

54. Act of March 2, 1867, 14 *USSL*, 541; acts of February 25 and March 3, 1885, 23 *USSL*, 321–22, 443. See also *Congressional Record*, 48 Congress, 2 Session (1884–85), 670–71; Report of the Committee on the Judiciary on appeals

If they urged more judges, Montanans also criticized the system which allowed judges on the supreme court to hear appeals of cases over which they presided at the district level. Critics called the arrangement "a wretched one," "inherently vicious," and the "so called Supreme Court . . . a sham."[55] But despite its obvious weaknesses, the appellate machinery did function reasonably well. Of 586 decisions by the district judges, the Montana supreme court affirmed 356, reversed 194, dismissed 16, and modified 20, certainly not a rubber-stamp record.[56] One proposed solution for a potentially unhealthy arrangement was to consolidate the appellate jurisdiction of the courts of Montana, Idaho, and Washington, each territory selecting one of its judges to sit jointly to hear appeals from district courts in all three territories.[57] This idea was never pushed very hard and the most common answer to the problem was simply to expand the judiciary by adding a fourth justice, with none to hear appeals from his own decisions.

From 1878 on, Congress was bombarded with various versions of this idea. Private citizens, judges, governors, and the Montana Bar Association pointed out that the territory was larger than all of New England and that "Even in so exhilarating a climate as Montana, there is a limit on human achievement."[58] Even with continuing support from the attorney general, bills introduced in Congress failed one after another, until finally, in 1886, and not without opposition, President Cleveland signed a law which provided four judges for Montana, none of whom was to sit on the supreme court in any appeal brought up from a judgment rendered by him at the district level.[59] Thus at the same time, the size of the court was increased and

---

from the supreme courts of the District of Columbia and the Several Territories, *House Report* No. 1260, 48 Congress, 1 Session (1883–84), 1–2.

55. *Weekly Independent*, July 10, 1879; James Callaway to Wilbur F. Sanders (Deer Lodge, February 17, 1889), quoted in *Herald*, February 22, 1889; Alexander Woolfolk to Maginnis (Helena, May 4, 1876), Maginnis MSS; Woolfolk to Brewster (Helena, February, 1883 [no other date]), Decius Wade file, APJ.

56. Guice, *The Rocky Mountain Bench*, 13.

57. *Weekly Independent*, January 20, 1876.

58. *Ibid.*, March 21, 1878; *Herald*, March 13, 1878; February 27, 1885; Blake to Devens (Virginia City, January 23, 1880), SCF, 1871–84; Sanders to Brewster (Helena, July 14, 1884), *ibid.*; memorial to Congress (n.d.), *LM*, 13 Session (1883), 209; Report of the Committee on the Territories to Reorganize the Judicial System of the Territory of Montana, *House Report* No. 470, 46 Congress, 2 Session (1879–80), 3–4; *Congressional Record*, 49 Congress, 1 Session (1885–86), 856; Report of the Governor of Montana, 1884, 264–65.

59. Act of July 10, 1886, 24 USSL, 138. See *Congressional Record*, 46 Congress, 3 Session (1880–81), 1901–2; *ibid.*, 48 Congress, 1 Session (1883–84),

one of its most evident evils eliminated. But the change came late, only after years of repeated effort, and many believed that even four justices were too few.[60]

It has long been fashionable to accept at face value blanket indictment of territorial judges as "broken-down politicians or men without capacity or integrity," to use the words of Delegate Martin Maginnis. Many of the judges, insisted Maginnis, "could not pass an examination for admission to the bar and could never earn a living in competition with our local bar. . . ." These, he said in 1876, "have not been exceptions, but the rule."[61] John Guice's 1972 book, *The Rocky Mountain Bench,* has gone far in correcting these stereotypes of the carpetbagger who lacked both talent and scruples.

Whether they admitted it or not, territorial judges were political appointees, and more than one, by chance or by choice, became embroiled in local politics. In Montana, where they were traditionally Republican in a Democratic constituency, this was not difficult to do. Holdovers from non-Republican administrations (i.e., Johnson's or Cleveland's) came under immediate fire, but attacks of one faction of Montana Republicans against Republican appointees could be equally as devastating. Governor Potts gave his blessing to a Republican directed drive to oust Chief Justice Henry L. Warren, "a bitter uncompromising democrat, of the most malignant type," who finally resigned in 1871 to go into law practice with Wilbur F. Sanders—surely an illustration of the no-party principle![62] Meanwhile, Potts and Delegate Cavanaugh, though of different parties, sought the ouster of Judge George G. Symes. Suggesting that "on the grounds of public interests," Symes be replaced with an Ohioan who was "an earnest and influential Republican," Potts wrote President Grant a

2777; *ibid.*, 49 Congress, 1 Session (1885–86), 6442; Report of the Committee on the Territories to reorganize the Judicial System of the Territory of Montana, *House Report* No. 470, 46 Congress, 2 Session (1879–80), 1; Report of the Committee on the Territories for extra Supreme Court Justices in the Territories, *House Report* No. 254, 48 Congress, 1 Session (1883–84), 1–2; Report of the Committee on the Judiciary on the revision of the Judiciary system of Montana, *House Report* No. 1454, 49 Congress, 1 Session (1885–86), 1; *Herald*, May 2, 1884; February 27, 1885.

60. *Herald*, November 9, 1887.

61. *Congressional Record*, 44 Congress, 1 Session (1875–76), 2425; *ibid.*, 48 Congress, 1 Session (1883–84), 2778. See also Wade, "Self-Government in the Territories," 304.

62. *Montana Democrat*, April 24, 1869; *Montana Post*, April 30, 1869; Matt H. Carpenter to E. R. Hoar (Milwaukee, May 24, 1869), Daniel Johnson file, APJ; Llewellyn L. Callaway, "Something About the Territorial Judges," *Montana Law Review*, IV (Spring, 1943), 7.

little pompously: "A new country recognizes a Judge of ability and nerve who will enforce the law and punish offenders. We need a civilizer here and not a demoralizer as we now have. An able Judge has more power for good here than all the Federal Officers put together. . . .[63]

Under great pressure, Symes resigned, but it was soon clear that his successor, John L. Murphy of Tennessee, was not Potts's idea of "a civilizer" either, and the governor played a central role in an ultimately successful movement of Montana Republican lawyers to unseat him.[64] Potts also figured prominently in the attempt in 1874 to oust Hiram Knowles from the bench, charging ineptness and intoxication; and he spearheaded the campaign to block the reappointment of Judge Henry N. Blake five years later.[65] In each instance, politics was important and Potts was striking as much as his arch-enemy Wilbur F. Sanders as at Blake or Knowles.

Another governor, John Schuyler Crosby, had been a party to the suspension of Judge Everton J. Conger in 1883 pending investigation of charges of incompetence, neglect of duty, gambling, drunkenness, and "keeping companionship of low, vile people." A man with a distinguished war record and brother of a United States senator from Michigan, Conger had few supporters, and he charged that Crosby and Wilbur F. Sanders wanted him out of the way for political reasons. Certainly staunch Republicans did argue that his retention would be inimical not only to justice, but to the cause of Republicanism in Montana as well. In the end, one day before the expiration of his term, Conger's suspension was lifted but he was not reappointed.[66]

63. Potts to Ulysses S. Grant (Virginia City, November 25, 1870); James A. Garfield to Grant (Washington, December 7, 1870), both in Francis G. Servis file, APJ; Potts to Garfield (Virginia City, April 29, 1871), Garfield MSS.
64. For this episode, see: John L. Murphy file, APJ; Potts to Wheeler (Virginia City, April 29, 1872), Wheeler MSS; Joseph Naphtally to Chadwick and Chumasero (San Francisco, December 20, 1884), William F. Chadwick and William Chumasero MSS, MHS; Potts to Garfield (Virginia City, September 23, 1872), Garfield MSS; *The Montanian*, April 18, 1872; *Herald*, April 23, 1872.
65. For the campaign against Knowles, see Merritt C. Page to George H. Williams (Radersburg, May 7, 1874), copy, BIA; Potts to Williams (Virginia City, October 20, 1874), SCF, 1871–84; Maginnis to Samuel T. Hauser (Washington, December 14, 1874), Hauser MSS; *New North-West*, January 8, 1875. For the Blake affair, see Blake file, APJ; Potts to Hayes (Helena, November 21, 1879), "personal," Hayes MSS; Alexander Woolfolk to Maginnis (Helena, January 12, 1879), Maginnis MSS.
66. The Conger suspension is documented in great detail in the Everton J. Conger file, APJ. See also Benjamin Brewster to Everton J. Conger (Washington, March 8, 1883; January 18, 1884), Letters Sent by the Department of Justice to Judges and Clerks, 1874–1904; John Schuyler Crosby to Brewster (Helena, April

Helena Democrats played a role in ousting his successor, John Coburn, in 1885 on charges of incompetency, a lack of knowledge of the law, an unwillingness to identify politically or economically with the territory, and an "offensive partisanship" in leaving a crowded docket to campaign for the Republican presidential candidate in Indiana. Coburn's head fell, thanks to Delegate Joseph Toole and the new Cleveland administration in Washington; his replacement, Charles Pollard, one of the most dismal of the judicial appointees, so came under fire that the Senate failed to confirm him.[67] This climaxed three years of turmoil for the first judicial district. In the interim, the chief justice from time to time stepped into the breach, but residents could only have been frustrated. As one of them wrote their delegate early in 1886, ". . . one thing to us is certain. We want a judge. We want one bad, and we want one as soon as possible."[68]

Given the heat generated by party affiliation and the distaste for "carpetbagger" officials, it is not surprising that public opinion often failed to recognize the positive contributions of the early bench. That some judges were inept or mediocre is undeniable; what is surprising is that so many were able appointees who came to understand the needs of the territory and who contributed much to the shaping of the body of jurisprudence connected with it. Their decisions were not always popular and sometimes they were as much political as legal. But within the handicaps of the system itself, most Montana justices were comparable in ability to their counterparts in sister territories or states and a few were superior to the general run.

Henry Blake thought every member "actuated by pure motives" during the eight years he was on the bench; in 1879, the editor of the *Herald*—no unbiased observer—believed Montana "especially favored" and that the bench at that time was "the ablest and purist

8, 15, 1883); Peter C. Shannon to Brewster (Washington, July 18, 1883), both in SCF, 1871–84; Brewster to Crosby (Washington, April 9, 1883, January 28, 1884), both in Dept. of Justice, Letters Sent, Gen. and Misc., 1818–1904; *Herald*, April 13, 1883.

67. For Coburn, see John Coburn file, APJ; Coburn file, Senate Papers re Nominations; Coburn to Benjamin Harrison (Indianapolis, January 30, 1886); Benjamin Harrison to Coburn (Washington, December 11, 31, 1885; May 3, June 24, 1886), all in Benjamin Harrison MSS; *Herald*, December 4, 17, 26, 1885; January 2, 1886. For Pollard, see Charles Pollard file, APJ; Benjamin Harrison to George F. Edmunds (Washington, January 13, February 1, 1886), Benjamin Harrison MSS; *Weekly Independent*, February 1, 1886; *Herald*, January 12, 28, February 1, 11, 19, April 14, 30, May 6, 1886.

68. J. L. Staats et al. to Toole (Bozeman, January 26, 1886), Robert P. Vivian file, APJ; *Herald*, May 10, August 6, 1886.

of which any of the Territories can probably boast."[69] Such paeans were no doubt overdrawn. Montana's judges displayed the petty foibles and jealousies of ordinary mortals; they had their personal quirks and eccentricities.

Some, like Murphy, were young and inexperienced. Newton McConnell, Tennessee prohibitionist, also had scruples against dancing and card-playing, and was "about as popular as a black bear in a bee settlement."[70] Henry Knowles was known for his sympathies for the defendant and some thought him biased. Blake followed the word of the law, so much the better if precedents came from Massachusetts, with ponderous arguments. Hosmer had the reputation of being "a learned man, with a literary turn"; Bach (pronounced "Baych") was known as an athlete, a sharp, precise dresser, and a good lawyer but "much affected by his dignity."[71] Galbraith, the six-foot Scottish American, was a lover of nature and a charming musician, but was accused of favoring the "land sharks" in his decisions.[72]

Undoubtedly the dominant figure was Decius Wade, chief justice for four consecutive terms. Although one colleague thought he had aspirations to Congress, although an editor piqued at his voiding of a printing law might call him "a usurper, a tyrant, a dictator, a Jeffreys, a Nero, the Czar of all Montana," and although he was damned as partisan and corrupt by Democrats each time he came up for reappointment,[73] history nevertheless records him as an able, conscientious jurist. In his sixteen years, he had presided over more than 116 terms of court, had sent 500 men to prison, and had sentenced an even dozen to the gallows—usually with a personal but pessimistic appeal for repentance.[74] Wade gave supreme court decisions in Mon-

69. Palidan, ed., "Henry N. Blake," 51; *Herald*, January 6, 1869; August 6, 1886.

70. *Herald*, April 26, July 8, 1887; *Weekly Independent*, May 5, 1887.

71. Callaway, "Something About the Territorial Judges," 6, 8, 9–10, 12.

72. *Herald*, August 6, 1886; Hiram Knowles to Angus McDonald (Deer Lodge, November 2, 1889), Knowles MSS; William Burton to Cleveland (Butte, April 12, 1886); William A. Clark to George A. Jenks (Butte, May 3, 1887), both in William J. Galbraith file, APJ.

73. Francis G. Servis to James A. Garfield (Virginia City, August 31, November 15, 1873), Garfield MSS; Woolfolk to Brewster (Helena, February, 1883 [no other date]), Decius Wade file, APJ. Wade's appointment file contains numerous letters from those who opposed his renomination.

74. *Herald*, December 29, 1886; February 26, 1887. "Does your soul now writhe in agony because of your bloody crime?" Wade once asked a convicted murderer. "Has your conscience become so awakened that it tortures you with horrors untold and indescribable, because of the innocent life that your bloody hand sacrificed for paltry gold?" Unidentified clipping (n.p., n.d.), Wade Scrapbook, Wade MSS.

tana "a weight and reputation that none other among the Territories enjoys or even approaches," insisted an admirer when the chief justice stepped down.[75] He wrote nearly half of the decisions in the first six volumes of the *Montana Reports* and few of his were reversed: of the seventeen which reached the United States Supreme Court, fourteen were upheld. With Henry Knowles, he played a major role in formulating court procedures and basic mining and irrigation law.[76] Despite a noticeable fault—"the expression of his views in many sentences"—he came to be considered the most distinguished member of the territorial bench. "The more I see of the work the larger he grows," a twentieth-century attorney would write. "He was an almighty fine lawyer."[77]

Whatever the caliber of its members, the court worked industriously throughout the territorial period to maintain its prerogatives, guarding jealously what it considered to be its legal rights and enhancing its own prestige if possible. It declared numerous laws invalid, some on the grounds that the legislature assumed powers that were judicial in nature.[78] In 1875, for example, after the legislature had required the governor, secretary, and marshal to canvass the votes of the capital election, the court not only ruled the action legal, but also declared its own power to order the provisions of the law enforced.[79]

It was in declaring the complete sovereignty of the federal government that the early judges were most vigorous, however. Chief Justice Wade in 1874 spoke without reserve in contending that the people of a territory retained no right of self-government; that depended wholly upon the will of Congress: "Congress could sell and dispose of a territory to a foreign power, and not only can it make all needful rules and regulations concerning the territories, but can abolish them, and the rules and regulations made by congress are enacted laws, and congressional rules for the territories can be made in no other manner."[80]

75. *Herald,* December 29, 1886; February 26, 1887.
76. *DAB,* XIX, 305–6.
77. Callaway, "Something About the Territorial Judges," 7–8; Blake, eulogy of Decius Wade (n.p., n.d.), Wade MSS.
78. See for example, Thorp *v.* Woolman, 1 *Montana Reports* (1870), 168–72; Commissioners of Custer County *v.* Commissioners of Yellowstone County, 6 *Montana Reports* (1886), 49–50.
79. Chumasero *v.* Potts, 2 *Montana Reports* (1875), 247. See also People *ex rel.* Robertson *v.* Van Gaskin et al., 5 *Montana Reports* (1885), 352, 375; *New York Times,* May 1, 1883.
80. Territory of Montana *v.* Lee, 2 *Montana Reports* (1874), 137–38.

At the same time the court was generally careful to protect individual rights, and sought to fit the constitutional amendments into the territorial scheme, an effort that was not always easy. When federal funds were not available to try a prisoner, Wade did not hesitate to release him.[81] In 1881, the Montana supreme court discarded a verdict returned by only eleven jurors in a criminal case, even though the defendant had agreed to the circumstances. It invoked the Fifth and Fourteenth Amendments to bar the seizure of property for delinquent taxes, assuming that the "due process" clauses had been violated, even though no state law and no law of congress was in question.[82]

When presenting Montana's brief before Congress in 1889, Delegate Joseph K. Toole listed as one of his grievances the weakness and deficiency of the judicial system. It was, he insisted, "inherently wrong," and "grossly inadequate. . . . We have outgrown a system designed only for a weak and sparsely inhabited Territory," he said, in words that showed insight into the problem.[83] For from the beginning the judiciary was hard pressed to meet the needs of its environment. At times, the court structure was too weak and inflexible to act effectively and the cutting edge of the sword of justice was more than once blunted. Hampered by limited funds, by an unfamiliarity with mining law, and by resentment stemming from local political cleavages and the dislike of "foreign" officials, Montana's territorial judges, good and poor alike, found their tasks not always easy nor pleasant. But under the circumstances, they generally handled them well.

Nor did the policy of the federal government in legislating for the territory provide much relief. If change came about, it was usually after years of supplication. Congress too frequently failed to judge the needs of each territory on its own merits. Seldom did national lawmakers recognize that changes taking place within Montana required additional legislation to expand the instrumentalities of organized government accordingly.

81. United States *v.* Fox, 3 *Montana Reports* (1880), 519.
82. Territory of Montana *v.* Ah Wah and Ah Yen, 4 *Montana Reports* (1881), 170–73; Chauvin *v.* Valiton, 8 *Montana Reports* (1889), 451. For another decision which took for granted the application of the Sixth Amendment, see Johnston *v.* Lewis and Clarke County, 2 *Montana Reports* (1874), 159. For a reversal of the Montana court's interpretation of the Seventh Amendment, see Kennon *v.* Gilmer, 131 *U.S. Reports* (1888), 28, 30.
83. *Congressional Record*, 50 Congress, 2 Session (1889–90), 821.

10

"... A Sort of Lying-In Hospital
for Political Tramps":
Territorial Offices and Officers

"He has erected a multitude of New Offices, and sent hither swarms
of Officers to harass our People, and eat out their substance." These
are the words from the Declaration of Independence, penned by
Jefferson in the year 1776. These are also the words spoken before
Congress by Delegate Joseph K. Toole on January 15, 1889, in presenting the case of the Territory of Montana for statehood.[1]

It was a basic grievance directed against the territorial system in
general that Toole was echoing and it was a complaint reiterated
many times before in those same halls. That the important administrative and judicial officers should be appointed by the president,
without consultation of the desires of the people over whom they
were to preside, seemed contradictory indeed to those schooled in
the rough independence of the frontier. Was there any reason why a
man capable of selecting his own officials while residing in Iowa or
Minnesota should be deprived of that right because he chose to move
a few hundred miles to the west or northwest? Montana, like her sister
territories, had from the first been granted a legislature. What logic
was there in permitting territorial residents to make their own laws
but regarding them as incapable of interpreting or administering
them?

1. *Congressional Record*, 50 Congress, 2 Session (1888–89), 821.

Throughout the period of Montana's territorial apprenticeship, these arguments were lost on Congress. Members of that body presented the stock argument of gradual preparation for self-government, but openly recognized the more realistic, if less commendable, matter of patronage as an element in prolonging territorial status. From the very beginning, offices in the remote West were regarded as political plums to be handed out for meritorious service above and beyond the call of duty. What better pasturage for spavined old war horses and disgruntled political hacks than the virgin meadows of territorial government?[2] For the recipient, such offices were often regarded, unjustifiably probably, as stepping stones to more desirable positions. As Senator Hendricks of Indiana commented in 1868, every territorial governor "was a candidate for Congress from the day he goes there."[3] Senator Benjamin Harrison believed politics could not be ignored: "I felt myself that the office of Governor of the Territory was a political office in its nature," he once wrote Charles Broadwater, "and that the discretion of the President in making an appointment was necessarily pretty wide—more so than in some administrative offices."[4] It was frankly and openly a system of patronage, admitted by president and congressmen alike, and resented by the territories.

The practice of appointing political favorites was particularly unpleasant because Montana tended to be strongly Democratic in an era of national Republican executive ascendancy. This fact undoubtedly accounts for some of the criticism that came from the territory, but protests were too broad and too often cut across party lines to be shrugged off as mere partisan politics. Delegate James Cavanaugh, a Democrat, could object vigorously in 1871 that the territories were "made receptacles for political convicts" who had been "spewed out at the mouth of honest constituencies" in the East. Chief Justice Wade, a Republican, complained of a system under which a governor might be a "political tramp without character, or the demented relative of some man of influence." The courts, said another, "might properly be called law schools where the Judges get a smattering of law at public expense." Congress never ceased to send out nonresident "pilgrims" and "carpetbaggers," who—according to Montanans—

2. Prior to 1883 retired army or navy officers were barred from holding territorial offices if receiving federal pay, but those not on the government payroll were still eligible, Act of March 3, 1883, 22 *USSL*, 567.
3. *Congressional Globe*, 40 Congress, 2 Session (1867–68), 2800.
4. Benjamin Harrison to Charles Broadwater (Washington, March 15, 1886), Benjamin Harrison MSS.

"have no interest in common with the people and are as ignorant of
their wants as are the Exquimaux of orange groves."[5]

TABLE 2. TERRITORIAL APPOINTEES OF MONTANA

Governors	Appointed by	Residence	Date of Confirmation	Reason for Leaving Office
Sidney Edgerton	Lincoln	Ohio	1864	Resigned
Green Clay Smith	Johnson	Kentucky	1866	Resigned
Nathaniel P. Langford	Johnson	Montana		Unconfirmed
James M. Ashley	Grant	Ohio	1869	Removed
Benjamin F. Potts	Grant	Ohio	1870	Term expired
			1874	Term expired
	Hayes		1878	Term expired
John Schuyler Crosby	Arthur	New York	1882	Resigned
B. Platt Carpenter	Arthur	New York	1884	Suspended
Samuel T. Hauser	Cleveland	Montana	1886	Resigned
Preston H. Leslie	Cleveland	Kentucky	1887	Resigned
Benjamin F. White	Harrison	Montana	1889	Statehood

Secretaries

Henry P. Torsey	Lincoln	Maine	1864	Declined appointment
John Coburn	Lincoln	Indiana	1865	Declined appointment
Thomas F. Meagher	Johnson	New York	1866	Deceased
John P. Bruce	Johnson	Montana		Rejected by Senate
James Tufts	Johnson	Montana	1867	Removed
Wiley S. Scribner	Grant	Montana	1869	Removed
Addison H. Sanders	Grant	Iowa	1870	Withdrew before taking office
James E. Callaway	Grant	Illinois	1871	Term expired
			1875	Resigned
James H. Mills	Hayes	Montana	1877	Term expired
Isaac D. McCutcheon	Arthur	Michigan	1882	Resignation forced
John S. Tooker	Arthur	Michigan	1883	Resigned
William B. Webb	Cleveland	Montana	1886	Removed
Louis A. Walker	Harrison	Montana	1889	Statehood

Judges

Ammi Giddings	Lincoln	Connecticut	1864	Did not serve
Lorenzo P. Williston	Lincoln	Dakota	1864	Term expired
Hezekiah L. Hosmer°	Lincoln	Ohio	1864	Term expired
Lyman E. Munson	Lincoln	Connecticut	1865	Resigned

5. *Congressional Globe*, 41 Congress, 3 Session (1870–71), 970; Wade, "Self-Government in the Territories," *International Review*, VI (March, 1879), 304; *Weekly Herald*, January 2, 1879; *Independent*, June 20, 1878.

Judges	Appointed by	Residence	Date of Confirmation	Reason for Leaving Office
Henry L. Warren°	Johnson	Illinois	1868	Resigned
William M. Stafford	Johnson	Montana?		Appointment tabled
Hiram G. Knowles	Johnson	Iowa	1868	Term expired
			1872	Term expired
			1876	Resigned
William W. Dixon	Johnson	Montana		Unconfirmed
George G. Symes	Grant	Kentucky	1869	Resigned
Lewis M. Burson°	Grant	Montana		Name withdrawn
John L. Murphy	Grant	Tennessee	1871	Suspended
Decius S. Wade°	Grant	Ohio	1871	Term expired
			1875	Term expired
	Hayes		1879	Term expired
	Arthur		1883	Term expired
Francis G. Servis	Grant	Ohio	1873	Resigned
Henry N. Blake	Grant	Montana	1876	Term expired
William J. Galbraith	Hayes	Iowa	1879	Term expired
	Arthur		1884	Term expired
Everton J. Conger	Hayes	Illinois	1880	Suspended: term expired
John Coburn	Arthur	Indiana	1884	Suspended
Charles R. Pollard	Cleveland	Indiana		Rejected
James H. McLeary	Cleveland	Texas	1886	Resigned
Thomas C. Bach†	Cleveland	Montana	1886	Statehood
Newton W. McConnell°	Cleveland	Tennessee	1888	Resigned
Stephen A. DeWolfe	Cleveland	Montana	1888	Statehood
Moses J. Liddell	Cleveland	Louisiana	1888	Statehood
Henry N. Blake°	Harrison	Montana	1889	Statehood

°Chief justice.
†Appointed to fill the office of fourth justice created by act of July 10, 1886.

That Montana's appointments were dictated by political considerations is undeniable. Was it not this that brought Lincoln's endorsement of Vice-President Hamlin's recommendation of Henry P. Torsey of Maine as the first territorial secretary in 1864? "The Vice President says I promised to make the appointment, & I suppose I must make it," Lincoln had written.[6] Was it mere concidence that the first three governors had all been members of the United States House of Representatives earlier in their careers?[7] Was it chance that three of the

6. Endorsement, Hannibal Hamlin to Abraham Lincoln (n.p., March 1, 1864), Torsey file, APS.
7. Edgerton had represented Ohio's 18th District in the 36th and 37th Con-

first five governors brought with them distinguished Civil War records?[8] Was it accidental that Chief Justice Decius Wade was a personal friend of James A. Garfield, a nephew of Benjamin Wade, and a brother-in-law of Vice-President Schuyler Colfax; that Benjamin Potts had studied law in the office of a three-term United States representative, was a close associate of James A. Garfield, and enjoyed "the most intimate friendship with Rutherford B. Hayes; or that John Schuyler Crosby and B. Platt Carpenter, both New York politicians, came to the gubernatorial chair in 1883 and 1884 respectively, just when another New Yorker, Chester Arthur, was in the White House?[9]

For any territorial vacancy, the president could expect a host of applications and pressure from senators pushing their favorites with "bushels of endorsements." For an opening for Montana chief justice in 1885, there were at least thirty applicants, plus at least a hundred others who sought a judgeship "in one of the Territories" without designating a specific one.[10] Nor were office-seekers always too selective: they took what was available. Justice James McLeary had really wanted to be U.S. Attorney in West Texas; Governor Preston Leslie had originally sought the chief justiceship of Arizona; Secretary John Tooker desired a land office position in Dakota, but came to Montana as a sort of consolation prize—probably as a concession to Senator Conger of Michigan, whose brother had recently been suspended from the Montana bench.[11]

Men applied for territorial posts for their own reasons. Here one argued poor health and the therapeutic benefits of a mountain climate; there, one sought change because of his wife's illness. Another

gresses but did not stand for reelection in 1862. Smith was in his second term in the House when appointed governor. Ashley had served ten years there, before being defeated. *DAB*, I, 389–90; VI, 20; Wold, *Biographical Directory*, 652, 939, 1536.

8. Smith, Potts, and Crosby.

9. Another uncle of Decius Wade, Edward Wade, also sat in Congress. *Herald*, March 15, 1871; July 6, 1885; *DAB*, XV, 135; XIX, 305; Wold, *Biographical Directory*, 932, 1653; Oliver W. Holmes, ed., "James A. Garfield's Diary of a Trip to Montana in 1872," *Frontier and Midland*, XV (Winter, 1934–35), 162; Benjamin F. Potts to W. Dennison (Helena, June 28, 1876), Hayes MSS; Potts to James A. Garfield (Virginia City, June 3, 1871; December 3, 1872), Garfield MSS.

10. See undated memorandum, signed J. M. Ewing, in Moses Liddell file, APJ; *Herald*, March 8, 1887.

11. *Herald*, October 23, 27, November 3, 1883; Edward Lacey to S. J. Kirkwood (Washington, February 15, 1882); memorandum received June 23, 1881; both in McCutcheon file, API; W. S. Pryor to Grover Cleveland (Frankfort, Kentucky, October 13, 1886), Leslie file, API; K. K. Legett to Cleveland (Austin, January 10, 1885), McLeary file, APJ.

wanted the governorship because his law practice at home was in the doldrums.[12]

Whatever his justification, any candidate was advised to come well fortified with credentials. Sidney Edgerton in 1864 had letters and petitions from Montanans buttressed by endorsements from half a dozen U.S. senators and twenty-five representatives; James Ashley had the support of 142 members of the House when he was nominated; and Benjamin Potts enjoyed the backing of John Sherman, the presidential electors of Ohio, and a long list of Republican legislators from the same state. When Francis G. Servis was named to the Montana bench in 1872 it was only after an active campaign in Washington on his behalf by James A. Garfield, Delegate William Clagett, and Governor Potts.[13]

If politics generally determined territorial appointments, they were the politics of the nation's capital, not of Montana. To be sure, Montana politicians like Fisk, Sanders, and George Pinney carried their local quarrels to Washington and sought to act as kingmakers, usually with marginal success if any.[14] Occasionally there was an exception, as in 1887 when a few words from a Montana Democrat to a Washington friend were sufficient to eliminate Sanders's law partner, W. E. Cullen, from any consideration for the chief justiceship of the territory at a time when the Sanders-Cullen firm was attorney for the Northern Pacific Railroad and Montana Improvement Company, then under fire by Land Commissioner Sparks for alleged timber depredations.[15] And two years later, when Louis A. Walker was named territorial secretary, his Montana confidant, Russell Harrison, son of the new president, was undoubtedly the key factor in the selection.[16]

12. See Thomas C. Buckley to James B. Beck (Falmouth, Kentucky, April 25, 1877), Thomas C. Buckley file, API; F. M. Cockrell to Stanley Matthews (Warrensburg, Missouri, April 12, 1877), Andrew W. Rogers file, API; R. L. Gibson to Augustus Garland (Washington, January 28, 1888), Moses Liddell file, APJ.

13. Nathaniel Langford et al. to Lincoln (Washington, March 17, 1864); J. H. Lane et al. to Lincoln (n.p., n.d.); Garfield et al. to Lincoln (n.p., n.d.), all in Edgerton file, APS; John Sherman to Ulysses Grant (Washington, March 8, 1869); Presidential Electors of Ohio to Grant (n.p., n.d.); Republican Members of the Ohio Legislature to Grant (n.p., n.d.), all in Potts file, APS; *New North-West*, December 24, 1869; see also Ashley file, APS; Brown and Williams, *Diary of James A. Garfield*, I, 356–57, 449, 463; II, 30, 31–32.

14. See Robert E. Fisk to Elizabeth Fisk (New York, March 12, 1869; Washington, March 27, 1869; February 24, March 9, 1881), Fisk family MSS.

15. Samuel Word to J. Haley (Helena, February 11, 1887); W. A. J. Sparks to L. Q. C. Lamar (Washington, March 14, 1887), Decius Wade file, APJ.

16. Isaac McCutcheon to Russell B. Harrison (Helena, April 2, 1889), Russell B. Harrison MSS.

Federal officials—Meagher, Potts, Hiram Knowles and Decius Wade among them—wrote influential friends in Washington on behalf of their own reappointment or advancement.[17] They sought to use their influence to block or oust other federal office holders, but even Potts, one of the most persuasive, had to admit that his success in this area was not "entirely satisfactory."[18] Potts was consulted on certain posts and no doubt his victory over the Fisk-Callaway-Sanders coalition in 1877 strengthened his hand. But his role was not focal: he might thwart some of his political enemies, but his favorites were not necessarily appointed.[19] Sam Hauser, of course, always cut an important swath in Washington; and Isaac McCutcheon, at least, believed that Governor Leslie had enough "clout" there to prevent his appointment as U.S. attorney.[20] But in general, recommendations of territorial officers on such matters were more likely to be ignored than accepted.

To be a serious contender, any hopeful had to be of the political party in power and preferably he should be active, although in 1886 the argument was successfully made on behalf of Thomas C. Bach for a judgeship that "He has never been a politician."[21] But this was atypical: normally, party loyalty was to be rewarded. This meant that under ordinary circumstances, Montana's wise men came from the east, with Ohio in the 1860s and 1870s furnishing more than her quota.[22] Administrative changes in Washington naturally brought sweeping displacements, even though of the same party, and when Cleveland's Democrats dispossessed the Republicans in 1885, Montana saw a notable influx of territorial officers from more Southern climes. Even his Civil War record did not save Judge John Coburn, but he was not alone. His friend Benjamin Harrison could write an-

17. Thomas F. Meagher to William H. Seward (Virginia City, December 14, 1865; February 20, April 22, 1866), TPS; James Tufts to W. E. Cullen (Virginia City, [?] 1868), BIA; Potts to Rutherford B. Hayes (Virginia City, June 9, 1874), Hayes MSS; Decius Wade to Hayes (Helena, October 24, 1878), Wade file, APJ; Hiram Knowles to Martin Maginnis (Deer Lodge, December 4, 1876), Maginnis MSS.

18. Potts to Hayes (Virginia City, November 6, 1870), Hayes MSS; Potts to S. H. Crounse (Virginia City, March 27, 1871), copy, Potts letterbook.

19. Zachariah Chandler to Potts (Washington, May 17, 1876), GEC; J. W. Andrews to W. K. Rogers (Chicago, May 28, 1877), Hayes MSS; Potts to Hayes (Helena, November 25, 1879), S. W. Munn file, APJ.

20. McCutcheon to Russell B. Harrison (Helena, March 6, 1889), Russell B. Harrison MSS.

21. Joseph K. Toole to Cleveland (Washington, July 13, 1886), Thomas C. Bach file, APJ.

22. For remarks on preponderance of Ohioans, see Potts to Hayes (Virginia City, June 9, 1874), Hayes MSS; W. F. Chadwick to Maginnis (Helena, January 29, 1879), Maginnis MSS.

other complainant from Washington, "You are very much mistaken in supposing that your case is the only one where an ex-soldier has been removed. They are thick as blackberries in August."[23] By the end of February, 1886, Cleveland had ousted three chief justices and seven associates in the territories and was being challenged by Harrison and other indignant Republicans in Congress; but politics was politics and party patronage won out.[24]

Cleveland's purge meant that any successful applicant had to have letters, as Moses Liddell did, proclaiming him "a Democrat (with a capital D) of the Jeffersonian stripe."[25] It meant also an invasion of southerners into Montana: a judge from Texas, another from Louisiana; a governor and a chief justice from Tennessee. These plus lesser federal appointments from border or former rebel states brought from local Republicans expressions of real concern about "Southern carpet-baggers" descending upon Montana "like a swarm of buzzards upon the carcass of a dead horse."[26] But soon, the positions were reversed. With Cleveland out of office, it was the Republican turn to wield the ax and the territory was not exempt.[27]

One of the characteristics of territorial office-holding in Montana was rapid turnover. Many of the "hot-house specimens" sent out proved "too frail to stand transplanting in a northern clime" and soon returned "to the genial influences of their own civilization," remarked Joseph Toole in 1888.[28] In the Grant era, according to another, Montana's officers swept in and out in bewildering succession: "As an Emigration Society the Administration has been an undoubted success."[29] A dozen years later, a Butte editor complained of the selection of a new governor who "knows no more about Territorial affairs than a Hindoo Chief. . . . His seat is scarcely warmed till some other . . . steps into the field and relieves him of his brief authority."[30]

During a quarter of a century, Montana had nine different gover-

23. Benjamin Harrison to Shelby Sexton (Washington, December 19, 1885); Harrison to John Coburn (Washington, March 31, 1886), Benjamin Harrison MSS.

24. *Herald*, February 24, 1886; Harry Joseph Sievers, *Benjamin Harrison* (Chicago, 1952, 1958), II, 285–86.

25. John C. Wickliff to Augustus Garland (Monroe, Louisiana, June 17, 1887), Liddell file, APJ.

26. *Herald*, October 12, 1885; *Semi-Weekly Inter Mountain*, June 10, 1885.

27. *Billings Gazette*, March 14, 1889.

28. *Congressional Record*, 50 Congress, 2 Session (1888–89), 821.

29. *Daily Rocky Mountain Gazette*, November 4, 1870.

30. *Inter-Mountains Freeman* (Butte), March 5, 1882. See also *Weekly Herald*, December 23, 1886.

nors, three of them from Ohio, and two each from Kentucky, New York, and Montana. At thirty-three, Potts was the youngest; Leslie at sixty-seven the oldest; the average age at the time of appointment was forty-six; the median about the same. Three, Smith, Potts and Crosby, were Civil War veterans; three, Edgerton, Smith and Ashley, had served in Congress; four, Potts, Carpenter, Leslie and White, had previously been members of a state or territorial legislature; Leslie had been governor of Kentucky. Smith, Potts, Carpenter, and Crosby all had some college education; five of the nine were lawyers by background, two were businessmen. Potts served more than twelve years—almost half of the territorial period—and the remaining time was divided among eight appointees, giving approximately one and a half years per administration to each. When the time served by secretaries acting as governor ad interim is deducted, the term average becomes even shorter. If Potts completed three four-year terms, no other governor finished even one. Two, Ashley and Carpenter, were removed or suspended; five resigned (Edgerton, Smith, Crosby, Hauser, and Leslie), several perhaps under pressure; and one, White, found his administration cut short by statehood.

Among the territorial secretaries, the record for tenure of office was little better. Of the nine different men who actually served in this capacity, five were Montana residents when selected; two came from Michigan and one each from New York and Illinois. At least four were Union veterans; an equal number had been members of legislatures earlier; at least three were college educated. Lawyers predominated: five were of that profession, one was an editor, one a bookkeeper, one a merchant, and Meagher defies categorization. Their median age was thirty-eight, somewhat below that of the chief executives. On the average, they each served about two and three-quarters years in office. Two, Callaway and Mills, served full terms; Meagher died while on the job; Tufts, Scribner, and Webb were all removed and McCutcheon and Tooker escaped removal only by resigning first.[31] One, Louis Walker, was secretary at the time of statehood.

An analysis of the territorial justices is more confusing. Nineteen men actually served. Information on the entire group is incomplete,

31. For Tooker's insistence that he had resigned and not been suspended see John S. Tooker to Cleveland (Helena, July 7, 1885); William Webb to L. Q. C. Lamar (Helena, November 17, 1885); Toole to Lamar (Washington, November 30, 1885); Tooker to Toole (Helena, December 23, 1885), all in John S. Tooker file, API.

but the median age was remarkably low—slightly over forty: Bach was but thirty-three when appointed, Wade only thirty-six. About half had served in the Civil War (one on the side of the Confederacy); at least half had previous political or judicial experience; and almost all were college educated. Three each came from Ohio and Montana, two each from Illinois, Tennessee, and Iowa, the remainder from Dakota, Connecticut, Kentucky, Indiana, Texas and Louisiana. One, Wade, completed four full terms; two, Knowles and Galbraith, finished two complete terms each; while three, Hosmer, Williston, and Blake, served at least one full term apiece. Six men resigned without completing their four years in office, one, Symes, probably only a step ahead of removal; three were suspended or removed, Murphy, Conger, and Coburn.[32]

Where the lesser territorial offices were concerned, United States marshal, attorney, and surveyor general, the same trends prevailed. But at whatever level, this rapid rotation of personnel was the product of several factors, not the least of which, of course, was the use of territorial posts as part of the patronage system. Changes in the White House or on Capitol Hill must invariably be reflected in Virginia City or Helena.

But beyond that, appointees often became disillusioned. Office seekers regarded territorial appointments as springboards to greater political glory. As James Fisk noted, when urging Wilbur F. Sanders to push for the governorship in 1868, "It will be the best stepping stone to Congress or to the Senate you can possibly expect." Chief Justice Wade was accused of seeking to use his official position as a means to the same end.[33] In some cases, perhaps, such expectations were borne out: George G. Symes, one of the early judges, later became congressman from Colorado; ironically, William W. Dixon, whom the Senate had refused to confirm for a judgeship in 1869, ultimately sat in Congress as a representative of the new state of Montana; former U.S. marshal Alexander Botkin would later become lieutenant governor of the state, and Robert B. Smith, who had been United States attorney, would serve as governor. Judges Knowles,

32. Although Conger was suspended, technically he was permitted to complete his term. There is some disagreement over whether Munson resigned or was removed. *Senate Executive Journal*, XVI, 310, 433.

33. James L. Fisk, to Wilbur F. Sanders, (Helena, March 26, 1868), Sanders MSS; Francis Servis to James A. Garfield (Virginia City, August 31, November 15, 1873), Garfield MSS.

Blake, Bach and Galbraith would all find places on the state bench,[34] but for the most part territorial offices in Montana did not prove to be gateways for more desirable positions either in state or national government. In many cases, the direct opposite was true: former officials were often satisfied with lesser positions, if indeed they remained in public life at all. Hezekiah Hosmer, the first chief justice, was for a time mayor of Virginia City and subsequently a federal warehouse inspector on the Pacific Coast; John L. Murphy, another justice, was later elected city attorney on the Workingmen's ticket in San Francisco; and former governor Preston Leslie in subsequent years became United States attorney for the state of Montana.[35]

It should be noted, however, that an impressive number of "imported" federal officials remained in Montana when their tenure was up. When Governor Sam Hauser planned his New Year's reception for 1886, he found himself in competition with similar functions sponsored by two former governors, Benjamin Potts and B. Platt Carpenter.[36] Potts had remained in Montana, and was elected to the legislature in 1885, when his "Potts & Harrison Horse Company" of Helena was billing itself as "Breeders of Clydesdale, English Draft, Thoroughbred and Trotting Horses; Jersey and Holstein Cattle of the best milking families."[37] Carpenter was in law practice. Interested in territorial politics, he supported Wilbur F. Sanders in 1886 and was active in "rounding up the voters" a few years later. He was a member of the 1889 Constitutional Convention and was seriously mentioned for the chief justice's post that same year.[38] After his ouster in 1877, former secretary James Callaway remained in Montana, was the first Republican speaker of the house in the legislature, and sat in both constitutional conventions of the 1880s.[39] Isaac McCutcheon, too, remained in the territory even after being forced out of the secretaryship. In a Helena law partnership, he became chairman of the

34. *Herald*, July 19, 1877; Wold, *Biographical Directory*, 911, 1592; "Directory of the Officers of the State of Montana," *Contributions*, VI (1907), 487, 488, 489, 490.

35. *Herald*, February 6, 1872, September 8, 1878; *Weekly Independent*, October 23, 1879; *Progressive Men of the State of Montana*, 176.

36. *Herald*, December 31, 1885.

37. Russell Harrison to Benjamin Harrison (Helena, May 8, 1884), Benjamin Harrison MSS; *Herald*, October 14, 1880; April 3, 1884; Waldron, *Montana Politics*, 45; see letterheads in Russell B. Harrison MSS.

38. *Independent*, October 24, 1888; *Herald*, January 5, 1889; entry for April 23, 1889, Diary of Frank Leonard Sizer (in possession of F. M. Sizer, Berkeley, California); *Progressive Men of the State of Montana*, 1319–20.

39. *Ibid.*, 86; Waldron, *Montana Politics*, 45.

Republican Territorial Committee, played an active role in politics, and from time to time wrote or visited Washington about Montana affairs, once even drafting a bill for Senator Benjamin Harrison, who promised "to try to give the matter attention."[40]

The turnover of territorial officers was also a function of the low prevailing rate of pay. By the organic act of 1864, the annual salaries of the governor and the three justices had been set at $2,500, while that of the secretary was $500 less. At various times, ostensibly to compensate for payment in depreciated greenbacks and for higher living costs, but actually to give a greater measure of control over appointed officials, the early legislatures had voted additional sums to augment salaries. However in 1873, after standardizing the pay of all territorial justices at $3,000, governors at $3,500, and secretaries at $2,500, Congress forbade the granting of extra compensation by territorial assemblies. But in practice, even these levels were not maintained: by limiting appropriations, subsequent Congresses, beginning in 1877, voted only $2,600 a year for governors and judges and $1,800 for secretaries. Justices were given a $400 increase commencing in 1880, but for the others the 1877 level prevailed to the end of the territorial period.[41]

Montanans realized that the pay scale was too low to attract and keep the best talent. The 1877 cut was viewed as a "very questionable, and certainly the very worst kind of economy." 'Our officers are, at best, poorly paid and as a rule, poor pay, poor preach,'" said the *Benton Record*. "The salaries of the Governor, Secretary and Judges are ridiculously small—less than average bookkeepers get in a commercial house," complained the *Independent* in 1878, noting that in the East job seekers were not so interested in Montana, where "most of the offices are not worth contending for."[42]

No doubt that was an overstatement: the scramble for Montana appointments was always lively, but not many officials could manage to live on their salaries alone. In 1877, Governor Potts urged his friend John Sherman, who was Secretary of the Treasury, if he could

40. *Herald*, September 30, 1884; May 19, 1888; April 1, 1889; Benjamin Harrison to McCutcheon (Washington, December 18, 1885; April 22, 1886), Benjamin Harrison MSS; Louis A. Walker to Russell Harrison (Helena, March 14, 1889), Russell B. Harrison MSS.

41. Act of May 26, 1864, 13 USSL, 90; act of June 17, 1870, 16 USSL, 152; act of January 23, 1873, 17 USSL, 416; act of March 3, 1877, 19 USSL, 309; act of June 15, 1880, 21 USSL, 225.

42. *Benton Record* (Fort Benton), March 23, 1877; *Weekly Independent*, May 23, June 13, 1878. See also *Herald*, February 18, 1876.

not support James Mills for the post of territorial secretary, to back some young bachelor of "good capacity and habits," because "a man of a family could not accept the place and live on the salary." And Mills, who took the job, agreed that it was "a meagre compensation indeed." In a letter to Maginnis, Miles wrote: "The fact is all salaries, or nearly all, are now too low to secure or retain good services, and I am not much worse off than the Governor, Judges, Collector and others." Even as late as 1885, one Montana politician writing President Cleveland about vacancies on the bench could insist "it is not easy to find men who are willing to serve at the salary paid."[43]

Even the mediocre salaries were not always paid on schedule; no salaries were paid for almost two years after the creation of the territory. When Chief Justice Hosmer went east on leave in the winter of 1865–66, he had to write Samuel Hauser about "where I am to get the means to defray the expenses of the passage" back. Hosmer confided to Wilbur Sanders that he had some $5,000 tied up in underdeveloped mining property, but that he was "really poor" and much concerned about "bread and butter." Nearly a year after he was appointed, Governor Ashley complained to the Treasury Department that he had received neither his fourth-quarter salary nor the governor's contingency fund, and that he was badly in need of both. "It has cost me thus far, more than I have received to get my family out here," he grumbled. A few years later, Justice Francis Servis, threatening to return "to my old stamping ground" in Ohio, also lamented irregularities in getting his pay. ". . . my illustrious predecessor *bilked* me out of part of my salary—which is little enough without," he complained.[44]

Delegate Cavanaugh argued in 1870 that "any lawyer in Montana" could make twice the salary Congress offered to judges and cited numerous examples that tended to bear out this generalization. Several years after Henry Blake left the territorial bench, his income was reported as three or four times "the amount Uncle Sam used to pay him while on the woolsack"; James H. McLeary twice told President Cleveland of the large discrepancy between his previous com-

43. Potts to Sherman (Helena, March 30, 1877), James H. Mills file, API; James H. Mills to Maginnis (Helena, November 19, 1877), TPI; Mills to Maginnis (Helena, January 26, 1878), Maginnis MSS; Sample Orr to Cleveland (Butte, August 8, 1885), Liddell file, APJ.

44. Hezekiah Hosmer to Samuel T. Hauser (New York, February 26, 1866), Hauser MSS; Hosmer to Sanders (Virginia City, January 24, 1867), Sanders MSS; James M. Ashley to R. W. Taylor (Helena, March 9, 1870), LT, Vol. 10; Servis to Garfield (Virginia City, December 18, 1873), Garfield MSS.

fortable practice in San Antonio and his judge's salary in "these mountains among strangers," as he called Montana. Once he said that the Texas law practice "paid me more than twice as much as the salary"; another time he said it exceeded the justice's pay nearly three hundred percent." The same was undoubtedly true for other officials, especially for a wealthy entrepreneur like Samuel Hauser. "We presume it would be a poor day for Hauser when he could not make more than his year's salary would amount to," remarked the *Herald*, pointing to pride and interest in the territory as explanations of why a man of such ability and character would take the office of governor.[45]

To offset poor salaries, Montana's federal officials often supplemented their incomes with sideline activities. Both Hosmer and Edgerton hoped to do so from mining, but with little apparent success. Secretary Callaway conducted a private law practice in an office adjoining his official quarters and soon had "a fine stock ranch" on one of the tributaries of the Stinkingwater. His successor, James Mills, continued to publish the Deer Lodge *New North-West*, though he longed to be prosperous enough to get out of editorial harness, move to Helena, and devote himself entirely to his duties as secretary. "It is a pleasant office," he wrote Martin Maginnis, "but there is not pay enough in it to justify me in relinquishing other business and camping with it." Others, including Secretary McCutcheon and Governor Carpenter, hung out their private law shingles almost as soon as they arrived in Montana, but this avenue was legally closed to court justices. Francis Servis continued as a partner in an Ohio banking enterprise, but when the firm went bankrupt, was forced to resign from the territorial bench, owing to "my financial embarrassment," as he explained to President Grant.[46]

Chief Justice Wade was one of the owners of the Second National Bank of Helena, organized in 1882; Governor John Schuyler Crosby

45. *Congressional Globe*, 41 Congress, 2 Session (1869–70), 1336; James H. McLeary to Cleveland (Bozeman, March 31, 1887; and San Antonio, February 13, 1888), McLeary file, APJ; *Herald*, December 16, 1886; July 13, 1887.

46. *Montana Mineral Land and Mining Company* (New York, 1866), 2, 4; William H. Miller to Hosmer (Bannack, July 14, 1865), Hosmer MSS, Beinecke Library; *Herald*, November 3, 1871; September 27, 1873; May 28, 1883; June 2, 1885; Leeson, *History of Montana*, 321; James E. Callaway to Robert E. Fisk (Virginia City, September 26, 1874), Fisk family MSS; Mills to Maginnis (Deer Lodge, January 6, 1878, October 2, 1881), Maginnis MSS; Servis to Ulysses S. Grant (Canfield, Ohio, July 15, 1875), SCF, Box 517; Garfield to Potts (Washington, January 6, 1873), copy, letterbook 12, Garfield MSS. An ancient statute of 1812 still forbade judges to establish private law practices as a sideline. Act of December 18, 1812, 2 *USSL* (1 Series), 788.

became a shareholder in Samuel Hauser's First National Bank and in his Fort Benton Bank. Secretary Tooker was one of the founders and the president of a mining and tunnel company on Red Mountain, while Benjamin Potts had a variety of enterprises going at different times in his gubernatorial career. At one time he served as agent for eastern groups interested in buying territorial warrants; by 1875 he was a director of the People's National Bank of Helena and accused by his enemies of speculation and Shylock money lending. Later, he also owned shares in Broadwater's Montana National Bank. Early he went into the sheep business, to the glee of editor Fisk; "The Governor is reputed to be an excellent fleecer." In 1878, Potts confided to Maginnis that the salary reduction "makes the position no longer desirable but as I can attend to a flock of Sheep and hold the office—I can make a living out of the two and a little money." By the 1880s, Potts was involved with both cattle and horses, importing blooded stock and eventually joining with Charles Broadwater and Russell Harrison to run 1,000 head of horses on a ranch near Townsend. Potts had confided to Rutherford Hayes in 1875: "I am having fair success here—and making some money with my means that I brought here."[47] But his prosperity was not based on his salary.

The officials themselves complained, the Montana legislature sent memorials to Congress, and the territorial delegate vainly toiled to boost salaries by about 100 percent. Delegate Toole denounced Congress and insisted that its salary slash of 1877 had been illegal, a position on which the United States Supreme Court disagreed.[48] Unperturbed, the nation's lawmakers sat supinely by, ignoring the high cost of living in the Rockies and unwilling to commit additional funds, even in time of a treasury surplus. Thus, even had the federal govern-

47. *Weekly Herald,* July 17, November 2, 1882; *Herald,* March 4, 1872; January 5, February 18, 1875; February 20, 1877; July 8, 1878; December 13, 1882; May 1, 1883; May 29, October 23, January 23, 1885; Hauser-Crosby agreement (Helena, February 21, 1883), copy, letterbook (1881–85), Hauser MSS; Potts to G. A. Baker (n.p., September 21, 1871); Potts to J. Kountze Bros. (n.p., January 14, 1873), copies, Potts letterbook; Potts to Maginnis (Helena, May 18, 1878), Maginnis MSS; Granville Stuart to Potts (Fort Maginnis, July 30, 1882), copy, letterbook 1, Stuart MSS; Potts to Hayes (Helena, November 20, 1875), Hayes MSS.

48. Benjamin Harrison to Coburn (Washington, July 4, 1884), copy, Harrison MSS; *Congressional Globe,* 31 Congress, 2 Session (1869–70), 1336–37; *Congressional Record,* 49 Congress, 2 Session (1886–87), 1737; *ibid.,* 50 Congress, 1 Session (1887–88), 4714; *ibid.,* 50 Congress, 2 Session (1888–89), 821. In a Wyoming case the court ruled that although the law of 1873 fixing salary levels remained on the books, it was superseded by each annual appropriation act. U.S. *v.* Fisher, 109 *U.S. Reports* (1883), 146.

ment been disposed to appoint the best available talent, the low financial return of territorial offices would have precluded all but the wealthy or the most dedicated.

Another chronic problem which hampered the effectiveness of territorial government and evoked criticism was absenteeism. After slightly more than a year's service, Governor Edgerton left Montana, never to return in an official capacity. Belatedly requesting a leave of absence, he subsequently explained that he had gone east "in the line of public duty," not only to place his daughter in school, but to help straighten out the territory's financial problems. In the meantime, Indian troubles erupted and the commissioner of Indian affairs believed it "'very probable that Governor Edgerton's presence might have prevented the outbreaks. . . .'" These remarks were passed on to the Department of State with slight embellishment: ". . . it is probable that the absence of the Governor will involve the Government in an Indian war, that may cost many millions of treasure, and hundreds of valuable lives for its suppression," wrote Secretary of the Interior James Harlan. Across the top of this letter Secretary of State Seward penciled "Deny the application. Make order for removal of Incumbnt"; to Edgerton, he wrote simply "that the reasons which you offer are not deemed satisfactory and that your absence cannot be sanctioned." His leave denied, Edgerton was forced to resign. Possibly it was he Delegate Maginnis had in mind when he referred contemptuously to territorial governors who "used their official position to borrow all the money they could obtain from respectable citizens and then decamped to the places from which they came."[49]

Two of the justices, Hosmer and Williston, were gone in the spring of 1866, both with financial complications that hampered their return. The third, Lyman Munson, went east in September of that same year to lobby for congressional nullification of the "bogus legislature" laws and to bring his family to Montana. Because of complications, he was not able to return for eight months. When Governor Green Clay Smith departed for Washington early in 1867 to do some lobbying of his own, crusty John Owen noted in his journal what many Montanans must have been thinking: "our Ter. officers Seem to have a fondness for Hibernating at the East."[50]

49. Sidney Edgerton to Seward (Talmadge, Ohio, January 30, 1866); Edgerton to Andrew Johnson (Washington, March 27, 1866); D. N. Cooley to James Harlan (Washington, April 10, 1866); Harlan to Seward (Washington, April 11, 1866); Seward to Edgerton (Washington, April 13, 1866), all in TPS; *Congressional Record*, 44 Congress, 1 Session 1875–76), 2425.

50. Message of the president in relation to the absence of territorial officers,

In an effort to discourage absenteeism the early Montana legislatures stipulated that officials must remain in the territory in order to be eligible for additional compensation.[51] Two federal laws of 1852 had provided that territorial officers might not leave their posts for more than sixty days without loss of pay, unless their absence was certified by the president.[52] Violations were so flagrant in the 1860s that at least twice bills were introduced in Congress to limit the legal period of absence to thirty days and to specify immediate removal for failure to comply. Neither bill passed, but Montana loomed large in the debates, and the executive branch of government cracked down vigorously, with Edgerton one of its victims.[53] President Grant issued an executive order in 1871, calling for an enforcement of the acts of 1852 and ordering that leaves be granted only in cases of extreme emergency.[54] Montana was governed several times after that by the secretary acting ex officio, and clearly absenteeism was not eliminated. Ordinarily, however, it was not by itself an issue, though in the removal of Governor Carpenter and Justice Coburn it became a pretext.[55] Most of the judges took extended leaves of several months each year and when two were absent at one time in 1884, local citizens protested that a territory as large as New England could not afford to have two-thirds of its court gone simultaneously. During the same year Secretary Tooker was out of the territory for nearly six months, spending much of the time on his son's farm in Dakota after having been injured in a railroad accident.[56] But probably one of the worst offenders was Montana's "home-grown" governor, Samuel Hauser, who seemed to spend about as much time in New York and Washington hotel suites as in Helena's executive offices.[57]

Senate Executive Document No. 6, 40 Congress, Special Session (1867), 5; Hosmer to Hauser (New York, February 26, 1866), Hauser MSS; Sanders et al. to Johnson (Washington, March 27, 1866); Lyman Munson to Henry Stanbery (New York, November 17, 1866; Helena, June 3, 1867), all in AG, 1864–70; Owen, *Journals and Letters*, II, 42–43.

51. Act of January 24, 1865, *LM*, 1 Session (1864–65), 391; act of December 7, 1867, *LM*, 4 Session (1867), 97–98.

52. Acts of June 15 and August 31, 1852, 10 *USSL*, 10, 98.

53. *Congressional Globe*, 39 Congress, 1 Session (1865–66), 35, 1928–29; *ibid.*, 39 Congress, 2 Session (1866–67), 790, 866. See also M. F. Pleasants to Henry L. Warren (Washington, February 11, 1869), Henry L. Warren MSS, MHS.

54. Executive order of March 31, 1871, in Richardson, *Messages and Papers*, IX, 4095–96.

55. See chapters 7 and 9.

56. Sanders to Benjamin Brewster (Helena, July 14, 1884), SCF, 1871–84; *Herald*, March 22, April 17, May 6, August 8, 1884.

57. See Chapter 7.

More serious as a basic grievance against the territorial apparatus was the practice of appointing alien, nonresident officers from outside Montana. Repeatedly Montanans protested the selection of "pilgrims," "foreigners," and carpetbaggers" and demanded that important offices be restricted to bona fide residents of the territory. Newspapers damned the "worthless demagogues from the States" who were appointed, and called territorial government "false in theory" and rendered worse by the vicious practice of making the places under these governments a sort of lying-in hospital for political tramps."[58] With the appointment of Isaac McCutcheon of Michigan as secretary early in 1882 came a wail of editorial anguish: "It is refreshing to know that we are to have a new secretary for Montana—one from the East, fresh and green. . . . Eastern people are better calculated to run the Western machinery than those who have been out here so long . . . besides the gentlemen from the East as a rule, are a little higher toned than the mountain stiffs."[59] And the *Herald* cried, "The Territories are farmed out among the Senators like pocket boroughs among English lords"; the editor was careful to deprecate the use of the term "carpetbagger" as one of Democratic vulgarity and southern origin.

Montana had sufficient talent, it was argued, "to run not only the Supreme Court of this Territory, but that of a half dozen more like it, without hunting among the prairies of the West for legal stock, which may, after all, prove nothing but a scrub."[60] Montanans would feel greater pride and concern in their own administration than did professional office seekers. Why not appoint local men, especially justices, and evoke "the gratitude of all the lawyers who have spent the past years in 'breaking in' pilgrim Judges from Eastern States who have known nothing of our people, laws and customs"?[61]

In Congress the same complaints were aired regularly. Delegate Maginnis especially denounced the territorial judges and executives, insisting—quite inaccurately—that they were often men "who could never earn a living in competition with the local bar." Potts thought

58. *Montana Post*, October 20, 1866; April 2, 1869; *Herald*, March 22, 1879. For other typical comments see *Herald*, May 3, 1884; January 29, April 19, 1887; March 8, 1889; *Weekly Independent*, May 1, 1869, January 17, 1878; *Semi-Weekly Miner*, January 8, 1887.
59. *Inter-Mountains Freeman*, April 9, 1882.
60. *Herald*, October 4, 1880; *Montana Democrat*, July 18, 1868.
61. William H. Childs et al. to Orville H. Browning (Virginia City, October 17, 1866), John P. Bruce file, API; William H. DeWitt to Joseph K. Toole (Butte, July 15, 1886), Thomas C. Bach file, APJ.

Maginnis's rousing speech on carpetbaggers in 1876 did him an injustice. "I have paid my debts, have borrowed no money and have stolen nothing from the territory but have tried to save every cent possible to the people." Delegate Toole injected a more modern note in 1889, when he asserted that the presence of "foreign" officials was "as poisonous and destructive to good government as the invidious growth of communism."[62]

Two solutions were suggested for the malady, both designed to make officials more responsible to the people of the territory. The first and most desirable proposal was to provide by federal law for the election of territorial officers by the residents of the territory concerned. That failing, the second remedy was to attempt to restrict appointments to bona fide residents. Throughout most of the territorial period, Montana's delegates worked vigorously but unavailingly to bring about either of these changes and were supported by frequent home editorials and memorials from their constituents.[63] Between 1868 and 1883 at least eight different bills were introduced in Congress to provide for the election of territorial officers, but none was accepted. Reporting adversely on an 1883 measure, the House Committee on the Territories stoutly maintained that "the appointing power of governors and secretaries has always been reserved by the General Government, and believing that said reservation of power is based upon wisdom and sound policy, it should not be disturbed or released."[64]

Nor were efforts to limit appointments legally to territorial residents any more fruitful although in the 1880s the movement had gained considerable momentum. Even earlier, at the beginning of

62. *Congressional Record,* 44 Congress, 1 Session (1875–76), 2435; *ibid.,* 48 Congress, 1 Session (1883–84), 2778; *ibid.,* 50 Congress, 1 Session (1888–89), 821; Potts to Maginnis (Helena, May 26, 1876), Maginnis MSS.

63. Memorials to Congress (n.d.), *LM,* 6 Session (1869–70), 122; *LM,* 11 Session (1879), 139; *LM,* 13 Session (1883), 199; *Weekly Independent,* October 28, 1871; December 4, 1874; May 11, 1876; January 17, 1878; *Herald,* January 21, February 22, 1878; April 27, 1880; November 2, 1882.

64. Report of the Committee on the Territories on H.R. 1666 to provide for election of the governor and secretary of the Territories by the people of the several Territories, *House Report* No. 212, 48 Congress, 1 Session (1883–84), 1. See also: *Congressional Globe,* 40 Congress, 2 Session (1867–68), 3580; *ibid.,* 40 Congress, 3 Session (1868–69), 458; *Congressional Record,* 44 Congress, 1 Session (1875–76), 213; *ibid.,* 45 Congress, 2 Session (1877–78), 319; *ibid.,* 45 Congress, 3 Session (1878–79), 59, 654; *ibid.,* 46 Congress, 1 Session (1879), 645; *ibid.,* 47 Congress, 1 Session (1881–82), 1653; *ibid.,* 48 Congress, 1 Session (1883–84), 121.

the previous decade, President Grant had been waited upon by ten territorial delegates "in force" and had pledged himself to appoint only residents to territorial posts. But when faced with reality, Grant reversed his position, arguing that the only way he could keep from alienating one or more factions within the Republican party in the territories was to send in outsiders unidentified with any local clique.[65] Montanans applauded a few years later when a rider to limit appointments to actual residents was added to a House deficiency appropriation bill of 1876, but it was quickly lost. In 1884 a similar bill was reported adversely by the Senate Committee on Territories, which pointed out that the existing law had stood without modification for nearly thirty-five years and that "party complications and unhealthy alliances" within the territories "'made impossible the selection of impartial and unprejudiced officers" from the ranks of residents.[66]

That the movement was gaining popular support was indicated by the adoption of its principle into the platform of both major parties in 1884 and the subsequent appointment of Sam Hauser as governor in the following year. But when Montana's delegate persisted in efforts to push a law through Congress, as he did in 1886 and 1887, that body, now that the chief executive, like itself, was Democratic, saw no reason to act.[67] Indeed in 1886, the House Committee on the Territories, which had previously been receptive to the idea, now did an abrupt about-face and reported unfavorably. This report, written by Congressman Charles Boyle of Pennsylvania, argued that wherever practicable residents should be selected for territorial posts but that "it would be unwise to require by statute that this should be done in all cases." Two years later, former representative Boyle threw a clean shirt into his carpetbag and started for Washington Territory and his new post as chief justice.[68]

65. *Herald*, July 22, 1872; December 24, 1873; Moses K. Armstrong, *The Empire Builders of the Great West* (St. Paul, 1901), 220, 270.

66. *Congressional Record*, 44 Congress, 1 Session (1875–76), 2424, 2425; *ibid.*, 48 Congress, 1 Session (1883–84), 994; Report of the Committee on the Territories on H.R. 4713 to require the Governors of Territories to be Residents, *Senate Report* No. 496, 48 Congress, 1 Session (1883–84), 1.

67. *Official Proceedings of the National Democratic Convention, Held in Chicago, Ill., July 8th, 9th, 10th and 11th, 1884* (New York, n.d.), 199; *Proceedings of the Eighth Republican National Convention Held in Chicago, Illinois, June 3, 4, 5 and 6, 1884* (Chicago, 1884), 93; *Congressional Record*, 49 Congress, 1 Session (1885–86), 529, 4891; *ibid.*, 50 Congress, 1 Session (1887–88), 235.

68. Report of the Committee on the Territories on Federal Officials in the

Party platform to the contrary, President Cleveland was a practical politician who well knew the value of patronage. When he insisted in 1887 that Montanans could not agree on a chief justice and so he found it necessary to choose an outsider, he was not being wholly honest. Perhaps the *Herald* was closer to the truth: "He had better have the manhood to say that he cannot stand up against the hungry hordes of Bourbons who are beseiging him for places." Soon, after a disgruntled Judge McLeary had resigned, in part because he had been passed over for the chief justiceship, Cleveland appointed Moses Liddell, purely because of political commitments to senators from Liddell's home state of Louisiana. "We don't know where Moses was when the light went out, but he was certainly on deck when McLeary went out," quipped one editor. "The President found him among the bull rushes in Louisiana."[69] Even so, Cleveland probably did better than his predecessors, for Hauser was his selection, as was Secretary William Webb and justices Thomas Bach and Stephen DeWolfe, all Montanans; but he named as many nonresidents to other important posts.

President Benjamin Harrison had a better percentage: he appointed one governor, one secretary, and one chief justice for the territory—and they were all Montanans. Harrison would stand by the Republican platform, his friends insisted, behind the principle of "No Non-Residents Need Apply."[70] How much of this was due to the influence of his son, Russell, the "Duke of Montana," as some called him, is difficult to say. When the elder Harrison was chairman of the Senate Committee on the Territories, Russell from time to time kept him informed of territorial matters and of political problems; he also asked for favors for Charles Broadwater; and, at least obliquely, made recommendations for possible appointments. After Harrison was inaugurated, "Puissant son Russell" was accused of unduly throwing his weight around in the White House, and of seeking to influence the distribution of offices for Montana. His correspondence indicates that he did serve as a kind of focal point for local aspirants for posts ranging from Indian agents and marshals to the governorship itself. Undoubtedly he had some influence, but how much is unclear. When the

Territories, *House Report* No. 2581, 49 Congress, 1 Session (1885–86); 1; Report of the Committee on the Territories on H.R. 4713, to require the Governors of Certain Territories to be Residents, *House Report* No. 477, 48 Congress, 1 Session (1883–84), 1; *Senate Executive Journal*, XXVI, 343, 353.

69. *Herald*, April 19, 1887; February 28, 1888; Garland to Cleveland (Washington, February 24, 1888), Liddell file, APJ.

70. *Herald*, March 8, 1889.

outgoing secretary refused to transfer the office to Louis Walker, young Harrison got the wheels moving in Washington and Walker could quickly telegraph back: "Took charge of office this morning—no trouble—take something my expense."[71] In any event, the Harrison administration came too late to have much impact on the territory.

On the surface and in principle, certainly, the insistence that Montana was "the chosen dumping ground for the parasites of power"[72] had some foundation. For the offices of governor, secretary and judges, nonresidents outnumbered resident appointees three to one. The ratio for governors alone was seven to two; for secretaries it was seven to five; and for justices sixteen to three. Five of the six persons rejected or unconfirmed by the Senate for these positions were Montanans.[73] Only in filling the lesser posts was there any noticeable tendency to favor local inhabitants: in 1868, in fact, the Senate disqualified James Marr, nominated for collector of internal revenue for Montana, on the specific grounds that he was a nonresident.[74] Even so, it would appear that for the total territorial span, the less important offices were about evenly divided between outsiders and Montanans.

But figures alone may be misleading. The administrations of the two resident governors, Hauser and White, together covered only slightly more than two years and were undistinguished and inconsequential. "Carpetbagger" Potts, who after the first few years was as much a native of Montana as they, for more than a dozen years gave a leadership and a direction to the territorial government brought by no other governor, domestic or imported. Members of the territorial bench, like Decius Wade or William Galbraith, may have come

71. *Semi-Weekly Miner*, March 23, June 26, 1889; *Herald*, March 7, 12, 1889; Benjamin Harrison to McCutcheon (Washington, March 8, 1886); Russell Harrison to Benjamin Harrison (Helena, May 8, 1884; July 28, 1888; New York, May 10, 1889); Benjamin Harrison to Charles Broadwater (Washington, April 16, May 8, 1886), copy; Benjamin Harrison to O. D. Conger (Washington, April 29, 1886); endorsement of March 23, 1889 on Thomas Carter to Benjamin Harrison (Washington, March 22, 1889), all in Benjamin Harrison MSS; Benjamin F. Marsh to Russell Harrison (Helena, February 27, 1889); George W. Irvine to Russell Harrison (Butte, March 2, 1889); George Steall to Russell Harrison (Sun River, March 9, 1889); McCutcheon to Russell Harrison (Helena, March 6, 1889), all in Russell Harrison MSS.

72. *Herald*, January 29, 1887.

73. Montanans included, for governor, Nathaniel P. Langford (1868); for secretary, John P. Bruce (1866); for justices, William M. Stafford (1868), William W. Dixon (1869), and Lewis M. Burson (1869). The outsider was Charles Pollard.

74. *Senate Executive Journal*, XVI, 372.

originally as "pilgrims," but as time passed neither they nor the public in general thought of them as other than Montanans.

Critics automatically assumed that nonresident appointees could not be politically effective in the territory. "Not Chester A. Arthur nor James C. Blaine could hope to succeed in Montana as Prefects sent from the central Government to rule over 100,000 American Freemen," commented one observer in 1884. "John Schuyler Crosby left here politically too dead to skin."[75] Residence champions also seemed to find a direct correlation between "imported" officials and ineptness or even malfeasance in office, a point of view which the evidence will not bear out. Charges of Meagher's immorality, Smith's gambling, and Potts's bribery and misconduct went unproved and were the work of political enemies. The references of Montana's delegates to "political convicts," governors "without honesty or character," or secretaries who squandered the appropriations"[76] were more rhetoric than fact. To blame the whole capital controversy on carpetbaggism, as Wilbur F. Sanders did,[77] was absurd. That there were occasionally irregularities or even corruption in office is undeniable, but these difficulties were not limited to men appointed from outside the territory. In fact, the most flagrant examples of fiscal trickery involved the removal of three different secretaries—all of them Montana residents.[78] All public officials, state or territorial, elected or appointed, "foreigners" or local citizens, were subject to the same human strengths and weaknesses. If some, like Sidney Edgerton, John Tooker, or John Coburn, were incompetent or indifferent, others, like Benjamin Potts, Decius Wade, or Hiram Knowles, proved honest and talented, respected by most responsible citizens of both parties. And when politics was pushed aside, Montanans recognized this fact. Bozeman's Democratic paper might complain of the "vicious system of appointments," but could note in the same breath that "it does not follow as a rule that persons sent are rascals and to be abused at every turn." Even Robert Fisk was willing to agree and to argue that the territories were in general "better governed than many of the states. There is more law and order in Montana than there is in Kentucky or Louisiana. There is less corruption

75. Sanders [?] to "My Dear Secretary" (Helena, January 5, 1885), incomplete letters, Sanders MSS.

76. *Congressional Globe*, 41 Congress, 3 Session (1870–71), 970; *Congressional Record*, 44 Congress, 1 Session (1875–76), 2425; *ibid.*, 48 Congress, 1 Session (1883–84), 2778.

77. Sanders to Garfield (Helena, November 14, 1874), Garfield MSS.

78. See chapters 5 and 7.

in Territorial Legislatures. There are fewer embezzlements among county officials in the Territories as a rule than in the States."[79]

If the crux of the criticism levied against Montana's appointed officials was that a basic principle was being violated, that the arbitrary filling of important posts without consulting the wishes and needs of territorial residents was incompatible with the fundamental precept that democratic government derived its just powers from the consent of the governed, it was the practical local political situation which so often brought complaints to a head. When the legislature asked the recall of justices Hosmer and Munson in 1866, when it redefined their judicial destricts to "sage-brush" them, when the Fisk-Sanders coalition sought to oust Potts and he in turn fought for the removal of Callaway in 1877, when the assembly fought the executive power of John Schuyler Crosby a few years later—these and similar episodes were as much manifestations of political or even personal differences within the territory as of protests against the system itself. Certainly the spectacle of a preponderance of Democrats, many of them unreconstructed rebels, presided over by Republican officers, sometimes outspoken Radicals like Ashley, could not be expected to make for an atmosphere of harmony. Even had the appointees consistently been of the same party designation as the majority of Montana's population, such purely local problems as the location of the capitol, allocation of printing contracts, concessions to railroads, and the demands of mining or grazing interests would still bring down a hail of abuse on the heads of officials. State officers, as well as territorial, would soon realize this.[80] But at least, under statehood, more of the patronage would be local; less would be controlled from Washington.

79. *Herald*, May 9, 1884, April 12, 1885.
80. In an analysis of some 160 territorial governors for the 1787–1912 period, Jack Eblen concludes that, when compared with state governors, these officials were reasonably good, even though limited in powers and unstable in tenure. Jack E. Eblen, *The First and Second United States Empires: Governors and Territorial Government, 1784–1912* (Pittsburgh, 1968), 319.

11

"... A Mere Foreigner for Every Purpose
Save That of Taxation":
Financing a Territory

In the eyes of Montanans, the operation of their territorial government was hampered by a continuous lack of financial support from
the federal treasury. Congress, they contended, understood neither
the economic facts of life nor the peculiar nature of governmental
problems in the West. No doubt such charges had some substance
about them and should not be dismissed lightly. Nor should they be
taken at face value without healthy skepticism. Though federal funds
were indeed lacking during the formative years, it was also true that
Congress from time to time bailed out the territorial legislatures
when special sessions were required to resolve questions of the legislators' own making, and despite repeated extravagances on the part
of the legislatures. And any careful assessment of Montana's financial
demands upon Washington and of responses to those demands would
indicate that the territory benefited in numerous ways from federal
largesse and could hardly be called exploited in an economic sense.

The governor, the secretary, and the judges received their salaries
direct from Washington without benefit of a dispersing officer. On
the other hand, funds for the legislature and the governor's contingency expenses went through such an agent—the secretary, who
had to be bonded for the purpose. The secretary sent estimates for
appropriations, apart from salaries fixed by law, but it is doubtful if

these meant much, since they were first revised and approved by the first comptroller of the Treasury before being passed along by the Secretary of the Treasury to the appropriate congressional committee. After appropriations were made, funds were then transferred by treasury warrants after requisition by the secretary. Supervision of disbursement was sometimes loose, with delinquencies and late settlements, although the Treasury was often strict in details.[1]

The financial troubles of the early territorial period stemmed in part from a natural lag between the creation of the territory and its actual organization on a working basis, and in part from Washington's inability to find a secretary willing to come to Montana. The first two men appointed to this post declined, and not until September, 1865, nearly sixteen months after passage of the organic act, did Thomas Francis Meagher finally arrive to take charge of financial affairs. Without this chief dispersing officer, governmental agencies were forced to struggle along as best they could, devoid of federal funds.

As ex officio superintendent of Indian affairs, the governor could handle monies for this side of his job, although Sidney Edgerton was slow in posting his official bond for this purpose.[2] But he could not substitute for the secretary as the fiscal officer of the territory to dispense funds apart from his own contingency fund, a mere $1,000 until 1877, when it was cut in half.[3] Edgerton therefore encountered difficulties in obtaining money both for Indian affairs and for the regular functioning of government. Indian agents complained that their employees were not being paid and were likely to leave; Edgerton protested to President Johnson that prior to his leaving Montana in October, 1865, ". . . not one dollar of the appropriations made . . . had ever reached my territory or been made in any way available therein. . . . The expenses of the first Legislative Assembly I had to a large extent borne myself out of my own private funds in the expectation then (1864–5 December to February) that I would be re-

1. For a general description of the mechanism of financing territorial governments, see Pomeroy, *The Territories and the United States*, 28–35.
2. Edgerton did not complete his bond until March, 1865. Sidney Edgerton to W. P. Dole (Bannack, December 24, 1864); Second Comptroller of the Treasury to Dole (Washington, March 14, 1865), BIA.
3. The last appropriation was made for the fiscal year 1876. Act of March 3, 1875, 18 *USSL*, 349; act of August 15, 1876, *USSL*, 159; memorial to Congress (n.d.), *LM*, 13 Session (1883), 210. Accounts for contingency expenses went semi-annually to the first auditor of the Treasury, with the funds put at the governor's credit where designated. William Hemphill Jones to Benjamin F. Potts (Washington, October 20, 1871), GEC.

imbursed in a few days."[4] According to Meagher early in 1866, "not a dollar" of the funds voted nearly two years before for legislative expenses had reached Montana, "nor has there been a single dollar in payment of the expenses of the Federal Officers. . . . We are in the midst of gold and silver, abounding in our streams and mountains to an exorbitant excess, in a downright destitute condition. We are living upon air, and the hope of some wholesome manna refreshingly visited us one of these days in the enchanted wilderness through which we are passing."[5] With laws and lawbooks unavailable because printing and expressing costs could not be met, Meagher confessed that he knew not what regulations to follow in handling financial affairs.[6]

Precisely how much Edgerton advanced out of his own pocket is difficult to determine. Early in 1866, he was repaid $3,646 from the territory, but claimed that the federal government still owed him more than $2,000 for his work with the Indians.[7] In the absence of a fiscal officer, the Bannack legislature issued warrants to meet its expenses and to pay the salaries of officers. As of April 2, 1866, a total of $85,004.50 in warrants had been issued, of which $29,809,05 had been redeemed.[8] According to Virginia City critics, Edgerton had been lax in forwarding vouchers to Washington and most of the drafts issued to pay off the first legislature as well as minor functionaries were not honored until Secretary Meagher arrived and belatedly filed his bond in the spring of 1866.[9] And Meagher immediately urged the legislature to redeem all outstanding warrants and put the territory on a firm financial footing. "No man of intelligence and substance now speaks of them but with distrust, mortifi-

4. See O. D. Barrett to O. H. Irish (Virginia City, July 1, 1865); Charles Hutchins to Dole (Jocko Agency, October 3, 1865); Edgerton to James Harlan (Washington, March 31, 1866), BIA; Edgerton to Andrew Johnson (Washington, March 27, 1866), TPS.

5. Thomas F. Meagher to Johnson (Virginia City, January 20, 1866), Johnson MSS.

6. *Message of Governor Thomas Francis Meagher* (March 6, 1866), 5; Meagher to Speaker of the House (November 9, 1866), *House Journal*, 3 Session (1866), 49.

7. E. B. French to D. N. Cooley (Washington, October 25, 1866), BIA.

8. A. Leech and W. M. Stafford, *Report of the Commission Appointed to Examine the Accounts of the Late Auditor and Treasurer of this Territory* (Virginia City, April 2, 1866), 1.

9. Entries for January 11 and 12, 1866, Howie diary; William H. Childs et al. to Orville H. Browning (Virginia City, October 17, 1866); John P. Bruce to Browning (Virginia City, October 15, 1866), both in John P. Bruce file, API.

cation and alarm," he said.[10] But his advice was ignored and the territorial debt began to mount.

Meagher's problems were soon compounded. His $2,000 bond was nearly all consumed in honoring the Edgerton-issued drafts to the first assembly; and, having spent most of the summer of 1866 touring the territory, he had neglected to file a new bond. In addition, he refused to follow proper governmental channels. As a result the warrants issued to pay expenses of the second legislature remained "almost entirely unpaid" seven months after the session adjourned, even though Congress had appropriated the funds.[11] The printers would not handle the copy of the journals of that and the following legislatures provided by Meagher "owing to the condition of his accounts and the protests of his Drafts."[12]

Again, in mid-1867, following Meagher's death, the territory was without a disbursing officer and in financial distress, its warrants dishonored, according to Governor Smith.[13] Before long, Smith had left the territory, with Secretary James Tufts in charge, having paid none of the governor's rent or incidentals and overdrawn where Indian affairs funds were concerned.[14] Soon Tufts was complaining of the fiscal irregularities of his predecessors, charging Edgerton with certifying inflated claims and feeling constrained to travel to Washington to straighten out the "unsettled and confused condition" of the secretary's office.[15] Governor Potts would make much of the rent and purchasing "scandals" of Tufts himself and of Scribner, who followed him, but how much of this was political, how much was carelessness, and how much was corruption is impossible to say. The

10. *Message of Governor Thomas Francis Meagher* (March 6, 1866), 4.

11. Bruce to Browning (Virginia City, October 15, 1866); Childs et al. to Browning (Virginia City, October 17, 1866), both in Bruce file, API; L. Daems to William H. Seward (Virginia City, July 26, 1866) TPS; R. Joseph to J. C. Cox (Washington, May 21, 1867), TPS; *Montana Post*, October 20, 1866.

12. James M. Cavanaugh to Hugh McCulloch (Washington, January 22, 1869), LT, Vol. IX.

13. Green Clay Smith to McCulloch (Virginia City, July 30, 1867), copy, telegram, TPS.

14. James Tufts to W. E. Cullen (Virginia City, September 30, 1868), BIA. Even as late as the mid-1870s, some of Smith's financial problems were still unresolved, with the government threatening to bring suit because of unpaid vouchers. See A. H. Barrett to Martin Maginnis (Helena, January 10, 1875); Maginnis to John Q. Smith (Washington, March 10, 1876); Green Clay Smith to Edward P. Smith (Frankfort, Kentucky, August 2, 1875), all in BIA

15. Tufts to R. W. Taylor (Virginia City, March 25, 1868), LT (Warrants), Vol. VIII; *Montana Democrat*, February 15, 1868.

Treasury Department, however, was persuaded at least that there was a need for change, and Tufts was removed from office, although official charges were never brought. But even after he was ousted, Tufts again went to the nation's capital in an effort to untangle "the somewhat extensive and complicated accounts" of his term.[16]

Evidence indicates that other secretaries were also untidy fiscal housekeepers. James Callaway reported that when he assumed the duties in 1871, he "found the government perfectly scattered over the country and in irresponsible hands." The records "were in bad shape, very imperfectly and carelessly kept."[17] Whether Callaway measurably improved the situation is debatable. In 1875 his failure to renew his bond delayed dispersion of treasury funds and consequently payment of legislators, who had to be given checks on the First National Bank of Bozeman, payable in thirty days.[18] When James Mills took over the office in 1877, he castigated Callaway, his predecessor, for his casual and inept keeping of records. Two safes, purchased in 1868, had both disappeared. ". . . to the date of my taking possession of the office," said Mills, "there never was but one entry on the books showing any item of expenditure since 1870, there is no entry of receipts or expenditures whatever since 1874, and only one account balanced since the organization of the Territory."[19] A later secretary, William Webb, who had carried a large banner in the 1888 Democratic parade, "Public Office is a Public Trust," was subsequently charged with embezzling $2,600 and investigated by a special treasury agent in 1889. During that audit, his successor observed confidentially: "We find several matters that is not exactly straight and when we get through which will take 3 or 4 days yet I am inclined to believe that Mr. Webb will wish he *was not.*" Although Webb sought to settle with the federal government out of court, the evidence was presented to a grand jury, which failed to bring an indictment— for political reasons, his enemies charged.[20] Certainly the investiga-

16. McCulloch to Tufts (Washington, January 17, 1868), Treasury Dept. Gs53 Ser., cited in Pomeroy, *The Territories and the United States,* 8; Taylor to Cavanaugh (Washington, November 16, 1869), LT, Vol. VIII; *Herald,* March 24, 1871.

17. James E. Callaway to Ulysses S. Grant (Virginia City, December 29, 1874), Callaway file, API.

18. *Herald,* March 25, 1876.

19. James Mills to Taylor (Helena, November 27, 1877), LT, Vol. XIV.

20. *Herald,* September 19, 1889; William Windom to W. H. H. Miller (Washington, July 1, 1889); George Batcheller to Miller (Washington, October 10, 1889); Elbert D. Weed to Miller (Helena, October 25, 1889); McConnell and Clayberg to Weed (Helena, April 1, 1890); Weed to Miller (Helena, May 22,

tion had revealed poorly kept accounts, and his replacement found almost nothing in the way of receipts or duplicate vouchers to indicate how many funds had been available and where they had gone since 1885.[21]

Since the secretary was the disbursing officer, the governor had little money at his direct disposal apart from his somewhat limited contingency fund. So long as he was ex officio superintendent of Indian affairs, his ability to draw upon treasury resources to support that side of his work gave him at least some financial flexibility, not only for himself but for the legislature as well. Governor Edgerton could justify employing a clerk at a time the legislature was in session, because, he argued, trouble was brewing with the Blackfeet.[22] A little later, the Office of Indian Affairs would reject Green Clay Smith's vouchers—advanced by Sam Hauser's bank—to cover $630 for three horses and a saddle and bridle, as "Commander in Chief of the Montana Volunteers"; but it would credit him with that amount toward the purchase of a team and an ambulance for his use in the Indian service.[23]

Financing the legislature also had its complications. Down to 1873, Congress customarily appropriated $20,000 for each legislative session in the territory.[24] For the next decade the sum varied from the $22,680 allotted in 1875 to the $14,000 of 1878, and after 1883 the amount remained at $22,000 per session. From 1872 on, Congress provided $2,000 annually for legislative expenses in years when the assembly did not convene and it was loath to increase this figure.[25]

1890; March 17, 1891), all in Department of Justice Year File 5348/89, Box 424; Louis A. Walker to Russell Harrison (Helena, May 25, 1889), Russell Harrison MSS.

21. Walker to John W. Noble (Helena, April 22, 1889), TPI; Walker to Russell Harrison (Helena, April 19, 1889), Russell Harrison MSS.

22. *Herald*, January 8, 1874; Edgerton to Harlan (Washington, March 31, 1866), BIA.

23. Charles E. Mix to Green Clay Smith (Washington, September 21, 1867), GEC.

24. Act of March 2, 1865, 13 *USSL*, 457; acts of July 23, 1866, and March 3, 1867, 14 *USSL*, 204, 455; acts of July 20, 1868, and March 3, 1869, 15 *USSL*, 109, 300; acts of July 12, 1870, and March 3, 1871, 16 *USSL*, 242, 486; act of March 3, 1873, 17 *USSL*, 299.

25. Act of March 3, 1875, 18 *USSL*, 349; act of June 19, 1878, 20 *USSL*, 194. In 1876, $22,000 was appropriated; in 1880, $19,710, and in 1882, $21,530. Act of August 15, 1876, 19 *USSL*, 159; act of June 15, 1880, 21 *USSL*, 225; act of August 5, 1882, 22 *USSL*, 236–37; act of July 7, 1884, 23 *USSL*, 178; act of July 31, 1886, 24 *USSL*, 192; act of July 11, 1888, 25 *USSL*, 277. In 1874, $2,282 was appropriated; in 1881, only $1,900 was set aside; and in 1887, the total of $2,450 included funds for a new safe. William Webb sought $3,300 for

Out of these annual appropriations came all legislative costs—per diem and travel payments to members and employees, the printing of the journals, rent, fuel, light, postage, and other incidentals.

Clearly Montana legislators considered these funds inadequate. A House committee of 1868–69 referred sarcastically to the "trifling sum" of $20,000, "erroneously supposed to be sufficient for the wants, comfort and convenience of this body. . . ."[26] And either because of extravagance, poor management, or unexpected contingencies, legislative expenses often did outstrip the money available. From the beginning, the assembly had indulged itself in petty luxuries, not to mention the accumulation of a debt of more than $109,000 before 1870. Secretaries Meagher and Tufts had both provided each legislator with "a fine pocket knife" at government expense. Meagher had promised each member six copies of both the *Democrat* and the *Rocky Mountain Gazette*; ten years later, Secretary Callaway rejected a request to furnish each councilman with four daily newspapers, a practice which seemed to have been customary.[27] On a number of occasions, when special sessions were without funds or when appropriations were momentarily held up, editors were willing to provide newspapers "without money and without price," taking their chances on future compensation.[28]

On one instance, at least, private citizens were permitted to borrow equipment purchased for the legislature when it was not in session, with the result that government property was "scattered all over the town and some of it *in the Country*."[29] This type of laxity may have been wasteful, but more expensive was the matter of printing, in Montana, as elsewhere, a political plum controlled by the secretary

---

miscellaneous legislative expenses for 1886, but received only $2,000, despite his appeal to the Secretary of the Interior. Act of June 20, 1874, 18 *USSL*, 99; act of March 3, 1881, 21 *USSL*, 400–401; act of March 3, 1887, 24 *USSL*, 614; act of March 3, 1885, 23 *USSL*, 409; William Webb to L. Q. C. Lamar (Helena, February 6, 1886), Letter from the Secretary of the Treasury Transmitting an additional estimate from the Secretary of the Interior of an appropriation for legislative expenses of Montana Territory, *House Executive Document* No. 123, 49 Congress, 1 Session (1885–86), 2.

26. After a resolution had been introduced to appropriate one dollar for the purchase of nails, the sum was cut in half, and finally the sergeant at arms was authorized to pull the requisite number of nails from an unused, unclaimed house in Virginia City. *House Journal*, 5 Session (1868–69), 54, 55.

27. *Montana Post*, November 10, 1866; Callaway to Council (January 5, 1876), *Council Journal*, 9 Session (1876), 24. Callaway to Taylor (Virginia City, October 27, 1871), LT, Vol. XI.

28. *Herald*, January 8, 1874; *House Journal*, 13 Session (1883), 31, 32.

29. Callaway to Taylor (Virginia City, October 27, 1871), LT, Vol. XI.

and/or the governor. Here, the first comptroller of the Treasury did exercise some supervision, even to small details: in 1869, he disallowed what he said was a $15.20 overcharge in composition and $150 for the making of an index to the statutes. "It is the duty of the Secretary to make the Index for the printers," he ruled.[30] But printing contracts were lucrative to the recipients and expensive to government; given the struggle between Potts and Callaway for its control in the seventies, it is not surprising that it was both important and a drain on the treasury. After 1872, at least, Congress set maximum limits on printing expenses for any single session, pegging these at $4,000 at first, dropping them to $2,500 six years later, then pushing them back to $3,750 in 1882.[31]

If printing costs were not the culprit, sometimes deficits were created by unexpected and unbudgeted special sessions, called either to meet an emergency or as in 1869 to adjust to a biennial schedule set by Congress. In the latter case, the Treasury Department indicated that no funds had been provided for a term in the 1868 fiscal year and that the secretary was not authorized to certify vouchers over the $5,900 already on hand, should the legislature convene in December as contemplated. Thus when the sixth assembly did meet, Secretary Scribner issued vouchers to cover legislators' pay, but had to reject requests for books, stationery, and other supplies.[32]

In general, though legislators were sometimes late in receiving compensation and printer's bills might be carried for long periods,[33] Congress was willing to provide supplemental appropriations. Delegate Billy Clagett appealed to the House in 1872 for $5,000 to cover the printing deficiencies for that fiscal year: not only was the request met, Congress added $3,117 to defray unpaid expenses of the sixth session.[34] In 1873 and 1874, the national lawmakers voted appropriations to meet the deficiencies of the third, fourth, and fifth assem-

30. Taylor to Wiley Scribner (Washington, November 3, 1869), LT, copy, Vol. VIII.

31. Act of May 8, 1872, 17 *USSL*, 73; act of June 19, 1878, 20 *USSL*, 193; act of August 5, 1882, 22 *USSL*, 236.

32. Taylor to Scribner (Washington, July 14, 1869 and November 22, 1869), copy, LT, Vol. VIII. *House Journal*, 6 Session (1869), 54; W. *Montanian*, November 24, 1870.

33. See Cavanaugh to George Boutwell (Washington, March 22, 1869), LT, Warrants, etc., Vol. IX; Mills to A. G. Porter (Helena, September 28, 1878); Maginnis to Porter (Helena, Sept. 30, 1878), LT, XIV; Mills to Maginnis (Helena, January 23, 1879) Maginnis MSS.

34. *Congressional Globe*, 42 Congress, 2 Session (1871–72), 1247; act of May 18, 1872, 17 *USSL*, 125.

blies.[35] Expenses of extraordinary legislative sessions were also met, belatedly, but usually with good congressional grace.[36]

Montanans complained briskly that federal outlays for legislative expenses were inadequate, but their criticism on that score was seldom as sharp as of some of the other aspects of territorial government, in part because they could not help but be aware of the shortcomings of their own elected representatives. Many were inclined to agree with Secretary Callaway, who, fighting for his political life in 1876, called the Montana legislature "proverbial for its extravagance."[37] To be sure, a Senate report of 1874 indicated that Montana's total governmental operating costs from the federal government for the fiscal years 1872 and 1873 were $60,674.34—as Table 3 shows, the costs were more than those of any other territory, but the margin was inconclusive.[38]

TABLE 3. FEDERAL GOVERNMENTAL EXPENSES OF THE TERRITORIES, FOR THE FISCAL YEARS 1872 AND 1873

Territory	1872	1873	Total
Arizona	$20,605.37	$36,664.59	$57,269.96
Colorado	34,300.00	14,051.08	48,351.08
Dakota	14,686.87	38,835.37	53,522.24
Idaho	22,218.65	35,301.79	57,520.44
Montana	43,206.75	17,467.59	60,674.34
New Mexico	37,498.84	17,349.23	54,848.07
Utah	36,697.18	14,198.90	50,896.08
Washington	42,564.00	16,788.79	59,352.79
Wyoming	31,075.05	17,293.73	48,368.78

35. In 1873, $122.50 was set aside for expenses of the third session; a large deficiency appropriation of the following year included $250 for the fourth, $316 for the fifth, and $5,052.32 for the 1874 session. Act of March 3, 1873, 17 *USSL*, 532; act of June 24, 1874, 18 *USSL*, 135–36; *Herald*, June 5, 1874.

36. In 1874, Congress appropriated $16,395 for expenses of the special session of 1873; in 1880, it set aside $8,640.31 for expenses of the extra session of 1879; and in 1888, $11,264.60 for the special session of 1887. Act of June 22, 1874, 18 *USSL*, 135–36; act of June 16, 1880, 21 *USSL*, 240; act of March 30, 1888, 25 *USSL*, 49.

37. James Callaway to Taylor (Helena, January 24, 1876), LT, Vol. XIII.

38. Letter from the Secretary of the Treasury to the Chairman of the Committee on Territories Accompanying Information in relation to the charge upon the Treasury for each of the Territories, *Senate Miscellaneous Document* No. 44, 43 Congress, 1 Session (1873–74), 2. Of the Montana expense, $31,353.69 was for legislative costs, $27,320.65 for salaries, and $2,000 for the contingency fund.

Other territorial critics sought more federal money for public buildings, for improved educational, penal, or curative facilities, or for expanding and improving the transportation network. Properly speaking, the desire for a branch mint in Montana had nothing to do with territorial status: it was simply the reaction of an isolated mineral area seeking to reduce the expense, delay, and danger in shipping bullion, which had to go to the nearest United States mint at Denver. Governors like Green Clay Smith failed to see the need for such an agency; petitions went regularly to Congress until 1877, but without success. After several abortive attempts, Delegate Maginnis steered a measure through in 1873, not for a mint, but for an assay office, only to have President Grant withhold his signature. But Maginnis persevered and early in 1874, $50,000 was set aside for the establishment of an assay office at Helena, an action that was much overdue.[39]

As early as 1866 a memorial called attention to the need of public buildings to house the various branches of territorial government and their records, and asked $50,000 for that purpose.[40] Despite a House committee recommendation in 1870 that $40,000 be appropriated to provide Montana with a capitol,[41] Congress took no action. Undoubtedly the unsettled location of the seat of territorial government was a factor at this time, but bills to provide a capitol at Helena introduced by Maginnis in 1882 and 1884 and by Toole in 1886 and 1887 fared no better.[42] A favorable report on the 1886 measure cited an annual rent of $5,485 for government buildings in Helena and urged Congress to appropriate $80,000 to construct a suitable edifice there. Governor Leslie complained in his annual reports of 1887 and 1888 that the territory was forced to rent part of the Lewis and Clark County courthouse for its government agencies.[43] And even

39. Smith to legislature (November 6, 1866), *Contributions*, V (1904), 133; memorial to Congress (April 13, 1866), *LM*, 2 Session (1866), 50; memorial to Congress (December 13, 1867), *LM*, 4 Session (1867), 269–70; memorial to Congress (n.d.), *LM*, 10 Session (1877), 443; *Congressional Record*, 43 Congress, 1 Session (1873–74), 2870; act of May 12, 1874, 18 *USSL*, 45; *Herald*, March 27, 1873; May 7, 1874.

40. Memorial to Congress (December 7, 1866), *LM*, 3 Session (1866), 93; *Council Journal*, 3 Session (1866), 118, 125, 139.

41. Capitol Buildings in Territories, *House Report* No. 27, 41 Congress, 2 Session (1869–70), 1–3.

42. *Congressional Record*, 47 Congress, 1 Session (1881–82), 5347; *ibid.*, 48 Congress, 1 Session (1883–84), 295–96; *ibid.*, 49 Congress, 1 Session (1885–86), 529; *ibid.*, 50 Congress, 1 Session (1887–88), 235.

43. Report of the Committee of the Whole House on Public Building, Helena,

though new, the courthouse could not handle all the county, territorial, and federal needs: it was ironic, protested the *Herald,* that "Though the Nation can get all the money it wants at two and a half per cent, the county pays six; the former miserably hoards its surplus and leaves its official representatives to rustle up cheap, pigeon-hole quarters in chance corners of the city."[44]

In vain, too, Montanans sought federal funds for a customshouse at Fort Benton, not a territorial matter.[45] They made efforts to gain appropriations for an insane asylum, with no better results. In the seventies, the territory did not have its own mental institution: the insane were contracted out, and both Governors Potts and Hauser were condemned for their veto of legislative bills to bring changes in the system.[46] Delegate Maginnis sought a federal subsidy of $25,000 in 1882; a popular drive a few years later urged the government to donate part of the abandoned Fort Ellis military reserve to create a mental hospital; and Governor Leslie repeatedly called for direct federal aid for an insane asylum, as well as an institution for the deaf and blind.[47] The press thought these ideas good ones—especially if Washington would foot the bill. The long existence as "a brevet commonwealth" should entitle "something for a dowry when Montana makes her debut as a matronly State among the stately throng free from the short dresses of Territorial minority," argued one editor in 1889.[48] But Montana was to be a poor bride in terms of worldly goods, if such were measured by public buildings.

She fared better where a penitentiary was concerned. In 1867

Montana, *House Report* No. 1689, 49 Congress, 1 Session (1885–86), 1–2; Report of the Governor of Montana, 1887, 868; *ibid.,* 1888, 831.

44. *Herald,* June 9, 1887.

45. Memorial to Congress (n.d.), *LM,* 12 Session (1881), 132; memorial to Congress (n.d.), *LM,* 13 Session (1883), 210–211; *Congressional Record,* 47 Congress, 1 Session (1881–82), 933.

46. *Herald,* February 17, 23, 1877; January 12, March 7, 11, 1887. In 1871, Potts wrote the governors of other states, Wisconsin, Kansas and Iowa among them, seeking a place to send Montana's insane. Apparently a few were sent out of state, but more responses indicated similar problems of overcrowding. Lucius Fairchild to Potts (Madison, November 11, 1871); James M. Harvey to Potts (Topeka, November 16, 1871); Samuel Merrill to Potts (Des Moines, November 11, 1871), all in GEC. In 1880 Montana statistics listed fifty-nine insane, forty-four of whom were in Deer Lodge and fifteen "at home." A *Compendium of the Tenth Census,* 1678, 1680.

47. *Congressional Record,* 47 Congress, 1 Session (1881–82), 5347; *ibid.,* 50 Congress, 1 Session (1887–88), 5596; Report of Governor of Montana, 1887, 868; Leslie to legislature (January 14, 1889), *Council Journal,* 16 Session (1889), 13–14.

48. *Herald,* January 16, 1889.

Congress stipulated that federal revenues up to a total of $40,000 per year be set aside for the fiscal years 1867 through 1869 to construct penitentiaries in certain territories, including Montana.[49] The legislature selected a site at Deer Lodge that same year, but work was not begun until 1870 and no prisoners received until the summer of 1871.[50] At first all federal penal institutions of this nature were under the jurisdiction of the U.S. Attorney General, administered by the federal marshals, with the territory paying a dollar a day for each prisoner so lodged. But since most prisoners were incarcerated for territorial offenses and since operating costs proved much higher than anticipated, the arrangement was not wholly to the liking of the Department of Justice. From November, 1872, to July, 1873, for example, maintenance costs for the Deer Lodge penitentiary totaled $21,429; yet only one federal prisoner was housed there.[51] As a result, Congress early in 1873 provided for the transfer of the penitentiaries in Montana, Idaho, Wyoming, and Colorado to the respective territories, retaining legal title in the process.[52] Governor Potts was not enchanted at the prospect. "I presume I shall be compelled to go to Deer Lodge City if the prison is turned over to the Territory," he wrote in March. "I don't want the accursed thing and shall avoid it as long as possible."[53] And with good reason: now the situation was reversed—the federal government paid the territory one dollar a day for each federal prisoner, while the territory bore the brunt of operating expenses. Fortunately for the Montana treasury, this arrangement soon broke down and in 1874 the prison reverted to its old status with the federal government in charge.[54]

As population expanded and as the judicial system became more effective, an increasing number of convictions for both federal and territorial crimes prompted demands for an expansion of prison facilities. Congress authorized $6,020 for completion of fourteen additional cells in 1874. In 1879 the penitentiary housed 34 inmates in its

49. Nebraska, Idaho, Colorado, Arizona, Dakota, and Montana were included to an annual limit of $40,000; Washington to $20,000. Act of January 22, 1867, 14 *USSL*, 377.

50. Act of December 19, 1867, *LM*, Extra Session (1867), 93; William F. Wheeler, "Montana Penitentiary" (Helena, October 23, 1877), 3, MS, Bancroft Library; Wheeler to Potts (Virginia City, April 18, June 21, 1871), GEC.

51. Wheeler to Potts (Virginia City, April 18, June 21, 1871), GEC; *Congressional Globe*, 42 Congress, 3 Session (1872–73), 410.

52. Act of January 24, 1873, 17 *USSL*, 418–19; G. H. Williams to Potts (Washington, February 20, 1873), GEC.

53. Potts to Wheeler (Virginia City, March 5, 1873), Wheeler MSS.

54. Act of June 20, 1874, 18 *USSL*, 112.

28 cells; five years later, in the same number of cells, there were 116 prisoners, many of them "desperate characters with long-term leases."[55] The old Deer Lodge county jail was purchased and set up within the prison enclosure to accommodate a dozen or so more persons and the legislature petitioned Congress repeatedly for a diversion of the territory's internal revenue funds to enlarge and improve the facilities.[56] Montana's governors and judges alike complained to the legislature or to officials in Washington.[57] Governor Crosby, who believed the penitentiary to be conducted "most loosely and in a reprehensible manner," and who unsuccessfully sought funds to improve security, estimated in 1884 that it would take $80,-000 to put the prison in shape to meet existing needs.[58] Crosby faced a crisis, for in October of that year, the U.S. Attorney General instructed the marshal in Montana to take no more territorial prisoners until proper facilities were added.[59] Thanks to the persistence of Martin Maginnis in the nation's capital, Congress responded with a skimpy $15,000,[60] but the penitentiary was never adequate, and

55. Annual Report of the Attorney General of the United States for the Year 1874, *House Executive Document* No. 7, 43 Congress, 2 Session (1874–75), 17; memorial to Congress (n.d.), *LM*, 11 Session (1879), 123; memorial to Congress (n.d.), *LM*, 14 Session (1885), 239; A. C. Botkin to S. F. Phillips (Helena, October 2, 1884), in Annual Report of the Attorney General of the United States for the Year 1884, *House Executive Document* No. 12, Vol. XXI, 48 Congress, 2 Session (1884–85), 168. The federal Census of 1880 indicated a total of 77 prisoners: 53 in the territorial penitentiary, 23 in county jails, and 1 listed under "miscellaneous." Only two were female and the eight "Colored" included three Chinese and four Indians. *A Compendium of the Tenth Census,* 1876, 1893.

56. See *Herald,* February 14, 1883; *House Executive Document* No. 268, 50 Congress, 1 Session (1887–88), 1; *House Executive Document* No. 1, 50 Congress, 2 Session (1888–89), 831; *Congressional Record,* 46 Congress, 2 Session (1879–80), 3936.

57. See Benjamin Harrison to John Coburn (Washington, February 3, 1885), Benjamin Harrison MSS; Report of the Governor of Montana, 1888, 831; Leslie to legislature (January 14, 1889), *Council Journal,* 16 Session (1889), 15; memorials to Congress (n.d.), *LM*, 11 Session (1879), 123; *LM*, 14 Session (1885), 239.

58. Crosby sought federal money to repair walls and employ additional guards, but a special agent sent to investigate advised greater care, rather than expenditure. John Schuyler Crosby to Benjamin H. Brewster (Washington, June 3, 1883), SCF (1881–83); S. F. Phillips to Crosby (Washington, August 3, 1883); Brewster to Crosby (Washington, October 16, 1883), copies, both in Department of Justice, Letters Sent, Gen. and Misc. (1818–1904); Report of the Governor of Montana, 1884, 564.

59. S. F. Phillips to Crosby (Washington, August 30, October 14, 1884), copy, Department of Justice, Letters Sent, Gen. and Misc. (1818–1904).

60. *Congressional Record,* 48 Congress, 1 Session (1883–84), 550, 1759; Annual Report of the Attorney General of the United States for the Year 1884,

Montana's governors continued, as Potts had done previously, to seek arrangements for housing prisoners outside the territory—with little success. The use of county jails and the farming out of convict labor were also advanced as solutions. Potts had done the latter in a most limited way but Crosby in 1883 vigorously vetoed a bill to give official sanction to the practice.[61]

In sum, federal contributions to the construction of public buildings in territorial Montana fell far short of expectations. An assay office and a penitentiary—and an insufficient one at that—represented the total. Although Utah, New Mexico, Nebraska, Washington, and Colorado had all received federal appropriations for the erection of capitols, territories created later did not.[62] However, the act of February 22, 1889, authorizing the formation of the Montana state government, granted 50,000 acres of federal land for the establishment of a deaf-mute asylum and 150,000 acres for a capitol.[63] In the long run Montana fared about as well as her sister territories of the same era, but her residents believed they deserved more.

Another locus of financial complaint was public education, both in terms of inadequate support and in terms of support that was unusable. By tradition and the organic act, sections sixteen and thirty-six of each township of government land in the territory were reserved for school purposes. In practicality, this meant little: as the superintendent of public instruction complained in 1868, the federal government merely set these lands aside for future use and had made no provision whereby the territory could sell, rent, or in any way benefit from them.[64] That same official, Cornelius Hedges, wrote a few years later: "We are baited with the bland assurance that when we have become richer and stronger—in fact, better able to supply our own wants from our own resources—then the Government will shower its benefactions upon us. . . . The Government assumes to be our guardian during our metamorphic infancy, and treats us as wards

House Executive Document No. 12, Vol. XXI, 48 Congress, 2 Session (1884–85), 167.

61. Potts to Council (July 21, 1879), *Council Journal*, Extra Session (1879), 80; Potts to Legislature (January 8, 1883), *Council Journal*, 13 Session (1883), 32; *House Journal*, 13 Session (1883), 288–89; Carpenter to legislature (January 14, 1885), *Council Journal*, 14 Session (1885), 15; *Avant Courier*, March 15, 1883; *Herald*, June 7, 1878; February 14, March 5, 1883; June 5, 15, August 17, 1885.

62. Capitol Buildings in Territories, *House Report* No. 27, 41 Congress, 2 Session (1869–70), 2.

63. Act of February 22, 1889, 25 USSL, 681.

64. *House Journal*, 5 Session (1868–69), Appendix, 290–93.

in most things; but while thus nominally fitting us to bear the responsibility of independent government, it totally neglects our educational interests, as if unimportant for the destiny that awaits us."[65]

Without avail, Hedges sought joint action by a number of territories to protest the "exceedingly shabby treatment" afforded by Congress in the matter of school aid. The legislature urged Congress either to sell a portion of the lands, retaining the principal and giving Montana the use of the interest, or to set aside for educational support the proceeds of other lands, with eventual reimbursement from the school lands. Private organizations petitioned for outright appropriations for school purposes, and Delegate Maginnis introduced such a bill into Congress.[66] Editors condemned the "absolute ruler of the Territories," Congress, for failing to provide positive financial aid for the present and suggested an appropriation of $100,000 per year for the public schools of the territory. By failing to permit Montana to lease its school lands, charged the *Herald* in 1886, Washington allowed its wards "to grow up in ignorance. Such a guardian in any Probate or Surrogate Court in the country would be deposed for gross neglect of duty."[67] Governors Potts, Crosby, and Leslie all condemned the arrangement, but Congress maintained a preoccupied silence.[68]

Nor was this the only criticism of the educational land-grant policy. Local land offices permitted individuals to patent mineral claims on school sections, leaving the territory with the alternative of finding substitute "lien lands," but with the complication that legal authority to relocate was vested in the federal government, which refused to act. By 1877, more than seven thousand acres of Montana school lands had been thus patented, each year more and more of the desirable lands "forever alienated from the *sacred* purpose to which they were originally dedicated."[69] A decade later, the superintendent

65. *Biennial Report of Hon. Cornelius Hedges, the Superintendent of Public Instruction for the Years 1872–3* (Cincinnati, 1874), 10; memorial to Congress (n.d.), *LM*, 10 Session (1877), 444–45; Report of the Governor of Montana, 1878, 1109; Emmet J. Riley, *Development of the Montana State Educational Organization 1864–1930* (Washington, 1931), 42.

66. *Congressional Record*, 44 Congress, 1 Session (1875–76), 303; *ibid.*, 47 Congress, 1 Session (1881–82), 3819; *ibid.*, 50 Congress, 1 Session (1887–88), 2327.

67. *Herald*, September 28, 1883; April 23, 1886.

68. Report of the Governor of Montana, 1878, 1109; *ibid.* (1887), 866; *ibid.* (1888), 826; *Congressional Record*, 50 Congress, 2 Session (1888–89), 821.

69. Report of the Governor of Montana, 1878, 1109; *Herald*, October 13, 1887; Riley, *Development of the Montana State Educational Organization*, 42.

of public instruction saw the grant lands in serious jeopardy "by the systematic scheming of unprincipled parties fraudulently taking up these lands as mineral claims, . . ." and Governor Leslie pointed out that timber as well as mineral land was being taken and that squatters were fencing and moving onto some sections for agricultural purposes.[70] This bold "robbery," as editor Fisk labeled it, was a strong argument for statehood: "The general government never has done anything and never will do anything to educate the people of the territories for the duties and responsibilities of citizens."[71]

Montanans also solicited federal support for a territorial university, a matter which was discussed in the legislature as early as 1866 and was the object of a memorial to Congress in 1872.[72] A bill introduced in 1878 by Senator Paddock of Nebraska would have granted public lands for such purposes in five of the territories, including Montana, as would another measure, equally unsuccessful, brought forward by Delegate Maginnis a year later.[73] Resistence was overcome, and in 1881 a national law permitted Montana, along with other territories, to select seventy-two unappropriated sections of the public domain within her borders to help establish a university once statehood was attained.[74] But Congress looked to the future, not to the present.

Even less fruitful were efforts to obtain grants for private institutions. Twice Maginnis introduced bills to cede government land to the Montana Collegiate Institute at Deer Lodge, but both measures were lost; an attempt by Delegate Toole early in 1889 to obtain the Fort Ellis military reserve for educational purposes met a similar fate.[75] No doubt there was much truth in the territorial indictment of

70. *Ninth Annual Report of the Superintendent of Public Instruction for the Year 1887, and the School Laws of the Territory of Montana* (Helena, 1888), 10, 11; Report of the Governor of Montana, 1887, 866.

71. *Herald*, October 13, 1887.

72. See *Council Journal*, 2 Session (1866); 41; *Council Journal*, 5 Session (1868–69), 18; memorial to Congress (January 12, 1872), LM, 7 Session (1871–72), 649–50.

73. *Congressional Record*, 45 Congress, 2 Session (1877–78), 3559; *ibid.*, 46 Congress, 1 Session (1879), 646.

74. Act of February 18, 1881, 21 USSL, 327. Originally the bill would have permitted a territory to sell one-tenth of the land almost immediately, but this was amended to prevent alienation before statehood. Subsequent efforts to modify the law to permit land selection in tracts as small as forty acres also failed. *Herald*, June 26, 1880; *Congressional Record*, 48 Congress, 1 Session (1883–84), 541; *ibid.*, 49 Congress, 1 Session (1885–86), 1219; Report of the Committee on the Public Lands on Lands to Dakota, Montana, Arizona, Idaho, and Wyoming for University purposes, *House Report* No. 1088, 49 Congress, 1 Session (1885–86), 1.

75. *Congressional Record*, 47 Congress, 2 Session (1882–83), 2104; *ibid.*,

Congressional attitudes toward education: "While the people of a Territory are poor and have everything else to do with the scant means they can acquire by hard work and constant peril, they are considered altogether unworthy of assistance."[76] In Montana, as elsewhere in the country, public schools continued to be supported entirely by direct taxes and proceeds from various local fines and penalties. In 1880, just under 22 percent of Montana tax money was earmarked for schools—roughly equivalent to the national distribution. The territory spent a total of $68,002 on public schools that year and in its per capita outlay ($1.74) and its per student enrolled expenditure ($14.57) it ran ahead of the national average but below that of the western states and territories.[77] But with some exceptions —notably the land grant colleges—Congress was not in the school business; certainly federal largesse seemed reserved for mature states, rather than probationary territories. Upon reaching statehood, Montana did receive substantial chunks of the public domain to subsidize a reform school, a normal school, a school of mines, and an agricultural college, as well as an institution for deaf mutes and a capitol.[78]

Such matters as postal service, road construction, river improvement or encouragement to railroads were not necessarily territorial questions. They were topics of concern to all regions, state and territory alike; yet circumstances—and especially distance and sparse settlement patterns—caused Montanans to look toward Washington for support. At the same time, with no voice in Congress nor in national elections, they could not hope to benefit from the normal log-rolling and pork-barrel politics. If the territory was not neglected where federal aid to transportation and communication was concerned, it

---

48 Congress, 1 Session (1883–84), 296; *ibid.*, 50 Congress, 2 Session (1888–89), 761.

76. *Herald,* June 26, 1880.

77. In 1880, 21.88 percent of Montana's levies were for school purposes; at the national level, 22.69 percent. The national average of per capita school expenditure was $1.59, the western average (including Montana), $2.63; the national average outlay per student enrolled was $7.99, that of the West $15.58. *Report on Valuation, Taxation, and Public Indebtedness in the United States, as Returned at the Tenth Census (June 1, 1880)* (Washington, 1884), 19; *Report on Wealth, Debt, and Taxation at the Eleventh Census: 1890* (Washington, 1895), Pt. II, 417.

78. The act authorizing formation of a state government set aside 100,000 acres for a school of mines, 100,000 acres for a state normal school, 50,000 each for a reform school and an agricultural college, plus grants for the capitol and the deaf-mute institution. Act of February 22, 1889, 25 USSL, 681.

was because of broad-thinking congressmen who looked beyond their own constituencies to national development.

From the establishment of the first post office at Virginia City in November, 1864, Montana's postal service expanded slowly along with population and transportation facilities. One of the earliest petitions of the Bannack legislature asked cheaper rates for newspapers and printed matter and more mail routes on a daily and weekly basis; subsequent memorials from assemblies of the sixties reiterated these requests, stressing that Montanans paid their federal taxes as promptly as others—an assertion which may or may not have been true.[79] Such memorials may have reflected impatience, for the postal system was indeed expanding: between March 3, 1865, and July 25, 1868, Congress authorized thirty-seven mail routes and thirty-six post offices for the territory.[80] As the structure grew rapidly, complaints were less of the need for new routes, but more of protests against expense or of poor "scrub mail service" that stemmed from the "old mossbacks at Washington" knowing little of Montana and its needs.[81] On the whole criticism of the postal system was limited and reasonable. Perhaps congressmen were more familiar with such commonplace problems and because they understood them, they responded more favorably with appropriations for the postmaster general.

Even before Montana became a territory, the federal government had undertaken construction of the Mullan Road, which despite rugged terrain, difficult weather, and inadequate funding, was completed as a wagon route linking Fort Walla Walla and Fort Benton

79. Stuart, *Forty Years on the Frontier*, I, 239, 264; memorial to the Postmaster General (n.d.), *LM*, 1 Session (1864–65), 718–20; memorial to Congress (December 15, 1866), *LM*, 3 Session (1866), 90–91; memorial to Congress (December 13, 1867), *LM*, 4 Session (1867), 270–71.

80. Annual Report of the Postmaster General, 1868, *House Executive Document* No. 1, 40 Congress, 3 Session (1868–69), 35, 262.

81. Post roads and routes established in the territory included: sixteen in 1868, one in 1871, three in 1873, seven in 1874, ten in 1876, three in 1877, 31 in 1879, thirteen in 1880, nineteen in 1882, and one in 1883. Act of March 30, 1868, 15 *USSL*, 49–50; act of April 20, 1871, 17 *USSL*, 17; act of March 3, 1873, 17 *USSL*, 593; acts of February 4 and June 23, 1874, 18 *USSL*, 11, 264; act of April 3, 1876, 19 *USSL*, 19; act of March 3, 1877, 19 *USSL*, 328; act of March 3, 1879, 20 *USSL*, 448–49; act of June 12, 1879, 21 *USSL*, 15–16; act of May 3, 1880, 21 *USSL*, 99; act of February 28, 1881, 21 *USSL*, 363; acts of March 6 and August 7, 1882, 22 *USSL*, 21, 360; act of March 3, 1883, 22 *USSL*, 578; *Montana Live-Stock Journal*, March 10, 1888; *Congressional Record*, 49 Congress, 1 Session (1885–86), 2783; *Herald*, August 29, 1888.

by 1863. More than six hundred miles long, this road was of considerable importance to the mining booms of both Idaho and Montana.[82] But within a few years the Mullan Road fell into disrepair and repeated Montana appeals for federal aid in reopening it were ignored until 1880, when $20,000 was appropriated for repairs between Fort Missoula and Coeur d'Alene.[83]

Early Montanans also sought congressional support for new and shorter links with the East. The northern route overland to Fort Benton was slow, seasonal, and dangerous; even more roundabout was the itinerary along the main transcontinental thoroughfare west along the Platte and across Wyoming, to swing sharply northward at Fort Hall to the settlements in western Montana. By 1866 one such shortcut, the Bozeman Trail, also known as the Montana Road, was in use, cutting diagonally northwest from the Oregon Trail across Wyoming, ultimately to Bozeman and Virginia City.[84] Congress was interested enough in 1865 to appropriate $50,000 to build a wagon road from Niobrara, Nebraska, on the Missouri near Yankton, Dakota, running northwest along the Niobrara River into Wyoming and joining the Bozeman Trail in the valley of the Little Big Horn. At the same time, an equal sum was authorized to connect Virginia City with Lewiston, west of the Bitterroots. Work commenced on both of these routes, but neither proved satisfactory.[85]

Meanwhile, in 1866, the War Department committed itself to protection of the water route along the Missouri, the line of the Bozeman Trail from the south, and a modified version of the Niobrara road from the east, and proceeded to build a series of military posts along these routes. But strong resistance of the Sioux would bring aban-

82. Report on the Construction of a Military Road from Fort Walla-Walla to Fort Benton, *Senate Executive Document* No. 43, 37 Congress, 3 Session (1862–63). See also W. Turrentine Jackson, *Wagon Roads West* (New Haven and London, 1965), 257–78.

83. Memorial to Congress (December 13, 1866), *LM*, 3 Session (1866), 92–93; memorial to Congress (n.d.), *LM*, 5 Session (1868–69), 115–16; memorial to Congress (n.d.), *LM*, 11 Session (1879), 124–25; act of June 8, 1880, 21 *USSL*, 166.

84. Grace Raymond Hebard and E. A. Brininstool, *The Bozeman Trail* (Cleveland, 1922), I, 219; II, 121. The most recent book on this subject is Dorothy M. Johnson, *The Bloody Bozeman* (New York and Toronto, 1971).

85. Act of March 3, 1865, 13 *USSL*, 519; Letter from the Secretary of the Interior, in answer to a resolution of the House of February 16, relative to a wagon road from Niobrara to Virginia City, *House Executive Document* No. 58, 39 Congress, 1 Session (1865–66), 28–32; Annual Report of the Secretary of the Interior, 1866, *House Executive Document* No. 1, 39 Congress, 2 Session (1866–67), 13; Jackson, *Wagon Roads West*, 281–296, 312–18.

donment of the "Bloody Bozeman" in 1868, leaving the old awkward Fort Hall approach the leading highway into the territory from the south and west.[86] Montana's legislature also petitioned funds for a wagon road from the mouth of the Yellowstone to Helena, another from the mouth of the Musselshell via the fertile Judith Basin to Fort Ellis in the Bozeman Valley, and a third to link the Union Pacific rail line at some point in Utah with Helena. The only fruit of these appeals was a preliminary survey by the Army Engineers, under Captain W. A. Jones, in 1873.[87]

Montanans also displayed an understandable interest in the coming of the iron horse and looked to the federal government to support railroad endeavors wherever possible. Both Governor Smith and Acting Governor Tufts suggested legislative petitions to Congress, urging completion of the Northern Pacific; the halting of that line at Bismarck in 1873 after Jay Cooke's failure in a financial panic brought dejection to the territory. "It is very discouraging," wrote a Bozeman resident, "for I see no hopes of better times for Montana until a railroad reaches us."[88]

That these were popular sentiments is evident both by the efforts within the legislature to permit subsidization of rail projects and by memorials to Congress asking that government bonds be issued to the Northern Pacific in lieu of the land grants already given. It was also argued that by attaching the southeastern portion of Idaho to Montana, Montana capital would be encouraged to flow into any north-south railroad undertaking that might be proposed to tie the Montana mines via Idaho to the transcontinental line in Utah.[89] Congress did grant charters on favorable terms to local railroads—at least eight were authorized in 1875—and by the end of 1888, the territory

86. Protection Across the Continent, *House Executive Document* No. 23, 39 Congress, 2 Session (1866–67), 20–21; Annual Report of the Secretary of War, 1867, *House Executive Document* No. 1, 40 Congress, 2 Session (1867–68), 45–49; Johnson, *Bloody Bozeman*, 310.

87. Smith to legislature (November 6, 1866), *Contributions*, V (1904), 136; memorials to Congress (December 31, 1868; January 14, 1869), *LM*, 5 Session (1868–69), 118, 120–21; memorial to Congress (n.d.), *LM*, 6 Session (1869–70), 126–27; Military Wagon Road in Wyoming and Montana Territories, *House Executive Document* No. 22, 43 Congress, 2 Session (1874–75), 1–4.

88. Peter Koch to Laurentza Koch (Bozeman, October 21, 1873), in Carl B. Cone, ed., "A Trading Expedition Among the Crow Indians, 1873–74," *Mississippi Valley Historical Review*, XXXI (December, 1944), 412; Smith to legislature (November 6, 1866), *Contributions*, V (1904), 134; Tufts to legislature (December 8, 1868), *House Journal*, 5 Session (1868–69), 22–23.

89. Memorial to Congress (February 13, 1874), *LM*, 8 Session (1874), 180; memorials to Congress (n.d.), *LM*, 10 Session (1877), 437, 440–41.

could boast of 1,784.9 miles of completed track, with 283.5 more under construction, most of the advance having occurred in the decade of the eighties.[90]

The coming of the railroad sounded the death knell for another form of transport—the major steamboat traffic on the Missouri waterway. From the arrival of the *Chippewa* and the *Key West* at Fort Benton in 1860, steamboats began to provide a comparatively cheap and easy transportation for both people and goods, and were instrumental in development of the growing territory. The number of steamers docking at the Benton levies jumped to 70 in 1866 and 1867 —the peak in river traffic—with a gradual decline until the late 1870s, when railroad competition began to be felt. A limited traffic also existed on the Yellowstone, on the Kootenai, on the Clark's Fork, and on Flathead Lake farther west, but none of this was of real significance.[91]

But during the heyday of the smoking, belching steamboats, Montanans actively sought federal funds for the removal of obstructions to navigation, mainly from the Missouri and to a lesser extent the Yellowstone. A memorial of 1867 noted that thirteen of the forty-eight vessels steaming up river the previous season could not land at Fort Benton because of low water, and asked that Congress appropriate $500,000 to clear the 450-mile stretch between the head of navigation and the mouth of the Milk River. The legislature of 1873 urged Montana's delegate to "use all honorable means" to achieve this end and subsequent petitions called for improvement of the Yellowstone as well.[92] A belated response came in 1878 when Congress provided $30,000 to clear the Missouri above Fort Union and touched off an intensive federal program which over the next decade put hundreds of thousands of dollars into improving the Missouri, although Montanans constantly complained of the slowness of the process and Delegate Maginnis had to fight in the House for every penny.[93] Much of this work came after the acme of steam naviga-

90. Act of March 3, 1875, 18 *USSL*, 482; Report of the Governor of Montana, 1889, 437.

91. Hiram Chittenden, *History of Early Steamboat Navigation on the Missouri River*, II, 273; Burlingame, *The Montana Frontier*, 141–44. See also William E. Lass, *A History of Steamboating on the Missouri River* (Lincoln, 1962).

92. Memorial to Congress (December 23, 1867), *LM*, Extra Session (1867), 271–72; joint resolution (April 26, 1873), *LM*, 8 Session (1874), 186–87; memorial to Congress (n.d.), *LM*, 9 Session (1876), 119, 200–2; memorial to Congress (n.d.), *LM*, Extra Session (1879), 134–35.

93. In 1879, an additional $45,000 was provided for the same project, plus $30,000 for a survey of the river from its mouth to Fort Benton. In 1880, $25,000

tion, at a time when the railroad had assumed the function of chief supplier of the territory. Perhaps some of the agitation for the maintenance of water routes may have been inspired by the hope—as voiced in the 1888 meeting of the Montana Stock Growers' Association—that river traffic could be used as a lever to force the reduction of railroad freight rates.[94]

Despite the grumbling of contemporary Montanans, federal subsidies should not be minimized. River improvements, the construction of roads, railroads, and even a few public buildings all brought employment and profit. The presence of Indians meant troops: both meant business. As provisioners of agency Indians and the score or so of Army posts that dotted the territory at one time or another, entrepreneurs like Tom Power, Charles Broadwater, and I. G. Baker employed hundreds of men ranging out from Fort Benton, that "Chicago of the Plains," and amassed fortunes in the process. If Montana's solid economic bases were minerals, livestock, and agriculture, her citizens too often failed to appreciate their federal aid, both direct and indirect. They were convinced that in practically all areas, Washington was niggardly—in funds for operating government, for public buildings, education, the penal system, transportation, even protection. Even though Montana was treated as well as other territories and better than some, Montanans did not hesitate to add financial grievances to the lengthy list against the territorial system in general—a system, which in their eyes, imposed an unnecessarily heavy burden of taxation upon them.

Few people like taxes, least of all those who believe their governments give them too little in return. Thus from the beginning, Montanans expressed a resentment of levies put on them. "Collecting taxes again to day. A good many objections raised," noted Neil Howie in his diary in July, 1864.[95] When a collector—it may have been

---

was voted to improve the Missouri above Fort Union and $15,000 for clearing the Yellowstone. In 1881, $40,000 was set aside for work on the Missouri and $30,000 for continuing the survey of its main channel. A year later, Congress authorized $100,000 for improvements on the Missouri, between Sioux City and Fort Benton, $40,000 for the survey, and $12,000 for the Yellowstone. Another $82,500 was voted in 1886 for removing obstacles in the upper Missouri. Acts of June 18, 1878, and March 3, 1879, 20 *USSL*, 154, 366; acts of June 14, 1880, and March 3, 1881, 21 *USSL*, 192, 479; act of August 2, 1882, 22 *USSL*, 205; act of August 5, 1886, 24 *USSL*, 327; memorial to Congress (n.d.), *LM*, Extra Session (1879), 21–22; *Congressional Record*, 46 Congress, 2 Session (1879–80), 1268; *ibid.*, 47 Congress, 1 Session (1881–82), 5042–44; *ibid.*, 49 Congress, 1 Session (1885–86), 1862.

94. *Montana Live-Stock Journal*, April 21, 1888.
95. Entry for July 1, 1864, Diary of Neil Howie.

Howie—tried to exact payment of a four-dollar poll tax, another diarist, this one a resident of Virginia City, recorded his own reaction: "I more than half wish, when I see such officers and the score of 'pettifoggers' going about seeking 'whom they may devour' in the country, that Uncle Samuel would let us severely alone, for it is a fact that miners can make their own laws so as to get along smoothly with each other, better than government laws enforced by such men."[96]

The situation was compounded by Civil War antagonism and the strong vein of "Secesh" attitudes in the territory. A federal wartime emergency measure of 1864 levied an income tax, a host of excise taxes, and license fees on most occupations, including all assayers of gold and silver, as well as "every person, firm, or corporation engaged in any business, trade, or profession whatsoever," provided that gross receipts were at least $1,000 annually. In March of the following year, this broad provision was revised to include a specific ten-dollar levy on all miners whose gross receipts exceeded $1,000 per year.[97]

Resentment ran high as a matter of principle. As the Montana collector of internal revenue commented in 1866, "Miners are the most independent class of people in the world—extremely jealous of the privileges they have always enjoyed—and they looked upon this requirement of the law as an aggression upon their privileges."[98] At Confederate and German gulches and elsewhere, irate Montanans held meetings and "passed resolutions threatening the lives of the Revenue Officer & his Deputies." The assistant assessor resigned in fear and the U.S. marshal advised against attempting to collect in some areas. "Sometimes a man was more violent than the others," Collector Langford wrote, "and would say that he owed no allegiance to any government, but that of Jeff. Davis, and that I need not expect to collect a tax from him, for he wouldn't pay."[99]

But when it became evident that Langford and the federal government meant business, most residents found it simpler to pay up. In 1865–66, nearly six hundred distress warrants were issued against the property of delinquents and some four hundred indictments found against persons whose possessions, such as merchandise, could not

96. Entry for July 16, 1864, Diary of James Henry Morley in Montana, 171, typescript, MHS.
97. Acts of June 30, 1864, and March 3, 1865, 13 *USSL*, 257, 473.
98. Nathaniel P. Langford to J. W. Taylor (Virginia City, May 20, 1866), copy, Langford MSS.
99. *Ibid.*; George W. Pinney to James Harlan (Washington, January 3, 1866), SCF, Accounts, 1865–71.

be located.[100] Merchants protested the seizure of goods by the collector of internal revenue, arguing that the merchandise had already been taxed in the States and that they had not seen the revenue law.[101] Federal officers continued to crack down on defaulters, and the majority of citizens ultimately paid their fees, but like John Owen, who viewed with regret the onrush of civilization over the Bitterroot Valley, they did so "under protest."[102] Taxpayers continued to complain, but nonetheless, as Table 4 shows, they contributed nearly $1,730,000 to the national treasury during the territorial period.[103]

TABLE 4. INTERNAL REVENUE RECEIPTS, MONTANA, 1865–89

Year	Amount	Year	Amount
1865	$ 36,022.93	1878	$ 27,103.88
1866	113,280.00	1879	30,084.53
1867	77,431.14	1880	33,714.17
1868	108,284.36	1881	44,881.67
1869	64,336.33	1882	68,001.31
1870	103,555.55	1883	75,542.81
1871	82,104.98	1884	125,369.68
1872	28,955.04	1885	90,565.20
1873	24,018.11	1886	90,840.37
1874	29,027.76	1887	101,158.38
1875	23,666.10	1888	145,835.38
1876	20,982.80	1889	162,642.81
1877	20,729.58	Total	1,728,134.87

Their protests were of two types: one an objection to taxes which hit certain interest groups—levies on lumber, printer's type, mailing paper, or on druggists, for example;[104] and one directed against the

100. Langford to Taylor (Virginia City, May 20, 1866), copy, Langford MSS.

101. See unidentified clipping, enclosure, with letter from Meagher to Seward (Virginia City, February 20, 1866), TPS.

102. Owen, *Journals and Letters*, II, 76; *Montana Post*, January 4, 1868. Apparently for a time, because of the lack of a boundary survey between Montana and Canada, customs duties were not collected. Helen Fitzgerald Sanders, ed., *X. Biedler: Vigilante* (Norman, 1957), 117.

103. Report of the Commissioner of Internal Revenue for the Fiscal year ending June 30, 1889, *House Executive Document* No. 4, Vol. XVIII, 51 Congress, 1 Session (1889–90), 314–15, 316–17, 318–19. Federal figures for 1865 seem incomplete. Truman Everts, Assessor of Internal Revenue, gave the sum of $81,-737.80 as collected that year. *Reports of the Auditor, Treasurer, and Indian Commissioner, of the Territory of Montana* (Virginia City, 1866), 5.

104. See *Congressional Record*, 45 Congress, 2 Session (1877–78), 1602, 1928; *ibid.*, 46 Congress, 2 Session (1879–80), 1352, 1422, 1493, 1573, 1657, 1861; *ibid.*, 50 Congress, 1 Session (1887–88), 4847.

principle of "taxation without representation." The first category of complaint was not against the territorial system; but the second, more fundamental, stemmed from the "colonial" bondage in which Montanans saw themselves. Since they were held in political subjugation by the federal government without a full measure of political rights, wasn't it unfair to ask territorial residents to contribute taxes on a basis of equality with inhabitants of the states? Delegate McLean in 1866 protested his constituents' limited representation and charged that Congress managed taxation in the territories "on a scale of grandeur and magnificance hereto unprecedented." Complained McLean, "If we are to be treated as wards in this great national court of chancery, we would respectfully petition the nation to allow us sufficient of our own funds to live upon until our estates are settled."[105] Delegate James M. Cavanaugh also believed that Montana was unfairly exploited. As he wrote the Secretary of the Treasury in 1869: "The people of Montana pay more taxes into the Treasury of the Nation than any other Territory belonging to the Government— and add more gold annually to the Country's wealth than any *four* Territories combined."[106] Since this was so, Montanans were convinced, the infamous system of taxation without representation was even more obnoxious. "Why should a citizen, when he goes to reside in a Territory, become an exile in the land of his birth?" asked Chief Justice Decius Wade in 1879. "Why should he become a mere foreigner for every purpose save that of taxation?"[107]

Where territorial taxes were concerned, the arguments concerning second class citizenship did not apply. Tax levies voted by the legislatures were relatively high and comprehensive. Yet inequalities and loopholes weakened the revenue program throughout the era.

The first revenue act of the Bannack legislature authorized a territorial levy of four mills on each dollar of assessed value of taxable property, county levies up to ten mills, and a county poor tax of one mill. "Taxable property" was a wide-ranging term: it included real estate, livestock, money, ditches and flumes, mortgages, and stocks and bonds, as well as furniture, watches, jewelry, and musical instruments. Noticeably mining claims were exempted, except "all machinery used in mining claims, which have an independent and

105. *Congressional Globe*, 39 Congress, 1 Session (1865–66), Appendix, 202.
106. Cavanaugh to McCulloch (Washington, January 22, 1869), LT, Vol. IX.
107. *Weekly Independent*, July 10, 1879; Wade, "Self-Government in the Territories," *International Review*, VI (March, 1879), 305.

separate value. . . ." Among other exemptions were federal or territorial property, courthouses and prisons, church buildings and
grounds, immediate property of the Masonic and Odd Fellow orders, and personal tools, libraries and household furniture to a fixed
value. Along with the ad valorem taxes went a poll tax of three
dollars on "every white male inhabitant" between the ages of twenty-
one and fifty, to be collected when property taxes were due and to
be divided two-thirds to the territory and one-third to the county.[108]
Equally as important was the licensing act passed a few days later
placing license fees on all professions and most means of city liveli-
hood, ranging from surgeons and peddlers to billiard tables, livery
stables, and hurdy gurdy houses.[109]

As at the federal level, at first there was a wide gap between the
tax laws and their enforcement. In 1867, Governor Smith called attention to the fact that in the previous fiscal year U.S. Internal Revenue Collector Langford had collected more than $113,000 out of
an assessed $114,023.56, while territorial and county collectors had
been able to gather in only about 30 percent of the total due.[110] Only
Madison County had paid in substantial property taxes in 1865, and
during the following year, Meagher and Beaver Head counties failed
to make returns to the territorial auditor. Chouteau County paid no
taxes at all, to the distress of Governor Smith. "Officers have been
appointed," he said, "but many of them, and especially the commissioners, refuse to act; hence there is no county government, and
the county is derelict in its duties." Smith urged that the legislature
provisionally wipe away Chouteau's county status and reattach it
to Edgerton County, "where there is organization, and where the
officers will do their duty."

Smith also suggested a change in assessment date. June 1 was the
date set by law, but large stocks of taxable goods coming up the

108. Exempted were the tools of miners to $50 value; those of farmers,
mechanics and professional men to $100; and libraries and household furniture
up to $100. Act of February 6, 1865, *LM*, 1 Session (1864–65), 411–13, 429.

109. A partial list might include: billiard tables, $100 annually; serenades,
operas, concerts, dance houses, hurdy gurdies and magicians, all $5 a day or
$50 a month; insurance companies, $50 a year; pawnbrokers, $50 a quarter;
gambling houses, $50 a month; assayers, $15 a quarter; lawyers, dentists, physi-
cians, and "persons of all other professions," $20 a year. Taxed also were mer-
chants, bankers, peddlers, butchers, artists, etc. Act of February 9, 1865, *LM*,
1 Session (1864–65), 523–28.

110. Smith to legislature (November 6, 1866; November 4, 1867), *Contributions*, V (1904), 130, 147.

Missouri River normally did not arrive until sometime in July or August, hence escaped taxation.[111] Revision of the tax schedule was made late in 1867, but in the meantime, collection was lax. As Table 5 indicates, the territory collected about four-fifths of the property tax due, but less than a third of the poll tax.[112]

TABLE 5. MONTANA TERRITORIAL TAXATION, 1867

Property tax due	$25,232.43
Property tax collected	19,126.38
Property tax delinquent	5,814.35
License fees collected	32,243.44
Poll tax collected	1,574.02
Poll tax delinquent	4,800.00

The new 1867 laws did eliminate some of the more flagrant abuses. The revenue act retained the old territorial, county, and poor levies, and included an increase for school purposes. The poll tax was reduced to two dollars and now applied to all males, regardless of race, between the ages of twenty-one and forty-five. In addition a new tax was added on the net proceeds of all mines and mining claims, and the assessment date was shifted to cover goods arriving in steamboating season.[113]

The license act of the same year left most earlier fees intact, but expanded the schedule to include taxation of all goods brought into the territory by water or land. This brought protests from the Oregon legislature late in 1868 against taxation and merchandise destined for the Pacific coast in transit across Montana, though Montana legislators saw nothing excessive about the measure and thought the whole business "undoubtedly exaggerated."[114]

But even after the 1867 revisions, the territorial auditor indicated that only about 65 percent of the property and poll tax due was collected in 1868.[115] Complete new revenue and license laws were en-

111. Smith to legislature (November 6, 1866), *ibid.*, 131–32.
112. "Annual Report of the Auditor of Montana Territory [1867]," *ibid.*, 154.
113. Act of December 23, 1867, *LM*, 4 Session (1867), 39, 45, 52.
114. Act of December 13, 1867, *LM*, 4 Session (1867), 237–40. Memorial from the Oregon Legislative Assembly (November 20, 1868); Report of the Committee on Federal Relations (December 16, 1868), both in *House Journal*, 5 Session (1868–69), 65–66, 67–68.
115. Of a possible $33,581.29, $31,730.53 was collected. Annual Report of the Auditor of Montana Territory, 1868, *House Journal*, 5 Session (1868–69), Appendix, 281.

acted in 1869, with a slight lowering in some rates;[116] even so, they remained high enough that the volatile Governor Ashley could refer to the "unnecessary and oppressive taxation which has eaten out the substance of the people and paralyzed the business interests of the territory."[117]

After 1872, with the adoption of a tax structure based on the California codes, the situation measurably improved. Levies tended to be revised downward in subsequent adjustments, and at the end of the era the territorial property tax was only two mills on the dollar, rather than the four of the earlier period.[118] Local editors maintained that Montanans paid higher taxes than those of any other territory,[119] a charge not born out completely by actual figures.

As shown in Table 6, census returns indicate that in 1870 and 1880 the territorial and local taxes on a per capita basis and the tax rate per $100 of total assessed valuation were higher in Montana than for the nation in general but lower than for other western states and territories.[120]

TABLE 6. COMPARISON OF STATE AND/OR TERRITORIAL TAXATION, 1870, 1880, 1890

Year	Montana total tax	Montana rate per $100	Western rate per $100	Montana per capita	Western per capita	U.S. per capita
1870	$ 198,527	$2.00	$2.55	$ 9.64	$10.51	$7.28
1880	383,947	2.06	2.23	9.80	10.73	6.26
1890	2,347,370	2.08	1.99	17.76	13.69	7.53

Never were the agencies of assessment and collection as efficient as was desirable—but neither were they in other parts of the United States. Governor Potts complained in 1873 of the negligence of county assessors and collectors and he reiterated these charges a few years

116. Act (n.d.), *LM* 6 Session (1869–70), 49–56, 99.
117. James M. Ashley to legislature (December 11, 1869), *House Journal,* 6 Session (1869–70), 36.
118. Act of January 12, 1872, *LM,* 7 Session (1871–72), 601–03; act of June 22, 1879, *LM,* Extra Session (1879), 10–11; Report of the Governor of Montana, 1889, 435.
119. *Herald,* August 29, 1889.
120. *Report on Wealth, Debt, and Taxation at the Eleventh Census: 1890,* Pt. II, 61.

later, arguing that the tax laws needed revision to eliminate many of their exemptions.[121] For tax purposes, according to the territorial auditor in 1887, there were only 173 pieces of jewelry and silverware in all of Montana—and none in Custer, Dawson, Gallatin, Jefferson, Silver Bow, and Yellowstone Counties! Only 11,080 board feet of lumber had been sawed in Missoula County, although it was a "known fact," at least to one editor, that one sawmill alone had cut over 20,000,000 feet. The gross receipts of quartz mills were "ridiculously low," less than one-third the amount turned out in the single city of Butte.[122]

This last charge, of course, touched upon one of the basic weaknesses of the tax structure: the failure to tax the dominant industry, mining, save for the levy on net proceeds and a small direct tax on patented claims. Certainly this arrangement was a boon to the metal industry and a tribute to the political acumen of its agents in the territorial legislature, but it meant a serious loss of governmental revenue. A report of the House Committee on Territories in 1888 noted a virtual lack of taxation on the mines of Montana, property which yielded over $25,000,000 in the previous year; within a few months, when it petitioned Congress to permit the sale of mining property to aliens, the legislature admitted that the territory's mineral product was up to $40,000,000 annually and the industry was "practically in its infancy."[123]

Vast expanses of unoccupied public domain or military and Indian lands remained untaxable, even after statehood. In addition, under its liberal federal charter, the Northern Pacific Railroad Company had been granted some 20,500,000 acres—one-fifth of the public domain in Montana—these holdings by law exempt from territorial taxation until surveyed. As long as the railroad was still being built, Montanans maintained a most condescending attitude; but the moment the line's completion was assured they began to clamor for a speed-up of the survey in order that additional tax revenue might be gained.[124] A legislative memorial of 1887 complained that the North-

121. Potts to legislature (April 14, 1873), *Council Journal*, Extra Session (1873), 16–17; Potts to legislature (January 3, 1876), *House Journal*, 9 Session (1876), 23–24; Potts to legislature (January 8, 1883), *Council Journal*, 13 Session (1883), 33.

122. *Montana Live-Stock Journal*, March 31, 1888.

123. Admission of Dakota, Montana, Washington, and New Mexico into the Union, *House Report* No. 1025, 50 Congress, 1 Session (1887–88), 9–10; memorial to Congress (n.d.), *LM*, 16 Session (1889), 242.

124. Report of the Committee on the Territories on Washington, Idaho, and

ern Pacific paid taxes on only 20 percent of its holdings, and Delegate Toole introduced a bill in Congress to facilitate collection of taxes on railroad grant lands.[125] But little could be done: federal surveys were always far behind schedule; when the territory made an attempt to tax the buildings and rolling stock of the company, the Montana supreme court barred the way.[126] Unable to tax the railroad lands, Montanans expressed alarm when the Northern Pacific included mineral claims within its property; they vowed that no substantial amount of such resources should pass into the company's hands.[127] Twice—once in 1888 and again a year later—organized conventions met in Helena to discuss ways of blocking these corporate mineral aspirations and to protest accordingly to the proper officials in Washington.[128]

It was the exemptions, rather than the underassessing of taxable property, that undermined the revenue base. Although there was always a substantial gap between assessed valuation and estimated true valuation of such real estate and personal property, Montana was no worse than the rest of the country. Indeed, apart from the important exemptions, the territory's per capita assessed valuation ran consistently above the national average, if not the western average. In 1880, according to federal computations, the ratio of assessed to true valuation was 64.7 percent for Montana, as opposed to a national average of 38.73.[129]

It should be noted, too, that territorial taxes, as such, made up a relatively small proportion of the total. In 1880, for example, internal revenue to the national government amounted to $33,714; taxes at the territorial and local level came to $383,947. Of that latter amount,

Montana Territories, *House Report* No. 3689, 49 Congress, 2 Session (1886–87), 6; Report of the Governor of Montana, 1883, 542; *ibid.*, 1886, 833–34.

125. Memorial to Congress (n.d.), *LM*, 15 Session (1887), 1252–53; *Congressional Record*, 49 Congress, 1 Session (1885–86), 529.

126. Northern Pacific *v.* Carland, 5 *Montana Reports* (1884), 199.

127. *House Journal*, 16 Session (1889), 234–35; *Herald*, February 4, 8, 1888.

128. See Thomas A. Clinch, "The Northern Pacific Railroad and Montana's Mineral Lands," *Pacific Historical Review*, XXXIV (August, 1965), 327–29.

129. In 1870, the per capita assessed valuation of real estate and personal property was $482.81 for Montana, $411.58 for the West in general, and $367.73 for the nation. In 1880 the figures were: Montana, $475.24; the West, $482.02; and the nation, $407.18. *Report on Wealth, Debt, and Taxation at the Eleventh Census: 1890*, Pt. II, 59. In 1880, assessed valuation in Montana totalled $18,609,802 and estimated true valuation $29,000,000. Ten years earlier, assessed valuation had been $9,943,411 and estimated true valuation $15,184,522, with a ratio of just over 65 percent. *Report on Valuation, Taxation, and Public Indebtedness in the United States, as Returned at the Tenth Census (June 1, 1880)*, 6, 16.

$55,829 was territorial; $317,337 county; and $10,781 of units below the county.[130] Thus only about one dollar in every seven collected went directly into the coffers of the territorial government.

Despite limited federal support and weak, often poorly administered tax laws, Montana's expenses remained large. Though some officials fared better than others and some legislatures were more extravagant than others, certain outlays could not be ignored. Early records show expenditures of $12,056 for the pursuit of fugitives— including $3,000 paid to Neil Howie "in search of Bucher."[131] By the 1880s, one of the largest items in the territorial budget was for the support of criminals, a sum which ranged as high as $60,000 per year, while maintenance of the insane, also a major expenditure, ran normally from $30,000 to $40,000 annually.[132]

Such legitimate expenses, plus the imperfect tax structure and the legislature's occasional flings into extravagance, combined to keep Montana in debt during most of its territorial years. Before the territory was a year old it had contracted a debt of more than $85,000, part of it necessary because of the absence of federal funds. Some $58,950 of this was funded and the debt began to rise rapidly year by year, with the most expensive reason the $130,000 deficit built up prior to 1872 to pay extra compensation to officials and to members of the legislature.[133] Governor Ashley had lashed out at the "immense sums of money collected and expended by county and territorial officials," and insisted that "the gross amount of money thus expended, when added to the gross amount of our indebtedness for all purposes, surpasses anything in the history of local civil government with which I am acquainted, for extravagance and reckless expenditure."[134] But by 1873, when the territorial debt reached nearly $160,000, Governor Potts's economy campaign, now three years old, was beginning to make an impact and a downward trend commenced. Preaching thrift, Potts refunded the debt several times at lower interest rates, and by 1883 could announce that for the first time the territory was free of

130. *Ibid.*, 25

131. Leech and Stafford, *Report of the Commission Appointed to Examine the Accounts,* 1.

132. *Herald,* March 30, 1885; January 12, 1887; March 15, 1888.

133. Leech and Stafford, *Report of the Commission Appointed to Examine the Accounts,* 1; *Council Journal,* 5 Session (1868–69), 269; Potts to James A. Garfield (n.p., October 26, 1872), copy, Potts letterbook.

134. Ashley to legislature (December 11, 1869), *House Journal,* 6 Session (1869–70), 36.

debt and had a surplus in its treasury.[135] Thereafter it continued in the black, although the counties ran up a collective deficit of nearly two-thirds of a million dollars.[136]

In 1887, however, when a new bounty law threatened to bankrupt the territory, Montana came close to fiscal disaster. Statutes of the 1870s had set bounties for bear and mountain lion, but counties had the option of whether to pay or not.[137] Stockmen under Granville Stuart's leadership had been responsible for an act of 1883 which required a modest territorial outlay in bounties for bear, mountain lion, wolves, and coyotes—the total cost of which ranged from $1,712.50 in 1883 to $13,764 in 1886.[138] But a revision, effective in March, 1887, decreased the bounties on bear and mountain lions, increased those on wolves and coyotes, and added new ones of ten cents each for prairie dogs and five cents each for ground squirrels.[139] Immediately costs shot skyward: by the end of August that same year, the territory had paid out $48,012.50 under the new law, of which $41,060.05 was for prairie dogs and ground squirrels.[140] "'Gopher the Treasury' is the war cry heard from every valley and hillside of Gallatin County," quipped the *Herald*, citing the "squirrel crop" as the prime new agricultural commodity of the region. "The ground squirrels have gnawed to the bottom of our Territorial treasury and will now begin to devour the resources of the future and our credit."[141]

135. *Herald*, December 15, 1873; act (n.d.), *LM*, 7 Session (1871–72), 578–81; act of May 1, 1873, *LM*, Extra Session (1873), 65–66; act of July 21, 1879, *LM*, Extra Session (1879), 12–14; Potts to Legislature (January 8, 1883), *Council Journal*, 13 Session (1883), 30.

136. In 1880, the territorial debt was $64,677; that of the counties, $659,696; and of the school districts $35,552. County debt ranged from the $26,282 of Chouteau to the $165,674 of Lewis and Clark. Montana's total figure was higher than that of any other territory except Dakota. *A Compendium of the Tenth Census*, 1572, 1623, 1624.

137. Act of February 19, 1879, *LM*, 11 Session (1879), 34–35.

138. Bounties were set as follows: bear, $8; mountain lions, $8; wolves, $1; coyotes, 50 cents, with the stipulation that they must not be taken on Indian lands. Act of March 8, 1883, *LM*, 13 Session (1883), 109–10; *Herald*, August 29, 1887; Granville Stuart to R. S. Ford (n.p., February 4, 1883); Stuart to John S. Crosby (Fort Maginnis, April 11, 1883); Stuart to Conrad Kohrs (Fort Maginnis, May 2, 1884), copies, all in letterbook 2, Stuart MSS.

139. The stipend for bear and mountain lions was reduced to $3; that on wolves went to $2 and that on coyotes to $1. Act of March [n.d.], 1887, *Compiled Statutes of Montana*, 15 Session (1887), 971–73.

140. Leslie to legislature (August 29, 1887), *Herald*, August 29, 1887.

141. *Herald*, April 29 & July 8, 1887.

Governor Leslie quickly convened a special legislative session to meet the emergency, pointing out as he did so that at the rate of bounty expenditures for June and the first week of July, the law would cost the territory nearly $200,000 by the time the regular legislature met.[142] Once assembled, the legislature went to work. "So far," chided the *Great Falls Tribune*, "the president of the council is ahead, having 2,150 scalps, but it is claimed that he stole 200 from the speaker of the house and 75 from the chairman of the committee on church extension."[143] After much discussion and at least one change of mind, the assembly repealed the bounties, leaving the question in the hands of county comissioners, cattlemen unhappy but the territorial treasury saved.[144] Early in 1889, a joint committee looking into finances noted that since the repeal of the laws, the volume of work in the auditor's office had so diminished that an additional clerk was no longer needed. At that time there was a treasury surplus of $114,000, although six months and one legislative session later it would have dwindled to $36,000.[145]

Democrats sought to take credit for bringing the territory out of debt, but most Montanans recognized that Republican Benjamin Potts was the man most responsible. They knew too that it was the legislature's thoughtlessness or its foolish extravagance that brought the deficits or from time to time threatened the surplus. Actually, the territorial debt of Montana was not out of keeping with public debts elsewhere. The 1880 debt at all levels, mostly county and with only a little left in territorial bonds, totalled $765,248, or $19.54 on a per capita basis, at a time when the national per capita average was $22.40. Statehood would bring Montana's per capita obligations well above the national figure.[146]

If the territorial revenue laws were never strong, if they mirrored interest groups and touched Montanans unfairly, Montanans had only themselves and territorial politics to blame. If they believed that

142. Proclamation of Governor Leslie (July 11, 1887), *Herald*, July 12, 1887.

143. *Great Falls Tribune*, August 3, 1887.

144. With what one editor called "the bungling for which that body is noted," the legislature first passed a county bounty law, then passed a general repealing act which swept away the new as well as the old statute. *River Press* (Fort Benton), December 26, 1888; acts of September 13 and 14, 1887, *LM*, Extra Session (1887), 58. See also *Herald*, September 6, 9, 14, 1887.

145. *Council Journal*, 16 Session (1889), 7–8; *Proceedings, Constitutional Convention, 1889*, 516.

146. In 1890 the total debt in Montana would be $2,918,893, a per capita average of $22.09, at a time when the national per capita average had dropped to $18.13. *Compendium of the Eleventh Census: 1890*, Pt. II, 325.

federal taxes were exorbitant and philosophically unfair and that the territory received less from Washington, they may perhaps be forgiven their myopia and occasional lapse of memory. Montana was at least on a par with her sister territories as a recipient of U.S. Treasury funds and benefited more than her residents would like to admit through federal subsidies of all types. Nor was Montana singled out: any national financial policy was general and directed toward the territories at large.

12

"...A Mighty State among the Mighty":
The Struggle for Admission

Territorial status meant relegation to an inferior political position on the national scene and Montanans protested accordingly. They saw themselves "Disfranchised and reduced to the position of serfs," as a Bozeman editor put it in 1880.[1] Why condemn a lack of self-government in Ireland, asked Delegate Toole a few years later, when the same situation existed at home? "We are accustomed to see States with far less resources and possibilities, mounted at it were, on steeds of steam, rushing swiftly past us, equipped with all the paraphernalia which sovereignty can invent or supply, contesting in a spirit of generous rivalry one with another for the first place in the race for political power and prestige, while we are compelled to 'sit solemnly astride a dead horse, in a reverential calm, with the reins held firmly in our hands' . . . ."[2] Under the circumstances, only admission to the Union could solve all grievances. "Without it," contended Toole, "there is nothing but political insomnia and internal unrest."[3]

The movement began early, and, while at times much more intense than at others, it extended throughout practically the entire territorial period. Commencing with humble requests in the 1860s, it emerged full blown in the 1880s, with demands strongly worded, even belli-

1. *Avant Courier*, August 5, 1880.
2. *Congressional Record*, 50 Congress, 2 Session (1888–89), 822.
3. *Ibid.*

cose in nature. And twice before being authorized by Congress, constitutional conventions would meet in Montana to draw up basic documents and request statehood.

In his message to the first legislative assembly late in 1864, Governor Edgerton had looked optimistically ahead to the day when Montana would be allowed her place in the Union on terms of equality with the sister states.[4] There were those present, however, who saw no reason to wait for the future. If eventually, why not now? As early as November, 1865, some of the leading Democrats of Helena urged Acting Governor Meagher to call an election to choose delegates to a constitutional convention. Meagher replied that his temporary assumption of the gubernatorial powers gave him no responsibility to comply, but he expressed a willingness to call a public meeting to petition Congress for statehood.[5] To the Secretary of State he wrote that if Montana were granted admission immediately, its congressmen would be traitorous Democrats and "flagrant mischief-makers."[6]

But the prospect of a senatorial seat just over the horizon was too much for the ambitious Meagher. When he decided to align himself with the territorial Democrats, he reversed his previous position and called an election and the subsequent convocation of a constitutional convention to give voice "to the wants and just pretensions of the Territory. . ." in March, 1866.[7] This action and the response it elicited were closely tied up with the controversy over the "Acting One's" right to convene the second legislature, and opinions on the matter were largely political.

Democrats rallied behind Meagher in favor of immediate statehood. In a preponderence in the territory, the party would be in a position to benefit from the patronage and elected offices that statehood would bring. "Admittedly, Montaña would not, indeed, dress up with the Republican line, but it would take rank among the staunchest of the President's Democratic supporters," Meagher now assured the administration.[8]

Republicans were wary: they questioned both the legality of

4. Sidney Edgerton to legislature (December 10, 1864), *Contributions*, III (1900), 342.

5. *Montana Post*, December 23, 1865.

6. Thomas F. Meagher to William Seward (Virginia City, December 11, 1865), TPS.

7. *Montana Post*, February 3, 1866.

8. Meagher to Seward (Virginia City, February 20, 1866), "Official & confidential," TPS.

the proclamation and the motives behind it. Meagher had called the convention, charged William Chumasero, "with the expectation that himself and a rebel Colonel formerly on Price's staff will be the Senators."[9] Henry Blake of the partisan *Montana Post* saw it as a party move inaugurated because "about three score Democratic politicians want office."[10] Admission would only enhance the power of the Democrats, but if delayed, future influxes of Republicans might offset "Bourbon" numbers and influence. Moreover, statehood would raise government costs and taxes, with "a corresponding increase of political cormorants to eat up the substance of our people." "Our present form of Government is 'good enough for poor folks,' " insisted one thrifty Bannack citizen.[11]

But plans went ahead. Elections were held on February 24, and nearly two months later a correspondent of the *Post* could announce that the constitutional convention, "Sired by the Acting-one, and damned by the people, having been helped along by a number of proclamations, is finally born."[12] Meeting in Helena, with Robert C. Ewing presiding, the body was able to get a quorum of its fifty-five elected members only by resorting to a proxy vote. It met six days, but had no public funds; while it did accomplish something, it gave the appearance to its opponents of being illy timed and premature. "At present, it reminds us of children playing soldier, with a broomstick for a rifle, and a sword of lathe, for a warrier's blade," scoffed Henry Blake.[13]

Borrowing the rules of the 1861 Missouri constitutional convention, the assembly used the proposed Colorado constitution of 1865 as a model, adding modifications from New York and California. Memorials were sent to Congress and a resolution adopted urging that all federal appointments be made from the "true working friends" of the Johnson administration and policy. Then, just before adjournment, the presiding officer requested members to remain in their seats for a Democratic caucus.[14] With the convention dissolved,

9. William Chumasero to Lyman Trumbull (Helena, March 12, 1866), *ibid.*
10. *Montana Post*, February 3, 1866.
11. *Ibid.*, February 10, 1866.
12. *Ibid.*, April 14, 1866. Apparently the group did not convene until early April, though a legislative effort to postpone it until July 9 or later was tabled. *Council Journal*, 2 Session (1866), 45–46.
13. *Montana Post*, April 14, 1866. See Margery H. Brown, "Metamorphosis and Revision: A Sketch of Constitution Writing in Montana," *Montana*, XX (October, 1970), 7.
14. *Montana Post*, April 21, 1866.

said the *Post*, "Saloon keepers have resumed the usual price for drinks, landlords have renovated their beds, and Helena once more rejoices in a respectable community."[15]

But the constitution that was drafted disappeared. It was presented neither to the people nor to Congress. Tradition has it that it was lost when delegate Thomas E. Tutt took the draft to St. Louis for printing; or it might have perished in a fire which destroyed the papers of Horace McGuire, secretary of the convention.[16] Modern historians, at least, have not seen a copy.

Thus it would seem that this premature statehood effort was actually something of a political escapade, sanctioned by Meagher and the Democrats without any real expectation of success. Shrouded in mystery so far as the details of its deliberations and its end-product are concerned, the convention becomes something of a legend, obscure and tantalizing, perhaps, but neither practical nor important in the long view of Montana history.

Meeting at the same time, the territorial legislature did not add its seal of approval to the constitutional convention, but petitioned Congress for an enabling act authorizing another such assembly preparatory to statehood. This was a mild memorial, mainly devoted to praise of the territory's "large and thrifty" population, its "pure air, and salubrious climate," and its limitless natural resources. It mentioned no specific grievances; only the general complaint that the territorial structure had in the past proved inadequate.[17] Its tone was felicitous, like that of a dutiful child respectfully asking favors of a benevolent parent.

During 1867, the legislature again considered the matter. Discussion now centered on dissatisfaction with the nullification by Congress of the laws of the two previous assemblies and in restricting private and special legislation. "Congress has seen fit to interfere with our local laws and institutions, thus seriously affecting the investment of capital" complained a House committee, which suggested statehood as the only remedy for this "state of political chaos." But the memorial actually sent to Congress omitted such specific complaints and was word for word almost identical with the one of the previous year.[18]

A bill introduced in the U.S. Senate by Oliver Perry Morton of Indiana early in 1869 advocated statehood for Montana, but realists

15. *Ibid.*, April 28, 1866.
16. Brown, "Metamorphosis and Revision," 8.
17. Memorial to Congress (April 14, 1866), *LM*, 2 Session (1866), 49.
18. *House Journal*, 4 Session (1867), 147; memorial to Congress (December

suffered no illusions that a Republican Congress would support action which would add two new Democratic senators—action which was "incompatible with the times." Nonetheless, most Montanans would by then have been pleased to accept admission to the Union, even with limitations set by the Radical Republicans. Their experience might be limited and expenses might be great, but statehood offered an opportunity to "cultivate our farm on our own account, independent of the abrogating powers of Congress, and to avoid being made the receptacle of Washington City's political excrement."[19]

When Morton's bill was lost, Montana spirits remained high. The sixth session of the legislature adopted a resolution calling for the establishment of a "State Convention Committee," authorized to call an election of delegates to a constitutional convention sometime after the completion of the federal census of 1870. In part because this resolution was for home consumption and in part because of increasing feelings that the territorial transitional stage had now been outgrown, this statement—like those of the newspapers—was far more critical than those of earlier years. But, though it sharply condemned federal taxation, appointments and lack of protection, it brought no results: the "State Convention Committee" did not carry out its delegated functions.[20]

By the end of the 1870s the clamor for statehood was being reiterated in more blatant tones. A legislative petition of 1879 listed a growing number of complaints, emphasized the weaknesses of territorial government, and demanded the "fundamental and inalienable rights of American citizens" for the people of Montana, with special stress on limited powers of the legislature and a lack of representation in Congress under the status quo.[21] Meanwhile the press was urging Congress to create five states out of the then eight territories and was pressing for the legislature to establish a "committee of correspondence" to work in unison with similar bodies from other territories.[22] Editor Fisk of the *Herald* displayed a versatility of thought when he

9, 1867), *LM*, 4 Session (1867), 267. Republicans again were opposed and Democrats in favor. See: *Montana Post*, November 16, 23, 1867; *Montana Democrat*, November 14, 21, 1867.

19. *Weekly Independent*, February 6, March 6, 1869; *Congressional Globe*, 40 Congress, 3 Session (1868–69), 731.

20. Act (n.d.), *LM*, 6 Session (1869–70), 122–23; *Weekly Herald*, January 29, 1870; *Daily Rocky Mountain Gazette*, July 4, 1870.

21. Memorial to Congress (n.d.), *LM*, 11 Session (1879), 139.

22. *Herald*, March 15, December 30, 1878.

insisted that the word "territorial" referred to land; that the Constitution named only two types of government—state and national; hence territorial government was unconstitutional.[23]

The Census of 1880 showed 28,177 males and 10,982 females—a total of 39,159—in the territory, an increase of over 90 percent since 1870.[24] This expanding population enhanced both the desire and the possibility for admission to the Union. One of the prayers of the chaplain in the lower house of the legislature early in 1881 was for Montana statehood; and Robert Fisk urged Benjamin Harrison, chairman of the Senate Committee on the Territories in Washington, to do something for those who had strayed far from home and had "become in these mountains aliens to 'the genial influences of civilization,'" to do something to benefit "the emasculated Territories, moving forward to the dignity of Statehood."[25] To Congress in general, Fisk proposed: "Just make two bites at the cherry, admit four of the Territories by one bill at once—Dakota, Montana, Washington and New Mexico. Then there will be four left for the next bite—say eight years hence—provided Utah is purged by that time." But he was wary of admission of a divided Dakota, fearing that would set back Montana's cause by several years.[26] Fisk undoubtedly spoke for the majority of his readers when he said "We feel as if we had served a long and hard apprenticeship and were fully entitled on higher grounds than simply the number of our people to an early admission as a State."[27] As delegate, Martin Maginnis had not pushed statehood, charged Fisk in the 1882 campaign: the "rings" behind Maginnis were not interested in early admission and Maginnis himself was concerned only if Montana stood to come in Democratic with him as senator.[28] The editor again urged concerted action of territorial legislatures to command the attention of Congress, but admitted that justice did not always prevail. "In all our history hardly a State has ever been admitted simply on the merits of the case." "Our strongest hope for Montana's admission as a State within the next two years comes, we are sorry to say it, from the fact that she has always been Democratic." Here, Fisk was thinking of Montana

23. *Ibid.*, January 6, 1879.
24. *Tenth Report of the United States Census Bureau, 1880*, I, 70.
25. *Herald*, January 20, 1881; Robert Fisk to Benjamin Harrison (Helena, January 21, 1881), Benjamin Harrison MSS.
26. *Herald*, November 8, 1881; January 19, 1882.
27. *Ibid.*, August 22, 1882. See also *Miles City Daily Press*, August 16, 1882.
28. *Herald*, October 27, 1882.

as a counterbalance to a Republican Dakota.[29] Other local newsmen pointed to the territory's financial solvency, newly won as the result of Governor Potts's efforts, as an indication of responsibility, but lamented of Montana that 'In the opinion of Eastern political economists, she has not yet drank the cup of political humiliation to the bitter dregs. . . .'"[30]

In 1883, the movement began to assume a more positive form. Meeting early that year, the thirteenth session of the legislature considered several approaches. One, apparently incorporated in a bill written by Wilbur F. Sanders and James E. Callaway and introduced by a friend, would have created a state government and elected senators who would then go to Washington to ask for admission. According to Callaway later, Democrats "smothered" this measure in the Council, thus preventing Montana from serious consideration at that time.[31]

In January of the same year, Richard Hickman, Democrat from Madison County, introduced a resolution condemning Maginnis for not pressing Montana's statehood claims more actively in Congress and authorizing the calling of a constitutional convention as soon as possible. The censure clause was quickly stricken, but debate on the proposal occupied much of the session. The House Committee on Territorial Affairs was pessimistic, pointing out that other territories, including Dakota, New Mexico, and Washington—all with greater population—had tried the same approach and had failed to move Congress with their arguments.[32] The Council defeated the constitutional convention bill, but on a reconsideration, the measure was ultimately passed in mutilated form—the result of Democratic opposition, according to the press. As enacted, the resolution provided for the election of delegates to a convention to meet early in 1884, with ratification of its work at the general election in November of the same year.[33]

Urging citizens to seize "an opportunity that will not present itself again for ten years or more," the *Herald* saw no reason why party machinery should not be used to elect delegates. To those who called

29. *Ibid.*, December 16, 1882; February 3, 1883.
30. *Semi-Weekly Miner*, February 7, 24, 1883.
31. Callaway to Sanders (Deer Lodge, February 17, 1889), quoted in *Herald*, February 22, 1889.
32. *House Journal*, 13 Session (1883), 52, 100–101.
33. *Herald*, February 28, March 1, 13, 1883; joint resolution of March 7, 1883, *LM*, 13 Session (1883), 199–200.

the movement premature because it did not originate in Congress, the newspaper replied: "Who ever knew or heard of anything originating in Congress? It is considered rare good fortune to bring Congress to give its attention and approval to the good and important things that are suggested from without."[34] And although counties and districts were admonished to select their best men, even though the job was thankless (and payless) like jury duty, or "serving on a Sheriff's posse, or being drafted into the army," the elections were disappointing. ". . . no general election ever transpired in this city," wrote the *Herald* editor, "in which there was manifested such general apathy and indifference."[35] Confided Granville Stuart, "The Constitutional Con. didn't bring out more than a third of the vote, on an average, & it don't amount to anything anyhow." Certainly, he said, such a turnout "won't look to Congress as tho we had population enough to entitle us to representation."[36]

Not everyone was so glum. Montanans were reminded that Monday, January 14, 1884, commemorated two important events: the thirty-sixth anniversary of the discovery of gold in California and the meeting of the constitutional convention on the second floor of Woody Paynter's new building at Main and Broadway in Helena.[37] A cross section of territorial talent, the forty-five elected delegates to that convention combined experience and ability. Together they formed "an admirable representative body—intelligent, zealous, careful, industrious and honest," said the *New North-West*. As a group they were "neither intemperate in habit or opinions."[38]

Veteran legislator Washington McCormick, who came to Montana in 1863, was elected temporary chairman, after which William A. Clark presided with aplomb and distinction. Anaconda mine magnate Marc Daly was also a member, but probably spent little time at the convention.[39] Tom Power was a leading figure from the Republican apparatus and the body included a wealth of political expertise.

34. *Herald*, September 28, 29, 1883.

35. *Ibid.*, October 1, November 7, 1883.

36. Granville Stuart to Thomas H. Irvine (Fort Maginnis, November 22, 1883); Stuart to Hauser (Fort Maginnis, November 22, 1883), copies, both in letterbook 2, Stuart MSS.

37. *Herald*, January 10, 1884.

38. Forty-five delegates were elected, but George Steele, member from Sun River, became ill and took no part in the deliberations, although he appeared on the final day. *Herald*, February 9, 1884; *New North-West*, February 15, 1884.

39. *Herald*, January 19, 1884; Proceedings, Constitutional Convention, January 16, 1884.

Three—McCormick, Elihu Waterbury, and William Y. Pemberton—
had been members of the 1866 convention and two others had served
in constitution-making assemblies elsewhere. At least fifteen members had sat in legislatures, either in Montana or outside; and James
E. Callaway and James H. Mills were both former secretaries of the
territory. Future territorial delegate Joseph K. Toole was regarded as
"the most forcible, fluent and impressive speaker when roused," Cornelius Hedges the "most scholarly," and Pemberton of Butte the
"readiest debater."[40] In age, they ranged from twenty-six to seventy-
one and at least one-third were college educated. Men born in the
North outnumbered those born in the South by a ratio of two to one,
and at least eight others were of foreign birth; and the assembly was
heavily Bourbon in flavor—thirty Democrats to fourteen Republicans
and one independent—according to the *Herald's* scorecard. Lawyers
made up the largest single group represented—roughly one-third of
the total—while mining and ranching interests each comprised about
one-fourth.[41]

Organizing itself into twenty-two standing committees, the convention set about its deliberations. It ignored a WCTU petition calling for a prohibition plank and passed over a suggestion that the
"obnoxiously monarchical" titles of "governor" and "lieutenant governor" be cast aside in favor of "the more republican terms of President and Vice President."[42] It spent far too much time debating
whether or not the state constitution should include an anti-railroad
pass clause, a proposal which William Y. Pemberton thought "a libel
on the virtue and patriotism" of Montanans.[43] It devoted a great deal
of time and generated much heat on the tax issue—especially the
status of mining property. In the end, despite petitions for equal
taxation, mines, as well as churches and cemeteries, were exempted,
except for improvements, machinery, surface ground, and net proceeds. Since mineral interests were so well represented, it was argued

40. *New North-West*, February 15, 1884.
41. Data on members comes from *Herald*, January 3, 16, 17, 18, 19, 21, 22,
1884.
42. Petition of Horatio Maguire (Bozeman, January 15, 1884); WCTU petition (n.p., n.d.), in Proceedings, Constitutional Convention, 1884; Minute
Book, January 14, 1884, pp. 42–43.
43. Said Pemberton: "I don't believe the man could be elected to the legislature who would sell his vote as United States Senator for a ticket on a railroad.
No sir. We want more money than that, if we sell." Minute book, January 16,
1884; *Herald*, January 18, February 1, 1884.

that unless mines were exempted, miners would vote against the constitution.[44]

Other provisions reflected some of the weaknesses of the territorial structure. The number of legislators, the number of judges, and the compensation for all would be increased. The powers of the judiciary were to be broadened and the right to tax the roadbed, the rails, and the rolling stock of interstate railroads running through Montana was specifically proclaimed.[45] The constitution was a relatively long document, drawn from many sources. Its preamble came from Massachusetts, its judiciary section largely from California, other parts from Minnesota and Alabama, "and probably more from Colorado than from all the rest together."[46]

After nearly four weeks, the convention came to a close and O. C. Bundy, Helena photographer, took a picture of all delegates and employees in their seats before it broke up. Forty signatures were affixed to the constitution and only Elihu Waterbury of Deer Lodge registered a negative vote against it.[47] Next came the process of "selling" the document to the voting public, for a strong showing at the polls—say, 40,000 in favor—was deemed vital in making the eventual case before Congress. The press believed it "a good instrument, taken as a whole," although some considered it too complicated. Labor spokesmen complained that worker's rights were inadequately protected and others felt that it favored mining unduly; but they urged adoption nonetheless.[48] Governor Crosby termed the constitution "a good one," though "there was a little too much Legislation embraced" and not enough taxation; but he gave his support at home and in addition urged the Secretary of the Interior to champion the statehood cause. In his annual report, Crosby noted that "With the constant and enormous increase of business pending before Congress, it is becoming each year more and more a physical as well as a moral impossibility for that body to give any serious attention to

---

44. Proceedings, Constitutional Convention, January 29, February 4, 1884; *Herald*, August 8, 1884; *Semi-Weekly Miner*, February 13, 1884; *Weekly Independent*, February 5, 1884; Constitution of 1884, *Senate Miscellaneous Document* No. 39, 49 Congress, 1 Session (1885–86), 23.

45. Senate Miscellaneous Document No. 39, 49 Congress, 1 Session (1885–86), 5, 11, 14, 16, 25.

46. *Herald*, January 28, February 11, October 25, 1884.

47. *Ibid.*, February 8, 1884; Brown, "Metamorphosis and Revision," 14.

48. *Herald*, February 3, 11, May 12, July 1, August 8, October 25, 1884; *Butte City Union*, February 10, 1884.

such legislation as the Territories need, even if the subject-matter of such legislation was within the knowledge of members, so that they could act intelligently thereon." By delegating these responsibilities to a Montana state government, Crosby insisted, Congress would benefit itself and the inhabitants of the territory as well.[49]

Having been printed and distributed for study, the 1884 constitution was approved in the November election by a margin of 15,506 to 4,266—roughly four to one—a showing that was not particularly impressive, for total balloting on the document ran 7,198 behind the combined votes in the Toole-Knowles delegate race on the same day.[50] A commission, which included Joseph K. Toole, was approved to present the case to the president, but a lack of money slowed progress. When an effort was made in the legislature to appropriate funds to pay members of the convention, a Council committee reported back that there was no money available but that when statehood became a reality "the first right to represent her in the halls of congress, or upon the floor of the United States senate, is hereby delegated to the members of said convention."[51] And Joe Browne, one of the deputation selected by the convention to wait upon the president, had to write Sam Hauser: "Now friend Sam I am out considerable on the Constitution 'racket'" and would appreciate help, he said, in getting a railroad pass "as far as possible in the direction of Washington D.C." Hauser obliged.[52]

But 1885 was not an auspicious moment. There was considerable delay in presenting the document to Washington; national politics hung in a precarious balance, the Senate Republican and the House Democratic. Hauser, the new governor, was in the nation's capital late in the year, "looking after the interests of Montana, and suggesting Montana as a good pair for Dakota"; and many thought that if statehood could be achieved, Hauser was the man who could swing it.[53] Even so, not all members of Hauser's own party were convinced that the time was ripe. Charles Broadwater was said to oppose admission—on the grounds that the increased expense of state government would raise taxes and that the Democrats could likely not carry Montana in an election. On the other hand, William A. Clark

49. John Schuyler Crosby to Martin Maginnis (Helena, February 13, 1884), Maginnis MSS; Report of the Governor of Montana, 1884, 564.
50. *Herald*, December 4, 1884; Waldron, *Montana Politics*, 44.
51. *Council Journal*, 14 Session (1885), 91–92.
52. Joe A. Browne to Samuel T. Hauser (Glendale, December 5, 21, 1884), both in Hauser MSS.
53. *Herald*, December 16, 1885.

was urging Hauser to "make a vigorous effort for admission" and to "talk with Vest, Gorman and others and prepare the way."[54]

Meanwhile, at the Forty-ninth Congress, Delegate Toole presented the ratified constitution and introduced a bill for statehood; at the same time Senator Voorhees of Indiana placed a similar measure before the Senate.[55] Since Montana was Democratic, which eastern newspapers saw as "no argument at all," the strategy apparently was to pair Montana with Republican Dakota, a maneuver Fisk's *Herald* believed ridiculous: "It is almost impossible to keep a sober face and hear such childish prattle about the promising scheme of our delegate to get Montana smuggled into the Union as a State."[56] Both bills were quickly lost and Voorhees then sought to amend a bill to admit Washington to include Montana as well, but after considerable Senate debate, the Hoosier was voted down by an almost solid Republican phalanx. Two days later the Washington admission bill passed the Senate, with all of the thirteen negative votes cast by Democrats.[57] Thus Senate Republicans rejected Montana, which was rated Democratic, but accepted Washington, which was Republican, for political reasons.

The second session of the Forty-ninth Congress (1886–87) also debated the propriety of opening the door to Montana, first in a House proposal to amend the Washington bill to include both Montana and Idaho, and this failing, in the omnibus idea brought forth by Representative Springer of Illinois to admit Dakota, New Mexico, Washington, and Montana, a proposal that was also in vain.[58] Other bills were introduced in the subsequent Congress and at least two Committee reports indicated general sentiment in favor of statehood, but Fabian tactics prevented any action in 1887 and 1888.[59]

54. William B. Webb to Hauser (Helena, January 30, 1886); William A. Clark to Hauser (New York, February 27, 1886), both in Hauser MSS.

55. *Congressional Record*, 49 Congress, 1 Session (1885–86), 700, 735.

56. *Herald*, October 20, 1886; *New York Times*, January 19, 21, 1886.

57. On the Montana amendment eighteen of nineteen negative votes were Republican; on the Washington vote, all "nays" were Democratic. *Congressional Record*, 49 Congress, 1 Session (1885–86), 3251, 3259, 3354.

58. *Ibid.*, 49 Congress, 2 Session (1886–87), 121; Report of the Committee on the Territories on Washington, Idaho and Montana Territories, *House Report* No. 3689, 49 Congress, 2 Session (1886–87), 7.

59. Late in 1887 an omnibus bill was introduced and lost which would have provided admission for Montana, Dakota, Washington and New Mexico. A month later, Delegate Toole proposed statehood for Montana alone. On January 10, 1888, Delegate Charles S. Voorhees of Washington Territory entered a bill which included Montana, and two weeks later, his father, Daniel W. Voorhees of Indiana, brought a similar measure before the Senate. *Congressional Record*, 50

Such setbacks were resented by Montanans, though most accepted defeat philosophically, confident that it was but temporary. Forgetting its earlier advice that the territorial legislature not meet again "until their powers are enlarged or the time comes for admission as a State," the *Herald* noted the hundredth anniversary of the Northwest Ordinance by citing the inevitability of change: "The doors of the Union may be barred for a time as the waters of a river may be dammed but they will gather head and force to sweep over any barriers, and all the powers, arts and genius of obstruction cannot long prevent it."[60] Even so, editor Fisk lost his composure and his patience when Governor Leslie's 1887 Thanksgiving Proclamation called upon Montanans to engage themselves in prayer "with the people of the United States."[61] With former delegate Maginnis and former Judge George Symes—now a Colorado Congressman—actively working on their behalf, Montanans had a right to be optimistic. Even more exciting was the rumor current in the spring of 1888 that a deal might be in the offing, with statehood for Montana and the Democratic vice-presidential nomination for Sam Hauser. "Stranger and worse things might happen," said the *Herald*.[62] But, just in case, the press suggested another constitutional convention; it proposed an inter-territorial assembly of delegates to take joint action; and it urged Montana "to get ready for housekeeping," for farseeing men predicted admission once the 1888 elections were over[63]—a prophesy that would be fulfilled.

By the summer of that year, the handwriting was on the wall. At the St. Louis convention early in June, the Democratic Party adopted a plank calling for statehood for Montana, Dakota, Washington and New Mexico; the Republicans followed suit later in the month and even added Wyoming, Idaho and Arizona to the list.[64] Infidel Utah

Congress, 1 Session (1887–88), 29, 235, 362, 649; Report of the Committee on the Territories on the Admission of Dakota, Montana, Washington, and New Mexico into the Union, *House Report* No. 1025, 50 Congress, 1 Session, 1–3; Report of the Committee on the Territories on Senate Bill 1619 to provide for the formation and admission into the Union of the State of Montana, *Senate Report* No. 733, 50 Congress, 1 Session, 1–2.

60. *Herald*, September 23, 1886, January 4, 1887.
61. *Ibid.*, November 8, 1887.
62. *Ibid.*, January 24, February 17, April 21, 1888.
63. *Ibid.*, November 6, December 6, 17, 1888; *Avant Courier*, December 13, 1888; Corvallis *New Idea*, quoted in *Great Falls Tribune*, July 9, 1887.
64. *Official Proceedings of the National Democratic Convention, Held in St. Louis, Mo., June 5th, 6th and 7th, 1888* (St. Louis, 1888), 101; *Proceedings of*

was shunned and Montana, like other territories, wanted no truck with being paired with the Mormon transgressors for admission.[65]

In 1888, as in 1884, both parties anticipated a close election and neither wished to test the balance that then existed. But at the polls in November, Republican Benjamin Harrison was elected president and a Republican majority was returned to both houses of Congress. The old lame-duck second session of the Fiftieth Congress then recognized the inevitability of the admission of at least some of the western territories and took action "to receive all the applause with several encores thrown in and at the same time to place the admitted territories under obligation to the republican party and a republican administration."[66] With this in mind, it set about passing an enabling act for Montana, Washington and the two Dakotas; and it was in support of this measure in mid-January, 1889, that Delegate Toole presented the brief of his territory in bold and dramatic fashion. Where the Declaration of Independence listed twenty-seven grievances, Toole enumerated but twenty-one, but at many points they were remarkably similar and his slashing attack earned him plaudits throughout the territories. As a constituent from Boulder wrote him: "It is the right kind of a *nail*, driven in the right *place*, with the right kind of a *hammer*, wielded with sufficient and the right kind of *force*."[67]

The president signed the Omnibus Bill on February 22, the seventieth birthday of Walter de Lacy, a pioneer who had arrived at Fort Benton nearly thirty years before. Toole called it "the grandest act of this administration and in the extent of constitutional government conferred is unparalled in the history of the republic."[68] The Montana press responded with applause and with solemn cautions that the approaching change of status carried responsibilities as well as rights. "Minerva, we are told, sprung full-armed from the head of Jupiter. Montana, after twenty-five years of travail, springs forth

the Ninth Republican National Convention Held at Chicago, Ill., June 19, 20, 21, 22, 23, and 25, 1888 (Chicago, 1888), 109.

65. *Weekly Independent*, December 20, 1888.

66. *River Press*, December 5, 1888.

67. *Congressional Record*, 50 Congress, 2 Session (1888–89), 821–22; George F. Cowan to Joseph K. Toole (Boulder, February 8, 1889), Joseph K. Toole MSS, MHS. See also: *Herald*, January 16, 1889; *Arizona Weekly Enterprise* (Tucson), January 27, 1889.

68. Act of February 22, 1889, 25 *USSL*, 676–84; Walter de Lacy to Fannie de Lacy (Helena, February 26, 1889), de Lacy MSS; Toole to Cleveland (Washington, February 22, 1889), telegram, Cleveland MSS.

equally well armed for a career of glory and prosperity, a mighty State among the mighty, even from her birth," sang the *Herald*.[69]

The enabling act of February 22 authorized the formation of a state government for each territory named. Some, like James Callaway, urged that Montana use the 1884 constitution, but prevailing sentiment was that it contained too much legislation and restricted too severely the powers of legislators and county officers.[70] Governor White therefore issued a call for the election of delegates to a constitutional convention to meet in Helena, the election in mid-May and the convention to meet on July 4.[71] But there was no repeat of the outcome of the 1888 delegate race. In a light turnout, due in part to storms, lambing season, and crop planting, the Democrats won a small majority of five or six, with one independent elected.[72] Local and personal influences proved stronger than party ties, although Republican stalwarts, who believed the outcome critical, blamed defeat on apathy, the Roman Catholicism of Delegate Tom Carter, and the unwillingness of Governor White to use the power of patronage.[73]

At the convention, William A. Clark again presided, having been chosen over Lewis Hershfield; in addition, seven others were present who had sat in the 1884 body. Former delegates Maginnis and Toole were there; former governor B. Platt Carpenter; and former justice Hiram Knowles. Of the seventy-five delegates, a surprising number, sixteen, had previous service in a state or territorial legislature. In age, they ranged from twenty-eight years to sixty-nine, with an average of just over forty-four. Eleven had been born outside the United States, but New York, Maine, Kentucky, and Missouri were the leading birthplaces. Four were Civil War veterans and the educational level was high: all had attended public schools and at least thirteen had gone to college. As in 1884, lawyers made up the largest single group (twenty); mining interests, led by Clark and by Marc Daly's

69. *Semi-Weekly Miner*, February 23, 1889; *Avant Courier*, February 28, 1889; *Billings Gazette*, March 7, 1889; *Herald*, February 23, 1889.

70. Callaway to Sanders (Deer Lodge, February 17, 1889), quoted in *Herald*, February 22, 1889; *Billings Gazette*, February 28, 1889.

71. *Herald*, April 15, 1889.

72. *Ibid.*, May 15, 23, 1889. One study, made in 1891, gave the convention breakdown as forty Democrats, thirty-four Republicans and one independent (Labor). A more recent study gives the Democrats a margin of thirty-nine to thirty-five, with one independent. Francis Newton Thorpe, "Recent Constitution-Making in the United States," *Annals of the American Academy of Political and Social Science*, II (September, 1891), 150; Waldron, *Montana Politics*, 50.

73. Isaac McCutcheon to Russell Harrison (Helena, May 28, 1889), Russell Harrison MSS.

associate John R. Toole, and merchants, headed by Charles E. Conrad, each had twelve representatives. Under the leadership of Con Kohrs, stockmen had seven members; and Peter Breen was spokesman for a small but vocal labor group. Farmers and small businessmen probably had less voice than their numbers in the territory warranted, for delegates tended to be educated, politically experienced, and personally successful.[74]

Using the 1884 rules and organizing themselves into twenty-three standing committees, the convention set to work. If it used the 1884 constitution as a point of departure, it re-debated almost every issue, even though with mineral interests pitted against stock interests as before it was a relatively harmonious group. Much of the long bill-of-rights section of 1884 was written into the new document but without the flowery reference to "the goodness of the Great Legislator of the Universe" from the preamble of the first. Among questions which precipitated debate were: the taxation of mines and irrigation facilities, possible abolition of probate judges and the grand jury system, the location of the capital, apportionment of state senators by county regardless of population, the desirability of woman suffrage, and the right of aliens to hold property. Efforts to bolster county powers were so strong that one editor sarcastically suggested for the "Confederacy of Montana" a great seal featuring a "bald-headed coyote, with the motto 'E Umbus Plurum.'"[75] Several visitors, including Senator William Stewart of Nevada, Senator Preston Plumb of Kansas, and Major John Wesley Powell, appeared before the convention to speak on land and irrigation problems, and by August 17, after Charles S. Warren, the wit of the assemblage, had thanked C. R. Middleton, who had given sixty-six speeches during the session, "for not taking up any of the convention's time," Chairman Clark brought down the gavel for the last time.[76]

The constitution produced was an amalgam of the one from 1884 and of much from the California constitution of 1879—which, while not ideal, seemed reasonable. "It bears upon its face the traces of the conflicts of contending interests," commented the *Herald*, which nevertheless found it an acceptable set of compromises. Like the constitutions of Washington, South Dakota, and North Dakota, drawn

74. Thorpe, "Recent Constitution-Making," 150–51.
75. *Herald*, August 5, 1889. For the debates, see *Proceedings, Constitutional Convention, 1889.*
76. *Herald*, August 9, 10, 17, 1889; Durfee, "Sidelights on the Making of the Constitution of Montana," typescript, MHS, 3, 4.

up about the same time, it tended to put limitations on legislative power and to exalt those of the executive—a "fixed tendency in American politics," according to an expert early in the century. But at the same time, it included strong safeguards to prevent corruption of both legislators and governor, with twenty sections to regulate corporations.[77]

By the terms of the enabling act, the constitution was to be submitted to the voters early in October and state officers were to be elected at the same time. Then, if the document were ratified and approved by the president, Montana would be proclaimed a state, its territorial officers continuing until then and its territorial laws remaining in effect until the new state legislature enacted statutes of its own. Both parties brought in prominent national politicians in vigorous bids to capture the machinery of government and Montana's seats in Congress.[78] Accompanying the constitution to the voting public went an "Address to the People," which in a nutshell described the major territorial grievances:

> The adoption of the Constitution will secure our admission upon an equal footing with the original States; it will give us adequate Courts for the administration of justice; it will permit us to tax large quantities of land now exempt from taxation; it will give us the immediate benefit of school and other lands donated by the United States; it will relieve us of that unjust inhibition by which we are prohibited from selling our mines in foreign markets; it will give us a representative in Congress and two United States Senators to represent us in Washington; it will give us the right of suffrage in national elections; it will give us a stable government; it will invite capital and emigration, in short it will break the shackles of territorial bondage and elevate us to the full dignity of American citizenship.[79]

The vote in favor of the constitution was clear-cut—24,844 for and 2,276 against; this count was promptly certified and forwarded to the president by Governor White.[80] Republicans promptly charged voting irregularities, coercion, and fraud in the preparation of offi-

77. *Herald*, August 17, 1889; Thorpe, "Recent Constitution-Making," 160–64, 173–74.

78. *Herald*, April 16, September 23, 24, 28, 1889; *Semi-Weekly Miner*, June 26, 1889; Alexander Botkin to Russell Harrison (Helena, April 17, 1889), Russell Harrison MSS.

79. "An Address to the People," in *Constitution of the State of Montana, as Adopted by the Constitutional Convention held at Helena, Montana, July 4, A.D. 1889, and Ending August 17, A.D. 1889* (Helena, 1889), 75.

80. Benjamin F. White to Benjamin Harrison (Helena, October 20, 21, 1889), Benjamin Harrison MSS.

cial returns; they lamented the "Dago Vote"—ignorant foreigners "marched to the polls and voted like cattle" to elect a Democratic slate in Deer Lodge County; and they decried the ballots "cast by a flock of birds of passage who happened to be located on the line of a new road then being constructed in Silver Bow county."[81] Not to be outdone, the Democrats filed counter-charges, accusing the Republicans of chicanery elsewhere, and with a writ from Associate Justice Stephen DeWolfe requiring that the Silver Bow returns be counted. DeWolfe was himself a Democratic candidate for office in the disputed district. While the county canvassing board carried out this order, the territorial one omitted the precinct in question, leaving Silver Bow with two sets of representatives, the acceptance of one of which would make the House Democratic, of the other, Republican. Meanwhile, Governor White accused Montana Democrats of deliberately seeking to withhold official returns, to delay statehood because they knew that when admission was proclaimed "the new State Officers would at once qualify and succeed them and these would all be Republicans."[82]

White's fears were unfounded, however. Despite pleas by Charles Broadwater, on November 8, 1889, President Harrison issued the proclamation which added the forty-first star to the American flag.[83] After twenty-five years, five months, and twelve days of "territorial vassalage," according to one editor's calculation, old timers could rejoice that "The gyves and fetters that have limited and cramped their movements have fallen away."[84]

Meanwhile, party strife dominated the first session of the new state legislature. On the basis of the disputed returns, both parties claimed seats and met in separate halls, each selecting their own favorites for the United States Senate. Some Montanans, like Walter de Lacy, were philosophical about the controversy. "I take no interest in it," de Lacy wrote. "It is a squabble between politicians, and it is two to one that both are wrong."[85] Ultimately the issue was decided by the Senate Committee on Privileges and Elections, which recom-

81. *Herald*, November 19, 25, 1889.

82. "This conspiracy to delay Statehood seems so determined that no effort will be spared in my opinion to carry it out," White told the president. White to Harrison (Helena, October 22, 1889), Benjamin Harrison MSS.

83. Broadwater to A. J. Davidson (Helena, November 8, 1889), telegram, Benjamin Harrison MSS; Executive Proclamation of November 8, 1889, Richardson, *Messages and Papers*, XII, 5459–60.

84. *Herald*, November 8, 9, 1889.

85. Walter de Lacy to Fannie de Lacy (n.p., n.d., envelope dated November 22, 1889), de Lacy MSS.

mended the seating of Republicans Wilbur F. Sanders and Thomas C. Power, rather than the Democratic claimants, William A. Clark and Martin Maginnis.[86]

The struggle for statehood for Montana is in essence the story of a reaction against the operation of territorial government and of the outgrowing of an apparatus designed for a weak, sparsely populated region. It is the story, too, of the unwillingness of Congress to recognize the inevitable changes taking place and to think in other than political terms for most of the decade of the 1880s. With at least one house Republican from 1881 to 1889, the possibility of admitting any Democratic state remained slight until a point had been reached—as was the case in 1888—where popular pressures were so great that neither party could afford to refuse. As bad as the fact that Montana was still predominantly Democratic, certainly, were the Free Silver sentiments of many of her citizens. Like other mining areas, the territory made no secret of its acceptance of the "silver heresy": residents and the legislature petitioned Congress on the subject; Governor Hauser bluntly scolded the administration for its betrayal of the silver interests to the "Rothschild Gold Bugs"; and Delegate Toole carried the bimetallic standard onto the floor of the House of Representatives with oratory as silvery as the metal he extolled.[87] These silverite infidels from the West were no more welcome to a Congress largely dominated by Republicans than were Protestant critics of orthodox Catholicism in the sixteenth century, and their presence could only retard admission to the Union.

As it was, because Montana's claims for statehood were merged with those of other territories, her case was not considered on its own merits and was finally decided on the basis of political expediency. In this, Congress acted in a fashion that was characteristic of much of its legislation for its western wards throughout the last half of the nineteenth century. At times it exhibited the same kind of salutary neglect toward the territories as had the British Parliament in the mid-1700s. Like those early colonials, Montanans complained of out-

86. Report of the Committee on Privileges and Elections in regard to the credentials of Messrs. Sanders, Power, Clark and Maginnis severally claiming seats in the Senate from the State of Montana, *Senate Report* No. 538, 51 Congress, 1 Session (1889–90), 13; William D. Mangam, *The Clarks: An American Phenomenon* (New York, 1941), 60.

87. Memorial to Congress (n.d.), *LM*, 13 Session (1883), 211; *Congressional Record*, 49 Congress, 1 Session (1885–86), 641, 739–40, 2160–63; Report of the Governor of Montana, 1885, 1002–3; *ibid.*, 1886, 832–33.

side interference and demanded more self-government; they resented the imposition of "foreign" officers upon them; they deprecated the right to national government to nullify local laws, however sparingly the power was used; and they consciously enhanced the powers of their own assembly. The Montana legislature was no mere creature of executive or judicial appointees chosen in Washington; it was a functional body of more strength than students of government have previously been inclined to admit.

On the other hand, if congressional inhibitions were usually more illusory than real, when Congress did respond, that response was generally belated or it failed to meet the needs and desires of Montanans. No coherent federal territorial "system" was apparent. Policies were ill defined and often ad hoc; actions too often came as a result of political agitation; too often they followed the dictates of party practicality.

To Montanans, admission came to mean the end of a quarter of a century of servitude, exploitation and neglect; it signified a new age of freedom, democracy, and home rule. Yet in actual practice statehood failed to cure automatically many traditional political grievances. Elected state officials could be as corrupt or as inept as federally appointed ones; state taxes could be as oppressive as territorial ones; and interest groups and powerful individuals played an even more important role than before. Indeed the 1890s would be dominated by the bitter struggle for political supremacy by mining tycoons William A. Clark and Marc Daly; and soon the giant corporation would exert its sway over the political as well as the economic realm. The Anaconda Company ("The Company"), Montana Power, Great Western Sugar, and the various railroads would vie with ranching, farming, tourism, oil, and labor unions for control of government in the twentieth century.

Kenneth Owens argues convincingly that the kind of no-party territorial structure that prevailed in Montana put into power an upper-class leadership based on a support relatively broad but hardly as democratic as that envisioned by Frederick Jackson Turner.[88] No doubt in Montana, as in the Dakotas, this experience helped influence political attitudes in the statehood era as well, for traditionally personalities have seemed to count more than party alignments and discipline. The impact of business interests and bitter intraparty

88. Owens, "Pattern and Structure in Western Territorial Politics," *Western Historical Quarterly*, I (October, 1970), 391–92.

strife were not new after 1889, but were part of what Howard Lamar calls the "politics of development." And Montanans would continue to nurture the same concern for federal aid without control that they displayed earlier. Party lines often blurred: in terms of vote, Montana has been classified as one of "the competitive middle" for the entire 1872–1970 period.[89] It was "neither principally Republican nor principally Democratic," but rather displayed an eccentricity of party politics that was unusual.[90] Although it had voted for William Jennings Bryan in 1896 and again in 1900, the state supported the winning presidential candidate—whatever his party—fourteen successive times between 1904 and 1956. Democrats served more terms than Republicans in the executive branch of state government and in both houses of Congress in the same period, but neither party dominated exclusively. The same kind of party irregularity that had characterized at least the second half of the territorial period persisted deep into the twentieth century.

To the extent that the Gilded Age was marked by corruption, crass materialism, industrialism triumphant, and close links between business and politics, Montana was a part of the era. After her initial years of turmoil, her government under the no-party system was dominated to a large extent by coalitions of appointed governors, like Potts, and powerful local enonomic interests, represented by Sam Hauser especially and indirectly by Martin Maginnis in Washington. In Montana, Hauser's influence was comparable to that of Francis E. Warren in Wyoming. The two, though of opposite parties, were the kingpins in political cliques made up of men of both parties and broadly supported. Hauser, Tom Power, or Charles Broadwater were the counterparts in Montana of, say, David Moffat in Colorado or Thomas B. Catron in New Mexico. Usually behind the scenes, they were shrewd, serious politicians, not without influence in high eastern circles, always willing to fight to enhance their own and what they believed to be the region's interests, even if it meant buying votes to do so. With cooperative governors in Helena and delegates of the effectiveness of Maginnis or Toole in the nation's capital, and support from the electorate, they functioned well, despite bitter fights and shifting within their own ranks. Political battles were real, with a

89. Paul T. David, *Party Strength in the United States, 1872–1970* (Charlottesville, 1972), 37, 50, 53.

90. Roland R. Renne, *The Government and Administration of Montana* (New York, 1958), 52.

blending of local and national issues. The Waving of the Bloody Shirt, Negro rights, the tariff, or currency reform were at times questions of some moment in the territory. But more acute were conflicts over personalities, offices or patronage; or the subject of federal monies for defense, internal improvements, or general economic development.

BIBLIOGRAPHICAL ESSAY

Rather than detail a complete list of all sources used in this study, this bibliographical statement focuses upon those which have been most important and most pertinent. These include manuscripts, government documents, books, periodicals, and newspapers, located in repositories as far flung as Helena, Berkeley, New Haven, and Washington, D.C.

MANUSCRIPTS

National Archives Holdings

For the study of any territory, the manuscript holdings of the National Archives are vital. They touch upon every aspect of territorial government and politics and are dispersed under many headings. Some of the most relevant are in the State Department materials (RG 59), especially the Territorial Papers, 1861–73; Appointment Papers of Territorial Governors and Secretaries; and Miscellaneous and Domestic Letters. Also of value are Territorial Papers of the U.S. Senate and Papers of the U.S. Senate re Nominations (RG 46). Of great importance are Interior Department records (RG 48), particularly the Territorial Papers (Patents and Miscellaneous Division), 1873–1889, and the Appointment Papers of Territorial Governors and Secretaries. Montana materials are scattered through the Justice Department files (RG 60): Records Relating to the Appointment of Federal Judges, Marshals, and Attorneys; Attorney General's Papers; Source-Chronological Files; Year Files; Letters Received; Letters Sent, General and Miscellaneous; and Letters Sent to Judges and Clerks. Information is also found in the Bureau of Indian Affairs (RG 75), Letters Received; and in the Treasury Department (RG 217), Letters Territorial and Division of Warrants of the First Comptroller's Office.

Montana Historical Society Collections

Private manuscript collections are scattered but the most important are at the Montana Historical Society in Helena. Especially significant there are the papers of Samuel T. Hauser, Martin Maginnis, Benjamin Potts, William F. Wheeler, Tom C. Power, the Edgerton family and the Fisk family. Also valuable are the General Executive Correspondence of the territory to 1876, the Allis B. Stuart collection, and the diaries of Cornelius Hedges, Neil Howie, James H. Morley, and Andrew J. Fisk. Smaller, but still useful, collections include those of Charles Hutchins, Decius S. Wade, Hezekiah L. Hosmer, Hiram Knowles, Thomas Francis Meagher, Wilbur Fisk Sanders, and Edward Warren Toole.

Other Collections

At the Bancroft Library of the University of California, the dictations of Sanders, Wheeler, Nathaniel J. Bond, and Francis E. Warren were helpful; at the Minnesota Historical Society, the Nathaniel P. Langford papers, and at Indiana University's Lilly Library, the Russell B. Harrison manuscripts give good insight into politics of the late 1880s. The Beinecke Library, Yale University, contains the papers of Hezekiah Hosmer and of James and Granville Stuart, both excellent collections. Correspondence of Benjamin Potts with Rutherford B. Hayes is found at the Hayes Memorial Library in Fremont, Ohio, and considerable Potts correspondence is in the James A. Garfield papers at the Library of Congress. The Library of Congress microfilm editions of the presidential papers of Lincoln, Johnson, Cleveland, and Harrison all contain pertinent Montana material.

BOOKS AND PERIODICALS

Basic to a general understanding of the history of any Far West territory is Earl S. Pomeroy, *The Territories and the United States, 1861–1890* (Seattle, 1969 ed.). Older but still sound is Max Farrand, *The Legislation of Congress for the Government of the Organized Territories of the United States, 1789–1895* (Newark, 1896). More recent is Jack E. Eblen's *The First and Second United States Empires: Governors and Territorial Government, 1784–1912* (Pittsburgh, 1968).

Earlier histories of Montana include Michael Leeson, ed., *History of Montana, 1739–1885* (Chicago, 1885); Hubert Howe Bancroft, *The History of Washington, Idaho and Montana, 1846–1889* (San

Francisco, 1890); Joaquin Miller, *An Illustrated History of the State of Montana* (Chicago, 1894); and Helen F. Sanders, *A History of Montana*, 3 vols. (Chicago, 1913). *Progressive Men of the State of Montana* (Chicago, n.d.) is useful for its biography.

More modern are Merrill G. Burlingame, *The Montana Frontier* (Helena, 1942), a fine book; K. Ross Toole, *Montana: An Uncommon Land* (Norman, 1959), the standard one-volume survey; Burlingame and Toole, *A History of Montana*, 3 vols. (New York, 1957); and James McClellan Hamilton, *From Wilderness to Statehood* (Portland, 1957). An excellent regional approach which includes part of Montana is Paul F. Sharp, *Whoop-Up Country* (Minneapolis, 1955). Of particular worth for this study is Ellis L. Waldron, *Montana Politics Since 1864: An Atlas of Elections* (Missoula, 1958). Robert G. Athearn, *Thomas Francis Meagher: An Irish Revolutionary in America* (Boulder, 1949) gives an objective appraisal of Meagher's Montana career; and John D. W. Guice deals fairly with the Montana territorial supreme court in his book, *The Rocky Mountain Bench* (New Haven, 1972).

Especially pertinent among contemporary accounts are Granville Stuart, *Forty Years on the Frontier, as seen in the Journals and Reminiscences of Granville Stuart*, edited by Paul C. Phillips, 2 vols. (Cleveland, 1925); Alexander K. McClure, *Three Thousand Miles through the Rocky Mountains* (Philadelphia, 1869); Andrew F. Rolle, ed., *The Road to Virginia City: The Diary of James Knox Polk Miller* (Norman, 1960); and C. C. Goodwin, *As I Remember Them* (Salt Lake City, 1913).

Materials on territorial Montana appear in periodicals too numerous to mention. Two, however, are basic: *Montana: the Magazine of Western History* (1951–), and the older *Contributions to the Historical Society of Montana; with its Transactions, Officers and Members* (9 vols., 1876–1923).

NEWSPAPERS

Among the newspapers consulted, the most important has been the *Helena Daily Herald*, the staunch Republican organ of the Fisk brothers during much of the territorial era. This has been balanced off with the rival *Independent* and with a number of others, including the *Rocky Mountain Gazette* (Helena), the *Montana Post* and the *Montana Democrat* (both originally in Virginia City), and the Deer Lodge *New North-West*.

UNPUBLISHED PH.D. DISSERTATIONS

Robert E. Albright, "The Relations of Montana with the Federal Government, 1864–1889" (Stanford University, 1933) lacks interpretation. A fine study of an important political figure is John W. Hakola, "Samuel T. Hauser and the Economic Development of Montana: A Case Study in Nineteenth-Century Frontier Capitalism" (Indiana University, 1961). Also sound is Kenneth N. Owens, "Frontier Governors: A Study of the Territorial Executives in the History of Washington, Idaho, Montana, Wyoming and Dakota Territories" (University of Minnesota, 1959). Incisive, but in need of trimming, is John Welling Smurr, "Territorial Constitutions: A Legal History of the Frontier Governments Erected by Congress in the American West, 1787–1900" (Indiana University, 1960).

FEDERAL AND TERRITORIAL PUBLICATIONS

The *Congressional Globe*, the *Congressional Record*, the *Reports* of the Bureau of the Census, and the *United States Statutes at Large* have been essential to this study. Among a large number of federal documents, none has been more useful than the *Annual Report of the Secretary of the Interior*, which in turn includes the yearly report of the territorial governors.

At the territorial level, *Laws, Memorials, and Resolutions* of the legislature has been of prime importance. Of much value also are the Montana House *Journal* and the Senate *Journal*. (The House *Journal* was apparently not printed for the first, eleventh, and fifteenth sessions, and that of the Senate not for the eleventh and fifteenth sessions.) Indispensable are *Reports of Cases Argued and Determined in the Supreme Court of Montana Territory* (9 vols., 1868–1889). Use has also been made of scattered reports of territorial officials, the messages of the governors, and the *Proceedings and Debates of the Constitutional Convention Held in the City of Helena, Montana, July 4th, 1889, August 17th, 1889* (Helena, 1921).

INDEX

Ackerman, S. F., 90
Adriance (penitentiary warden), 106
Alcohol: study of, 186
Alien Land Law, 204–5
Aliens: discrimination against, 200n
Anaconda Company, 176, 309
Anthony, Daniel R., 58
Anti-Semitism, 178
Arthur, Chester A.: 148–49, 155, 160, 236, 254
Ashley, James M.: 45, 47, 195, 237; introduces Montana bill, 11; administration of, 57–73; nominated for governor, 58; biography of, 58–59; reaction to, 60–61; promotes immigration, 63; appointment difficulties of, 64–67; vetoes by, 66; Indian policy of, 68; removal of, 68–69; criticism of, 71; assessment of, 72–73; supports Greeley, 72; ignores successor, 76; opposes special legislation, 183, 184; condemns Anti-Chinese discrimination, 200; protests unpaid salary, 244; protests high taxes, 283
Assay office: established, 265
Avant Courier (Bozeman), 162

Bach, Thomas C., 217, 229, 238, 252
Baker, Isaac G., 277
Baker, Major Eugene M., 68
Bannack: founding of, 7; named temporary capital, 20
Barkley, William G., 65, 89, 90
Bass, William E., 193

Beaman, Fernando C., 12
Beidler, John X., 9
Belknap, William W., 82, 84, 160
Benton Record (Fort Benton): cites poor official salaries, 243
Big Hole, Battle of, 113–14
Blackfoot (Chief of the Crows), 114
Blackfoot Indians, 33
Blacks in Montana: numbers of, 14; discrimination against, 200–201
Blaine, James G., 87, 254
Blaine, John E., 87–88
Blake, Henry N., 229, 244; challenged to duel, 42; effort to block appointment of, 227; on judges, 228
Board of Livestock Commissioners, 209
"Bogus" legislature, 38–39
Bonds: posted by secretary, 257, 258
Botkin, Alexander: in 1882 election, 96; becomes lieutenant governor, 241
Bounty law, 208–9; could cause bankruptcy, 287–88
Boyce, James B.: *Facts about Montana*, 119
Boyle, Charles E., 251
Bozeman, John: asks protection of Bozeman Valley, 52
Bozeman Massacre, 52
Bozeman Trail, 274
Breen, Peter, 305
Broadwater, Charles A., 95, 151, 160, 161, 162, 167, 172, 176, 211, 252, 277, 300, 307; on railroad subsidy, 121; opposes Hauser, 165

Officers: salary augmentation for, 28,
245–46; appointments and problems of, 232–55; turnover of,
239–40; salaries of, 243–45; absenteeism of, 247–48; nonresident
appointments of, 249–54; bills to
provide election of, 250; bills to
limit appointment of to residents,
250–51
Omnibus Bill: signed, 303
Orem, Con, 10
Organic act: summary of, 15–17; bill
to amend, 41
Orr, Sample: and 1878 election, 95
Owen, John: establishes post in the
Bitterroots, 5; on Indians, 32; on
absenteeism of officers, 247; protests taxes, 279
Owens, Kenneth N.: on western
territorial patterns, 1, 309; on
Hauser's importance, 159

Pacific railroad survey, 5–6
Packard, Mrs. E. P. W.: lobbies on
women's property rights, 201
Paddock, Algernon S.: bill for land-
grant universities, 271
Pemberton, William Y., 298
Penitentiary: transfer of to territory,
267; expansion of facilities of,
267–68; criticism of, 268. *See also*
Prison facilities
Pierce, E. D.: discovers gold, 6
Pinney, George M., 18, 237
Plumb, Preston B., 166, 305
Plummer, Henry, 9
Pollard, Charles R.: appointment
unconfirmed, 228
Poore, Ben Perley: describes Ashley,
59
Post offices: establishment of, 273
Potter, John, 142
Potts, Benjamin Franklin, 2, 67, 236,
238, 253, 266; administrations of,
74–149; biography of, 74–75; ap-
pointment of, 75; describes Montana, 75–76; clashes with Ashley,
76–77; vows to beat Cavanaugh,
79; praises Clagett's victory, 81; on

patronage, 82–83; seeks ouster of
judges, 83, 226–27; criticizes Ashley
clique, 84; describes Sanders, 85;
criticized by Fisk, 86–87, 102;
condemns Fisk, 88–89; and cooperation with Democrats, 98; com-
plains of printing, 101; fiscal
policies of, 104–11; urges cut in
extra compensation, 105, 188; en-
dorses Hardie report, 107; vetoes
by, 108–9, 122, 187, 193, 198;
criticizes fees of county officials,
110; Indian policy of, 111–15; and
capital controversy, 130; praises
Callaway, 136; criticizes Callaway,
137–38; attempts to oust, 140–45;
exoneration of, 144; reappointment
of, 147; relations of with legislature, 195; urges Sunday blue laws,
198; influence of, 238; later career
of, 242; on appointments, 243–44;
additional activities of, 246; com-
plains of fiscal irregularities,
259–60; and farming-out of convict
labor, 269; condemns school land-
grant policy, 270
Potts and Harrison Horse Company,
242
Powell, John Wesley, 305
Power, Thomas C., 161, 162, 177,
277; member of 1884 constitutional
convention, 297; seated in U.S.
Senate, 308
Prison facilities: inadequacies of,
219–20. *See also* Penitentiary
Probate courts: expansion of jurisdiction of, 222, 223. *See also* Court
system
Probate law: enactment of, 26;
inadequacies of, 193
Public buildings: federal funds
sought for, 265–69
Public education, 269–72. *See also*
School lands; School laws
Public printing: disputes over, 98–
104, 263

Railroads: movement for subsidies,
116–28, 275–76. *See also* Northern